KAZUCHIYO
BATTLE FOR TWO BRIDGES

BY
MELANIE SCHOEN

CONTENTS

PROLOGUE 1
CHAPTER ONE 12
CHAPTER TWO 25
CHAPTER THREE 35
CHAPTER FOUR 47
CHAPTER FIVE 61
CHAPTER SIX 73
CHAPTER SEVEN 86
CHAPTER EIGHT 93
CHAPTER NINE 104
CHAPTER TEN 114
CHAPTER ELEVEN 127
CHAPTER TWELVE 138
CHAPTER THIRTEEN 147
CHAPTER FOURTEEN 163
CHAPTER FIFTEEN 176

CHAPTER SIXTEEN 191
CHAPTER SEVENTEEN 209
CHAPTER EIGHTEEN 221
CHAPTER NINETEEN 228
CHAPTER TWENTY 242
CHAPTER TWENTY-ONE 252
CHAPTER TWENTY-TWO 267
CHAPTER TWENTY-THREE 273
CHAPTER TWENTY-FOUR 285
CHAPTER TWENTY-FIVE 298
CHAPTER TWENTY-SIX 306
CHAPTER TWENTY-SEVEN 317
CHAPTER TWENTY-EIGHT 330
CHAPTER TWENTY-NINE 339
CHAPTER THIRTY 356
CHAPTER THIRTY-ONE 367
CHAPTER THIRTY-TWO 380
CHAPTER THIRTY-THREE 393
EPILOGUE 402

PROLOGUE

It was deep into the chills of autumn when two great armies clashed for the last time on the fields of Shimegahara. All told, forty-thousand soldiers, divided in near equal measure between two fools, fought a gruesome battle in worship of the petty grudges of their ancestors. They met with blades and bows and stained the mud red. Even when drizzle turned to downpour, neither side would relent. For miles in every direction, villagers retreated to their row houses, listening to the distant thunder of drums.

Well-fortified in the shelter of a wooded mountain temple, Tatsutomi Shigenaga, lord of his clan, awaited news of the battle in the company of three thousand reserves. He sat perched on the edge of his stool at the center of the war tent, clad in his full, crimson armor, spear in hand. The polish put to his helmet's gold crest did nothing to hide the scratches and dents earned from decades of war. He was in every appearance a perfect rendition of his samurai title, broad-shouldered and firm-faced, ready to march to the field at the first word from his scouts. One would expect no less from the Red Dragon of Suyama.

What a brave, indomitable sight he should have been for

his young son, Kazuchiyo, but Kazuchiyo would not be the hero of this tale if he were lacking in perception, or if he were easily swayed by a guise of confidence. It did not escape his notice how heavily his father's hand shook around his spear.

"Father," said Kazuchiyo, "won't you let me fight beside you?"

His father grunted, adjusting his grip on the spear. Perhaps he had realized that Kazuchiyo could see his struggles. "You are not yet a man," he said. His lip quirked with good humor. "If you were to take a head, you wouldn't have a man's name to claim it with."

Kazuchiyo was not a boy easily swayed by humor either. "Then we can hold the ceremony now," he said. "Grant me a name and a sword so I can fight for our family."

"When you are old enough," said his father.

"All my elder brothers had their ceremonies by the time they were thirteen, and I'm thirteen now."

Tomonaga, third of Kazuchiyo's elder brothers, stood at his father's other side. He was also clad in full armor bearing the dragon crest, and all the more smug because of it. "Don't be eager to rush out onto the field, little tadpole," he teased. "You may have the dragon's mane, but not its fangs. Not yet."

Made self-conscious by his brother's teasing, Kazuchiyo reached back to fuss with the thick, black locks of his hair. The soldiers around them smirked in amusement. "I'll cut it with Father's permission," he retorted. "When it's time."

"It will be time soon enough," said their father, and he cast his gaze again before him, as if he were somehow able to peer through the downpour to his troops. His fist tightened around the spear. "Believe me, you will one day have your fill of war."

A cry arose from the lookouts, and Kazuchiyo's father straightened his back, waiting with hard-forged anticipation in his brow as the ranks made way for a messenger. The man came on horseback nearly all the way to the war tent before dismounting. The dragon's banner hung limply from his back; his helmet was cracked and askew. "My lord!" he cried as he rushed inside and threw himself to the ground. "My lord, news from the front!"

"Let's have it, then."

The man raised his head, and it was then that Kazuchiyo realized he was little more than a boy himself, no more than two or three years past his own age. His face was heart-shaped and soft and unbefitting of a soldier. "My lord, Master Yatamoto has turned against us and joined Aritaka," he said, and his audience went stiff with shock. "He launched an attack against our southern flank and has divided our forces in two. Soon they'll have cut the vanguard off entirely."

Shigenaga rose from his stool. The rustle of his armor impressed upon young Kazuchiyo a sensation like coils drawing tight. "And my sons?" he asked as his soldiers gathered themselves in kind. "They still fight?"

"They do you proud at the front," the boy replied, "but they're in desperate need of reinforcement."

"They will have it." Shigenaga strode forward and called to his generals, ordering them to make their soldiers ready. As all rushed to comply, he turned back to his younger sons. "You will remain here with the final regiment," he instructed them. "Protect this camp at all costs."

"Let me go with you to the front," said Kazuchiyo. "Let me fight to defend my brothers!"

"Your brothers have more than enough fight in them," his father assured him. "This temple has none of its own." He set his hand heavily on Kazuchiyo's shoulder. "If the vanguard falls, there is always retreat."

Kazuchiyo nodded with resolve and resignation. "But if a rearguard falls, there's nothing," he finished the saying obediently. "Good luck, Father."

Shigenaga nodded in return. It would be sentimental foolishness to pretend either of them knew then what fate awaited them, but he touched his son's hair and smiled, saying, "When this battle is over, I will have a grand name for you." And Kazuchiyo smiled, eager for it.

The Lord of the Tatsutomi mounted his horse, and with trusted generals at his side, he rode away from the safety of the temple camp. The thunder of their hoofbeats and war chanting disappeared beneath the hills. In the company of the five hundred remaining men, Shigenaga's third and fourth sons faced their duty with all due seriousness, commanding scouts to increase the diligence of their patrols.

An hour passed, as the rain intensified, with no news.

"What name do you think Father will pick for me?" Kazuchiyo wondered aloud, tightening his robes and trying to make them feel more like armor.

"Part of his own name, of course," said Tomonaga. "Kazunaga, probably. Mother was always pleased with your name."

"Tatsutomi Kazunaga," he said, rolling the name about in his mouth, imagining the brush strokes. The battle raged on, yet already his boyish mind was cast into the future, to a time when he could be called upon to defend his family and home with more than merely his presence at his father's side. He longed to bear the twisting curves of his clan's dragon sigil upon sturdy armor, as his brothers did, and to uphold his father's justice. His fantasies were cut short by the memory of that very banner torn and crooked, hanging from the back of the soft-faced messenger who had come to warn them of betrayal. He glanced about and could not remember what had become of that boy.

A shout arose from the perimeter, and both sons turned toward the tent entrance, holding their breath. Tomonaga grabbed up his spear, and showing none of his father's caution, he hurried to the enclosure's entrance. He was greeted there by an arrow carving into his skull.

You mustn't blame poor Kazuchiyo for what he did next.

His father had warred with the Aritaka since before he was born, and he had for thirteen years been saturated with tales of samurai valor. He had watched the bodies come back on carts, bloated and bloodied, limbs askew or missing. He was no

4

stranger to death. But upon seeing his closest brother stumble back, a shaft of wood piercing his skull just below his right eye, a panic overcame him. Without thought to who had fired the arrow, he caught Tomonaga in his arms. By the time he had lowered him to the ground, Tomonaga's body was limp and the spear was tumbling from his hand.

Out from the unceasing rain came their attackers: soldiers in patchwork armor, with patchwork loyalty. They cut down every Tatsutomi in their path with the ferocity of beasts. A son of the Dragon ought to have stepped over his brother's body, taken up his spear, and met his death with courage, but Kazuchiyo knelt in the mud, shocked, Tomonaga twitching and gurgling against his chest.

He would tell me later that he fought. He would have liked for me to tell you that now. But it is my reluctant duty to confess that he did not, and that it would haunt him for the rest of his days.

One of the Aritaka struck him across the temple with the butt of his spear. Kazuchiyo should have been prepared after years of his brothers' training, but the blow sent him crumbling to the ground and robbed him of his sight and sense. In breathless darkness he tried to draw himself upright, his only anchor Tomonaga's wet hissing. Hands grabbed him from all sides, wrenched his arms behind him to be tied. The spots cleared from his vision just in time to watch a sword cleave through his brother's neck.

"The head should be mine," said one soldier. "I shot him."

"Head goes to the general," said another. "If you're lucky, he will reward you for it."

Kazuchiyo was hauled upright. On his feet, face to face with his brother's killer, some strength came back to him. Too late he struggled; with arms bound he was an easy target for a fist in his gut. He doubled over, gagging.

"Keep your eye on him," said the gnarled man, and he took a fistful of Kazuchiyo's hair as he dragged him from the tent. "Lord Aritaka said to take him alive if we can."

Kazuchiyo stumbled after. A thousand questions preyed on his tongue, but none would have done him any good to ask. He couldn't understand how it had happened so quickly, that his father's most stalwart troops had fallen to lordless mercenaries, who were now shaking his brother's head to drain it of blood. His stomach crowded against his throat, and he wanted to scream.

They threw him over the back of a horse. The gnarled man mounted behind him and took him again by his hair. As they rode away from the camp, every movement of the animal bore into Kazuchiyo's stomach and ribs, and he nearly vomited. But it was shame more than pain that burned his eyes as he was carried away from the temple, through the sparse forestry of the foothills and down muddied slopes to the field. Even when he tried to struggle, there was nowhere to go.

What few attempts Kazuchiyo did make at escape ceased when they came to the battlefield. In the waning light Shimegahara was sickly and gray, its grasses matted down by bodies strewn in all directions, an unceasing drone of dying men accompanying the patter of raindrops. Men in dark, indigo armor walked up and down the plains with swords in hand, putting an end to any enemy breath they came upon. The corpses were piled so high that the figures moving among them may as well have been hellish *oni* overseeing the torture of the damned. So many of his father's men, slaughtered and rotting. The stench was enough to make him choke.

Above it all there rose a voice—a cry, bellowing and piercing at once, roiling like ocean waves across the weary plain. Someone still fought, more creature than man by the sound of it. Kazuchiyo could not lift his head to see, could not know whose soldier wailed with such agony and hate, if even it were a human being at all. A mad hope overcame him that it was somehow his father, a dragon transformed, made furious with revenge for his fallen army.

The horse stopped, and Kazuchiyo was yanked roughly from the saddle into the grabbing hands of yet more soldiers.

They dragged him over bodies and broken banners, and one of his sandals came loose, trapped by a man's armpit. It was all he could do to stay upright, and still he didn't fight, until their passage over an embankment brought him to his father.

It was not the Red Dragon of Suyama who still fought. He knelt in the sludge, the tufted shafts of arrows sticking straight out from his chest and back in half a dozen places, his armor hanging off, his helmet shattered nearby. It was not the arrows that had felled him; two Aritaka soldiers stood on either side of him, their spears plunged into his hips keeping him pinned. The earth surrounding him was stained black. Kazuchiyo could only stare, uncomprehending. His father's silhouette broken among the heaps deadened him, and it wasn't until he was shoved to the ground himself that he realized the man was staring back at him.

Shigenaga's eyes were so heavy. He was past the point of feeling pain, and he shivered, half slumped against one of the spears buried in him. When he opened his mouth, only blood came out, no strength in him to voice words. Kazuchiyo tried to push to his feet, to run to him, but the surrounding men swept his legs out from under him. They pushed his chest into the dirt.

"There," said a deep voice. Kazuchiyo strained to find the source. "He lives, as promised. And he will continue to live, from now until the end of his life, as *my* son."

Shigenaga coughed and gagged to follow. As he struggled, Kazuchiyo managed to raise his head, and at last he laid eyes on his enemy: Aritaka Souyuu, the Great Bear of the North. His body was broad and hulking, his dark armor weathered and stained, and atop his head sat the helmet passed to him by his father, crafted from oxen horns. Kazuchiyo had seen him only once before, and at the time found in him no reason to be impressed. Now, he was frozen, and at Aritaka's mercy.

Lord Aritaka was not alone. In addition to his many surrounding generals and foot soldiers, a figure stood beside him that Kazuchiyo had never seen, nor had he any inkling of their origin. In the dark and rain it was impossible to tell even if it was man or woman or something else, their form being draped in the thick robes of a holy mystic, their long hair swept back from a narrow, sloping face. The stranger was entirely unconcerned with Aritaka's boasting or Shigenaga's slow and agonizing death, their attention instead fixed on something in the distance. Perhaps they were listening to the howl that even then continued to ripple across the battlefield.

"You were always a worthy rival," Lord Aritaka was saying, and Kazuchiyo watched in mounting horror as he motioned two of his generals forward. "And you deserve a worthy death."

Both unsheathed their swords. The first moved behind the prone Shigenaga, while the second squatted before him, offering up his blade. Kazuchiyo shook, helplessly transfixed, as his father accepted it. But then the two spear-bearers stepped back, wrenching their blades from Shigenaga's torso, and he lurched. Fresh blood spilled out from beneath his armor, and his already pale face went white. Though he caught himself on his palms, keeping himself partially upright was the most his strength could bear. He couldn't angle the sword toward his belly as honor dictated.

"Kazu..." he choked out, and he lifted his head, his eyes pleading. Kazuchiyo pulled against his bindings in futility. "Kazuchiyo, you—"

The first general struck. His katana cleaved through Shigenaga's vertebrae in one clean stroke, severing his head from his body. Kazuchiyo watched, numb, as it rolled a few meters down the slope to rest at Aritaka's feet. Though the eyes went swiftly dull, they stared back at Kazuchiyo relentlessly, locked in a final image of anguish.

Lord Aritaka sighed. "Put it with the others."

"Yes, my lord," said the figure beside him, in a deep and craggy feminine voice. She removed a silk bag from the inside of her *kariginu* and collected Shigenaga's head with as much respect as could be shown given the circumstances. "And the boy?"

"Like I said, he comes with us."

The gnarled man hauled Kazuchiyo to his feet, which could barely hold him. The field smeared into black and gray and the stench of blood, and Kazuchiyo swayed dizzily as his father's body became one of the thousands. A small cart beyond Aritaka and his entourage carried more silk bags, enough for every one of Shigenaga's sons and generals. To Kazuchiyo, it was an impossible outcome, and he felt that at any moment he would slip away into some terrible dreamscape.

But then, that scream. Over the rolling field that wrathful cry continued unceasing, and in fact sounded more forceful than ever. Kazuchiyo's bleary ears clung to it. His throat vibrated around it, as if it spilled from his own lungs. He could not make a sound, but the furious stranger did it for him, and he quaked with emotion.

They marched him north across the field, into the ranks of Aritaka's foot soldiers. Here the scream grew louder and with time more ragged, interspersed with clashing iron and men cursing. Before long they came upon a circle of Aritaka soldiers, each shifting anxiously even as they shouted orders at the man at its center: the source of that thunderous voice, the howling creature.

To anyone he would have been a ferocious sight, but to Kazuchiyo, torn asunder by an evening of traumas, he was godlike: nearly two meters tall, shoulders broad as a *torii* gate, legs planted in the earth as sturdy as a centuries-old oaks. Indigo Aritaka armor was fastened haphazardly across his muscular frame as if he had outgrown it in moments, bursting the seams. However, the Tatsutomi spear he brandished suggested that all his armaments had been scavenged from those fallen on the field of battle. His wild crop of brown hair was matted down by blood, and his chest plate was stained with gore. A dozen failed challengers lay at his feet.

As Kazuchiyo watched, one of the surrounding Aritaka men fired an arrow, and it struck deeply in the woven plates of the warrior's shoulder guard, enough to draw blood. Still he did not slow. He snapped the arrow shaft with his fist and then charged, scattering Aritaka's bravest. With a vengeful bellow he thrust his spear into the offending archer's throat. One soldier advanced, hoping to find some opening in the warrior's defense, only to quickly realize there was none. The spear whipped about with incredible speed, its blunt edge cracking the soldier's jaw from his face. A second blow felled him onto his back before the blade stabbed clear through his armor to his heart.

The circle widened. The soldiers looked to each other in helpless confusion. For some time a stalemate dragged on as the warrior caught his breath, his dark eyes flashing from one man to the next in challenge.

"What's taking so long?" said the gnarled man holding Kazuchiyo captive. "Shoot him and be done with it."

"But you saw—" replied the soldier closest, who flinched in alarm when the warrior turned his eyes on him. He gulped. "There's gold for you if you can take his head."

The warrior's penetrating eyes fell on Kazuchiyo next, but he did not flinch. He stared straight back, more fearful *for* than *of* the madman. Already Kazuchiyo had watched invincible men killed by easy strokes. It may have injured his father's pride to know that watching a stranger felled by Aritaka arrows and spears would be his final, unbearable burden, but to Kazuchiyo this was more than a stranger, this was rage incarnate. This was the fist around his throat, the burning behind his eyes. This was vengeance and fury in human form, a demon, a dragon, a weapon. All the hate he could not raise to his surface was already a force in the world, with dozens of corpses to its credit. If his enemy snuffed even that out, he would have nothing left.

The warrior charged without warning. His face twisted in rage, and he roared, lightning and thunder at once. The gnarled man cast Kazuchiyo down and drew his sword, but his assailant was inescapable. The man's worn katana snapped like a twig beneath the spear's crossblades; then his arm snapped, severed at the elbow. All around the soldiers reeled and panicked, those with arrows knocked loosing them on their unstoppable foe. Kazuchiyo shuddered at the sickening *thunk* of the few that found their mark, but still the warrior fought, gutting and cleaving, while Kazuchiyo watched in awe. He fought until his voice was raw and his mighty knees shook, the Aritaka retreating so far that he couldn't cross the distance. Even Lord Aritaka himself came to watch the spectacle draw to its inevitable conclusion, the mysterious, robed woman beside him. The vision of a young, fearless warrior driving back the Aritaka soldiers was a fitting beginning for what would one day become his unapproachable legacy.

At last he was spent, collapsing to his knees among his victims. Kazuchiyo was there to catch him. Though neither had arms free or strong enough to bear the other, they leaned chest to chest beneath the cool autumn rain. The warrior trembled, and Kazuchiyo with him. Strangers, then, but only for a while longer.

"Thank you," whispered Kazuchiyo, thinking that at any moment his champion would crumble at his seams like all the rest. "Thank you—he killed my brother."

The warrior panted, each hoarse breath stirring the hair against Kazuchiyo's cheek. "You're samurai?"

"Yes. My name is Kazuchiyo."

"Kazuchiyo," he repeated, blood on his lips. "I'll kill you, too."

At the time, he must have meant it. I wondered often, at the end of it all, if he regretted making that promise. But I do know that Kazuchiyo believed him. He always believed in him.

CHAPTER ONE

This violent beginning to Kazuchiyo's tale was not an uncommon one for its time. For nearly a century the country of Shuyun had been embroiled in civil war, as the great samurai *daimyo* vied for land and influence amongst themselves. Emboldened by the lack of any meaningful leadership from the ailing shogunate, let alone the emperor and his court, they sent thousands of men to their deaths over petty slights as often as grand ambitions. For a young boy to lose his father, three of his brothers, and any claim to his ancestral home was no greater tragedy than any of the other similar misfortunes spread out over decades of reckless arrogance.

So, regretfully, the near-complete obliteration of the Tatsutomi clan in the autumn of 1482 disturbed very little of the natural order of things, for a time. Lord Aritaka claimed their principal castle as his own and instilled his younger brother as its master. Kazuchiyo's mother and youngest brother were ejected and forced into religious exile in a remote mountain temple. Families who had once sworn undying loyalty to the dragon banner bowed to their new lord. The peasantry noticed no difference at all. What was one samurai lord traded for another, other than a new emblem on the tax collector's purse?

As for Kazuchiyo, he was taken deep into Sakka Province, to the castle town of Gyoe, of which he had only ever heard stories. Its white plaster walls and gold-tipped eaves shone like a beacon even in the cloudy gloom. The main keep, which stood four stories tall upon a great stone base, sank into the mountainside and was heavily fortified, the sprawling town below interspersed with thick barriers and baileys to confound invaders. Built by Lord Aritaka's father, the castle had never been breached by the enemy—unless one agreed to count Gyoe's own lord personally conveying Tatsutomi Kazuchiyo across the threshold.

Kazuchiyo spent his first day at Gyoe in a silent haze. He was cleaned and dressed and fed, two of Aritaka's finest always at his side with hands on their katana. Whether they were diligently preventing his escape or his suicide, it mattered very little, as he followed their instructions without question. He listened to the rain on an unfamiliar roof, concentrating on its monotony to drown out memories of the death-littered field, straining his ears for a distant voice.

They put him in a small room with a thick futon and stood guard while he allowed exhaustion to smother him in sleep. By morning he was sweat-drenched and shivering from dreams he couldn't remember.

In the morning a new pair of soldiers came to fetch him, and they led him up to Lord Aritaka's audience chamber. Kazuchiyo's first step onto the tatami put a chill through him, and he lifted his head to stare back at the assemblage of generals and advisors filling the room. The two factions were easy to tell apart, but all viewed him with disgust and mistrust, their eyes boring into him as surely as arrows. He did not even have scavenged armor to protect himself, but he had no choice but to continue forward, submitting to their weasel-eyed judgment.

At the far end of the chamber sat Lord Aritaka himself in handsome, indigo robes bearing the round, white crest of his clan, and beside him again knelt the long-faced woman from the field. Kazuchiyo had not laid eyes on either of them during the several days of journey from Shimegahara, and to see them calm and unscarred from the battle churned his stomach. Though he managed to walk down the line of their audience, by the time he knelt before the bear he was shaking.

What could he have done? His family had been destroyed. He was trapped in the enemy's lair. Even if they had given him a sword to cut his belly open, his hands were too weak to wield it. So Kazuchiyo bowed his head to the floor before his father's killer, and he waited.

"Kazuchiyo," said Lord Aritaka, his deep, coarse voice filling the chamber. "I trust you have not been mistreated since your arrival."

"No, sir," replied Kazuchiyo, not that he could have said otherwise.

"Good. You may be my hostage here, but you are also the eldest remaining son of a man I much respected. I will not tolerate your mistreatment."

His words reassured Kazuchiyo not at all, given how still and silent the surrounding advisors remained. "Thank you, sir."

"Do you know why I've kept you alive, boy?"

Kazuchiyo's heart thundered. He had expected to be tested, but in his numb exhaustion had yet to formulate any strategy. Cautiously he started to lift his head, hoping a glimpse of the man's face would give him some clue. But before he could raise his gaze, the woman kneeling beside him drew his attention with a flick of her wrist and tapped the floor with two fingers. He quickly returned to his prostrate position.

"I am a hostage," said Kazuchiyo. "You can use the threat of my death to prevent my father's vassals from rising against you."

Lord Aritaka grunted. "You hold your father's vassals in high regard? You trust that if they *did* have designs against me, they would let your death stand in their way? They would only need your younger brother, if they truly wished to raise the dragon banner again." He shifted, the rustle of his robes making him sound larger than he was. "Do you know why it was your father lost?"

Kazuchiyo clenched his fists against the tatami and hoped that Aritaka would not see him shake. The image of his father slumped in the rain was so heavy on his eyes that he could not have seen anything else even if he *had* lifted his head. "The scout," he said, hating that he couldn't keep the hurt out of his voice. "The one who came to tell us that Master Yatamoto betrayed us. He was lying. The vanguard had already been defeated by the time he came to us." His shoulders ached as he tried to sink deeper into himself. "You lured my father and his men away from the temple so you could finish him off."

"That is perceptive of you," confirmed Lord Aritaka.

Kazuchiyo licked his lips, but his mouth was dry. "It wouldn't have worked if not for the rain. If Father had had accurate information from the front—"

"It wasn't the rain that killed your messengers," Aritaka interrupted him. "Yatamoto didn't pledge allegiance to me on account of the weather, nor did Waseba and his brothers for that matter. The Tatsutomi army was doomed to fail."

Kazuchiyo had yet to reconcile with the knowledge of even one of his father's generals betraying him; that there had been several was unfathomable to him. He had thought a samurai's honor much stronger. He tried to remember if he had seen any familiar faces upon entering the chamber, but the inside of his head had begun to melt and smear, and he couldn't be sure of anything.

"Your father's instincts for war had been dulling for a long time," Lord Aritaka continued. "I thought at first that I alone could see it, but clearly that was not the case. You should see this as a valuable lesson, boy. No daimyo can go on without the confidence of his generals."

Kazuchiyo thought instead that some generals were not worth having confidence in. Yatamoto, Waseba, and anyone else who would betray their lord in his moment of need were cowards and nothing more. Even Aritaka was a coward for having courted them. He would have said so, except that when he trembled, he remembered his father's hand around the spear. "Lord Aritaka," he said, only when he could be sure this weakness would not be apparent in his voice. "Why have you kept me alive?"

Aritaka did not answer immediately. His assembly grew tense at Kazuchiyo's back as they, too, waited to hear his mind. Kazuchiyo stewed in apprehension and began to wish he'd had the strength to meet his death on the field. And then Aritaka spoke.

"Your life is a mercy I grant to your father," he said, with righteousness Kazuchiyo hated him for. "We may have been rivals, but he was a man of great valor, once. I held him in such regard as I have very few others. And in light of that, I have decided to accept you as my son. You will take a portion of my name and be trained into a mighty warrior, as your brothers were before you. It was your father's last request."

"Liar," Kazuchiyo whispered into the floor. His memory was a muddied hell, but his father's face twisting toward him in anguish would never leave him.

"Lift your head, boy."

Kazuchiyo flinched, but he obeyed. He was not proud of his composure in that moment, certain that Lord Aritaka could see the frustration and pain etched very clearly in his face. Aritaka's own countenance was a rough blank of emotion, with no hint of the nobility of greater lords. He was only an animal struggling to hide his greed, and they regarded each other for several long minutes while the generals watched uneasily.

"I keep your father's swords in my chamber," said Lord Aritaka. "If I gave them to you now, would you cut me down?"

Kazuchiyo wound his fists in his *hakama*. For his father's sake he wanted to swear that he would. He had long admired the red-corded blades that had hung from his father's hip, and he imagined the katana in his grip, the weight and the strength of it guiding his arm. But then he thought of the field. He imagined Aritaka's blood gushing down over his hands, his body collapsing to join corpses laid end to end like tatami mats, and his stomach turned. Even with those prized weapons at his side, he knew he could not have struck his enemy down. Not until he became stronger.

"No," said Kazuchiyo. "I would not."

"And why not?" Aritaka prodded.

Kazuchiyo swallowed back bile. "Because I would not want to dishonor my father's last request by letting any harm come to you, my lord."

Lord Aritaka regarded him a while longer, and then he grunted. "Don't lie to me, boy," he said, but his lip turned up in an appreciative smirk. "At least not until you're better at it."

Kazuchiyo bowed his head again to the floor. "Forgive me, my lord."

"No matter. I wouldn't expect any less of you so soon." Lord Aritaka resettled. "You are dismissed. You are permitted to roam the castle, as it is your home now. My men will accompany you wherever you go, for now."

"I understand," said Kazuchiyo. He knew very well that even if he managed to breach the walls, he could never navigate the unfamiliar town or the wilds beyond on his own.

"Your age ceremony will take place in three days' time," Aritaka continued. "As my son, your future as well as your mother's and younger brother's will be secure. Take this time to consider the kind of man you will be."

"Thank you, Lord Aritaka," Kazuchiyo said, the words acid on his lips.

Lord Aritaka dismissed him, and as the soldiers escorted him out of the chamber, he looked one more time over the gathered loyalists. There were several familiar faces among the generals after all. General Yatamoto averted his eyes, but General Waseba stared straight back at him, unashamed.

Once in the hall, free from the eyes of Lord Aritaka and his honorless traitors, Kazuchiyo felt much of the strength rush out of his knees. Already he was exhausted and heartsick, his mind aflame with too many worries. He refused to wonder what Tomonaga might have done in his position; every thought of him reminded Kazuchiyo of the arrow piercing straight through him. There was nothing to do but allow Aritaka's men to take him back to his room, but as they headed for the stairs, he heard it: a familiar voice, crying out.

The warrior from the field. Kazuchiyo's heart pounded in his ears, and he worried for a moment that he was hallucinating. Then he looked to the men alongside him, and their wary looks confirmed that they heard it as well. The warrior's bellows may as well have shaken Gyoe down to its stone foundations, but as far as Kazuchiyo was concerned, they were meant only for him, like an unearthly beacon. Whatever dread he might have felt at the thought of another battle dissipated beneath the knowledge that he would not be alone; someone in Gyoe hated Aritaka as much as he did.

Kazuchiyo turned on his heel and stepped toward the voice, eager to follow it to its source. He was halted almost immediately by one of the soldiers seizing his shoulder. The man let go just as swiftly—captive or no, he dared not bruise the son of a samurai so high above his own station—but he did fix Kazuchiyo with a disapproving eye.

"Your chamber is this way, young lord," he said, indicating the opposite direction.

"Who is that?" Kazuchiyo asked, his focus unwavering. "Someone is screaming. Shouldn't you go and see?"

"That's no concern of ours or yours."

The soldier gestured for them to continue on, but Kazuchiyo could not, such was his desperation for a face that did not belong to an enemy. "Lord Aritaka said I am allowed to roam," he said, wishing his voice were stronger, more commanding. "Please, won't you escort me there?"

The soldier frowned severely, but as the wailing continued he, too, was moved enough by curiosity to relent. "Very well," he said. "Do not leave our side."

Kazuchiyo hurried down the narrow castle corridors as quickly as decorum allowed. He traced the voice down the stairs and past what appeared to be the healer's chambers, to a small room at the base of the main keep. By then he could no longer hear the raging cries, but two more soldiers were already standing at the open doorway. Kazuchiyo shouldered past them, eager to see.

He was rewarded with the man from the battlefield, but not quite as he remembered. Though still of an impressive stature, he was no hulking demon, and he was younger than he had seemed, no older than a teenager himself. His jaw was stern, but his brow was drawn tight with strain, and he groaned and panted atop a thin mattress of straw. Dried blood stained the bandages covering his otherwise bare arms and torso, and sweat soaked the rest of him. Even though he had stopped his shouting he was shaking in the grip of a grueling recovery, and he wasn't alone.

A woman knelt at his side, clad in a flowing indigo kimono. Her hair was rich and dark and fastened at the nape of her neck with a shimmering gold comb, her face soft and round, old-fashioned in its beauty. She hummed a gentle melody as she stroked the young warrior's hair, and gradually, he calmed. With shuddering breaths he grew lax at her side.

"There," said Kazuchiyo's guardian. "Now you've seen. It's time to go."

The woman lifted her head and fixed Kazuchiyo with eyes wide and round as ink droplets. "Oh!" she said, and she smiled at him. "Is this him? Lord Tatsutomi's son?"

The soldiers hesitated. This was a woman who lay outside their natural chain of command, and they were unsure what amount of deference they were meant to show her. She took an unseemly amount of amusement in their confusion. "Let him come in," she said, waving Kazuchiyo forward. "There's no danger."

Kazuchiyo hurried to join her at the young warrior's side, heedless to the soldiers' disapproval. "I didn't know if he survived," he said, gaze leaping between each of the many bandaged wounds. The *thunk* of striking arrows echoed between his ears. "Will he live?"

"He's survived this long already," said the woman with a

wistful smile. "As long as someone is here to watch over him, I think he will live."

Kazuchiyo spared another look at the woman. She was too finely dressed to be a servant, but he could not imagine the lady of the castle waiting on an unknown foot soldier—an enemy, at that. "*Are* you here to watch over him?" he asked.

She hummed enigmatically. "Does it not appear so?"

"Lady Satsumi," one of the soldiers interrupted. "We're to take that boy back to his room."

"He can stay a while longer. I will watch over him, too." She turned her smile on Kazuchiyo. "You wouldn't harm me, would you, young Tatsutomi?"

Kazuchiyo instinctually lowered his gaze; if this was another test, he could ill afford to fail it. "I only wanted to see that he still lived," he said honestly.

"Then you ought to stay a little longer, just to be sure." Satsumi motioned for the soldiers to stand back. "He's only a boy. Give us a few moments, won't you? And send someone to fetch water and more clean cloth. He will need fresh dressings soon."

The men all shifted in frustration, and after they shared a squeamish glare, one hurried off for the supplies while the rest took up positions just inside and outside the doorway. It mattered to Kazuchiyo very little; his only care was for the young warrior before him, smothered in fitful unconsciousness.

Satsumi soothed the heavy crease from between his eyebrows. "Do you know him?" she asked. "Was he one of your father's?"

"I don't know," Kazuchiyo admitted. "He was wearing Aritaka armor." He watched the rise and fall of each breath, each time praying another would follow. "But he was fighting Aritaka soldiers. I don't know anything about him."

"The rumor is that he stormed onto the field shortly after the fall of the vanguard. He had no armor or weapon until he stole them from his victims. And then he killed indiscriminately until it was over." Satsumi's round eyes gleamed with curiosity.

20

"Like some kind of demon."

Kazuchiyo had witnessed enough of the young man's strength to believe in such a theory. He reached out, drawing his fingertips across the curve of his bicep, feeling out the muscles; the skin was undeniably rough, but still fleshy, still human. "Has he said his name?"

"I don't know that he's said anything to anyone," replied Satsumi. "Except maybe, *AAURRGHH*, like you heard just now."

She cast him a look, expectant, but Kazuchiyo was far removed from even the concept of humor. She sighed apologetically. "Well, that will be the first thing I ask of him, once he's awake enough to speak sense."

Servants came into the room then bearing fresh water and clean rags, but Satsumi welcomed them only long enough to accept their offerings. "Come help me, Little Dragon," she said instead, urging Kazuchiyo to take one of the rags. "Have you tended the wounded before? Not too wet, now. What's your name?"

"It's Kazuchiyo." He squeezed water from the rag and, following Satsumi's guidance, began to wipe the sweat from the young warrior's forehead and brow. "Excuse me, but are you...Lady Aritaka?"

Satsumi laughed, but there was venom behind her amusement, a twitch in her eye. "Goodness, no. Not *yet*." She unwound the bandages around the warrior's shoulder, revealing a deep bruise and a healing arrow wound. "Not unless I can give my lord an heir. For now he has to content himself with the Lady O-ran and her brood."

"My lady," said one of the watchful soldiers. "Please don't fill his ears with that kind of talk."

Satsumi smiled politely at him and then leaned in again to Kazuchiyo. "You see, Kazuchiyo," she said conspiratorially, "best you not listen to the prattling of a courtesan, even if she is our lord's favorite." The man glowered back at her, but she ignored him, returning her focus to the wounded boy. "You

21

must have spoken to Lord Aritaka by now, yes?"

Kazuchiyo watched closely as she applied a rosewood ointment to the shoulder wound. "Yes," he said, not wishing to dwell on that meeting.

"And did he tell you why he chose to keep you alive?"

Kazuchiyo's attention snapped back to her. There was no reason for him to trust anyone residing at Gyoe, much less a loose-tongued courtesan with aims at improving her status, but he was helplessly eager for any information as to Aritaka's unfathomable motives. "He did," he whispered back. "But he lied."

"Of course he lied." Satsumi smiled secretively as she continued to apply the ointment. "The truth is much too obvious to share aloud."

"Lady Satsumi," the soldier warned again, distraught.

But Satsumi paid him no heed, leaning suddenly closer to speak directly into Kazuchiyo's ear. "Lord Aritaka is in need of a proper heir," she said. "His son is famously impotent, and his daughter? Too ferocious for a husband. He has always been jealous of your father for breeding so many sons of great prowess. All he needs from you is a grandson, and then he'll kill you."

Kazuchiyo listened with eyes downcast, his ribs drawn tight. "Why would he not adopt a son from among his generals?"

Satsumi scoffed. "And split his retainers in two as they take sides? His samurai are little more loyal than your father's were, I am sorry to say. Not to mention the harm to Lady O-ran's pride. Strange as it may seem, a son of his enemy will do more to unite than divide these petty war-brains."

The soldier marched forward. "What are you telling him?" he demanded. "I *will* report this to Lord Aritaka."

Satsumi leaned back, all flashing smiles. "Have some pity on the poor boy," she said, sing-song, as she made fussing adjustments to her kimono. "He's all alone in the world, now. He ought to have some idea of who his enemies are."

"He has no enemies here," the soldier retorted, though his tone was less than convincing. "He is our lord's guest, and soon, his son."

"Indeed." Satsumi pushed gracefully to her feet and smiled down at Kazuchiyo. "Remember, Little Dragon, you also have friends here."

Kazuchiyo returned her gaze, and though he counseled himself on restraint, he could not hold his tongue. "Only until *you* can provide Lord Aritaka an heir."

The twist of Satsumi's rouged lips grew sharp. "Keep applying that ointment to his wounds like I showed you," she said, "and he'll recover soon enough. He's lucky to have a clever boy like you watching over him."

Satsumi departed, to the relief of the guards. Their leader gestured to Kazuchiyo. "Come on, now. Back to your room."

"Please let me finish tending to him," he quickly replied, going so far as to bow his head to the floor. "Please, sir. I'll return straight to my room after."

The guard shifted and sighed, and finally he relented. "Well, be quick then. And don't pay any mind to whatever it was that woman told you. She talks more than a monk doesn't."

"Yes, sir," Kazuchiyo replied automatically, and he returned to the warrior, peeling back his remaining bandages. Dedication to his task kept his mind centered, driving out whatever emotion would have tried to build in the aftermath of Satsumi's warnings. He wiped away the sweat and applied the ointment just as she had done. In better days he had done similar for his brothers after long afternoons training in the yard, bruised from wooden *bokken*, but there was no time for those reminiscences, so he thrust them aside as well. There was only the one man in Sakka Province who may have as much of a reason to hate Aritaka as he did.

The young warrior flinched, and his hand snapped around Kazuchiyo's wrist. His palm was clammy, his grip shuddering, but when he opened his eyes, they blazed. He glared up at his caretaker with as much malice as he would an enemy. It gave

23

Kazuchiyo a chill, but then the young man relented, licking his lips. "Water," he said hoarsely.

With his wrist still captured in a tight grip, Kazuchiyo twisted to the side to drag the bottle closer. He spilled some in the effort of tipping it to the man's lips, who drank, ravenous and with eyelids fluttering. When it was gone, the man collapsed onto the mattress and seemed to pass out again.

Kazuchiyo watched him with breath held. "What's your name?" he finally asked.

The young warrior grunted and shuddered. "Fisherman," he said without opening his eyes. "Tree cutter. Boy."

"Those aren't names," Kazuchiyo protested. "Please, I want to know who you are."

"Villager," he continued. "Peasant. Tall one. Slave." Another shudder passed through him, and when his head fell to the side, his temple rested against Kazuchiyo's knee. "Practice."

Kazuchiyo could only speculate as to the young man's meaning then, but a glimpse of old scars surrounding the new gave him enough clue as to be mortified. Gingerly he touched the man's hair, as Satsumi had done, hoping to convey some solace or sympathy, but by then the young warrior was unconscious again, giving no indication that the sentiments were felt.

Kazuchiyo slipped his arm free and returned to his work, dressing the remaining wounds as best he could. Afterward he allowed the soldiers to escort him to his room.

That night, as he curled tight beneath heavy sleeping robes, he could hear the young warrior again, howling throughout the castle.

CHAPTER TWO

In the morning, new soldiers came to relieve the others, and Kazuchiyo asked in the humblest language if he could be allowed to meet and tend to the young warrior again.

"Oh, you mean Yagi-douji?" the man said with a squeamish look and Kazuchiyo straightened up, eager for even a moniker to refer to the stranger as. "He's dangerous." But Kazuchiyo persisted, and at length, he gained permission.

The basement room was in a terrible state compared to how Kazuchiyo had left it the morning before. The futon was torn, its stuffing spilling out and stained with dried blood. One entire sliding door had been broken through, leaving wooden splinters everywhere. The young man himself was stretched out awkwardly amidst his bedding, flushed, his breath shallow. Servants and samurai huddled nearby and stammered to each other over what was to be done.

"He woke last night in some kind of fit," Kazuchiyo's guard told him. "Threw a man straight through that wall, broke his arm. It took General Ebara striking him to put him down. We were lucky he was near."

Kazuchiyo glanced between the men, but he did not see anyone dressed well enough to be a general. "There's more blood than yesterday. He must have torn open his wounds. Has anyone tended them?"

"You're welcome to try," the guard replied, only to recant when Kazuchiyo started forward. "Wait, I didn't mean—"

Kazuchiyo ignored him. To some it may have looked like fearless courage that allowed him to kneel at the boy's side, but to Kazuchiyo, it was only that his life meant less to him than the fate of his champion. When he touched the young warrior's shoulder, he startled, and he fixed Kazuchiyo with the same hateful glare as the morning before. It was no less frightening but Kazuchiyo did not flinch away.

"Water?" he suggested, and the young warrior nodded warily.

When Kazuchiyo was not immediately thrown against a wall, the guards relaxed. "You all have chores to get to," one samurai said, and he shooed the onlookers away. "Back to your duties. And find the beast a new room."

The crowd reluctantly dispersed. A few guards remained but kept their distance, sidling closer only to deliver the requested water and fresh dressings. As the young warrior gulped down his drink, Kazuchiyo took the opportunity to investigate his wounds. He discovered a gash just over his hip with a fresh, oozing scab.

"You'll never heal if you move so much," Kazuchiyo said quietly, and though he had no more ointment, he wet a cloth with the remaining water to dab the wound clean.

"I wasn't trying to," he retorted, but he did calm, relaxing onto his side as Kazuchiyo worked.

"You broke a man's arm. Were you...having a nightmare?"

He didn't answer. Kazuchiyo let him be until there was nothing left to do but try and bind the wound. "Can you sit up? So I can wrap it?"

The young warrior grumbled wordlessly, and it soon became clear, as he tried to maneuver his arms beneath him, that his stubbornness was meant to hide his weakness. He propped himself up on one elbow so that Kazuchiyo could thread the gauze wrap beneath him.

"Won't you tell me your name?" Kazuchiyo tried again once he was finished. "I won't tell anyone, if you don't want me to."

He offered another sip of water, which the young warrior accepted eagerly, even as his eyes darted away. "I already did," he muttered.

"'Practice'?" said Kazuchiyo, and they were nestled so closely together that he felt the other shudder at the word. A heavy weight fell over him. "No one's ever named you? Not even as a boy?"

"Leave me alone." He shoved Kazuchiyo's hand away, spilling the rest of the water, and thumped onto his back once more. His temper cost him; the drop made him hiss and rub his wounded shoulder. When Kazuchiyo reached for him, he shoved him away again. "Go away! I don't want your help!"

Kazuchiyo leaned back, but he moved no farther than that. He wished he had the luxury of showing his anger so easily. "One of the soldiers called you Yagi-douji," he said. When the young man glared at him, confused, he explained. "He must think you have the strength of a horde of oni."

"Yagi," he repeated, his brow furrowing. "Yagi-douji." He snorted and closed his eyes. "I don't hate it."

Kazuchiyo smiled. The expression felt strange, as if he couldn't hold onto it. "*I* think you're as strong as *one hundred* oni."

The so-called "Yagi" frowned, unmoved. "It's not so hard to break a man's arm."

"I mean on the field," said Kazuchiyo, goosebumps on his skin as he remembered the howl rippling out through the rain. "You must have killed dozens of men. I'll never forget it."

Yagi blinked up at him. "You were there?" he asked, bewildered and squinting. "At the battle?"

"Well...yes. Of course." Kazuchiyo frowned at him in return. "I'm Kazuchiyo. You don't...remember me?"

We can easily blame blood loss and fevered sleep for the

uncommon length of time it took Yagi to assemble his wits. Once he had, he sat up so quickly they nearly collided. "That was *you?*" He immediately wilted, wrapping his arm around his chest. For once, he did not protest when Kazuchiyo moved to support him, and the close quarters must have stirred his memory into place. He looked upon Kazuchiyo with fresh eyes, sobered by shock and disgust. "That was *you,*" he said again, breathless as he gripped Kazuchiyo's sleeve. "But...you're just a boy."

Kazuchiyo swallowed, feeling the lump crawl down into his stomach. He thought of Tomonaga's teasing face splitting open beneath an arrow. "I wasn't there to fight," he said quietly.

Yagi stared, seemingly baffled. As if for the first time he gazed about the room, eyeing the guards on the other side of the broken door and the Aritaka crest on their armor. "Where are we?" He tried to use Kazuchiyo's shoulder to stand, but his legs would barely heed him, let alone hold him, and he had to abandon the effort before he'd halfway begun. Instead, he launched into a series of progressively anxious questions. "Who are you? Whose son are you—why did they bring me here? Why am I here!"

"Calm down," Kazuchiyo urged, doing his best to prevent Yagi from attempting to stand again. "Move too much and you'll reopen your wounds."

"Why do you care?" Yagi continued to holler, growing ever more agitated with the furious panic of a wounded animal. Unable to move as he wished, he settled with grabbing up Kazuchiyo's collar while the guards shifted in indecisive anxiety. "Why is a samurai boy looking after me? Why haven't you killed me!"

"I can answer that," said a woman in the doorway.

Both boys looked to the open entrance: it was Aritaka's female advisor again, dressed in a handsome, forest-green *kariginu* with gold cords. Her long hair was swept back and topped with a tall, black cap. Though finally given a clear vision of her face, Kazuchiyo could discern very little about her age or demeanor. Not young, but not aged; not concerned, but not disinterested. She strode into the room with two young women in pleated skirts following, each carrying a tray of supplies.

"The hell are you?" Yagi grunted, and Kazuchiyo, already bowing his head, cringed at his disrespect. But the woman was unperturbed, and she lowered to her knees just beside the pair of them. She pressed her open palm to Yagi's shoulder.

"Lie down," she said, and Yagi's back hit the floor with a great *smack*, leaving him gasping and wincing.

Kazuchiyo flinched as well, hate stirring in his belly as he listened to Yagi's ragged breath. "Please don't punish him too harshly, honored master," he said, praying she would hear only his sincerity. He found Yagi's hand and gripped it tight. "He's very nearly delirious from his wounds."

"Then once he is cured of that, there should be no excuse for future rudeness," she replied, her voice rough like a bullfrog. "Lift your head, Kazuchiyo. You ought to see me at work."

Kazuchiyo did so, watching as the two assistants set out their tools. One poured a bitter-smelling broth into cups, while the other prepared an inkstone and paper.

"Don't touch me," Yagi growled, gripping Kazuchiyo's hand so hard that it ached. "Fucking demon!"

"A compliment indeed, coming from Yagi-douji, the howling oni of Shimegahara," said the woman with a tilt of her head. She regarded the boy as one might a delicious meal offered by a disliked acquaintance. "Hush now. I have very little patience for time wasted."

One of the assistants pushed the tray with the ink and paper over to her, and with swift elegance she took up the brush and began to write. The other offered up the steaming cups to Kazuchiyo. "Drink," said the woman without looking up from her calligraphy. "One for each of you. He'll need your help, Kazuchiyo."

"I'm not drinking that," Yagi said.

Kazuchiyo accepted the first cup. The memory of this mysterious priest sliding his father's head into a silken bag

29

was tempered somewhat by her warning him of impropriety in Aritaka's hall, and he couldn't bring himself to believe she truly meant them harm. There were plenty of less obvious ways she could have done away with them, if that was her goal. Still gripping Yagi's hand, he drank.

The first gulp was bitter, and he grimaced, forcing himself not to gag. The rest went down easier, warm and earthy, and he managed it all in one breath. When he finished, he was surprised to see the intensity with which Yagi was watching him. It did not seem to be paranoia for his own safety, but rather concern for his young guest, and it warmed Kazuchiyo all the more.

"It's not pleasant," he warned, trading his empty cup for the second dose. "But it will do you good to have something in your stomach."

"Then have her bring saké," Yagi retorted, but he did not resist much longer. With a great effort to appear rebellious, he allowed Kazuchiyo to support him while he drank. Just as the last drop was spent, the woman swept up the rectangular paper tag she had written on and pressed it to his chest.

Yagi jerked away, and his cup clattered to the ground. "What is this?" He scratched at the paper but couldn't get his fingernails beneath it. "Get this off me!"

"Leave it be," the woman scolded him. "It's there to help you heal." When Yagi continued to paw and scrape, she sighed and put her hand again to his shoulder. "Lie down."

Yagi's back hit the floor again, and he hissed, teeth bared. "Stop that!"

He looked ready to say more, and the woman ready to punish him for it, so Kazuchiyo covered Yagi's mouth and bowed over him. "Thank you for your kindness toward my undeserving friend," he said, relying on manners instilled in him by his mother. "And for your kindness toward me when I was in audience with Lord Aritaka. I am very grateful."

The woman chuckled, sharp and brief, her coarse voice giving it an eerie tone. Her assistants giggled beside her. "I had high hopes for you having sense," she said. "Do you know who I am?"

Yagi huffed against his palm, and the pair exchanged a look. Only once Kazuchiyo was confident that Yagi would not cause them further trouble did he remove his hand. "Forgive me, I do not. Though if you'll permit me a guess, I suspect you're an *onmyouji* in Lord Aritaka's employ."

"Employment does not accurately describe our arrangement," the woman replied. "But yes, I have offered him my advice on celestial and other matters. Are you very familiar with onmyouji?"

"No, honored master. Though my father sometimes consults...*consulted* with the temple monks."

"Wise men usually do." There was a hint of sarcasm in her tone that set Kazuchiyo on edge, but she gave him no opportunity to dwell upon it. "I am called Iomori no Jun. You may address me as Master Iomori. Make sure your friend leaves that *o-fuda* alone. His bloodlust is attracting the spirits of the men he's slain, and they very well might possess him through his wounds without it."

Yagi stiffened, his eyes quite wide. Though Kazuchiyo was unsure if she spoke in earnest, seeing Yagi's anxiety raised his as well. "I will, Master Iomori." He bowed more deeply. "Thank you, again, for your help."

The assistants gathered up the supplies, and Kazuchiyo was glad for it, eager for the woman to move on. Her bland stare was beginning to dig beneath his skin. To his disappointment, she motioned for the two women to depart ahead of her, and with bows they did so. "Your oni friend here asked a question as I was arriving," she said. "I think it only fair the two of you know the truth, it being the same for both of you."

Kazuchiyo lifted his head cautiously, neck hairs on end. "'Why are we still alive?'"

"I'm sure you recognized that Aritaka did not tell you the truth," Iomori continued, matter-of-fact bordering on smug. "And you've likely heard other speculations." The subtle downturn of her lip convinced Kazuchiyo that she specifically had the Lady Satsumi in mind. "But the truth is very simple: you're alive because I convinced Aritaka that you should be."

Yagi made no sound, but Kazuchiyo could feel him seethe. He himself was unsure of his reaction. "May I ask why, Master Iomori?" he asked.

"Because," she leaned closer as if imparting a grave secret, "I have read your future, Young Dragon. I see great things for you yet to come." Her eyebrows quirked. "And for your fearsome ally here. Both of you have destiny written in your names that you must yet fulfill. And I would see it done."

"My name?" Kazuchiyo flushed with heat, and his throat went unexpectedly tight. "I don't...have my full name yet."

"Kazuchiyo." Iomori traced the characters against the floor with her finger. "'A thousand ages of peace.' Aritaka would say your father chose such a name out of cowardice, eager to put his lifetime of war behind him before you came of age, but to the wise, peace is never cowardice. Only the strong can afford peace." She narrowed her eyes on him, and he felt their grip harden around his chest. "And you will be strong. I have seen it."

Kazuchiyo could not respond, and none could blame him for that. One question with three answers, and none of them he could lay his trust upon. To his credit, he bowed his head in acknowledgment. He did not trust his voice, no matter what he could have said.

Iomori took pity on him. "It is fine if you do not fully understand yet." She leaned back. "Know only that I am held highly in Aritaka's favor, and that I want you alive." She glanced to Yagi. "Both of you. That should be all that matters to you now."

She stood, and instinctively Kazuchiyo lowered his head again. "Thank you, Master Iomori," he murmured. Yagi offered nothing, and without a parting word, Iomori removed herself from the room.

"Liar," Yagi grumbled once she was far gone. He raked his

nails across the o-fuda a few times before giving up. "A noble like that will feed us to her dogs as soon as we're not useful to her. Whatever she's after."

Kazuchiyo nodded, but he still had no strength to speak his mind. Her talk of names had shaken him more deeply than he could have prepared for, and all around him the unfamiliar castle echoed with pounding rain and the voices of dead kin. He would never take the name his father had prepared, a thought that already haunted him, like a ghost dragging him away from a world he no longer belonged to.

"Are you all right?" Yagi startled him from his melancholy. "You're pale."

"I'm fine," Kazuchiyo reassured him, eager for the excuse to lie. "Please don't worry about me. You have your own healing to do."

Yagi stared up at him, unconvinced. "Why are you here?" he asked again bluntly. "You're a samurai's son. Why look after me?"

"Someone has to." He tugged the wrinkles out of Yagi's bedding as best he could and checked to make sure his bandages were tight. "If you ask me to leave, I will," he offered reluctantly. "But I would rather stay."

In truth, Kazuchiyo was too frightened to go back to his room. He feared that in solitude the memories raised by Iomori's words would rise up and drown him in his grief; he feared even more that Aritaka or some other might call on him and find him in such a state. But Yagi was strength incarnate as far as his young mind was concerned, and as long as he stayed by his side, he could stave off the urge to weep a while longer.

Whether or not Yagi understood, he snorted quietly. "I'm not going to order you to do anything."

"Thank you," said Kazuchiyo, and for the remainder of the afternoon he stayed in Yagi's room. The poor youth was not very good company, spending many hours fitfully asleep. Kazuchiyo soothed him as best he could. By making Yagi's care his duty, he was able to distract himself for a time.

And when Kazuchiyo grew weary, he stretched out on the floor alongside Yagi's bedding. He watched Yagi's chest rise and fall, trying to imagine from where the young man drew his indomitable strength. Could he have been more than human after all, to defeat so many, to survive blows that would have killed lesser men? Perhaps Iomori had spoken the truth, and Kazuchiyo owed her his life—but not Yagi. His life he had fought for and won through sheer force of skill, and any envy Kazuchiyo might have felt toward him was swallowed by awe.

Kazuchiyo slipped his hand into Yagi's while he slept. His palm was so broad, his fingers so long, his knuckles so sturdy. Kazuchiyo squeezed him tight as if that firm hand were his only lifeline, engraving the weight and the warmth of it into his memory.

Eventually the footsteps of a patrolling guard convinced Kazuchiyo he had better return to the seclusion of his room. That night, he held his hand close to his chest, depending on the lingering imprint of Yagi's strength to grant him sleep.

CHAPTER THREE

The next day was devoted to preparations for Kazuchiyo's coming-of-age ceremony. He was fitted for a new wardrobe, particularly the handsomely embroidered robes he would wear before Lord Aritaka. He was given extravagant meals he barely touched and introduced to a dozen different generals. Though he thought to look for the man that had severed his father's neck, his memory could not place him, and in the end he only took particular note of General Ebara, a squat but muscular man with a woolly beard and wide-set eyes. The sternness of his frown made it easy to picture that he had been the one to strike Yagi down from his fevered state.

Then came the advisors. They tested him on history and calligraphy, asked him all manner of questions about his home province, his family, his father's vassals. Iomori was present for much of it, judging his responses. He answered dutifully, depending on the lessons drilled into him by childhood tutors. By the time evening drew close and Lord Aritaka summoned him, he was exhausted and buzzing, like a sleeping limb struggling to draw blood back to it.

"I'm told that you've given no trouble to anyone in your time here," said Lord Aritaka as they shared supper together.

"I am pleased to hear it, though it also makes me suspicious. I want to know what's on your mind."

"My only concern is for the ceremony tomorrow, Lord Aritaka," Kazuchiyo replied.

"So you say." Aritaka regarded him stoically over the lip of his sake cup. "Well. You've given me no reason to doubt you. After tomorrow, you're to address me as Father."

His wife, the Lady O-ran, had deliberately avoided looking in Kazuchiyo's direction throughout the meal, but she glanced to her husband then. Her dark eyes were heavy with resentment. Kazuchiyo still had no choice but to reply, "Yes, Lord Aritaka."

"I'll relieve the guards that have been following you about all this time," Aritaka carried on. "You're free to move about the keep only, for now. I trust you already understand what the consequences would be if you were to overstep your bounds."

Kazuchiyo pushed his rice bowl aside. "Yes, Father."

After supper, Kazuchiyo was escorted to his room. He stayed as long as he could stand, listening to the guards returning to their normal patrols. The buzz was spreading through him, leaving numbness in his limbs. If he let it settle any deeper he was sure he would never be able to expel it again. And so, once the night was at its darkest, he lit a candle lantern and snuck out of his room to head for Yagi's.

He wasn't there. Kazuchiyo shuddered with panic, but it wasn't long after that he heard a familiar voice groaning in complaint. He followed it to the southern corridor where the rooms faced the outer wall, and there discovered Yagi in fresh bedding, enduring the same nightmares.

"Yagi," Kazuchiyo called, hushed, placing the lantern far out of reach as he made a careful approach. He had not forgotten the threat of a broken arm, but he had no idea what Aritaka's men would think of finding him out and about in the castle so soon after being unleashed, and he was eager to wake the young warrior before he advanced to howling. "Yagi." He knelt a little ways away and stretched his arm out to tap the back of his hand. "Wake up."

Yagi immediately lashed out, and he might have caught Kazuchiyo by the wrist if he wasn't already expecting it. His eyes snapped open a moment later, wild like an animal's. Then he spotted Kazuchiyo, and after a momentary confusion, he sobered. Shame flashed across his face as he drew his hand back. "It's you."

Kazuchiyo edged closer. "Do you always have nightmares?" he asked quietly.

Yagi got his arms beneath him, and though it took visible effort on his part, he sat up. He was still breathing hard, sweat on his lip, but when he looked to Kazuchiyo, something in his regard of him had changed. The pinch of his eyebrows was strained and sympathetic. "Should you be here?" he asked, keeping his voice low as well. "Don't get yourself in trouble for me."

His concern was encouraging, though Kazuchiyo could not fully appreciate it. "Someone told you about me."

"One of the generals, Ebara. He told me what Aritaka plans to do." Yagi scowled and twisted the bedding between his knuckles. "Fucking samurai. What kind of man would demand this of a boy? If only he'd come down here, I'd cut his throat for you."

"No," Kazuchiyo said quickly, and then hushed himself, fearful of nearby ears. "No, please. If anything happens to him *or* to me, it's my mother and brother that will suffer for it."

"Cowards! If only..." Yagi looked plenty ready to continue his rant, but a glance at Kazuchiyo held him back. "If you don't want me to take his head for you, why do you keep coming here?" he asked instead.

Kazuchiyo lowered his eyes. He was certain he could not put his true thoughts into words without exposing himself as a childish fool. "There isn't anywhere or anyone else," he said.

"Every soul in this castle is loyal to my enemy. Except you..." He took a deep breath. "I feel safer with you here."

He expected sarcasm or scorn, but when he peeked, Yagi was sighing, his jaw working anxiously. "You shouldn't," Yagi said. "I killed just as many dragons out on that field, you know."

"Why?" Kazuchiyo edged closer. Of all the mysteries he had yet to solve, this was closest to his pounding heart. "If you're not a soldier for either side, what were you doing there?"

Yagi did not answer for some time. He stared fixedly at his knees. The muscles in his face and neck constricted, then relaxed, then constricted again, battling through anger and guilt and confusion. "I was..." He started, but then his face screwed up again, and to Kazuchiyo's surprise his eyes were glossy with fury. "Something happened to me," he tried again. He touched his chest, and upon being reminded of the o-fuda still sealed there, he dug his fingernails into it. "Something... broke in me. I don't remember most of it after storming the field."

"And before?" Kazuchiyo prompted, half expecting Yagi to confess that he crawled out of some portal to the afterlife.

Yagi clenched his fists and again took his time answering. "The morning before the battle, I was out hunting fowl along the riverbank with a few men from the village," he said carefully, as if it took effort to remember. "A troop of soldiers stopped us, soldiers working for Aritaka, I think. They stole everything we'd caught. The old village headman begged me not to fight back, but when we returned to the village..." His lips pulled back in a sneer. "We found out they'd already been there. They'd already beaten that old man's son half to death stealing their harvest. I wasn't going to let him talk me down again—not *again, never* again. Not after everything I've—"

He took in a deep breath. He looked ready to storm out of the castle and recreate those moments on the muddy field, and Kazuchiyo watched, transfixed. Then he let it out again. "Samurai," he muttered. "Hypocrites and butchers, but *I'm* the oni. I guess that's not wrong."

He collected himself then, scraping the back of his hand across his face. "Fuck. That man Ebara that was here—he said he wants to adopt me."

Kazuchiyo straightened his back. "General Ebara wants you as a son? What about your home?"

Yagi shrugged raggedly and then winced, rubbing his shoulder. "The village wasn't my home. It was just a place to earn food. They're probably happy enough to be rid of me." He snorted. "Aritaka was never going to let me leave anyway, not if they can get some use out of me. That woman said she wanted me alive, but she didn't say anything about becoming a samurai, the fox."

Kazuchiyo licked his lips and waited until he had caught his breath to reply. "Then you'll be staying," he said, relief making him faint. "Even if you don't like us, a son of a general is—"

"It wouldn't be here," Yagi interrupted. He looked to Kazuchiyo with an apologetic frown. "Ebara serves at Ninari Castle on the western border. He's taking me there."

Kazuchiyo's hopes melted away, and that prickling buzz crept back into his fingertips. All morning they had tested him on his knowledge of geography, yet he could not remember how far Castles Gyoe and Ninari were from each other. "So you'd...become an Aritaka vassal." He clawed after his better sense. "West of here is Kibaku Province. Is he already planning on attacking them? Is that why Master Iomori wanted you alive? To fight in another war?"

"If I refuse they'll probably just execute me," Yagi said. "Compared to that, killing more samurai isn't so bad. Or I'll kill my way out if I don't like it. I've done it before." He eyed Kazuchiyo with curiosity. "If you do become Aritaka's heir, I'll be taking heads in your name after all. What will *you* do?"

Kazuchiyo cursed himself for not being more astute; he wasn't losing an ally after all. Once he was lord of Castle Gyoe, he could order Ebara and his sons to any post or command of his choosing. All he need be was patient. The thought of being separated from the only man he could begin to trust was a bitter one, but he took a breath and recited it silently to himself: *all he need be was patient.*

Yagi flinched suddenly, his nostrils flaring. His head whipped toward the door, and he yanked at Kazuchiyo's robe. "Get behind me." Kazuchiyo had no idea what had triggered his caution until the door slid open.

A man and a woman stood in the opening, dressed in close-fitting robes and pleated trousers of Aritaka's colors, hair slicked back beneath peasant scarves. They might have been mistaken for castle servants if not for the man cleaning blood from the blade of a short sword. As the woman came forward, Kazuchiyo caught a glimpse of a third man behind them tying Aritaka armor over his chest.

Yagi gave him another tug, but before either of them could properly brace themselves, the woman dropped to one knee before them. "Master Tatsutomi," she said with hushed urgency. "Please come with us, quickly."

"What?" Kazuchiyo glanced to her belt where her own *kodachi* was sheathed. "Who are you?"

"I can explain once we're away from the castle." She offered her hand. "But we have to go now, before the next patrol comes."

"This is some kind of rescue?" Yagi said incredulously. "Who sent you?"

"One of my father's vassals?" Kazuchiyo guessed. Without thinking he took the woman's hand and allowed her to draw him to his feet. "My mother's family?"

"It doesn't matter," the woman said, with such hurried carelessness that it served as its own answer: no dragon had sent them. "We need to get you out of here before tomorrow."

"But Yagi…" Kazuchiyo stumbled as he tried to look back; Yagi was struggling to his knees in bewilderment. "He has to come with us."

The man with his sword still unsheathed grabbed him by the arm. "There's no time. Just go before we're all caught."

They propelled Kazuchiyo toward the door, and the hands digging into him, their bruising insistence, reminded him too clearly of the gnarled man dragging him from his army's tent. A terrible weight tried to settle in his limbs, and for an instant he was helpless, just as he had been watching his family slaughtered before him. His breath caught several times before he could give it voice.

"My brother," he gasped out. "My mother—if I leave Gyoe, Lord Aritaka will have them killed!"

"That's not our concern," said the man, confirming even further that these were no allies. He gave Kazuchiyo a shove to keep him moving and then turned back into the room, fingers flexing around the handle of his weapon. "Go on," he told the woman. "I'll take care of this."

Yagi was on his knees, but he was watching Kazuchiyo, looking to him to know how to act. As much of a beast as he was, his movements were stiff with recovery and the stranger within easy striking distance. There was so little time to think and Kazuchiyo felt so heavy, but he could not bear to stand by and do nothing yet again. Yagi's voice—not again, *never again*—thundered out of his chest and before he was aware of his own actions, he had snatched the kodachi out of the woman's sheath and spun about, stabbing it into the man's back.

He didn't cry out. He arched beneath the blow, and Kazuchiyo shuddered at the impact of blade to flesh that swept up his arm. As he started to twist about, shocked, Kazuchiyo wrenched the sword free. The stench of blood that should have turned his stomach only heightened his determination, and he swung again.

The woman yanked him back. They tumbled out into the hall together and grappled for the sword, hitting the far wall. She was taller and stronger than him, and her fist across his temple knocked him to the ground. The kodachi skittered out of his grip. "You crazy fool!" she shouted at him, her words blurring in his rattled ears. "We hate Aritaka as much as you do!" She took fistfuls of Kazuchiyo's robe and hauled him to his feet. "Come on before—"

Yagi barreled out of the room with a roar, and in the next moment the woman was gone, ripped away as Kazuchiyo was thrown to the ground again. With strength and momentum in defiance of his many injuries, Yagi heaved her straight off her feet and flung her, sending her crashing through the nearest barred window. Wood snapped with an incredible percussion, and she screamed as she rolled down the tiled eave and out of sight.

The last of the trio gaped at them. When Yagi turned toward him with a face contorted in rage, he panicked and lunged with his sword. Yagi batted it aside with his already bandaged forearm and punched him in the face hard enough for bones to break. The man hit the floor, and Yagi struck him dead with his own sword.

Kazuchiyo grabbed up the kodachi once more and clawed to his feet. His lungs heaved and his hands shook, but both sensations were dulled, like distant echoes, as he took in the scene. The castle was already shouting in answer to the commotion, and soon the soldiers would come seeking explanation.

"Kazuchiyo," said Yagi. It was the first time he had said his name since the field, and Kazuchiyo shivered. "Do you know who they were?"

Kazuchiyo looked to the dead man in stolen armor, to the shattered window, to the man back in the room who was still alive and struggling to his knees. For them to have infiltrated Gyoe at all was a tremendous feat and could only mean that they were shinobi of some skill, that Kazuchiyo and Yagi were lucky to have survived at all. If they were not free agents sent by Tatsutomi clan to retrieve their fallen lord's son, they could have been from a neighboring province, hoping to steal away the North Bear's new pawn before he could solidify his power any further. They could have been sent from within, meant to drag Kazuchiyo away from the castle so that their master had an excuse to have him and his remaining family done away with; they could have even been sent by Aritaka himself, if he had changed his mind over Kazuchiyo's fate but with no graceful way to dispose of him. There were many options, but only one that could be cast in Kazuchiyo's favor. It startled him how clearly he could see it now that he held a bloodied sword in his hand.

The guards rushed forward. "Yagi, please, get on your knees," Kazuchiyo said quickly. "Please, this once, bow your head and don't say anything."

Yagi eyed the approaching men with their spears warily, but he lowered himself to his knees. "What are you going to tell them?"

"Please, just keep your head down and don't speak."

Kazuchiyo returned to the room. The man he had stabbed had been stabbed again by his own sword, this time through the throat—Yagi's doing, no doubt—but he was clinging to life, blood pouring from his mouth. His eyes rolled up as Kazuchiyo stood over him, confused and hateful. But he had no strength left with which to fight, and with his nerves steeled, Kazuchiyo stabbed him through the heart. The force of it rattled the small bones in his wrist, but that, too, reached him only as ripples from the far end of a pond.

"What goes on here?"

Kazuchiyo released the kodachi. He turned from the body and stretched to the floor in a full bow. "We've killed two men," he answered dutifully. "And a woman was thrown from the window. I think she's dead, but someone should confirm, just in case."

He expected a volley of questions, but none came. Thankfully, neither did the sound of Yagi getting himself killed for sneering at Aritaka soldiers when one wearing their armor lay dead at his feet. Some time passed, and Kazuchiyo's sight began to blur, but then a new set of footsteps joined the baffled soldiers. A deep voice said, "Kazuchiyo, what have you done?"

Kazuchiyo let even the echoes and ripples fall away. "These

three were wearing my lord's colors," he said, "but they were not acting in my lord's interest. They were sent to kill me."

"Kill you?" Lord Aritaka repeated. "Sent by whom?"

"That I do not know, as they wouldn't say." He took in a deep breath through his nose and placed his wager. "But I find it hard to imagine they were intruders. The mighty Castle Gyoe has never been breached."

Aritaka went silent, and with Kazuchiyo cooling his forehead against the floor, there was no way to gauge his reaction. At length, the lord cleared his throat loudly, and Kazuchiyo took that as a cue to lift his head. Their gazes meet across the short space, and he felt the old bear judging him. Then Aritaka's lip curled in a subtle, dry smile.

"That's much better," he said, and he continued to judge a few beats more, waiting for Kazuchiyo's composure to break. It did not, and by the time he turned away, the smile was gone.

Lord Aritaka ordered his men to investigate the bodies and dispose of them, and to fetch the physician for Yagi's freshly wounded arm. None could have envied the position Kazuchiyo had put Aritaka in: whether to admit his beloved Gyoe's impenetrable defenses had been breached by an outside enemy, or to admit his own confidence had been breached by an enemy within. More than one eye would turn to the Lady O-ran and those loyal to her in the aftermath. To sow discord between a lord and his wife was quite bold for Kazuchiyo's first foray into politics, and I am exceedingly proud of him for that.

Kazuchiyo and Yagi were herded into another room where they were tended, wounds cleaned and bandaged, fresh clothing brought to them. They had only moments of privacy, but Kazuchiyo took full advantage, leaning in close to Yagi's ear.

"Thank you," he whispered. "If anyone asks, please tell them they were here to kill us and that you don't know anything else."

"As far as I'm concerned, that's the truth anyway," Yagi replied. He wrinkled his nose. "You probably saved my life."

"I *know* you saved mine," Kazuchiyo replied. "Thank you."

Yagi looked even more uncomfortable, and he scraped his fist across his mouth. "Whoever this was, it won't be the last time they try to kill you. What will you do?"

Kazuchiyo glanced to the hall where the soldiers were milling about, occasionally looking in their direction. All were in Aritaka colors, but there was no telling which could be trusted, if any. He was certain Lord Aritaka and Master Iomori were somewhere close beyond them, conspiring, Ladies Satsumi and O-ran plotting somewhere above. Every one of them had already claimed his life as theirs one way or another, and he could not allow himself to be numb. Not even for one moment longer.

"I have to be stronger," he said, facing Yagi with all the conviction he could muster. When his hands threatened to shake, he took a deep breath and twisted them in his hakama to keep them steady. "I'll be as strong as you, and as clever as—" He gulped and shook his head. "And *more* clever than my father. No one will be able to say I'm only alive because of them. Never again." He quaked with emotion broiling just below his surface, saving and savoring it. "Until the day comes when I can finally ask you to take Aritaka's head."

Yagi stared back at him. To Kazuchiyo he was steadfast and inspiring, but I like to think he was overwhelmed then, a little in awe of this mysterious young boy trying so hard to take hold of his destiny. Whatever misgivings he might have harbored were pushed aside, and he nodded to Kazuchiyo seriously. "I'll be ready," he promised.

The next day, Kazuchiyo was washed and fed and dressed in handsome indigo robes. He followed a procession of Aritaka loyalists to the city's large temple complex where the ceremony would take place. All the generals and advisors he had met were in attendance, as well as O-ran and Satsumi, Master Iomori, and a slew of others. Even Yagi was there in the company of his soon-to-be-father, pale but alert, his robes a bit too short for his long limbs. His brows were tightly knit, and Kazuchiyo took great comfort in his sympathetic frustration.

He said not a word through the ceremony. He drank the saké given to him, accepted his Aritaka armor and a pair of handsome swords. For the last time that he would ever allow, he stayed still and silent as they cut his hair.

At the end of it, he faced his new father and their vassals as Aritaka Kazumune. But in his heart his name never changed.

CHAPTER FOUR

K azuchiyo lived at Gyoe for five years after that, and there are a great number of stories I could share with you about his life then. Though he was never allowed to journey beyond the limits of the surrounding town, there are plenty of adventures both exciting and mundane with which a teenaged lord can entertain himself in a castle keep. More mundane ones than exciting, perhaps, but enough to fill a pillow book. He studied and trained among Sakka's finest, learning the arts of war from aged generals, clashing swords with elite masters. He explored every corner of the castle, unearthing texts of ancient tales and battles past, and spiriting them away to rooftops and alcoves where he could steal moments of privacy. He learned the habits of Gyoe's occupants both high and low and curried favor wherever he could. By necessity he was obedient and humble whenever called upon, never so much as before his adoptive father. In all things he dedicated himself with impeccable conviction toward the secret goal he carried, ears ever keen for news from the western border. Every grain of knowledge, every favor earned and skill obtained, was a weapon for his growing arsenal.

And I would happily sing praises for his youthful fortitude, but as far as Kazuchiyo was concerned, he was still a prisoner. He was a spy among his enemy, a shameful spectacle too weak to do anything but bow and grovel before his family's killers.

So let us not dwell on those painful years. Let us resume instead in the budding spring of 1487, just after Kazuchiyo reached eighteen years of age. He had grown into an admirable man by any measure: handsome, with thick, coal-black hair and eyes bright as gold; clever, with wits nearly sharp enough to rival a fox; even-tempered to the point of stoicism. Even if some among Aritaka's ranks suspected he still harbored resentment toward his situation, he gave them no reason to act on it. He woke before sunrise every morning and hurried to complete his tasks with the utmost proficiency, and on one such morning, after a night of rainy sleeplessness, those duties conveyed him to the chamber of Lady Satsumi.

Satsumi greeted him warmly, as she always did, but her face was still pale after a week of illness following the loss of her most recent pregnancy. "I have breakfast for us," she said as she swept him inside, where two trays awaited them. "Come sit with me, Kazu. Forgive me if I keep you in suspense for a while, but I've missed your company and I'm determined to do what I can to prolong it."

"My company is yours whenever you require it," Kazuchiyo replied as they took their seats. Satsumi's maid was already kneeling nearby, ready to serve them, and he acknowledged her with a short bow of his head, which she returned. "I hear you're still recovering, but you look very well."

"I wish you would smile when you say things like that," Satsumi replied, though already there bloomed a bit more color in her cheeks. "Flattery is far more effective that way."

"It's only the truth," Kazuchiyo said as the maid set out bowls of rice and soup for them. "Given the circumstances, it might be insensitive for me, in particular, to offer flattery."

Satsumi's eyes lost some of their shine as they flicked away. "Once you're finished, you can leave us," she told the maid. "I'll call if you're needed."

"Yes, Lady Satsumi."

The maid hurried to complete her duties, and with everything poured and prepared, she showed herself out. Kazuchiyo and Satsumi each took a moment of silence to sip their tea and be sure of no more lingering ears before the latter spoke.

"You've grown so careful in your words, Kazu," she said. "You ought to be commended."

"I'm not a boy any longer, Lady Satsumi," he replied, helping himself to the rice first. "I understand the position you're in. Do you believe your illness this time to have come from the same source as before?"

Though Satsumi did not look to have much appetite, she made an effort to nibble at the vegetables. "No, I am well convinced it was that horse-faced friend of yours," she said breezily. "I don't suppose you could reassure her from me that I mean you no harm? Even if I *was* left alone long enough to bear one of these children, it would be quite a long time before we knew for certain if Lord Aritaka would accept them. All this meddling is frightfully premature, and speaks to, frankly, an embarrassing level of insecurity on her part. And on the part of dear Lady Aritaka, for that matter."

Kazuchiyo continued to watch her as he ate, and he could not help but glance down to the loose fit of the obi across her abdomen. "Master Iomori is very protective of me," he agreed, "but that doesn't always mean she listens to me. Still, I'll do what I can."

"I would appreciate it." Satsumi paused in her eating to face him with greater seriousness. "*You* believe it, don't you, Kazu? That I mean you no harm?"

"It's as you say. Even if you have a fine son, Lord Aritaka would not claim him as an heir until he came of age. As long as I prove myself to him before then, he can have no reason to choose a child of yours over me." Kazuchiyo returned her gaze with a smile. "As far as I can see, I'm in no danger from you at all, Lady Satsumi."

Satsumi smiled as well, though her eyes were in conflict. Kazuchiyo did believe that it would grieve her to do him harm. "Nor I you," she said. "I'm very fond of you, Kazu."

She meant it, and he believed it, even if that mattered very little in the grand scope of their peculiar friendship. Still, with that reassurance they could continue a while longer.

"When we're finished," Satsumi changed the subject, "would you mind playing for me?"

"Only if you fulfill a request of mine first," said Kazuchiyo.

Satsumi made a long-suffering face as she reached into the front of her robe. "I supposed I've held you in suspense long enough," she said, back to her teasing. She pulled out a folded strip of paper and flipped it open with one hand while continuing to eat. Kazuchiyo continued his meal as well, though his attention was fixed very sharply on the letter as she began to read.

"'To my dearest sister,'" relayed Satsumi with an effort toward drama. "'The days here at Ninari Castle continue to be fraught with trials. Though I do not wish to alarm you...' Hm, he rattles on and on." Satsumi paused to sip from her tea; it would seem she was not so finished with her play at suspense after all. Kazuchiyo forced himself to continue eating as if his heart wasn't rising slowly up his throat.

"Ahh, here we are," she said at last, and she flashed Kazuchiyo a smirk. "'As for Ebara Motonobu, whom you know better as Yagi-douji, he is as ferocious as ever. General Utsukawa has ordered him to assist in the extra fortifications to the castle, and the workers claim to have seen him hoisting the beams across his shoulders. Every day I am more convinced he lives up to his nickname! Just ten days ago he brought a man before the general that he claimed to have been a Kibaku spy, and on orders beat the man to death. They say he looked like a vision of hell! Even the blacksmith promises to craft him a proper club. I do not know why...'"

Satsumi trailed off with a chuckle. "He goes on to scold me for asking after such a terrible brute so often. His calligraphy

50

is atrocious—I do believe his hand was shaking when he wrote this."

"May I see?" Kazuchiyo asked with enough insistence to elevate request to demand. Satsumi raised her eyebrow as she passed it to him, and he pored over the text. The tremble in each character made it extremely easy for him to picture Yagi poised over the helpless carcass of an enemy scout, blood speckling his bare skin. The gleam of his eyes sharp with malice was ever at the front of Kazuchiyo's memory.

"I'm happy for you," Satsumi said. "I know you've worried after him, but from the sound of it, he hasn't changed one bit."

Kazuchiyo read over the rest of the letter, absorbing all the information he could from what was said and, almost as importantly, what was not. He then reread the description of Yagi twice over before returning the letter to its recipient. "I am very grateful to your brother," he said. "And to you, for sharing his letters with me."

"I would ask him to illustrate it for you," Satsumi teased, "but from the sound of it, his courage would be even less up to the task than his artistry." She tucked the letter back into her kimono. "Once the construction on the castle fortifications is finished, I'm certain that Lord Aritaka will want to survey the work personally. You ought to ask that he take you with him."

Kazuchiyo flushed with heat. "Leave Gyoe?"

"He will have to allow it at *some* point," Satsumi reasoned. "What good does it do him to have an heir who has seen nothing of the world? Besides, if he starts a war with Kibaku Province, it will be yours to finish."

"Let us hope it won't come to that," Kazuchiyo said, distracted.

Once they had finished, Kazuchiyo fulfilled his promise, but he did not play for her in the room. She fetched the wooden flute from its case for him, and he opened the chamber windows to the south. On feet light as a cat's he stepped out onto the tiled roof and took in a deep breath of morning air still crisp from rain. He watched sunlight stream through gaps in the cloud cover and highlight the roofs of the town below: the rows of shops and peasant homes, the broad pagoda of Gyoe's largest temple, the statues of local deities lining the guardhouses and baileys. Gyoe was a lively town, a crowded town, crammed into terraced roads that spilled down the hillside.

Every day it became a little harder for Kazuchiyo to remember the view from the castle he'd been born in.

He sat on the edge of the sill and played. The sound of the flute rang clear from the lower keep, and he liked to think that samurai and peasant alike were turning their eyes upward in search of him. As often as he could, he reminded Gyoe's citizenry that he lived among them. He played lullabies from his youth, songs that had drifted to him from the river villages, melodies that only a dragon would know. He wanted the voice of his mother in their ears even if they weren't aware.

When Kazuchiyo paused to catch his breath, he spotted a caravan approaching Gyoe from the road to the southeast, comprised of over two dozen horses. Their riders bore Aritaka banners. He continued to watch them as he resumed his music, up until Satsumi reached through the window to tug his shoulder.

"You're being summoned," she said, indicating the chamber's entrance where a young page waited.

"I'll come back later," Kazuchiyo said as he returned the flute to her, "so I can finish playing for you."

"You've played enough for me," she replied. "Look after yourself some, Kazu."

"I will. And someday when I am lord of Gyoe, I'll make sure you're looked after, too."

He meant it. She didn't believe it, though through no fault of his, and she wished him good luck as he departed with the page.

Lord Aritaka awaited him not in his usual audience chamber, but in the courtyard. Kazuchiyo wondered as he approached if he had summoned him after hearing the flute, perhaps even as a means of silencing him, but there was no

52

consternation in his expression as they greeted each other.

"You look very well this morning," Lord Aritaka said as they made a slow circle of the grounds. "I wondered after you last night. I know you are not fond of the rain."

Perhaps he thought he was being considerate. Certainly five years was long enough for a prisoner's malice to dissolve. Kazuchiyo didn't bat an eye. "Thank you for your concern, but if I lost any sleep it was only because I've been looking forward to today. I could see the caravan approaching."

"Oh?" Aritaka glanced to the southern wall. "It's been a long time since you've seen your siblings. There'll be a feast tonight. I hope you'll help me keep them on their best behavior."

"Of course." For almost a year Aritaka's two children with O-ran had been sent to the eastern border, aiding in Sakka's defense against their seaside neighbors—an area that had long been controlled by the port-town merchants more so than any samurai lord, its wilderness teeming with bandits and thugs. The remoteness of the post well suited Lord Aritaka's cubs, though there was little glory in it. Though Kazuchiyo spoke in earnest in claiming he looked forward to seeing them, there was only one among them whose company he would enjoy.

"Have you heard any news from Ninari Castle?" he asked. "I heard a rumor that they've apprehended Kibaku spies at the border."

Aritaka cast him a sideways glance. "Your ears are as keen as ever. The rumors are true. There's no doubt that Lord Koedzuka is searching for weaknesses in our new defenses. So much for his claims of wanting peace."

"If he were expanding his border defenses, I would want our spies to investigate as well," Kazuchiyo reasoned. "Maybe you should let them find some weakness, if only to draw out their true intentions."

"That's bold of you," Aritaka said, though he smirked with approval. "You're learning more all the time." He regarded Kazuchiyo silently a moment, thoughtful, before continuing. "The construction will be completed in three weeks' time. I intend to oversee the finalization in person. That may be the best test of Koedzuka's resolve."

Kazuchiyo's breath caught, though he quickly regained his composure. "Who will you leave in charge of Gyoe?"

"O-ran can handle the daily administration," he said. "And Hidemune will remain here as well. It will be good for him."

The prospect of remaining behind with Aritaka's son and his mother made Lady Satsumi's advice all the more potent. "Father, with your permission I'd like to accompany you to Ninari Castle."

"I thought you might," said Aritaka. "Though I'd like for you to tell me why you want to."

"I haven't been outside this town in five years," Kazuchiyo replied. "Isn't that reason enough?"

Aritaka smirked again. "I suppose it is. Though maybe you're also thinking you'll get a glance of Suyama along the way."

"The road to Ninari doesn't go south enough to see the Suyama border. Even if it did I wouldn't recognize it." Kazuchiyo stopped walking so that he could fix Aritaka with an even look. "You don't have to test me anymore, Father. No one from Suyama has come for or asked after me since I've been here, and I've never tried to leave because we're all under one banner now. We're all Aritaka." He narrowed his eyes with determination. "And I want to know the state of our western border before Kibaku decides to go to war."

Aritaka eyed him, but Kazuchiyo had spent the years by his side well, and it did not take much to convince him. He nodded, pleased. "I'm looking forward to the day you take the field with me. It may be sooner than later." He jostled Kazuchiyo's shoulder. "I have high hopes for you."

A bird called from just beyond the wall. Kazuchiyo knew that it wasn't a bird; his first mornings at Gyoe he had woken to unfamiliar songs, and he still held resentment toward them, enough that he knew each chirp by heart. He looked to Aritaka. "Was I not the only one you summoned?" he asked with eyebrows raised.

Aritaka grunted in amusement. "Go on down to the town, Kazumune. You ought to greet your brother and sister."

"Yes, Father."

Kazuchiyo bowed to him and then turned to leave. He had nearly reached the courtyard gate when he heard a quiet thump of feet landing on soft ground, and Aritaka saying, "There you are. What do you have for me?"

"My lord," said a man's voice, "I have news from the western border."

Kazuchiyo stopped in his tracks. He knew that voice. It seized him by the throat, and he knew that if he turned, he would see a young scout with a heart-shaped face, telling his father lies. But he couldn't turn. The two voices blurred into a deafening roar, and he couldn't breathe let alone move. He told himself to turn, *commanded* it of himself. It wasn't until he heard Aritaka dismissing the man that he was able to jar himself into motion, and he turned just in time to see a figure leaping to the courtyard wall. He caught a glimpse of brown robes and dark hair pulled back, and then the stranger disappeared down the other side.

Kazuchiyo ran. For five years he had wandered Gyoe's halls leery of all enemies, save this one he had never known to look for; the old connection to his former life was reforged so suddenly and unexpectedly that it urged him onward. He streaked out of the courtyard and followed the wall as quickly as he could, tracing it back to where the man had crossed over. He caught another glimpse of silky, black hair whipping around a corner, and he gave chase, only to find the man gone again. Kazuchiyo continued regardless, following the twisting paths through the castle grounds toward the town. As he reached the final gate he saw him again, crawling through one of the windows meant for archers. A sheer drop lay beyond, and once again, as Kazuchiyo raced to look through, he found no trace of him.

Cursing, Kazuchiyo hurried to the gate. It might have

been wiser not to pursue a creature of such obvious skill, but his heart was thundering in his chest, overriding all reason. He was compelled, and he ran, ignoring the curious stares of guards. There was no one clinging to the outer wall, no one in the street below. Kazuchiyo ran to the nearest shop, and using a cart freshly returned from the market, he climbed to the roof. It may have drawn a few eyes, but Gyoe was mostly used to his rooftop antics. He hopped from one building to the next and finally spotted the dark robes and darker hair: the man was strolling down a lane toward the west, unaware of his pursuer.

Kazuchiyo hurried to the edge of the roof and dropped down to a parallel street. He had no reason to think the man was less familiar with the city than he was, but he hoped he still had surprise on his side. What he intended to do with it, he did not know; he only knew that he needed to confront this specter from the past, and he rushed down the line of shops. As soon as he found an opening he turned down it, and he spotted the man heading away from him, down an alleyway across the road. It was the best opportunity he could have hoped for.

Kazuchiyo approached, slowly at first, making an attempt to mask his footsteps. As soon as he was clear of the main road, he charged. He was confident in his speed, and he caught the man before he could turn, digging his fingers into his brown robes at the shoulder. But just as he found his mark, the man went limp, sliding out of his grip. The robe came off in Kazuchiyo's hands and his target rolled, propelling himself backwards and out of range.

"Well, shit," the man said, unimpressed. "If it isn't the tamed dragon."

Kazuchiyo spun toward him. The man was not very different from what he remembered: older than him, but still in possession of a youthful, heart-shaped face, and pale, gray eyes. He didn't look at all disturbed to have been attacked in the open and showed no sign of appreciation for the significance of their meeting. It boiled Kazuchiyo's blood, and he charged again, throwing the man's robe back in his face.

That caught him off guard, if only a moment—just long enough for Kazuchiyo to take advantage. He threw his weight into the man's chest and shoved him back against the alley wall. It wasn't any different than his years of training, he told himself. He was taller; he had the advantage. But as he pinned the man to the shop wall, he felt something jab at his abdomen, and he glanced down to see the man pressing the tip of a steel *kunai* into him.

The man shook his head to free himself of the robe and let out a huff. "I guess you recognize me after all," he said, doing a very good impression of unconcerned despite Kazuchiyo's hand on his throat. "I didn't think you would."

"You were at Shimegahara," Kazuchiyo said, and despite his own efforts his voice shook. "Your lies to my father got him and all his men killed."

"I was following orders," he retorted, a roughness to his voice, an almost buzzing that grated on the nerves. "Not my fault your old man fell for it."

Kazuchiyo tightened his grip, and the man tensed, the corner of his eye twitching. With the two of them pressed so close together Kazuchiyo could feel his body coil in readiness to fight. It sent his heart pounding. Despite my abridgments to his tale, for him it had been years since he'd been embroiled in any real combat outside the sparring room, and he was eager to test his adult mettle against a true opponent. That it could be against one of the instruments of his family's demise increased his eagerness all the more.

"Okay," the man said, and he touched Kazuchiyo's wrist—gently, as if to soothe him. "Okay, I've said too much. But I was only doing what I had to, just like you are now."

"Who are you?" Kazuchiyo demanded. He couldn't feel the kunai against his stomach any longer, but he wasn't about to break eye contact to search for it, not when the slippery weasel was watching him with such cautious intensity. "Tell me your name."

"Let go of me first, won't you?" The man relaxed into the

wall at his back. "It's not like you're going to kill me, so we might as well have a conversation like men."

He started to withdraw his hand; in the process his fingertips skated along the inside of Kazuchiyo's wrist, and the slow, deliberate caress of rough to tender skin spread goosebumps up Kazuchiyo's arm. Suppressing a shiver, Kazuchiyo at last withdrew.

"All right," he said. "Now tell me—"

The man jabbed him hard in his diaphragm, and for a moment Kazuchiyo thought he felt the kunai slice through flesh and muscle, but it was only the blunt of the handle. Even so the breath rushed out of him, and a kick to his shin brought him to his knees. Before he could gather himself let alone retaliate, the man had snatched up his robe and, bracing his foot to Kazuchiyo's shoulder, vaulted up to grab the roof of the shop and pull himself up.

"You may be Aritaka's son, but you're no one's lord yet, let alone mine," he taunted as he tugged his robe back on. "Touch me again, and I'll be collecting a fat reward for your head. There are plenty willing to pay for it."

"Wait!" Kazuchiyo wheezed as he struggled upright. "Your name!" But the man only turned his back and disappeared over the roof.

Kazuchiyo reached his feet with every intention of giving chase, but then he realized that a pair of shop hands had entered the alley in response to the commotion. Upon seeing Kazuchiyo they hurried forward with concern, only to stop short at the sight of Aritaka's crest embroidered across his back. "Lord Kazumune," one called hesitantly, bending at the waist in deference. "Are you all right?"

"I'm fine," Kazuchiyo replied, tidying himself as best he could. He no longer had any hope of pursuing the disrespectful snake. "Thank you for your concern."

He headed back to the main road. By then the caravan he had spotted from the rooftop had reached the town, and people were gathering along the street to see. Two dozen Aritaka samurai entered through the gate on horseback, some of them dragging supply carts, all clad in full armor that was more for display than defense. At the front rode Aritaka Hidemune, Lord Aritaka's biological son. He was broad-shouldered like his father, but there the similarities ended: his face was round and sour, his whiskers sparse and uninspiring, his posture limp. He had no hint of a lord's bearing nor did he seem to gather any hint of a lord's respect. The admiration of the crowd was reserved entirely for his sister, and Kazuchiyo pushed forward to better see her.

Mahiro. Also known by such exciting and enviable nicknames as "Bandit Slayer," "Iron Arm," and "Oeyo's Unyielding Gate," her prowess was well known all across the eastern quarter of Shuyun. In height and build she easily challenged Sakka's best warriors, in bravado even more so. Her armor was splashed with vibrant yellows and greens, strips of animal fur patched between them. Her helm was crowned with broad, gold horns, and a wild mane of white horse-hair spilled over her chest and back. Unlike the rest of her comrades with their weapons sheathed or loaded on the carts, she carried her famed *naginata* in hand, sometimes bracing it to her shoulder, sometimes brandishing it to the awe of the crowd. As she made her way down the street behind her brother, she flashed grins and laughter at every onlooker, and they adored her for it.

Kazuchiyo did not expect to catch Mahiro's eye, but she spotted him almost at once, and her grin grew wider still. "Kazumune!" she bellowed, and she waved him forward. "Come to greet us, eh? Come jump on my saddle. I'll deliver both my brothers together!"

Mahiro's stead, the mighty Suzumekage, had as strong a back as her owner, and could have borne Kazuchiyo's added weight easily. Kazuchiyo contented himself with walking alongside. "Welcome home, sister," he greeted her. "Did you have any trouble on the road from Oeyo?"

Mahiro snorted dismissively. "What trouble would dare?" She smacked the length of her naginata against her armor.

"And you, cub? Trouble rarely finds you, but you make a habit of seeking it out."

"I only seek what finds me first," Kazuchiyo replied, secretly offended by her suggestion. To his mind, his captor's family's attempts to abuse and discredit him were no fault of his. "I'll tell you about the latest over dinner."

Mahiro laughed some more. "I'm looking forward to it!"

Hidemune turned his head just enough to cast the pair of them a hateful look. Even after he had faced forward again, Kazuchiyo could feel his bitterness emanate all the way to the keep.

CHAPTER FIVE

Gyoe was abuzz as it received its awaited guests. Though
Hidemune traveled often between his home castle and
Oeyo on the eastern border, Mahiro had not graced its halls in
almost a year. She swept through like a typhoon, going room to
room greeting old friends and rivals, her laughter echoing the
halls. More than one scuffle broke out: some playful, some less
so. Kazuchiyo followed along the whole while, taking particular
note of which of Aritaka's servants and vassals received her
favorably.

She sobered only when taking an audience with her
parents in the upper keep. After a brief exchange behind closed
doors she burst out again and bellowed for wine.

"Come to my room after you've shed your armor,"
Kazuchiyo offered. "I have some saké."

"I'll come right now," Mahiro insisted.

She held her tongue until the pair of them were safe in
the privacy of Kazuchiyo's modest chambers, privacy being a
relative thing when in a castle made of wood and paper. No
one would have missed the heavy thumps of Mahiro's helm and
armor pieces hitting the floor. "That old man is no bear!" she
declared as she shed her battle gear. "He's a toothless old ferret.

What does he know about what I've done for him in the east? He knows shit, that's what! He thinks men could do better, he's welcome to send some. Rotten horse shit."

Kazuchiyo poured the saké, and Mahiro sprawled beside him, snatching hers up. She drank the full cup at once and then passed it back for more. "I thought our eastern border was secure," Kazuchiyo said as he obliged. "Were there problems at Oeyo?"

"Not hardly, thanks to me! We have been securing that border for years, and we finally have enough soldiers in place to guard checkpoints against their smugglers. He ought to be praising us."

"And he's not?" Kazuchiyo prodded, handing over the refilled cup. "The banquet we're having tonight is in your and Brother Hidemune's honor."

Mahiro rolled her eyes and drank again. "Hidemune's honor, my ass. He's only putting on airs because it will be the first time Hidemune's had run of Gyoe without him. I'm only here because he wants me marching west. There's the smell of another war brewing."

Kazuchiyo took a long sip from his own cup. "I thought you would look forward to that."

"Hell, I do! I am!" She thrust her closed fist forward, wrist tilted as if her naginata were in her grip. "Been waiting all my life to put my blade through those yapping crows in Kibaku. But fuck, Kazu, he could at least…"

She was quiet for a moment, dragging her fingernails across her scalp. Her brown hair, matted from the helm, stuck in strange places as she fussed. She looked much younger than her years then, maybe even sullen. Then the fire returned to her eyes, and she looked to Kazuchiyo with smirking mischief. "You'll be joining us, won't you, Kazumune?"

"If Father allows it. I want to." He watched his sister drink for a moment, ill ease in his stomach. Despite the bitterness he was determined to hold against his "family," her eccentricities had cultivated a fondness in him. There were few people in

Sakka with as little interest in using him as Mahiro, and he disliked having to make use of her himself.

"I've heard that the Koedzuka clan have been sending their spies to keep track of Castle Ninari's progress," he said. "They're well known for their shinobi, aren't they?"

"The best you'll find outside the capital, probably," Mahiro agreed. She snorted. "Or, you won't find them, because they're shinobi and that's the point, right?"

She elbowed him, and Kazuchiyo couldn't help but smile along. "Not much like ours, then," he said, watching for her reaction.

"Oho?" Mahiro focused on him intently. "You've met one of father's little foxes?"

"In broad daylight," Kazuchiyo said, trying to sound much less interested than he was. "A young man with long hair and gray eyes."

Mahiro threw her head back with a laugh. "So you've met *the* fox!" she declared. Kazuchiyo winced, knowing that if he asked her to lower her voice it would have the opposite effect. "And got a good look at him, too, from the sound of it. He doesn't care so much about the 'be not seen' thing, does he? I'm surprised it took this long for you to catch him."

Kazuchiyo forced himself to take another drink so that his impatience would be less obvious. "So, you know him? What's his name?"

"If he has a name he's not about to tell anyone, let alone me," Mahiro said as she stretched out against her elbow. "But he goes by Amai." Her eyebrows arched with amusement. "Why do you want to know?"

"Only because he wouldn't tell me himself."

Mahiro laughed some more at that. "There's a stubborn side to you, Kazumune," she complimented him. "I've always liked that."

"Can you tell me any more about him?" Kazuchiyo asked, his pretense of mild curiosity failing him. "Does he live in Gyoe?"

63

"Do you have need of a shinobi? That's a bit suspicious, isn't it?"

Mahiro fixed him with a look she perhaps thought to be intimidating, which was diminished by the smirk tugging her lips. Even so, Kazuchiyo took her teased warning seriously. Even a careless mention from Mahiro's lips could turn eyes his way, and the fear of that throbbed between his temples. "He's going to be *my* shinobi before long," Kazuchiyo said, and he straightened up, emulating a bit of Aritaka's gravitas. "After the way he treated me this morning, I want to make sure he knows that."

Mahiro was surprised a moment and then resumed laughing. She even slapped her knee. "I'd pay to see it!" She pulled herself upright and scooted closer. To Kazuchiyo's relief, she even lowered her voice. "In the outer wall, there's a window west of the guardhouse where the slats are loose. Beneath one is a small alcove large enough to stow a rolled paper. Whenever Father wants to pass instructions to his foxes, he has a servant tuck a message there. But any one of them can find it, so if you're going to leave something for your little kit, be careful what you say."

Kazuchiyo had no inkling what such a message would even entail, but he simmered with anticipation nonetheless. "I suppose I shouldn't use the name 'Amai' then."

"'Black Fox,'" Mahiro wagged her finger at him, "if you have to use a name at all." She slapped him heavily on the back and leaned away. "You're clever; I'm sure you'll have no trouble."

Kazuchiyo nodded. He was eager to move the conversation away from himself and so poured Mahiro a bit more drink. "You have as much confidence in me as Father does. He's asked me to manage you and Brother Hidemune at tonight's banquet."

Mahiro grunted mightily and finished off her cup. "What does he think I'll do to dishonor him this time? Am I an animal now?"

"You could prove him wrong by behaving yourself," said

Kazuchiyo, faintly teasing.

"Don't think I wouldn't!" She made a face at him. "Though you were so obvious just now that it makes me want to misbehave *more*."

"Fair enough," Kazuchiyo replied, and they chuckled together.

Mahiro passed the rest of the morning in Kazuchiyo's room, regaling him with her tales of adventures on the eastern border: fierce battles with brigands, forest beasts felled, men and women drawn to her bed. Kazuchiyo was very content to listen, volunteering only a few stories of his own. His mind was far away, and by the time Mahiro left with her armor to seek out fresh clothes and a bath, he was eager for a few moments alone.

"Amai," he murmured, tracing his fingertip over the tatami in the shape of various symbols the name could be made from. Did he spell his name like *rain*? Like *sweetness*? Like *heaven*? It mattered not at all because he had no reason to write it, and more importantly, no reason to seek the man out ever again. As eager as he was to know everything about his father's pawns, there could be very little gained from associating with such a temperamental shinobi. He ought to have set his focus on more important potential enemies.

But that soft-featured face peering up at him from beneath an ill-fitting helmet had pursued his sleepless nights for five years. So many of the details of that horrid evening had smeared in his memory to indecipherable demons, but not that face. He wanted to hear from the man's own mouth what his orders had been, who had passed them down, who he had killed to obtain the scout's armor. He wanted a slender throat beneath his palm again, letting righteous anger refuel his desire for vengeance.

Kazuchiyo went into his closet and fetched paper, brush, and ink. For as long as he had been cautious he now chose instinct, and he scrawled a few lines straight from his pounding heart.

A black fox, fearless,
stalks through the rain, unaware
his helm is broken

Before he could lose his nerve or regain his caution, he blew the ink dry and folded the paper to tuck into his robe. With only a pale effort to appear unhurried, he made his way back down through the keep and past the twisted streets to the gate. He easily found the same window he had seen Amai pass through earlier, and when it appeared that no guards were within eyesight, he nudged the loose slats out of the way. Just as Mahiro had described there was a small alcove cut into the wood. With a tremor he tucked the paper inside, replaced the slats, and returned to his chamber without making eye contact with another person the whole way.

That evening, Lord Aritaka summoned his family and close samurai to the central keep for the promised banquet. They formed long rows seated before the serving tables, the men dressed in fine robes bearing their family's crests, the women draped in colored layers. The meal was served in several courses, consisting of rice, soup, grilled fish brought fresh from the eastern caravan, pickled vegetables, and dried plums—a lavish affair for samurai far removed from court. It spoke to the lofty aspirations of the host, and that significance was lost on no one.

Kazuchiyo sat across from Hidemune, and thus endured a great deal of narrow-eyed glares throughout the meal, even a few from his mother. Contrary to his fears, Mahiro contained her typically savage good humor to the occasional guffaw, her restraint in no small part owed to the Lady Satsumi seated beside her. As was Satsumi's way, she soothed and engaged with a near flirtatious elegance that earned her Mahiro's attention most of the evening and, more to her goal, Lord Aritaka's relief and appreciation.

Partway through the meal, Lord Aritaka motioned for silence, and the assembly was swift to comply. Each already knew what he meant to say and listened with rapt anticipation. Even Kazuchiyo leaned forward to get a proper view.

"In two weeks' time, construction on the new armaments to Castle Ninari will be complete," he declared. "I will be traveling to the castle myself in order to oversee the final outcome of their work, and with me will travel six of my generals, as well as two thousand of our soldiers and their families from around Sakka province, to reside in the nearby towns and foothills."

The six generals he spoke of, including General Waseba, bowed their heads in acknowledgment. "Also accompanying me," Aritaka continued, "will be two of my children, Mahiro and Kazumune. In our absence, Hidemune has complete authority of Gyoe, and the remainder of you will heed his every command."

"Yes, sir!" the gathering said in unison, bowing their heads.

"Very good." Lord Aritaka lifted his cup to them. "Here's to Master Utsukawa and his brave men at the border."

They all drank, and Kazuchiyo hoped the saké would help drown his thundering heart. There could be no mistaking Aritaka's intentions that night: he was preparing each of them for war.

As the gathering dispersed late in the evening, Kazuchiyo fulfilled a promise by seeking out Master Iomori, who had remained at her lord's side all through the meal without a word. "Master Iomori," he greeted her, and when he bowed, she bowed lower.

"You needn't show such deference to me," she said, though with very little actual humility. "You are the lord's son, as I continue to remind you."

"I myself am not yet lord of anyone," Kazuchiyo replied, hopeful that any thought to Amai's taunting did not show too plainly in his face. "And I owe you my life, which you also continue to remind me of. Often."

Iomori's lip gave a quirk that some might mistake for a smile. "Let us hope you don't waste that life I've given you at the border," she said as they made their way toward her chambers in the east tower. "Gyoe has been treacherous enough for you. I fear what might become of you so far from home."

"If treachery can reach me within the walls of Father's newly fortified castle, that would not reflect well on General Utsukawa's craftsmanship," said Kazuchiyo.

"No, indeed." Again, Iomori betrayed a glimpse of near-human amusement. "But you are a clever young man. I know you can handle yourself, and you have powerful allies awaiting you there."

The thought of Yagi-douji prowling the halls of the border fortress filled Kazuchiyo with eagerness that was difficult to hide. "Will you not be joining us? I would feel more at ease if you were." He watched her closely. "And away from Lady Satsumi."

Iomori fixed him with a sharp eye. "You don't need to play word games with me, Lord Kazumune. You can speak your mind."

"I'd like for you to leave Lady Satsumi alone," Kazuchiyo obliged her. "I know you're acting in my interests, but I don't want to see her suffer because of me."

Iomori held her tongue as they passed a few servants, waiting to speak until they were in relative privacy again. "If she bears a child, it will be O-ran that suffers. You would be satisfied with that outcome instead?"

As they reached the tower, Kazuchiyo allowed Iomori to take the lead. "My very existence is suffering to Mother," he said as they ascended. "Any child of Lady Satsumi's cannot harm her more than me. Will you please leave her be? If for no other reason than I ask it of you?"

Iomori turned on the stairs to look down at him. With only dim evening light easing through the tower's windows on the floor above, her silhouette was tall and striking. "Is that an order?" she asked.

Kazuchiyo stared, and not for the first time felt his courage falter before her. She was testing him, and he was loath to fail. The potency of her disapproval had always been fierce. He squared his shoulders and said, "Yes, it is."

Iomori did not reply at once, as if waiting for him to retract. When he did not, she gave a short nod and turned to continue up the stairs. "Very well. I'll interfere with the ladies no longer." She chuckled then, her voice raspy. "Ah, it so does remind me of court."

Kazuchiyo followed close behind, up to her chambers. "You were at the Emperor's court?"

"Did I never tell you that? Well, it was very long ago." She let them into her room and guided him to a far closet disguised by a hanging scroll. "But never mind that now. I have something for you."

Iomori removed the hanging scroll and then slid away the panel behind it, revealing a stock of small boxes and writing supplies. It was less carefully arranged than Kazuchiyo would have thought for a woman of Iomori's bearing. First to be retrieved from the piled collection was a folded paper which she handed to him with very little ceremony. "This is a messenger *shiki*," she explained. "If ever you have need to contact me— from the border, especially—write a message on the paper, fold it back up, and set it outside. It will reach me."

"Less conspicuous than sending a messenger," Kazuchiyo said. He tucked the paper into his robe. "I thank you."

"I'm not finished." Iomori reached back into the closet, and despite the piles of items, she plucked a small box out of the slew as easily as if someone on the inside had presented it to her. The box was made of simple wood with no engravings, and when she opened it, Kazuchiyo was puzzled to find the inside lined with some kind of thin, tempered metal. It was full of small, lacquered beads of various earthy colors, each with a length of dark ribbon laced through it.

"Hold out your arm," she said as she selected a small red

bead from the rest.

Kazuchiyo did so, pushing back his sleeve. The red reminded him of Tatsutomi banners, and when Iomori pressed the bead to the inside of his wrist, goosebumps rippled up his arm. "If I'm seen wearing this color—"

"Don't fret," Iomori interrupted, and as she wound the ribbon around him, she was sure to disguise the bead beneath it. "If anyone asks, you can tell them it was a blessing from me." Once she finished tying it off, she met Kazuchiyo's eyes and held them with unblinking intensity. "Wear it as often as you can. It just might save your life."

She let him go, and as Kazuchiyo drew his arm back to his side, he shivered at the almost imperceptible weight of it. "Thank you, Master Iomori. Even if you are not traveling with us to Ninari, I know you are with me."

"No more pretty words. I'm only doing my duty." She bowed to him, and following her lead, Kazuchiyo's bow was shallow by comparison. "Good night, Lord Kazumune."

"Good night, Master Iomori."

Kazuchiyo departed, and his heart beat swiftly all the way back to his chambers in the main keep. In five years he had never owned a piece of red clothing for fear that it would speak too openly of his continuing devotion to the Tatsutomi banner. He could never be seen with a dragon motif of any kind, was in possession of nothing crafted in Suyama save his mother's old lullabies. Even a small red bead tucked against his wrist was the greatest declaration of loyalty he had ever kept outside his own heart, and it filled him with exhilaration and terror in equal measure.

Once back in his room, Kazuchiyo shut himself in and changed quickly into his sleeping robes. He curled up beneath his layers of bedding and there tried to catch his breath after a long day of stirring revelations. Running his thumb back and forth over the hidden bead, he thought of the road through the mountains that would take him to Castle Ninari, and the dangers he might face there. He thought of Lady Satsumi at war with her own security, of Mahiro's struggles to impress their father, of Iomori's mysterious gifts. He thought of a pale-eyed shinobi caressing the inside of his wrist, and wondered with a knot in his stomach if his message would provoke a response—wondered why it mattered to him at all.

But mostly, he thought of Yagi. He repeated the description from the letter over in his mind, remembering the tremor in the script. He well recalled his own shudder of awe at first meeting Yagi, and it was so easy for him to draw memories of the man back to him: his broad shoulders, his sturdy limbs and eyes fierce as a wolf's. Kazuchiyo believed that in their time apart his champion had grown only fiercer. Emboldened by the details from Satsumi's brother, his imagination supplied him with vibrant speculations of a beast of a man, bearing great beams of heavy wood across his bare, muscular shoulders.

Soon, they would be reunited, and his anticipation for that meeting fueled in him eagerness that easily gave way to arousal. With every effort toward quiet he slipped his hand down between his thighs, pleasuring himself with the fantasy of a firm chest and heavy breath at his back. His memory of Yagi's wide, strong palm, which had once been a source of encouragement and strength for him, took on new meaning now that he was fully grown.

In the morning, after a night of shallow sleep, Kazuchiyo stirred from his bedding and discovered that a piece of folded paper lay beside his pillow. He jolted upright but then hesitated, his heart fluttering. He hadn't expected a reply so soon, and he turned to and fro, seeking some evidence in the room of an intruder. Finding none besides the paper itself, he at last reached out and drew it toward him.

It was the same paper that he had delivered to the alcove, and alongside his message from the day before was written the lines:

Good thing the fox only needs
wit to escape the hunter.

It was not the most elegant poetry, following only the basic rules of format and written in brush strokes that would have infuriated Gyoe's tutors. Kazuchiyo shivered all the same, even licked his lips as he reread the simple lines over and over. His black fox had responded, was taunting him. This fact alone meant something. Perhaps if he pressed a bit more, he could tease from the responses some insight into the man's nature and intentions.

But first, he would have to be very certain of his own response. He hurried to gather brush and ink as possible verses coursed through his mind.

So swift, so clever,
He crosses the battlefield
No care for the dead

Once Kazuchiyo was finished he hurried to put his supplies away and then took his breakfast in his room. After his discussion with Mahiro that morning, he was anxious of drawing attention to himself, even more so with Iomori's secret blessing, and he would have to plan how best to approach the alcove again. The thought of so many suddenly tangible secrets for him to carry left him almost light-headed, and he hurried to his chores to keep him focused.

CHAPTER SIX

After a morning of studies, sitting in with Lord Aritaka and his advisors, and aiding in preparations for the approaching march, Kazuchiyo made his way toward the castle gate. He found himself casting long glances at the rooftops in search of a familiar silhouette. He wondered if his verse could stir the conscience of a cold-eyed agent of deceit. The distraction was very nearly a costly one, as he rounded the last corner and spotted a figure already at the slatted window. It would have been suspicious to pause, so he continued on, his excuse for business in the town already prepared. However, as he passed, the man turned, and he could see that it was his brother, Hidemune, noticing him.

At first Hidemune's expression was one only of disgust, which Kazuchiyo had been on the receiving end of many times before. But then something gave him pause, and he tucked both arms into his robes as he approached. "Kazumune," he called.

Kazuchiyo obediently stopped. "Brother," he greeted, and he bowed. "I was just heading into town."

"What for?" Hidemune eyed him with suspicion. "Why not send a servant if you have errands?"

"I was going to offer prayers at Ishiyama Temple," Kazuchiyo answered easily enough. "For safe travels on our journey."

"Your journey is weeks away." Hidemune jutted his chin back toward the castle. "Come train with me, little brother. I'm in need of the exercise."

Without waiting for an answer, he headed back into the compound interior. Kazuchiyo cast the window one last glance, but he had no choice but to abandon his mission for the time being.

Hidemune led him back up the path toward the lower keep. They passed a servant on the way, who skittered off after receiving a few whispered instructions from Hidemune. This tightened Kazuchiyo's nerves.

They entered the practice dojo, a broad room with wooden floors and low ceilings, thick panels lining each wall to dull the endless clack of swords. A few boys were already going through the motions of training *kata*, each of them heirs to powerful Sakka families. They were quick to move to the sides upon the approach of their lord's sons. All eyes fell on the two brothers.

"I'm not well dressed for this," Kazuchiyo said, careful to keep his voice as neutral as possible. Already his mind was hard at work, calculating just how much of his skill was wise to show before his bitter elder brother.

Hidemune gestured to the trainees along the wall. "Lend us your wraps," he said, and a pair hurried to comply. With deep bows they handed over their straps, and Kazuchiyo used them to tie up his sleeves before removing his sandals. By the time he had selected a wooden practice sword from the racks Hidemune was already taking to the center of the floor.

A palpable tension came over the hall as Kazuchiyo joined him. It was not his first time going through training with his brother, with varying experiences; he had very few means of predicting how Hidemune's mood would affect this session. Even so, he refused to falter in front of even the young trainees, and he kept his chin high as he moved to take his stance.

"You're not worried about this excursion of yours, are you?" Hidemune said as the two of them braced their feet in unison, one in front of the other, their wooden swords aimed ahead of them.

"I'm not worried," Kazuchiyo replied.

Each raised his swords above his head slowly, in total control. With deep breaths they lunged forward, feet smacking loudly against the wood, swords cleaving the air. The tip of Kazuchiyo's sword traced an elegant arch and stopped exactly where it had started; Hidemune's dipped a few finger widths lower before snapping back to the proper position. Even an untrained eye would have noticed the difference between Kazuchiyo's effortless efficiency and Hidemune's brute carelessness. Luckily, it neither took a trained mouth to keep it to oneself, and their audience made not a sound.

"You haven't left Gyoe in years," Hidemune continued to press as they drew their feet back in and returned their swords over their heads. "Sakka's countryside is vast. I hope you don't get overwhelmed."

"I won't be overwhelmed," said Kazuchiyo, and they lunged again.

They went through a set of ten in similar fashion and then changed stance, poised for a lateral strike. As they continued the exercise, the far door slid open, and Kazuchiyo's heart skipped as the Lady O-ran entered. She was simply dressed that morning, one robe pulled up over her head to serve as a veil. In her youth she had been lauded as a great beauty, but an adulthood of bitterness and pride had pinched her sloped features into jagged crags, and her once lovely, dark eyes were squinted in perpetual irritation. She watched her two sons moving in unison throughout the exercise with a predator's unfaltering glare.

Hidemune stood taller in her presence, though it did very little to correct the poor form of his strokes. "I hear you've spent a great deal of time with Lady Satsumi lately," he prodded.

Even a lowered voice would carry to O-ran's ears given

the echoing space of the chamber, and a raised one would only strengthen Hidemune's unspoken accusation. Kazuchiyo remained as even-toned as he could as he answered, "Lady Satsumi and I are fond of each other. I wanted to share with her my condolences for her latest miscarriage."

Both of them lunged in the final move of that set, their swords slashing. As they moved into the next stance, Kazuchiyo glanced to his brother's hands: tight and angry around the grip. He adjusted his footing slightly to prepare his defense, should it become necessary.

"How unfortunate for her," Hidemune grumbled.

"I should offer my condolences to you as well, Hidemune," said Kazuchiyo, because sometimes a man can hold his patience only for so long. "You might have been a brother again."

Hidemune pivoted and swung toward him. His swordplay was not refined, but he had enough weight to put strength into it. Kazuchiyo would not have been able to parry if not for how prepared he was. It only took the proper angle to divert Hidemune's blade, and then he hopped back out of range.

The surrounding trainees held their breath, and when Kazuchiyo spared them a glance, he realized there were more than had been there before. O-ran continued to watch with an eagle's eyes, and General Waseba was in the process of joining her. Apparently word was spreading of their sparring match.

Hidemune straightened up, though now that Kazuchiyo's guard was up he had no chance of landing a strike. "Or maybe an uncle."

Kazuchiyo was less prepared for that than he was for the sword, but his face remained unchanged. "You only embarrass yourself inventing gossip." He moved to the next position: sword held low and angled, along his right side away from Hidemune. "Lady Satsumi is devoted to our father."

"Are you?" Hidemune retorted, reaching desperately for any possible barb in lieu of genuine wit. He followed Kazuchiyo's example in taking the new stance, thinking incorrectly that he was at an advantage. "I'm sure you're looking forward to being outside of Gyoe's protection with him."

"I don't know what I've done to offend you, for you to make these insinuations against me," said Kazuchiyo, "but whatever it is, I humbly apologize."

The wood creaked beneath Hidemune's foot, and again he turned to strike. He had a clean opening that any skilled swordsman could have easily exploited. But therein was the point; anticipating him, Kazuchiyo moved far more swiftly, the slice of his sword catching Hidemune's at its most vulnerable point. The clashing wood echoed across the chamber, and Hidemune's sword was flung from his grip. It clattered to the floor several meters away.

"If you wanted to spar," Kazuchiyo gathered himself, "you could have honored me by saying so."

Hidemune stood dumbstruck. Their audience gaped, and long seconds passed in utter silence. Then Hidemune's temper flamed to life, and he turned on Kazuchiyo with a scowl twisting his wide face. He took a step forward as if meaning to try again with his fists alone. "You disrespectful—"

"Kazumune!" Mahiro bellowed from the sidelines. Both men startled as she marched out onto the floor. How she had managed to hide her entry from them was almost as much of a shock as their confrontation. Without care or hesitation she flung her arm around Kazuchiyo's shoulders and hauled him off his feet, carrying both of them to the floor in a tangle.

"I'll spar with you!" she roared before breaking out in laughter. She hooked her arm through his elbow with enough force that he was forced to drop his bokken, not that he would have preferred to keep it. He was too startled to do much but follow her lead, and they grappled like children.

"Ridiculous," Hidemune grumbled above them. Abandoning his sword, he yanked the ties off his sleeves and stalked from the floor. Kazuchiyo tried to watch him leave to see if he might say something to Lady O-ran, but Mahiro captured him in a headlock, and by the time he slipped free, both of them had departed with General Waseba.

Mahiro let him go, clearly without any intent of leaving him be. "Get those boys back out here!" She snatched up the ties Hidemune had abandoned, fastened her sleeves, and motioned impatiently for their onlookers to join. "If you're going through your kata, you might as well see how it's done right. Come on, now, form ranks! I haven't got all morning!"

The others hurried to comply, returning to the rows they had been training in before the interruption. Kazuchiyo took a bit longer to join them as he swept back the locks of hair tousled by Mahiro's wrestling. It was not until he picked up the wooden sword again that he realized his hands were shaking, and all at once it occurred to him the terrible risk he had taken in provoking his temperamental brother. Certainly he and his mother would find their own way of retaliating for their embarrassment. It made him afraid for the tiny bead pressed to his wrist, throbbing along with his heightened pulse, and he smoldered with anxiety and bitterness for the hundreds of petty abuses he had suffered at their hands.

Then Mahiro thumped him on the shoulder, and he let the emotion flow out of him. He joined the younger pupils and, under Mahiro's instructions, started the series of exercises again.

The indomitable Mahiro worked them like mochi, hours later at last allowing them to retreat, groaning, toward the bathhouse. But she did not release Kazuchiyo as easily, insisting that he join her for a trip to the stables. Exhausted from the exercise of both body and mind, he had no means to refuse. In truth he appreciated her distraction more than he could yet admit, and a drink of saké from the gourd she perpetually carried on her person almost as much.

"She's the most magnificent steed in Shuyun," Mahiro said as she greeted Suzumekage in her stall. They rubbed noses and snorted happily like beastly sisters. "Isn't she, Kazu? She's itching to go west as much as I am. She's never been so deep in those forests."

"You're well matched," Kazuchiyo agreed. "Fortunate, as

they say she won't allow anyone else to ride her."

"Because I spoil her," said Mahiro, scratching beneath Suzumekage's chin. "And she's just as bloodthirsty as I am. It would be a waste for anyone else to ride her." She gave the horse a hearty pat and led Kazuchiyo deeper into the stalls. "She could use some grooming, but first I want to introduce you."

Kazuchiyo followed, curious. "Introduce me?"

Mahiro stopped in front of a different horse, which moved to the front of the stall to greet her as well. Her fondness for animals had always been well-reciprocated. It was a tall male with cloudy gray hair, which darkened around its muzzle and legs. As Kazuchiyo approached, the animal regarded him with what he perceived to be pleasant curiosity.

"This is Hashikiri," Mahiro introduced happily, encouraging Kazuchiyo closer. "Adorable, isn't he? He's young, but he's the fastest little shit I've ever seen. Other than Suzumekage, of course. But he's got to come close if you're going to keep up with me."

Kazuchiyo held out his hand, letting the horse sniff and then nose at it, looking for treats. He wished he had some to offer. "Excuse me?"

Mahiro rolled her eyes, though she was grinning. "He's yours! He's my gift to you. You'll need a horse of your own if we're leaving Gyoe, you know. We'll break the two of you in together."

Kazuchiyo blinked at her in surprise. "You're giving him to me?"

"You need a horse," said Mahiro impatiently. "And he's mine to give, so I'm giving him to you." Seeing Kazuchiyo's continued misgivings, she finally surrendered. "Yes, I have approval from Father. Do you want him or not?"

"Yes," Kazuchiyo said quickly, embarrassed that he was letting paranoia dampen his enthusiasm. "Yes, he's beautiful." Kazuchiyo patted Hashikiri's forehead gingerly and was relieved that he did not seem to mind. "But I don't have much experience with horses."

Her grin returned in full force. "And I have three weeks to teach you. We start in the morning."

They stayed in the stable while Mahiro gave Suzumekage a much-needed grooming, instructing Kazuchiyo as she did. It was all but impossible for him to waste concern on the altercation in the training hall with four immense hooves and more than two thousand pounds in need of his attention. He devoted himself to his tasks, and it wasn't until they were leading Suzumekage out of her stall that Mahiro found a way to broach the subject.

As much as she could, anyway. "Kazu," she said clumsily. "Maybe you should...just stay out of Hidemune's way for a while."

"I'll try," Kazuchiyo said with a weary smile. "Thank you for your help today."

He walked with them as far as the gate and watched with a bit of envy as Mahiro took to the saddle and raced out into the town. He could well imagine the people and their carts leaping away from the road to avoid her exuberant gallop. The thought that he would be alongside her sometime soon came to him late, and was quickly drowned out by other concerns.

Kazuchiyo moved to the slatted window, peering through at first as if he were still watching Mahiro's descent through the town. When there didn't seem to be any guards watching, he nudged the proper slat and reached into the alcove. He was certain that earlier Hidemune had been delivering some message of his own, but there was nothing inside. Were the Sakka shinobi always so swift, or had he been mistaken? The question left him boiling, and he hurried to deliver his note before returning to the castle.

The rest of the day he spent recuperating after the morning training. He studied in his room and played a bit of his flute when it suited him. By the evening meal he was summoned to join his father, and he worried that he would be forced into another confrontation with members of his family he was not yet prepared for. However, Lord Aritaka was alone that evening, and the two of them ate in privacy while discussing the road to Ninari Castle.

Much like his daughter, it was not until they had all but finished that Aritaka sought to comment on that morning's events.

"I heard that you and Hidemune had an exchange while training earlier," he said stiffly. "I wish that you would not quarrel."

"It was not my intention to quarrel with anyone," Kazuchiyo replied. "But I must have done something to offend him, and for that I am sorry."

"I have put you both in an unenviable position," Aritaka said, and Kazuchiyo was startled by the unexpected frankness. "I know the burden it is to you, but I hope you are aware of the burden it is to me, too, that I might have to choose between you."

Kazuchiyo had practiced too well for too long to let his frustration show. "I am aware. I will abide by your decision, whatever it is."

"And I promise there *will* be a decision, in due time. If there can be no reconciliation between you..." Aritaka took in a deep breath. "I will not abandon you to fight amongst yourselves after I am gone. The future ruler of Gyoe will be decided long before then."

Kazuchiyo's heart thumped and fluttered. He wondered at how low he would have to sink to be the kind of man that could so easily discuss abandoning one of his sons. "If there is anything I can do to help ease your burden, I will gladly do it."

"You do it now," said Aritaka, and they finished their meal without another word on the topic.

Kazuchiyo's sleep that night was restless, and he awoke to the disappointment of finding no return message in his room.

Perhaps the mysterious shinobi was offended by his accusations or else had tired of entertaining him. It was more likely that no one had returned to the alcove a second time after accepting Hidemune's message; part of him was curious enough to want to check. His better sense convinced him that doing so might draw too much suspicion to himself, and he resolved against it, despite the temptation. He would have to depend on Mahiro's tutelage to occupy his mind.

Fortunately, Mahiro's tutelage was unceasingly engaging. With boundless energy she instructed Kazuchiyo in the horse's anatomy and manners, how best to greet a horse and read its body language. She named each piece of equipment and proudly displayed those that she had procured for his use. By the time they were saddled and ready to begin riding, Kazuchiyo was eager to put her advice into practice. Mahiro boosted him into the saddle and helped him to get situated before taking to Suzumekage, and she led the way out onto the street.

"Keep your back straight," Mahiro instructed as they started at a slow pace toward the gate. "And stay calm. He's better at this than you are, and he knows it. He'll take care of you."

Kazuchiyo leaned forward to give Hashikiri a pet before straightening up. "Has he been ridden much?"

"Oh, sure, by the stable hands." Mahiro cast a smirk over her shoulder. "I took him out myself, yesterday. We'll be taking it nice and easy today, so you'll be fine."

"I'm not worried." Kazuchiyo tried to not be intimidated by the sway of the animal beneath him. They were coming close to the town, and he didn't want any of the people there to see him less than composed. "I trust you, and him."

They made their way down the central street and attracted more attention than Kazuchiyo was eager for. Though every inhabitant of Gyoe was well acquainted with Aritaka's youngest child, the sight of him on horseback was exceptionally rare, even more so as they were heading closer to the town's border. He began to feel anxious as they approached and felt like a fool because of it. There was nothing to stop him now from passing through that barrier, and no one to scold him for it. Soon he would be expected to cross half the province, in fact, but his heart still pounded fiercely as they rode at an almost painfully slow pace through the gate.

There was no fanfare, of course. No gust of wind or breaking of clouds to signify the breach of five years of isolation. Even so, Kazuchiyo's heart thumped and sped as they passed beyond the gates, onto the open road. He followed Mahiro down the twisting path, taking in the smell of the hillsides, of new grass growing exuberantly in the wake of much rain. Travelers made way for them, and birds sang unceasingly from the sparse trees. Tiny stone statues of lucky gods and guardians dotted the roadside, worn smooth and in some cases faceless with age. It evoked in Kazuchiyo a rush of freedom, much as he had found playing his flute from the rooftops, and at the same time it infuriated him, that his father had denied him a simple pleasure like this for so long.

Kazuchiyo's hands tightened on the reins, and for a moment he was overwhelmed by the fantasy of spurring young Hashikiri into a sprint, racing south through the sloping countryside, past the rivers and forests to the great Shimegahara field that separated his prison from his home. He could set free his mother and brother, as he had been; he might even find a loyal samurai to draw to his banner. With wits and strength he might even expel the northern invaders from the dragon's lands, refortify, and never again be felled by traitors and their lies.

He allowed himself to indulge in that hope for only a moment. There was no need to rush to rebellion and strife. As long as he remained in Aritaka's favor, he would one day be granted rulership of Sakka and Suyama together, just as his false father ruled them now. As cathartic as it was to imagine indigo Aritaka banners trampled into the earth, to wrest his homeland back under Tatsutomi blood mattered far more than simple vengeance.

They spent several hours outside the city, never going faster than a gentle walk. Mahiro chatted along the way, giving him pointers and telling stories both instructional and humorous about her many experiences riding with Suzumekage. By the time they returned the horses to the stables Kazuchiyo could feel the soreness settling in, and she offered him advice for that as well. They tended to the horses and then separated to their respective chores.

Kazuchiyo returned to his room, and his heart skipped: the piece of folded paper was pressed between the closed window panes.

He rushed forward and tugged it free. The poem had been continued after all, and it read:

He avoids even his kin
leaving no trace behind him

"Avoids," Kazuchiyo read aloud, glancing to the window and back. "No trace." Was Amai asking him not to use the alcove again? Or to cease trying to contact him? If the latter were true, it would have been better that he not respond at all. Kazuchiyo could only assume he was being cautioned against letting their correspondence be intercepted by Hidemune or others. Though it would have been wiser to let the *renga* conclude with such a definitive verse, he could not. As night fell, he tucked his response into his window panes.

Where does he call home?
Where does he take shelter from
this unending rain?

Kazuchiyo turned his mattress to better face the window, determined that he would settle in and pretend to sleep until the crafty shinobi came to take the bait. He had every intention of vigilance, but when the sun rose he found himself rubbing sleep from his eyes, and the paper was gone.

Another day of study and chores and riding instruction followed. Kazuchiyo sped from the lords to his sister and even to Lady Satsumi for an afternoon of music and tea. He kept his mind full of present duties and allowed nothing to distract him. He even managed to avoid all gossip concerning Hidemune. Still, it disappointed him when he returned to his chamber that evening and found nothing waiting for him. How foolish he felt, to be letting a childish and dangerous game take such hold over his thoughts.

He awoke the next morning to the paper folded next to his pillow, nothing else in the room disturbed. It continued:

Closer than the hunter knows
Too close to ever be caught

"I'll catch you yet," Kazuchiyo whispered, his face hot and pulse aflutter when he thought of Amai delivering such a challenge directly to his bedside as he slept. "Just you wait."

CHAPTER SEVEN

They continued on in that manner for some time. Kazuchiyo's days were full of learning, planning, and training, far removed from his elder brother whenever possible. He visited Hashikiri often even on the days they did not ride, bringing treats in the hopes that his new friend might look forward to seeing him. He took tea with Lady Satsumi and convinced Master Iomori to describe to him some of the topography of Kibaku, a province he had never seen. His anticipation mounted with each new morning: for the journey into unknown territory, for the challenges he might face, and especially for the reunion for which he had waited five long years. He spent many nights with the memory of Yagi's broad, strong hands to give him comfort.

And all along he and Gyoe's black fox continued their game, leaving the folded poem for each other. Sometimes Amai would come soon after Kazuchiyo had laid his bait; sometimes he would not retrieve or leave the paper for days. Kazuchiyo tried more than a few times to keep a late-night vigil, but he never succeeded in catching so much as a glimpse of a shadowed figure. If he managed to stay alert until dawn, Amai would not appear, and Amai would only appear when he lost his fight with exhaustion. He began to suspect a supernatural root to the man's prowess or, at the very least, that his carelessness in being seen that first day they met was an intentional misdirection as to his abilities.

He taunted:

Though catching the fox
cannot be the only way
to learn its secrets.

The reply came:

What could a hunter offer
that would tempt a clever fox?

These literary liaisons were the most reckless Kazuchiyo had engaged in during his five years within his castle prison. The promise of so many firsts fanned his courage and dulled his caution.

No juicy morsel
would be enough, no trinket,
no loyalty pledged.

Once, Amai attempted to usurp the leading verse from him.

A fox needs no loyalty.
He fends for himself alone.

But don't you believe
that he has no currency.
He trades in secrets.

But Kazuchiyo quickly claimed it back.

For knowledge can be costly,
the pursuit of it, lethal.

Curiosity:
A weapon and a weakness
fox and hunter share.

And thus the game went until Kazuchiyo returned late to his room one night after hours at study, pleased to find a reply waiting for him. His breath tangled around his ribs as he read.

Perhaps together they can
sate this sinful desire.

He remained still for a long time, reading and rereading as his face grew hotter. The words seemed to crawl off the page toward him, like long, slender fingers stroking the inside of his wrist. Days of careful prodding and phrasing, and suddenly all he could think of was this salacious invitation. He even neglected to recall that he had first sought Amai out, seeking revenge for a murdered father and brothers.

But Kazuchiyo's youth got the better of him, and he hurried to fetch his brush and ink. By candlelight he responded:

Secrets for secrets,
whispered straight from lips to ear,
swallowed by the rain

Exasperating, but also charming, that even in his attempts to answer Amai's blunt overture, Kazuchiyo felt the need to preserve the poem's central theme. In his mind, the cohesiveness of the imagery was more evocative that way. He tucked their paper into the window, embarrassed at himself for what he considered a bold reply. This time, he was certain Amai would come, and that he would be ready for it. He rushed through his evening preparations and into his futon.

It was one of the longer nights of Kazuchiyo's life. He kept his vigil through the darkest hours, watching his poem clutched by the window. He knew each line by heart, and he repeated them over in his mind, plucking from them every possible innuendo. This could not have been Amai's aim from the start, and so what had swayed him? Was he simply so enamored by well-staged poetry? Kazuchiyo burned with curiosity fit for the players in their ad-libbed drama as the hours wore on. With each passing moment he was more and more convinced that soon Amai would creep through the window, that he would see silver eyes flashing in the dark. The anticipation kept him simmering through the chill spring night, and he changed his posture—or rather, his pose—many times.

By dawn Kazuchiyo had lost hope, and he glared spitefully at the unclaimed message, exhausted and irritated and tantalizingly unfulfilled. An impulse to rip up the poem seized him, but luckily, a servant came to fetch him first. His efforts to hide the paper from her reminded him of how precious it was to him, and he abandoned all thoughts of destroying it as he hurried to dress himself.

Lord Aritaka had summoned him to his chambers for the morning meal, and Kazuchiyo dutifully joined him. His father wasted no time in stating his point. "I've received word that the construction is complete as scheduled. Our men throughout the province are already on the move toward Ninari. Mater Iomori tells me that tomorrow is an auspicious day for travel. We will complete our preparations and set out."

"Tomorrow?" Kazuchiyo echoed, straightening up. "Has it been three full weeks already?"

Aritaka smiled. "I'm not surprised that time has flown for you. You've always been studious, but these last weeks, especially so. I hope you enjoy the reprieve of travel."

"I'm looking forward to it," said Kazuchiyo, hurrying through the rest of his meal. It turned his stomach to have Lord Aritaka look on him so fondly.

After breakfast he visited Hashikiri in the stables, but not to ride; he only wished to bestow a few treats, even a few words of encouragement, before he would have to call on him for the journey ahead. He met with the head of the porters to ensure their supplies were prepared, even though his father would have seen to that already. In the afternoon he visited Lady Satsumi, and was surprised to find that Master Iomori had called on her already.

"Was it not your wish that we be amiable in your absence?" Iomori asked as one of her assistants poured out tea for them. "I am making an effort."

"She's making an effort," said Satsumi with a dubious slant of her brow. "This is the most hospitality I've received from this woman in years."

"If I can take credit for that, I'm honored," said Kazuchiyo. "I believe you have more in common than you might see."

Satsumi accepted her tea but waited until all three of them had been served before taking a sip. "What we have in common is *you*," she said, a note of seriousness beneath her teasing. "And our interest in your well-being. I'm sure that Master Iomori has offered you some good-luck trinket for your journey already, but I have one of my own to give you."

She reached behind her and pulled forward a wooden box, plainly decorated, which she slid toward him. Kazuchiyo took a polite sip of his tea before devoting his full attention to the gift. He opened the lid to reveal a *tanto*: a short, sturdy dagger in a handsome wooden sheath. The first character of his name was set into the grip in gold leaf. Kazuchiyo drew his fingertip over it, goosebumps rising along his skin.

"It's beautiful." He lifted the weapon from its casing. He drew the blade and touched it to his fingernail to test its expert sharpness. "Thank you, Lady Satsumi."

He slid the blade back into its sheath and looked to her, unable to hide the question in his face. As timely as the gift was, he had to wonder at her choice of label: it might have been more appropriate to decorate the dagger with the Aritaka family crest, or a character from his surname. Even his full given name would have made more sense. But one character alone—*peace*, ironic for a weapon—seemed a particular choice, hinting at intentions he could not yet work out.

"You're very welcome," replied Satsumi, and though she was smiling, her eyes were grim. "I hope that you don't find need to use it too soon."

"It would not make much sense as a gift if he didn't use it," said Iomori, dispelling the brief moment of tension. "I, for one, hope he finds an opportunity."

Satsumi shot her an exaggerated glare, and the pair traded dry barbs throughout the rest of Kazuchiyo's visit.

When Kazuchiyo returned to his room, the poem was where he had left it. He unfolded it to confirm that Amai had not taken and returned it, but only his latest verse stared back at him. Trying to quell his disappointment, he returned the poem to its place and left again.

He spent the remainder of the evening out on the courtyard wall, playing his flute. To some it may have appeared that he was offering a final serenade to his home of many years, but the truth was he only wanted Amai to know he was not in his chamber, should he want to retrieve their poem. He told himself that he had no real concern that Amai's delay was a rejection of any kind; he had on occasion taken days to make his appearance and, more importantly, Amai himself had been the one to change the tenor of their wordplay. But come morning he would depart, with no telling how long he would be gone. If Lord Aritaka was eager for warfare with the neighboring Kibaku province, a campaign could easily stretch for weeks or months. Certainly Amai would realize as much and know that they had very little time left to enjoy their correspondence, but by nightfall, the poem had not moved.

Determined not to waste another night's rest, especially considering the long day that would follow, Kazuchiyo put himself to bed and resolved not to think of Amai at all. He found sleep that was restless and dreams that frustrated. By morning he had resolved not to even look to the window. If Amai discovered his acceptance of the invitation too late to act upon it, then it served him right to remain just as unsatisfied for months on end.

Of course, curiosity got the better of him, and when he discovered the poem finally gone, his heart beat hard with elation and also regret. It would be a long time before he could know the response. Or so he assumed, at the time.

CHAPTER EIGHT

The castle bustled with activity all through the morning. Lord Aritaka hosted a hearty breakfast in his chambers, receiving the well wishes of those who would be staying behind. While the servants finished loading the carts and horses, he led his entourage to the shrine within Ishiyama Temple to receive a blessing from the mountain gods, headed by Master Iomori. When every preparation was complete they gathered just within the gate, forming their ranks. Kazuchiyo took his place next to Mahiro as they mounted their horses.

Mahiro winked at him, and he smiled back. They both sobered themselves when looking to the line of their father's generals and advisors come to see them off; O-ran and Hidemune were among them, watching with sour expressions. Kazuchiyo made only enough eye contact to prevent any claim that he was avoiding them.

Then Lord Aritaka spurred his horse, and the procession was underway. They rode out of the castle gates at an easy pace and into the town, where the citizens had gathered to bid their farewells. Though the older townspeople lowered their heads in respect, the young faces beamed up at the decorated horses and riders, much like Kazuchiyo had done as a child watching his father and brothers march from the keep. He had hoped to feel a swell of pride and accomplishment as he joined his first cavalcade, but instead he was uneasy beneath all the attention. He wanted to be free of the town as quickly as possible.

Mahiro, on the other hand, relished having an audience. She had dressed in her breastplate and helmet for the occasion, with its mane of bright white hair, catching every eye and earning her cheers from the bold among the crowd. Even her father could not discourage her as she flexed and posed for the approval of her supporters. It made for a rousing exit, and by all accounts, a memorable one.

At last they passed through the city gates, taking to the dusty path that twisted down among the foothills. The chatter quieted, and there was only the monotonous clomp of the horses and occasional squeals from a wagon wheel. Kazuchiyo was grateful for the calm; he had grown familiar with the road after his weeks of training, and with Mahiro catching her breath he had time to reflect.

The countryside was undeniably beautiful: sloping hills and towering pines, flowering trees just starting to bud. Their caravan followed the sunlight-dappled trail west into the forest, eventually journeying farther than Kazuchiyo had ever been. He found himself reminiscing about stories the old generals had told him in his youth, of days long past when the Tatsutomi army was at its strongest, its vanguard advancing deep into Sakka territory. Five years he had lived within its borders, and his knowledge of the terrain was poorer than their memory of thirty years past. He kept a keen eye on all his surroundings as they went, committing as much to memory as he could.

Someday, he would rule this stretch of land. All he need be was patient.

In the early evening they arrived at the private homestead of General Waseba Houshin, the second of three brothers who had at one time served under Tatsutomi's dragon banner. Unlike his elder brother, he was not often seen at Gyoe, preferring a life of prayer and farming in solitude. Kazuchiyo had not laid eyes on him since the battle at Shimegahara and was startled by the change he observed in his make and manner. Though Houshin had always been uncommonly tall, he was a great deal thinner than Kazuchiyo remembered, and he greeted Lord Aritaka and his procession with humble servitude. His head was shaved in the manner of his newly adopted religious piety, and even his current name, Houshin, was a choice to reflect his desire for enlightenment.

Lord Aritaka greeted him amiably enough, the elder Waseba less so. Nevertheless Houshin welcomed lord, family, and generals into his home, while the foot soldiers and porters made camp around the modest property.

"How is Hashikiri holding up?" Mahiro asked as she and Kazuchiyo were guided toward the guest house. "He didn't give you any trouble, did he?"

"No trouble at all," Kazuchiyo replied gladly. "Though there were a few times he seemed a little restless. I think he was itching to run."

Mahiro laughed. "Of course he was! He'll have the chance, you can tell him that from me." Her grin turn mischievous. "How's your *ass* holding up?" she teased, and she gave him a smack.

Kazuchiyo jumped with a very inelegant yelp, and Mahiro guffawed, earning her glares from the surrounding generals. But her humor would not be dampened by something as inconsequential as disapproval. "There's a natural hot spring up the hill from the guest house. We'll take a trip this evening, eh? That'll get you right."

Kazuchiyo gave his backside a discreet rub and continued on with her. "All right."

After granting them the opportunity to relax for a while in the guest house, Houshin accepted them in the main house for a modest supper. There were no meats, only rice and pickled vegetables. Kazuchiyo did not mind, but the elder Waseba had plenty to remark on.

"You must have grown these yourself," he said as they ate; on a kinder tongue it might have sounded like a compliment. "There are plenty of them."

"We were gifted with a fine harvest," replied Houshin with patience befitting his lifestyle.

"Were your forests not gifted with game?"

Houshin kept his eyes downcast as he ate, the rest of the assembly watching with varied sympathy and scorn. "We were gifted with healthy livestock," he said. "Once they have lived out their time, I will have meat to serve."

Waseba harrumphed. "I hope you at least allow the men that serve you a proper diet. They will need muscle weight on them if they're to go to war."

"You didn't get that tall eating just radishes," Mahiro agreed with a taunting smirk.

Lord Aritaka cleared his throat. "Every soldier in my army will be well fed," he said, signaling the end of that subject.

After supper, Mahiro led Kazuchiyo up the wooded path behind the guest house, there finding another smaller building for bathers to disrobe and wash. After scrubbing themselves of road dust and the smell of their horses, they sank into the naturally heated waters of the mountain spring. Though the bath was wide there was only one, and Mahiro thought nothing of them sharing it. "It's not as if I have any modesty or even decent tits," she reasoned as she stretched her arms across the rocks and settled in. "But I promise not to piss in it."

"I would hope so," Kazuchiyo replied, and her laugh echoed among the pines.

"You know," Mahiro said after they had had some time to soak, "I think when we reach Ninari, I'm most looking forward to meeting Yagi-douji."

As startled as Kazuchiyo was to hear the name from her, he managed to keep his expression fairly neutral. "You mean General Ebara's son?"

"I've never been far enough west to run into him." There was a tone of wistful curiosity in her voice that Kazuchiyo disapproved of. "But they say he has the strength of twenty men, and his spear is the size of a pine trunk. What do you think?"

"I think he's the strongest man I've ever met," Kazuchiyo said honestly, "but I don't think you'll care for his demeanor."

"Well, all the better, then." Mahiro's grin was devilish as she stared into to the darkening sky. "I'm only interested in testing my blade against his anyway."

Kazuchiyo was tempted to say she didn't stand much of a chance, but that would only increase her interest, and he didn't want to dwell on the subject of Yagi any longer, not when his heart was so full of anticipation it was ready to burst. As he struggled to think of some way to distract her that would not rouse her teasing nature, they were interrupted by footsteps approaching from the bathhouse, and a moment later Waseba Houshin himself joined them at the pool's edge.

"I hope you don't mind my intrusion," he said.

"It's *your* bath," Mahiro replied with a shrug.

Houshin discarded his robe and slid into the water with them. He looked heavy with thought that Kazuchiyo could feel on his own shoulders. How was he meant to feel about this man he had last seen when he was a boy and Houshin was a towering pillar of his father's army? Now, a somber pacifist shyly sought Kazuchiyo's eye.

"This might be my last chance," Houshin said, "so I had hoped that I could speak with you."

Kazuchiyo stared back at him, anxious and trying to hide it. Houshin looked pained, and he did not know if it would give him any comfort to hear whatever he had to say. "Mahiro," Kazuchiyo said, "would you mind going on ahead of us?"

"He has something to say I can't hear?" Mahiro retorted,

but when Kazuchiyo looked to her, she sighed. "I'm going to find us a drink. But I *will* be back." She regarded Houshin with suspicion as she climbed out of the bath; he averted his eyes. "And soon."

"Thank you," said Kazuchiyo. Once she had disappeared into the bathhouse, he returned his full attention to Houshin expectantly.

Despite having requested Kazuchiyo's ear, it took Houshin some time to collect himself and make use of it. "I want to apologize to you," he said at last, with a tremble of emotion that Kazuchiyo did not expect. "For the shameful betrayal of my family against yours, five years ago at Shimegahara. If not for the inconvenience it would cause you, I would cut my belly open to make amends. But the best I can do now is do you no harm, and pray for their souls."

Kazuchiyo stared back at him, stunned and unable to respond. In his years of captivity he had not once been offered condolences for his lost kin, let alone an apology, and his heart could not trust it. But Houshin's downcast eyes were so earnest in their grief that he could not think him a liar either.

"Is this some kind of test?" he asked, fearful that the elder Waseba, or one of his servants, was waiting for him to express too much resentment.

"No," Houshin assured him. "Though I understand how you would think so." He smiled in a frail, self-pitying way. "You must despise me. I betrayed my lord to a gruesome end, and now here I sit, claiming to be a man of piety. But I saw enough death on that field to last me a lifetime, and I am sorry for my part in it. I hope never to lift a sword again."

Kazuchiyo shuddered, fingering the bead still tied to his wrist; he had been afraid to loosen the ribbon even before Mahiro, and feeling its slight indent against his pulse gave fuel to his righteous anger. "If you were sorry," he said, his voice rough with the effort of restraint, "you would have cut your belly open on the field, like my father did."

"I know. And I will now, if you ask it of me." Kazuchiyo's

heart began to pound fiercely, but before he could fully consider the words, Houshin continued. "I would hate to do anything that could jeopardize your standing with Lord Aritaka. Though it pains me to admit, I know my elder brother would not overlook any opportunity to discredit you."

"Why did the Waseba clan betray us?" Kazuchiyo pressed. He couldn't begin to ponder what kind of penance he desired from this man, but information he was in desperate need of. "If it was your brother's decision, what did Aritaka offer in order to coerce him?"

Houshin cringed and glanced about in sudden paranoia. If there were spies lying in wait on his order, he was doing an enviable job of acting. "He offered what your father wasn't willing to," he said in a quieter voice. "A greater war than the settling of a grudge between two provinces." He took a deep breath and lowered his voice even further. "Lord Aritaka promised us that he has plans to march to the west."

To the west, of course, lay Kibaku province. Its eastern border was mountainous and heavily forested, making it a natural barrier that both Sakka and Suyama provinces shared. But past that, Kazuchiyo's tutors had claimed, was a great plain that produced enough rice to feed one hundred thousand men a year. If that prize were not tempting enough, beyond Kibaku lay the inner territories, the riverlands...and the capital.

Kazuchiyo swallowed. As inadvisable as it was, he found himself speaking the implication aloud. "Aritaka has designs on becoming the shogun."

Houshin leaned away. "You mustn't," he said, and Kazuchiyo quickly nodded in understanding. "I should not have said anything, but now you know. You ought to understand the motivations of those that would wish you harm."

Kazuchiyo sank deeper into the pool, his thoughts in a whirl. He would have liked more time, but he could hear Mahiro pacing about in the bathhouse and knew they wouldn't have privacy for much longer. "You're right," he said, too many emotions turning like a water wheel within his chest. "I do despise you. But it won't serve me if you take your own life five years too late." He fixed Houshin with stern eyes. "If you would make amends, do it by taking up your sword when your master calls on you."

Houshin's shoulders sagged with resignation. Though he clearly dreaded the thought, he climbed from the bath and turned to Kazuchiyo on his knees, lowering his forehead to the wet stone. "I will," he promised, and Kazuchiyo believed him.

He hurried upright as Mahiro returned and excused himself. Mahiro threw suspicious glares at his back as she slipped into the water. "What did he want?"

"He wanted to reminisce," Kazuchiyo said, and he waved for his portion of the saké with uncharacteristic eagerness. "I knew him, in my former life."

Mahiro poured Kazuchiyo a cup and watched closely as he gulped it down. It wasn't characteristic of her to be quiet either, but an awkward silence stretched between them before she furrowed her brow and said, "Hey, Kazu. You like me, don't you?"

Distracted as he was by Houshin's provocative declarations, Kazuchiyo could only answer, "Of course. You're my sister."

Mahiro's face scrunched up, and she took a swig of alcohol from the bottle. "Do you like me *because* I'm your sister?" she persisted. "Or *in spite of* it?"

"Does it matter?" he asked, but upon seeing her crestfallen, a pang of guilt forced him to take her seriously. "I don't resent you for anything, if that's what you're asking."

Mahiro relaxed, though she still looked troubled. "Good," she said, and then she changed the subject to how skinny and drooping she would look if she only ever ate roots and shrubbery like Houshin, and how she was looking forward to a feast at Ninari. Certainly the border samurai would feed them pork and venison poached from Kibaku woods.

The sky was nearly black by the time the pair returned to the guest house to sleep, no moon and few stars to light their way down the path. As they parted, Mahiro looked to her brother once more with a pitiable expression, but she still worked up a cheerful good night.

In his room, Kazuchiyo let his hair down and huddled under his bedding. They had not yet reached Ninari and he was already simmering with concerns and secrets he had never expected. He thought of the Tatsutomi's grand keep where the Red Dragon and his generals used to gather when he was young, their eyes and hearts ever seeking war. At the time he had never considered a battle greater or an enemy more imposing than their northern rivals, the competition that had captivated his family for generations. Now, the truth was set loose upon him: Yatamoto and the Waseba brothers, greedy for a greater war, had judged his father lacking in ambition and destroyed him for it. With fresh insight Lord Aritaka's haste to make war on Kibaku made complete sense, and even lent gravity to the petty conflicts between O-ran and Satsumi, Hidemune and Kazuchiyo himself. It was not merely Gyoe that hung in the balance.

A thousand ages of peace, his father had named him. An expression of hope and cowardice his vassals had killed him for, and one that Lord Aritaka was determined to stamp out of his stolen son. Kazuchiyo curled his knees to his chest and shuddered with frustration that burned his lungs. Even if he survived long enough to best Hidemune for their father's affection, what would that earn him, if generals north and south betrayed him for not seeking more than that?

He lay there, hoping for sleep, until he heard a creak on the wooden floor just beyond his doorway.

Kazuchiyo went very still. The night was so dark and windless that he hadn't noticed before, but with his senses intensely focused he realized that the quiet chirp of the crickets was a little bit louder. He held his breath and knew, with frightful certainty, that he was not alone in the room. With movements slow and subtle to keep the bedding from rustling, he reached into the waistband of his robe where his tanto was hidden. His palm sweat around the grip, and he was convinced

101

he could feel his own name branding itself into his palm.

He waited there for minutes that dragged on for hours, but nothing stirred, and he heard and sensed no more indication of an intruder. When at last he turned, the sliding door to the outside was open a mere two inches, and in the very dim light he could barely make out the shape of a folded paper leaning in the gap.

Kazuchiyo shot forward and snatched it up. He stumbled over his robe as he threw the door open, but he could make out no figure retreating from the grounds, no disruption in the line of ferns or low-hanging branches. The night air cooled the sweat on his neck, and with a shiver he ducked back into the room, making sure the doors were closed and that he had not roused anyone else in the building. Thus reassured, he lit a candle and crowded over the tiny flame to read.

It was not the same poem that he and Amai had shared over the past three weeks of secret correspondence. The paper was rough and torn, as if it had been ripped from a note or a ledger, and the words were scrawled in great haste. But it was unmistakably familiar handwriting, and it read:

Helm and bow laid down for a
new hunt no less passionate

Kazuchiyo read the lines over several times until the distant call of an owl startled him into blowing out the candle. He folded the paper as small and thin as he could and tucked it into Iomori's ribbon for safekeeping before hurrying back into bed. Fourteen syllables and all his earlier worries scattered like petals in the wind. Huddled beneath his robes he imagined a young shinobi trailing their caravan through the woods, ever out of sight as proof of his title, ever focused. He marveled at Amai's careful wording—calling back to the first verse, completing the narrative so efficiently. That attention to detail had to have been for his own sake, and that in itself excited him as much as the accepted invitation.

Surely Amai was following them to Ninari Castle. There Kazuchiyo would have a proper chamber of his own, perhaps even with an outside window like at Gyoe, where a clever fox could sneak in undetected to all but his rival, waiting, willing…

If not for the wine Kazuchiyo might have never found sleep that evening, and even then memories of the rainy field threatened to cloud his mind as he drifted off. His dreams were electric and full of running, and he woke up more eager than ever to be underway.

CHAPTER NINE

Thankfully, come morning Lord Aritaka was no less impatient. Breakfast was served, and soon after the camps were broken down and preparations made to depart. Houshin was there to see them off, and though his elder brother did not make an effort to share any parting words, Kazuchiyo thanked him for having hosted them for the night. Houshin bowed his head.

"I am yours to call upon, whenever you have need of me," he said, and Kazuchiyo bowed in return.

Then they were on their way again, along the twisting road to the west. The trees were denser than the day before, allowing only sparse sunlight to warm Kazuchiyo's back. He tried to devote his concentration to the grade of the path, only to find that his mind was too full of anxious anticipation. He looked continuously to the trees, hoping to see a shadowy figure giving chase. Then he looked ahead, imagining a taller, broader figure he knew to be waiting, and his heart tangled.

By midday they came to a rise in the hills, the forest peeling back to reveal an uninterrupted view of the countryside. Kazuchiyo gazed out over the slopes, trees, and fields beyond. How he wished to feel peace, faced with flowing green in infinite shades, winding paths with peaceful travelers, the outlines of fields in the distance preparing for spring planting. Instead he found his gaze drawn to the south, and the shape of a village among the trees where the citizens were likely finishing their morning chores. He wondered if any of their youths were being offered up to Lord Aritaka's war plans.

Though Castle Ninari was not as expansive as Gyoe, it was no less impressive. The main keep with its coal-black walls stood four stories tall atop a twenty-foot base of stone. Its eaves were jagged and striking, confusing to the eye. It was accompanied by a single lower tower that was nearly as tall and just as sturdy, but the real defenses were inside the ward: an immense bailey with smooth walls and stone base surrounded the entire structure, with long overhangs to prevent breaches, and diamond cutouts up and down its length for archers. The closest pines had been hacked down so that the defenders had a long range of visibility. Kazuchiyo did not envy any advancing army that chose to lay siege to such a well-constructed fortress.

The gates opened for them, and as Lord Aritaka led the way through, they were greeted by rows of samurai and their underlings. Many of the subordinates were dressed for labor rather than presentation, as if they'd been dragged from their posts, and a keen eye would have noticed that a few of the scaffolds leaning against the inner wall were not quite complete. But Generals Utsukawa and Ebara were at the height of their manners, each bowing deeply at the waist as they accepted their lord.

"Allow us to lead you to the interior," said General Utsukawa.

They guided the procession on foot along the inner wall toward a second gate that led them into the compound's interior proper. Along the way Kazuchiyo looked to the workers coming down from their scaffolds, his eyes darting from one to the next. Just before reaching the gate, his gaze found its prey: a tousled mop of brown hair and broad shoulders tanned from the sun and glistening with sweat, just like his every imagining. His heart pounded so thunderously he was sure the man heard it. Yagi-douji lifted his head from his bow, and for the first time in five years, they faced each other.

At first, Yagi's dark eyes were just as Kazuchiyo remembered: fierce and contemptuous, as if he could have sprung to violence at any moment against a despised enemy. But then his brow arched in surprise and recognition, and the flutter of his eyelashes sent chills rippling across Kazuchiyo's skin. Did his appearance warrant such a stunned reaction?

Too soon they rounded the second gate, and the contact was severed. Kazuchiyo took a deep breath and assured himself that now that he had arrived, he would have many chances to properly greet Yagi, as soon as the pleasantries were over with.

They dismounted just outside the keep, and as servants came to tend the horses, Lord Aritaka, his children, and his generals were led on a tour of the grounds. "I noticed the construction was not as compete as your letter led me to believe," Aritaka was quick to scold General Utsukawa. "Your men are still hard at work."

"It is only the stairs and rails for the archers," Utsukawa quickly assured him. "We still don't have a complete count of how many soldiers we'll have to man the walls."

"As many as they will hold, General. We have the men."

"Those Kibaku crows will have to be idiots to throw themselves at a castle like this," said Mahiro as she surveyed the armaments with approval. "Are you sure you'll be able to seduce them into it, Father?"

Aritaka frowned at her choice of words. "The Koedzuka samurai are a greedy lot. They won't be able to resist."

His assessment did not match the stories Kazuchiyo had heard from Master Iomori over the years, but he paid it little mind. Though he stayed close to his father's side throughout the tour of the castle, he did not devote an appropriate amount of attention until they reached his chamber in the upper floor of the main keep.

"This room will serve you while you are here," said Utsukawa as he introduced Kazuchiyo to the modest space. "I hope it does not displease you."

Kazuchiyo noted the room's broad window with slats that could be deployed or pushed aside as needed. "It suits me very well," he said.

The tour continued, and once completed, Utsukawa bowed again to his lord and guests. "Supper will be prepared shortly. Your rooms should be well stocked, if you would like to change clothing before the meal."

Kazuchiyo glanced between the two generals and could not stop himself. "Will your sons be joining us?"

"Yes," Utsukawa replied while Ebara pulled a face. "They are very eager to meet you, Lord Kazumune."

"Mine is not well suited to ceremony," said Ebara, "but he will be present, yes."

"I look forward to it," said Kazuchiyo, and he excused himself back to his room to prepare.

As promised, the room was already well stocked, and Kazuchiyo dressed in a handsome, indigo *hitatare* robe tailored to his size. He would have liked a bath, but had to make do with a wash basin for his face. His long hair he spent the most time on, brushing and tying it to perfection. By the time he was finished he was all but giddy, thinking of the many stories he had to share, the stories he hoped to hear. It did not occur to him that Yagi might have felt differently. To him, this was a destined reunion, one that could forever change his fate. As naive as it may seem, in this he was not mistaken.

Kazuchiyo was finishing his preparations when a slip of his sleeve reminded him of the ribbon tied around his wrist and the folded note that had remained tucked inside it throughout the day. With a pang he drew it toward him, thinking then how fickle and greedy he was. What would either man say if they could see him drawn so powerfully in two directions?

Kazuchiyo moved to the window, propping it open half a hand's width before heading to supper.

Lord Aritaka received his children and generals in the hall of the keep, and there they were seated for a hearty banquet. Kazuchiyo's place was not nearly as close to Yagi as he would have liked, with Utsukawa and his sons between them. He had to content himself with glimpses of the man's profile whenever he leaned forward to take up his wine cup. Which, granted, was often.

"This is a real meal," Waseba declared as they were served strips of pork. "Fine game from the deep woods. Men become tigers on meat, not on radishes."

Utsukawa bowed happily, thinking his words compliments rather than a condemnation of an absent brother. "My eldest son fired the arrow that felled this boar," he bragged as humbly as possible. "We owe a great deal of our storehouse to his efforts."

"On your next hunt, you ought to take Kazumune with you," said Aritaka. "He is very keen with a bow."

"My sons would be honored," said Utsukawa, and Kazuchiyo bowed his head to express the same. He already found Utsukawa rather exhausting.

"I'm coming, too," Mahiro spoke up. "I'm anxious to see how the hunting here compares to the eastern border I'm used to." She cast a sly eye farther down the group. "I do hope your beast of a boy will be joining us, General Ebara."

The other Ninari generals shifted uncomfortably; Yagi continued to eat as if he had not heard. "Motonobu is not well-suited to hunting," Ebara answered for him, and Kazuchiyo wondered just how many times he had used that phrase to describe his ill-mannered foster son. "He hasn't the patience for it."

"You cannot use a beast to hunt a beast," agreed Utsukawa's

eldest. "With respect."

"That's not what I heard," said Mahiro. "They say he caught and executed a Kibaku spy single-handedly—*barehandedly*. Isn't that a kind of hunting?"

Ebara's lip quirked, and suddenly Kazuchiyo could perceive the pride he had been trying not to express all along. "That kind of hunting does not require patience."

"What does it require?" asked Kazuchiyo. Seeing Yagi flinch at the sound of his voice made his skin crackle. "Kibaku spies are famously skilled. I would like to know how your son was able to capture one."

"That's not—" Utsukawa started to say, but Lord Aritaka silenced him by clearing his throat.

"I would like to know as well," he said. "How does one catch a crow?"

Ebara leaned back, and all eyes diverted to Yagi. It took an almost uncomfortable amount of silence for him to acknowledge their attention. At last he placed his cup down. "I smelled him," he said plainly.

"Smelled him," Lord Aritaka repeated. "How so?"

"The man cut himself on an unfinished beam when scaling the wall," Yagi explained. "I happened to pass by and smell the blood. I followed it and discovered him."

The assembly listened with grave curiosity, except for Mahiro, who laughed and slapped her knee. "He happened to smell a drop of blood in passing!" She elbowed Kazuchiyo. "That's a proper oni for you, eh?"

"It's very impressive," he said, watching as Yagi resumed eating.

"He doesn't deserve your praise," said Ebara, though there was praise in his tone. "We are all honored to serve."

"I look forward to his further service," said Aritaka, and the conversation continued on about the arrogant foolishness of Kibaku province and the Koedzuka samurai that governed it. Kazuchiyo absorbed the conversation as best he could whilst casting covert glances Yagi's way. Yagi did not look up even once, which did not deter him.

At the meal's end, more empty flattery was shared, and everyone dispersed. Despite the possibility of appearing rude, Kazuchiyo deliberately dodged any eye contact from his father and hurried to Yagi before he could stalk off. "Motonobu," he said, and the way Yagi wrinkled his nose at the name threatened to make him smile. "If you don't mind, I would like to see the area of the wall that the spy passed through."

"I don't mind," said Yagi. The two of them shared an unspoken understanding as they avoided Mahiro's attention to sneak away as quickly as possible.

Once they were finally alone, Kazuchiyo felt more at ease and yet somehow more anxious at the same time. His steps were light but his heart tight and heavy, and he had no idea where to begin. "It's good to see you," he managed clumsily. "You look very well."

"I guess. Well." Yagi scratched the back of his neck. "Compared to the last time you saw me, I'm sure. How long has it been?"

"Five years."

"Shit." Yagi shook himself. "I mean, it's good to see you, too. You really startled me when you rode in like that."

They exited the keep together and there slowed a bit, taking their time across the courtyard to the inner wall. There were still workers along the scaffolding, taking turns serving themselves from a pair of rice pots, and a few of them glanced their way. Kazuchiyo was too absorbed in his companion to think anything of their attention. "What do you mean?" he asked, reliving that shiver when their eyes met upon his entrance. "Didn't you know I was coming?"

"Of course," Yagi said awkwardly, "but you're a lot taller than I remembered."

A laugh bubbled out of Kazuchiyo, and he blushed, embarrassing himself. It sounded strange to him, and he assumed it did to Yagi as well. "It's been five years," he reminded him. "It'd be a shame if I wasn't any taller."

"Sure, but…" Yagi heaved a great sigh. "What I mean is, you look well, Kazuchiyo."

Kazuchiyo's breath caught, and before he knew it he had stopped walking. It had been so long since he had heard the name in his heart spoken aloud, and he wasn't prepared for the power those syllables still held over him. Emotion strangled him, and he couldn't bring himself to respond.

Yagi stopped, though it took him a moment to recognize that he was the cause of Kazuchiyo's distress. "Oh—sorry. I'm not supposed to call you that now. It's Kazu—"

"Kazu," Kazuchiyo interrupted. He took a deep breath to dispel the grip on his ribs and faced Yagi with determination. "When it's us alone, just Kazu is fine."

Yagi nodded, his brow heavy with understanding. But then his expression eased, and he reached out. Kazuchiyo held very still as Yagi gave a gentle tug to a lock of his bangs. "It looks like you haven't cut your hair at all since then, either. I'm glad that old bear didn't get his teeth in you."

He let go and turned to continue on. When he realized that Kazuchiyo was not following, he glanced back. "Did you really want to see the wall? Or was that just an excuse to lose the old men?"

"I do!" Kazuchiyo spurred himself forward, light as air. "I want to hear all about it."

"It's not much of a story," said Yagi. He, too, seemed invigorated by their exchange. "He was careless and I was angry. It's okay if you call me Yagi, by the way, even in front of the old men. Everyone else does."

"Good," said Kazuchiyo, unable to help his bluntness. "I don't believe 'Motonobu' suits you at all."

Yagi grunted. "There's lots of things that don't suit me, as you've probably heard."

They reached the wall, now complete, and they climbed the planks together. Kazuchiyo peered through the arrow slit. As he had noted earlier, thirty feet of forestry had been cleared away from the wall, leaving a long stretch of unprotected land to cross. "He must have been very bold to have crossed that land without being spotted."

"I assume he was watching us for a long time," said Yagi. "Memorizing the guard rotations." He grumbled under his breath. "Or it was magic."

"Magic," Kazuchiyo echoed, reminded of Iomori's gifts to him. "Not magic enough to save him from your keen senses, though." He turned back to look at Yagi, who was rubbing his nose self-consciously. "Did he confess anything about his master? Or his mission?"

"Not a word. Though I'm sure Utsukawa will tell Aritaka that it was a declaration of war. All they're waiting for is an excuse."

Kazuchiyo nodded solemnly and looked toward the keep once more. Up and down the walls the men and women of Sakka province toiled at the scaffolding, some placing the crates that would be used to hold arrows for the defending archers. They were dutiful but cheerful as the sun dipped toward the western wall, and they lit torches to continue working. Before too long it would be bows in their hands instead of hammers and chisels. Kazuchiyo watched them move about in the shadow of Ninari's central keep, their darkened figures blending into the earth, their voices an incomprehensible drone to his ears.

"If Kibaku can't provide one, Lord Aritaka will use an excuse of his own making to go to war," he said distractedly. "He doesn't have a choice."

"He could always lose his head on the field," Yagi grumbled with the same blunt carelessness that Kazuchiyo remembered fondly. "Then you'd be lord of Sakka, and you could make war or peace or whatever you want."

Kazuchiyo watched a young teen hurrying food and drink to his elders, who were nailing the final railings into place. They could not have been far apart in age, but to Kazuchiyo's eyes he appeared very young. "I don't have a choice, either," he said. "All of Aritaka's vassals are fixated on the west. I can't survive them if I turn my back."

"You think you have better chances surviving war?" Yagi's expression twisted. "Your first father died at battle, you know."

Despite his apparent insensitivity, Kazuchiyo smiled. "That's the irony of it. My father survived thirty years of war. It was only when he dreamed of peace that it killed him." He took in a deep breath and faced Yagi with renewed determination. "But as long as you're in our army, I'm not afraid."

Yagi leaned back, brow intensely furrowed. He didn't seem to know what to make of his young lord, who had grown so much and changed so little since their last encounter. "All right," he said, with clear effort to rise to Kazuchiyo's confidence in him. "At least it's more interesting than building a wall."

Kazuchiyo's heart swelled with relief. Having invested possibly too much faith in this brief acquaintance from his youth, even Yagi's artless attestation of loyalty bolstered his spirits as nothing else could have. "Thank you," he said, as if having been offered a priceless gift. He shifted his weight back and forth, overwhelmed with all he wanted to express. "There's so much I want to tell you," he confessed. "So many things that have happened. And I want to know everything that's happened here, too—everything you've been through." He felt a touch of color in his cheeks. "I've thought of you often these five years."

Yagi scrunched his nose. "There's...not much to tell. But I guess we'll have plenty of time, if you're going to be here with Aritaka for a while." He took a step back to urge them away from the wall. "For now we should head in before they think we're colluding out here or something."

"All right." Kazuchiyo smiled and followed him back toward the keep, though Yagi's words had struck him. He wondered if the man remembered that night in Gyoe's keep, promising to one day take Aritaka's head for him.

CHAPTER TEN

Once inside the keep, the pair parted ways. Kazuchiyo climbed the stairs to his room on the upper floor, alight with hope and energy. He was so pleased with the encounter that it wasn't until he was curling up under his bedding that he remembered he might be entertaining another reunion that night.

He looked to the window. The sky was not as fiercely dark as before, but there was still very little light by which to make out the shape of the opening. Nothing had moved and nothing had been left for him. Kazuchiyo rearranged his bedding so he could better face the window. If Amai had been bold and impatient enough to deliver his message on Houshin's property, Kazuchiyo had no doubt that he would be just as punctual now that he had arrived. Lying on his back, he closed his eyes and pretended to sleep. This time for certain he would catch his quarry.

Sure enough, when the moon was at its highest Kazuchiyo sensed a nearing presence. The window made no sound as it was opened, but something in the air shifted, and for a moment he thought he smelled the familiar tang of blood. His heart raced as the tatami conveyed to him the subdued vibrations of approaching footsteps, slow and cautious, testing the unfamiliar room. Soon, an intruder stood at Kazuchiyo's bedside.

Kazuchiyo did not move. He held his breath and kept his eyes closed as he felt the figure shift, placing a foot on either side of him. His heavy pulse stopped up his ears as the man lowered himself onto the bedding. For the first time since their meeting in the alley, they touched: Kazuchiyo held his every muscle tight as weight settled over his stomach, pinning him. At last he could hear the other's breath, and then he could feel it, soft and shallow against his face. Before he could decide whether to spring or submit, a pair of soft, full lips touched his in a kiss.

It wasn't Kazuchiyo's first, but he almost wished that it was. A dark room, night air whistling through the open window, a warm body covering his—a warm mouth, gentle and teasing. Kazuchiyo returned the kiss without opening his eyes, thrilling with the illicit mystery of it all. But when he tried to reach up, his wrists were captured in a tight grip. Slow to comprehend any danger, he allowed them to be pushed back to the mattress. It wasn't until his intruder had shifted, trapping Kazuchiyo's hands between his ankles and thighs, that it occurred to him that something was wrong. By then, a hand was snaking around his throat.

"Shh," Amai soothed, and Kazuchiyo's eyes flew open, finally granting him a look at the man's soft face and bright eyes. He tightened his fingers around Kazuchiyo's neck as he pulled a sharpened kunai from his belt and tucked the point under his jaw. "Shh, don't struggle."

Kazuchiyo didn't, sensing that it would be wasted effort. Even then his brain was muddled with excitement, bitterness and betrayal slow to penetrate. He stared up at Amai and realized that his nose hadn't been mistaken: there was a splash of blood drying against the collar of Amai's robe. He swallowed. "Is this revenge for the alley?"

"This is me acting under orders," Amai replied, his voice

115

the same buzzing drawl Kazuchiyo remembered from their only other meeting. "Your brother told me to kill you."

Kazuchiyo's mind became a coil of snakes. Cold crept up his limbs, and he stared at Amai as if from outside himself. Visions of a young fool paraded across his bleary sight like illustrations from a rolling scroll—every time he had dashed to his room in search of a poetic reply from a mysterious stranger, all those anxious nights spent lost in imagination and anticipation. He felt ill all over.

"Your death would serve him in so many ways," Amai continued to whisper, the cords on his gloves digging into Kazuchiyo's throat, though not yet enough to hamper his breathing. The greater threat was the point of the kunai so close to his vein. "If Aritaka's son were to be murdered by a Kibaku shinobi, that would mean the war he's so eager to get on with. And it would leave Hidemune to take his rightful place below his father."

Kazuchiyo thought of Hidemune at the message alcove and felt emotion crush against his chest with far greater weight than Amai's slender frame. "Since the beginning?" he asked, his voice hushed and already raw. "You were waiting for this all along?"

Amai snorted quietly. "Worked pretty damn well, didn't it? Your guard couldn't be any lower than it is now."

He scraped the tip of the kunai back and forth against the point of Kazuchiyo's jaw, just enough so that he could feel its expertly filed sharpness. Rather than intimidate, his taunting only fueled Kazuchiyo's anger and hurt. Five years he had spent coiled and cautious, his head spinning around like a fearful owl's; to have been outdone by youthful indiscretion was a shame he was in no way able or willing to bear.

"I warned you to stay away," said Amai. "It's not as if I *wanted* to—"

Kazuchiyo lunged, but not at Amai. He rocked to the side so that the kunai pierced his neck. It was only a shallow wound, nothing vital ruptured, but blood welled immediately to trickle into the bedding. With a hissed curse Amai drew the weapon back and shifted his grip, trying to staunch the flow with his thumb.

"I said *don't struggle.*" For a brief moment Amai's expression twisted with concern before he was able to wrangle his apathy back into place. "Shit, I was just getting to the good part, too."

"Then kill me," Kazuchiyo retorted, squirming enough that Amai wouldn't be able to let the wound close over quickly. "If you've come for my head, take it, you duplicitous vermin!"

"Quiet down; I'm trying to tell you something." Amai leaned closer, though using his ankles and feet to keep a tight hold on Kazuchiyo's wrists. "The truth is, I did enjoy our little game." He gave another snort, and a strand of his hair fell loose from its tie to brush Kazuchiyo's temple. "When have I ever needed to write poetry? In fact, I'm thinking now it would be a shame to kill you after all."

Kazuchiyo held very still against the mattress, cursing how his body throbbed with every pulse of his heart, masking any sign he might have felt of vibrations through the floor. "If you are expecting me to beg," he said, "I won't give you that satisfaction."

"I don't want you to beg, I want you to *pay me,*" said Amai. "Make it worth my while to betray Hidemune for you."

Kazuchiyo glared back at him in disbelief. "You want me to bribe you with coin to spare my life?"

Amai rolled his eyes. "It doesn't have to literally be coin. Come on, Kazumune, you're clever."

"If honor alone, cannot sway a traitor fox, what else can I give?" Kazuchiyo replied coldly.

"Did you just—?" Amai's lip twitched, and he sat up, regarding Kazuchiyo with a strange mixture of curiosity and irritation. He was quiet for a moment, and Kazuchiyo could see him counting the syllables of Kazuchiyo's improvised poetry under his breath. He shook his head. "You have some nerve."

"That's only four syllables," said Kazuchiyo.

"You want to do this *now?*" Despite looking wary in the

dim light, Amai could not help showing that he was impressed. "I'm here to kill you and you want to make poems?"

"Give me my sword and I'll fight," Kazuchiyo continued his verse. "If not, words are all I have."

Amai licked his lips. He was concentrating, and Kazuchiyo relaxed so as not to distract him. If he were more alert, he might have noticed the subtle creak of a nearby stair. "Not all that you have," Amai said at last, counting the syllables as he spoke them. "There's that tanto in your belt. Unless that's..." He scoffed. "I can't do this on the fly like you."

"Then get off me," said Kazuchiyo, "and I'll write it down for you." He twisted his wrists. "My hands are numb."

Amai hesitated; he did look tempted. Uncertainty tugged at his brow, and he leaned closer again. Despite his precarious state, Kazuchiyo couldn't help but swell with anticipation for whatever he was about to confess. But he didn't get the chance—there were footsteps in the hall.

In an instant Amai had the kunai poised at Kazuchiyo's throat again. "Don't say a word or I'll go through with it."

Kazuchiyo tensed. "I won't have to."

The door clattered open, and there stood Yagi.

Amai's eyes went wide. He flipped the kunai in his hand as he hurried upright, and as Yagi stormed in, he swung his arm, trying to catch him with the blade. The flash of steel did not deter Yagi for an instant. He grabbed Amai by the hand, his fingers and palm broad enough to smother Amai's beneath them. All he needed was a tug to drag Amai off his feet and grab him by the throat.

"Kazu—" Amai tried to say, but then Yagi yanked him about by the neck and forced him up against the nearest wall beam. The smack of his head against the wood made Kazuchiyo's stomach lurch. Amai's struggles were ineffective against Yagi's might, no claw of his nails or wild kick enough to hamper or dislodge him.

Kazuchiyo put his hand to his neck as he climbed upright. His fingers were tingling painfully and his heart was in a tangle, but watching Amai choke and grow weak within Yagi's grip made him colder still, and he could not bear it. "Yagi, stop!" He ran to them and pried the kunai out of Amai's shaking hand. "Let him go!"

Yagi's lip curled in a sneer; he did not seem willing to relent for anyone, but when Kazuchiyo touched his shoulder, he let go. Amai crumpled to the floor in a heap, gasping and coughing. Even so Yagi was sure to urge Kazuchiyo behind him as he took a step back.

"Are you all right?" He reached for and then hesitated over his wounded neck. "You're bleeding."

"It's not deep," Kazuchiyo assured him. He stared up at Yagi, warmth blossoming behind his ribs, but footsteps on the stairs cut short any time for expressing his gratitude. He looked to the doorway, then to the open window, and finally, to Amai, still regaining his breath. Their eyes met, and he saw fear.

"A Kibaku spy broke into my room and tried to kill me," Kazuchiyo said, his voice hollow even to him, "but you interrupted and he fled out the window."

Yagi looked to the window and back. "What?"

Kazuchiyo grabbed Amai by the collar of his robe and dragged him to the nearby closet. He was shaking but resolute, and there was very little time to act. "Hide," he said, shoving Amai into the narrow enclosure. "Don't make a sound, or *I'll* go through with it."

"But—" Amai tried to say, but Kazuchiyo closed the door on him.

"What the hell is going on?" Yagi demanded. "Who is that?"

"A Kibaku spy tried to kill me," Kazuchiyo repeated, "but he escaped out the window." He straightened up and took hold of Yagi's shoulders. "Please, just tell them that."

"Again with—" Yagi groaned in exasperation. "I'm no good at this!"

"What was all that noise?" said a voice, and a pair of guards peered into the room.

119

Amai was still wheezing in the closet, loudly enough that anyone who drew close would hear. Without a thought Kazuchiyo doubled over, coughing violently. Yagi flinched and rushed to support him as he lowered himself to his knees, and the guards crowded in with alarm.

"Kazu!" Yagi took him under his arm, but when Kazuchiyo tugged at him, he caught on. He looked to the guards, panicked, and bellowed, "It was a Kibaku spy!"

The men lurched back; Yagi was making such an effort to lie well that his face contorted into a look of fury that had both shaking. "He fled from the window!" Yagi carried on. "Don't just stand there!"

"Wake the general!" one guard shouted to his fellow, seemingly affected by Yagi's volume. "I'll rouse the soldiers!" He looked Kazuchiyo. "My lord, are you—"

"He's fine," Yagi snapped. "Go after the bastard!"

"Yes, sir!" White-faced, the men ran to their tasks.

Very soon there were more footsteps drawn by the commotion, more voices rising in alarm. Kazuchiyo quieted his acting to listen as the entirety of the castle came to an uproar. His heart raced, speeding a fearsome energy through his system until he quaked with it. Yagi's broad palm against his back was a welcome anchor, and he feared he might have vibrated apart without it.

"Kazu," Yagi said close to his ear. "What the hell is going on?"

Kazuchiyo leaned into him, a fire beneath his skin. "I'm going to start a war," he said.

Mahiro came next, barely dressed and brandishing her naginata. She fretted over Kazuchiyo with flustered rage before storming off again, rallying more to her and shouting for the intruder's head. More guards came in and out, along with the castle's head physician, who cleaned and applied ointments to the shallow wound in Kazuchiyo's neck. Kazuchiyo and Yagi both professed that they had not clearly seen the shinobi that had threatened them—only that he was slight of build and very swift. By then Amai had gone quiet inside the closet, but Kazuchiyo could sense him tense with every question put to them.

Then Lord Aritaka came, and Kazuchiyo bowed his head. "Father, forgive me for my carelessness."

"It's no fault of yours," Aritaka assured him. His expression was a slate of stone, making his son very curious as to what emotion he was careful not to show. "We will find the shinobi and discover how he was able to breach our defenses. I am only glad that he did not succeed."

"I owe my life to brave Motonobu," Kazuchiyo said, and Yagi, who had remained at his side throughout, shifted uncomfortably. "If not for his keen senses again, surely the man would have killed me."

Aritaka looked to Yagi, who lowered his head. "When I said I looked forward to your service, I did not expect it to be so soon," Aritaka said. "You are to be commended."

"I don't…" Yagi swallowed down a disgruntled expression. "Thank you, Lord Aritaka."

"Did he say anything about his mission?" Aritaka asked them. "Did he leave behind any clue of his intentions or origins?"

"He said only that he was ordered to kill me. He left this." Kazuchiyo set Amai's kunai between them, his blood on its tip. The sight of it hardened his conviction, and he stared back at his father without fear. "I thought at first that he was from Sakka, but I'm convinced now that he was actually from Kibaku. Just like five years ago."

Aritaka leaned back, and that mask he had so carefully constructed showed its cracks. He understood every syllable of Kazuchiyo's intent. The war he sought so passionately lay at his feet, but at a heavy cost: he could no longer ignore the implication of treachery within his walls, much less within his own family. "Then there can be no reconciliation," he said, words carefully chosen to recall their conversation in Gyoe.

"No," said Kazuchiyo, in turn knowing full well that he was calling for Hidemune's death. "If Sakka is to remain strong, we must meet them in kind."

Aritaka nodded, his weariness showing through only for a moment before he gathered himself. To someone less invested in his eventual demise than Kazuchiyo, he may have even elicited sympathy. "Then we will meet them in kind," he said. "Blood for blood." Aritaka pushed to his feet. "We'll have you moved to an interior room, well-guarded so that you can rest after your ordeal. Come morning there will be much to prepare for."

"Thank you, Father, but I'm fine here. I have brave Motonobu to look after me."

Aritaka looked to Yagi, who bowed stiffly. "As you wish," he said. "But stay within this room until the shinobi is caught."

Kazuchiyo bowed his head. "Yes, Father."

Aritaka left . Yagi glared at the door, and when he was certain that the remaining guards were at a suitable distance, he leaned close to Kazuchiyo again. "Can you explain now what's going on?"

"Soon," Kazuchiyo promised. "When there are fewer ears."

He stood using Yagi's shoulder and moved to the window. He could see very little of the courtyard below, but the walls were alight with torches, and the shouting voices of Aritaka's soldiers echoed between them. They continued in that way for another hour, searching every square meter of the grounds and each of the rooms and chambers without discovering any sign of the mysterious, would-be assassin.

General Utsukawa came to offer his most heartfelt apologies for the breach, along with his life as reparations, if need be. Kazuchiyo rejected that offer in favor of swift retribution, to the man's great relief. Gradually the commotion began to subside, as all came to the conclusion that the intruder had escaped back over the wall, perhaps by use of supernatural means. Though the guard remained heavy, Kazuchiyo at last convinced those stationed outside his room to allow him to shut the doors up, so that he might catch a final hour of sleep before sunrise. At long last, Kazuchiyo felt secure enough to crack open the closet door a few inches to check on his uninvited guest, but Amai was not there.

Kazuchiyo trembled, fury strangling him with greater force than Amai had inflicted on him. Before he could rouse the guard all over again, he heard a scraping overhead, and he drew his candle closer to see.

Rather than content himself in the closet, the cunning vermin had crept up into the ceiling. His eyes flashed in the candlelight as he peered down at Kazuchiyo from behind a wooden beam. "Is it safe?"

"For now," said Kazuchiyo, and he backed away so that Amai could creep down. Even so Amai stayed in the closet's opening in case there was a need to duck inside again. He wore one of Kazuchiyo's robes, but only loosely, and only the upper half, so that it hung lewdly off his slender frame. When Kazuchiyo and Yagi regarded him in confusion, he shrugged.

"I couldn't stay in the Kibaku robe," he reasoned, pointing to the bundle of green cloth stuffed up in the closet ceiling. "And if anyone finds me here, you can say General Ebara was kind enough to offer me to comfort you in your stress."

Yagi folded his arms, and Kazuchiyo sat beside him, his manners no less intimidating. "You would try humor with me now?" he said. "With all of Ninari crying for your blood, your life in my hands?"

"I spared you first," Amai reminded him quickly, though he kept his voice low. "If not for my conscience you wouldn't have survived past that kiss."

Yagi frowned. "Kiss?"

Kazuchiyo's face went hot with embarrassment. "And you wouldn't have made it that far if not for your treachery all this time." He trembled with bitter emotion. "You used me."

"I played along," said Amai. "It's not my fault you took it

so seriously."

"Kazu," Yagi interrupted impatiently. "Who the hell is this?"

Though Kazuchiyo still had plenty of accusations to hurl, he reined himself in. "This is Ebara Motonobu. Son of Ebara Toranobu."

"I'm very familiar with Yagi-douji," said Amai, gingerly rubbing his bruised neck. "I suppose he lives up to his name well enough." Yagi glowered.

"Yagi," said Kazuchiyo, "this is one of Lord Aritaka's shinobi, Amai."

"Amai," Yagi grunted. "Well? And are you?"

Amai was thrown by his gruffness. "Am I what?"

"*Amai*," Yagi repeated, with a slightly different inflection to imply the syllables' meaning. "Are you *sweet*?"

Amai reddened; it was strange to see him off guard. He leaned back on his palms as he stared back at Yagi, as if he needed to recollect his wits. "Don't I look it?" he replied.

Yagi's eyes narrowed as if he were considering this, and Kazuchiyo squirmed with discomfort the longer they regarded each other. "Amai was sent to kill me," he said, eager to bring them back to the matter at hand. "By my brother, Hidemune."

"By your..." Yagi's chest swelled with righteous anger. "Why did you not tell Aritaka that?"

"Because he's smart," said Amai. Kazuchiyo could not help but feel flattered by the praise. "Getting me and Hidemune killed for treason would solve one problem but put him in a dangerous position. Because...?"

He looked over to Kazuchiyo expectantly. Kazuchiyo bristled at being led by the nose, but he took over the explanation anyway. "Because if Hidemune is feeling confident enough to have me killed, he must have allies among Aritaka's generals. If I retaliate against him now, with all Aritaka's generals gathering their forces, we would be fighting a war within our own borders rather than against Kibaku."

Amai nodded his approval; Yagi shook his head in

124

frustration. Kazuchiyo continued. "With this, I've given him the war he wants with Kibaku. At the front, I can distinguish myself among Aritaka's most trusted generals, while all Hidemune can do is wait." He fixed Amai with a stern look. "Though I *did* tell my father of Hidemune's betrayal. Perhaps you were not keen enough to hear it."

Amai frowned slightly, his eyes growing dim as if in the midst of recalling that conversation. Yagi was not patient enough to bother, grumbling, "Samurai double-speak. It's no wonder they're always at each other's throats."

"He promised me that he would not let Hidemune and I fight among ourselves," said Kazuchiyo. "I'm certain he told Hidemune the same. To keep his trust I cannot be the one to start that fight, not publicly. But as long as I can prove my worth, once the Kibaku threat has passed, Aritaka will destroy Hidemune himself. Finding an excuse that doesn't directly relate to me will serve him better when it comes to silencing Hidemune's allies as well."

Amai watched him with greater appreciation. "I shouldn't have expected any less from you. You've got it all figured out."

"So what happens now?" asked Yagi. He jerked his chin toward Amai. "You're just going to let this fox go?"

"He can't go back to Gyoe empty-handed. I don't see that he has any choice but to join my service."

Amai cleared his throat. "Begging your pardon, but I have *plenty* of choices remaining."

"I disagree," said Kazuchiyo. His heart was still bitter over the reveal of Amai's true intentions, and he had little trouble transforming his hurt into pressure. "Killing me should have been easy for you—there's no downside for Hidemune with me dead—but you betrayed him and your shinobi comrades to spare my life. Those aren't the actions of a man with many options."

"You have no idea who I have or haven't betrayed," Amai countered. "And if you're trying to trick me into saying more, it won't work."

Yagi reached out abruptly, grabbing Amai by his shoulder to shove him back into the closet. Just as he closed the panel, the door to the room clattered open, and Kazuchiyo startled. Mahiro stormed inside for the second time, still clutching her naginata, and she dropped to her knees next to Kazuchiyo.

"I couldn't find him," she admitted, furious and guilty. "I'm sorry, little brother."

"You don't have to apologize." Kazuchiyo struggled to cast aside all his frustration and face her with the calm patience she was used to. "He's not an adversary to be taken lightly."

"I don't understand why Kibaku would want you dead!" Mahiro dropped her naginata, clearly intent on staying a while. "Are they really that eager to throw themselves at this castle? Fuck those bird-brained warmongers!"

"I don't care what they're after," said Yagi. "We'll meet them blood for blood."

Mahiro agreed with passion, and the two of them carried on speaking of the terrible fate that awaited their hostile neighbor. Kazuchiyo silently promised himself that he would find the time and privacy to properly thank and apologize to Yagi for having him play along with the charade. But Mahiro remained with them until dawn, and by then their fathers had returned, summoning them to confer further on the intrusion. Kazuchiyo only had a few moments in his room alone to change his clothes and prepare for the day ahead.

By then, Amai was long gone.

CHAPTER ELEVEN

In the spring of 1487, Lord Aritaka Souyuu of Sakka Province gathered his army on his western border, intent on making war with the neighboring Kibaku. Due to the deceptive efforts of his son, Kazuchiyo, he did not want for an excuse.

"He could not have trespassed into Kibaku without some justification," Kazuchiyo explained to Yagi in the stables, the day before their scheduled march. Though there were plenty of workers to tend to the horses, he took pride in attending to Hashikiri personally, and it afforded him some degree of privacy with Yagi without drawing attention to themselves. "Kibaku is a long and narrow province, and it shares a border with many smaller provinces. Once Lord Aritaka advances, each of them will have to decide whether to send or withhold their aid. Who began the fight and for what reason will play a part in that decision."

"Samurai war games," Yagi grumbled. He was content to stand back while Kazuchiyo carried out the grooming. "As if any excuse would justify their slaughter."

"If not for the emphasis the lords place on appearances, there would be even more war," Kazuchiyo said. "People have to believe there is reason to all this conflict."

Yagi leaned against the door to a vacant stall, arms folded. "Do you really believe there's a good enough reason for this war you're about to help start?"

Kazuchiyo paused in his brushing. In truth, his young mind was aflame with conflict he dared not express. Every night since learning the truth from Amai, he had dreamt of the death-littered field of years past. Even so, he faced Yagi with conviction. "This war is a boulder tumbling down a mountainside. It cannot be stopped until it has run its course. But if I am a part of it...at least I might be able to help guide it."

"I hope you're not overestimating yourself," said Yagi, but then he shrugged. "Though I guess at this point, it's not as if either of us have a choice."

Thus on the dawn of the fourth day after the "attempt" on Kazuchiyo's life, Generals Ebara and Waseba roused their soldiers to prepare for the march. Kazuchiyo dressed in his full armor, fastening around his waist the pair of swords Lord Aritaka had gifted him at his adulthood ceremony. They had never seen use.

"This will be little more than a skirmish," Lord Aritaka reassured him as they gathered in the courtyard. "Kibaku is on guard, but they will not be expecting an assault this soon. Under General Waseba's command you should have no difficulty taking the outpost, and I don't expect you to fight personally."

"I'm prepared to do whatever I need to, for Sakka's sake," Kazuchiyo replied. "I want you to be proud of me."

"I am. I know you'll do well."

He then dismissed Kazuchiyo, who bowed and joined the growing ranks.

They marched from Ninari Castle with the barely-risen sun at their backs, down the road through the forested hills. Kazuchiyo rode between Yagi and Mahiro as part of General Ebara's second battalion, well protected by the two thousand soldiers accompanying them. Hashikiri seemed calm and pleased with the exercise, but Mahiro's proud Suzumekage was hurried and eager, and Mahiro had to check her often.

128

"This old mare has seen enough battle to recognize a march to war." She grinned as she gave Suzumekage's neck a hearty pat. "She loves it as much as I do."

"This will be your first time fighting in Kibaku," said Kazuchiyo. "Do you think it will be much different from what you're used to?"

"I hope so!" Mahiro threw her head back in a laugh, her helmet's mane flowing out behind her. "I'm tired of picking off bandits and mercenaries. These crows had better give me a challenge." She leaned forward to see Yagi on Kazuchiyo's other side. "What about you, Yagi-douji? That nose of yours must be itching for more battle."

"I've only been in 'battle' once," Yagi replied. "I barely remember it, other than that I wasn't very good."

"Wasn't very good?" Kazuchiyo echoed, affronted. "I watched you defeat more than twenty of Aritaka's finest with only a spear and ill-fitting armor, and that was *after* you had been at it for an hour at least."

"And just as many of Tatsutomi's finest, but not half as many as I wanted. It's not as if I accomplished anything."

Mahiro laughed again, loudly enough to draw attention from the surrounding foot soldiers. "Now that's what I call a proper oni." She swung the bottom of her naginata around to smack against Yagi's back, jostling him in his saddle and almost striking Kazuchiyo in the process. "If being declared the fiercest warrior of the fiercest battle Shimegahara has ever seen wasn't enough for you, prepare to be disappointed by Kibaku. Any glory to be had there will be mine."

"Have it," Yagi grunted, stretching his shoulders. "I don't care."

Kazuchiyo waited until Mahiro had been distracted by the banter of the foot soldiers. "Yagi," he said quietly. "Do you resent me for bringing you into this war?"

Yagi harrumphed. "I'm the one that stormed the field and got myself snatched up by a samurai. If not for you, I'd either still be here or I'd be dead. So no, I don't."

"Still," Kazuchiyo pressed. "I know you do not have the love of war some think you do."

"Not like some, no." Yagi cast Mahiro a sideways glance as she laughed at some bawdy joke, but when he looked back he must have seen the guilt in Kazuchiyo's face, because he shifted atop his horse uncomfortably. "But I am...curious," he admitted, only loudly enough for Kazuchiyo to hear. "I *want* to take the field, if only to know...if it suits me."

Kazuchiyo nodded, though his heart was in conflict. He did not know if he hoped Yagi would live up to his name, or if it was cruel of him to hope for anything at all.

They came out of the forest into the rolling hills late in the afternoon, and there General Waseba drew their ranks to a halt so all could rest their feet and water their horses. Kazuchiyo was called to a hastily raised enclosure to confer with the generals. He kept his chin held high.

"On the other side of that hill is the residence of General Oihata," Waseba explained. "It's no castle, but the center compound is bordered by a deep moat and tall palisades. We cannot afford to wait them out, and we want to keep damages to the surrounding town to a minimum. Those are our lord's orders."

"How many armed warriors can we expect to fight back?" Kazuchiyo asked.

"Two hundred at the most. The rest of Oihata's men are scattered about the countryside." General Waseba grunted with disdain. "By now they'll know we're coming, but it won't make any difference. We'll attack from two fronts and force their surrender before nightfall."

Ebara nodded approvingly. "With ten times the advantage they may surrender before we even cross the moat."

"Oihata is a stubborn old goat. I won't accept any surrender unless it's directly from his own mouth."

"If he tries to take his own life, you mustn't let him," said Kazuchiyo. "His son is close in Lord Koedzuka's favor, and they will bargain for his safe return."

The generals turned to stare at him, but Kazuchiyo kept his posture straight and chin high. Experience he may not have had, but in rank he was at least their equal, and he was anxious to have them appreciate it. Though Waseba did not appear moved, Ebara gave a short nod.

"I agree," he said. "As much as I'd enjoy testing my mettle against his, we must take Oihata alive if possible."

"So be it," grunted Waseba. "Circulate those orders to your men: none are to harm General Oihata under penalty of death. I'm sure he'll make his identity plenty clear."

The council disbanded, each of the generals returning to their troop commanders to spread the word. Before Kazuchiyo could get far, Waseba called him to his side. "You will hold position among my troops on the hill," he instructed. "This is your first engagement, and you ought to observe as closely as possible without taking to the field yourself."

"If that is your command," said Kazuchiyo. "But will you not take to the field yourself? I thought you were eager for it."

Waseba regarded him coldly, sensing the accusation against his wrathful character beneath Kazuchiyo's words. "There will be plenty of battles ahead for you to watch me on the field," he said, and he stalked off.

After the soldiers had finished their rest, the samurai took to their horses again, and the soldiers to their march. They crested the hill and Kazuchiyo caught his first glimpse of the Oihata residence that was their target, nestled in the valley's sloping fields. It looked like any other town: the general's mansion at its center, short and broad with many outbuildings, surrounded by the moat; rows of shops, guardhouses, and civilian homes; fields flooded for the spring planting bordering the town on all sides. Normally the farms would be bustling with activity, the roads bearing all manner of travelers, but not a soul was visible beyond the village borders.

The two-thousand-strong forces of Sakka Province struck out according to Waseba's instructions. General Ebara took eight hundred men toward the main road in the south, Yagi with him. Mahiro joined the smaller troop set to attack from the east. Kazuchiyo remained alongside General Waseba, perched on the top of the hill overlooking it all among five hundred reserve troops. After what felt like hours, they saw movement within the town as trails of smoke began to rise along the compound walls.

"They're boiling water and oil." Waseba swatted a fly from his horse's neck with his war fan. "But none of the buildings are more than two stories high. It's not as effective defensively as when poured from the spouts of a castle wall."

Kazuchiyo had to remind himself not to hold his breath as he watched, hands tight on the reins. "Normally I would have ordered the archery units to fire flaming arrows over the walls," Waseba continued, "but Kibaku is known for its fertile land, and we are at the beginning of a campaign. The less we do to damage their rice production, the more rations we'll have access to, if this campaign stretches into the winter."

"You've planned for this war to go on that long?" asked Kazuchiyo without taking his eyes off their soldiers closing in on the village.

"Lord Aritaka would not enter into a war of this magnitude lightly." Waseba eyed him for a moment, steely and contemplative. "This plan of his is not that dissimilar from wars your father and I discussed when you were a child."

Kazuchiyo grew tense, and though he did not turn or otherwise move, Hashikiri pawed the ground in answer to his distress. "All the lords east of the capital have dreamt of conquering Kibaku," he said.

"I remember when I was your age. Your father and I stood on a hill not unlike this one, while your grandfather explained to us the flow of the battle. I always assumed I would have you at my side like this eventually, though not under these circumstances."

Those circumstances being, of course, a bloodthirsty betrayal followed by a violent end. Were Kazuchiyo even a hair's width closer to his dear Yagi in temperament, he might have turned his sword on the man. To be gutted on the doorstep of small village governed by an old man was the only kind of shameful fate a traitorous snake like Waseba deserved, and no one would have blamed Kazuchiyo too harshly had he acted. But as was his way, he clenched his teeth and bided his time and watched the archers in the distance, loosing their arrows on the town.

The battle, such as it was, lasted only a few hours. Kazuchiyo observed from the hilltop, never taking his eyes from the conflict: the back and forth of projectiles, followed by the assaults on each of the two main gates. The sounds of shouting voices and splintering wood echoed all the way to his vantage point, and he could feel each pluck at him as if he were made of stretched koto strings. He could have sworn he heard Yagi's roar above the rest. The soldiers swarmed into the village streets. Even with the heat of the evening sun fierce on his brow, the ringing of steel took him back to the rainy fields of Shimegahara, and he told himself to remain very still until the fight was over. He knew he would not be able to move anyway.

Gradually, the thunder of warfare died away. Among the smoke indigo Aritaka banners rose from the general's mansion. General Waseba raised his fan to signal his men forward. He led them down the hillside to see the outcome.

Later, Kazuchiyo would remember very little of his first post-battle survey. He depended heavily on Hashikiri's fine training, who followed General Waseba's horse through the remnants with a stout heart. He himself was flung far away, the smell of the dead drowning out his keen senses. The streets were glutted with Sakka soldiers who were working to pile corpses onto carts. Wounded from both sides huddled, moaning and crying, against the storefronts. Families were prodded into the village square at swordpoint. Kazuchiyo followed the procession past the wailing, groaning, shouting cacophony, barely seeing, barely hearing, as if he were thirteen years old again, the helpless captive of a man with a gnarled face.

They reached General Oihata's mansion and dismounted, but it wasn't until Kazuchiyo heard Mahiro bellowing from within that he jarred back into his proper composure. Though still breathless he followed the sound of her voice, and together he and Waseba discovered the source of the commotion in the compound's courtyard garden.

"Dishonorable!" an elderly voice bellowed. Kazuchiyo rounded the corner and spotted General Oihata at last, face down in the sand with Mahiro pinning his arms behind his back. "Disgraceful! Impudent!" The shoulder guards of his armor had been torn free and there was blood on his face, but otherwise he did not appear injured, save for his sizeable pride. "Has the Bear in the North lost his mind?"

"No, but *this* bear might," Mahiro retorted, giving his arm a yank. "If you don't quit your weeping, that is."

Kazuchiyo took in the rest of the scene: a dozen dead samurai from either side of the conflict lay strewn across the trampled garden, while half that number sat on the outskirts with their wrists bound and heads low. Yagi was among the Sakka soldiers standing guard over the captured men, and Kazuchiyo breathed a sigh of relief to see that he was unharmed—scowling, blood-splattered, but unharmed.

"Master Oihata," Waseba said contemptuously as he stopped in front of the fallen general. "It has been a long time."

"Who is that?" Oihata struggled against Mahiro's hold. "Let me up, you honorless beast!"

Waseba harrumphed, taking an unseemly amount of amusement in his enemy's defeat, as far as Kazuchiyo was concerned. "Let him up, Mahiro. But watch him close."

"Yes, sir," said Mahiro with a vicious grin. She let go and stood, offering no help to Oihata as he pushed up onto his knees. His face was haggard with age; what little hair he had left pure white and cropped short, one eye blind. What was left of his armor hung loose on his once formidable frame, but as he glared up at Waseba in defiance there was enough heat in his passion to mark him as a powerful warrior, and a continuing threat. When Waseba caught him eyeing the sword at his hip, he took a step back.

"Cowards and thieves," Oihata spat. "Attacking an ally without warning, without offering me the respect I deserve!"

"I'll offer you your respect once you've been of use to me," Waseba replied coldly. "Hand over the shinobi you sent to infiltrate Ninari Castle."

"It was just the one, and he's *dead*." Oihata glared at Yagi across the courtyard. "Thanks to that damned oni of yours."

The mention of Yagi helped to restore the rest of Kazuchiyo's focus, and he straightened up. "You would have no way of knowing that unless you had more spies in the castle," he said.

Oihata turned his one good eye on Kazuchiyo, and his brow furrowed. "*This* is Hidemune?"

"No, my lord. I am Lord Aritaka's youngest son, Kazumune."

"Ha! I thought so." Oihata leaned back against his heels. "That shaggy bear could only ever father *animals*."

Mahiro snatched her naginata out of the hands of a nearby soldier, and all around the soldiers tensed. Oihata didn't flinch. Kazuchiyo thought to intervene, but before he could even take a step Mahiro drove the blunt end of the weapon's staff between Oihata's shoulder blades, throwing him face first again into the sand.

"Better a beast than a plucked pigeon!" she snarled.

"Mahiro," said Waseba, though without much concern or admonishment. "Enough."

Mahiro stepped back again, and as Oihata pushed himself up, his eyes went to each of their swords, gauging the distance. If they left him alone anywhere for too long Kazuchiyo was sure he would find a way to take his own life. "You sent a spy into Ninari to kill me," Kazuchiyo said, trying to distract him from making the attempt. "This retaliation was warranted. No more of your soldiers or the villagers need to die, if only you cooperate."

"Kill you?" Oihata scoffed. "If one of my lord's spies had been sent to kill you, you wouldn't be standing there with a head on your shoulders, beasts and demons be damned."

"That's not a denial," said Waseba, and before the man could protest, he signaled to Mahiro. "Take him to an interior room and have him bound and well-guarded. We need him alive."

"Yes, General." Mahiro tossed her naginata back to the soldier. "Come on, you bald old goat." She dragged Oihata to his feet. "Try anything and I'll break both your arms."

"Dishonorable!" Oihata snarled in return. Two more men had to come forward to help Mahiro wrestle him from the courtyard, despite his thin stature. "You'll burn in the Fifth Hell for this, Waseba! My son will destroy you!"

Waseba was already turning away. "Now we secure the compound and village," he told Kazuchiyo, who followed him. "Letting Oihata's officers know that he still lives should discourage them from taking their own lives. All the village weapons are already being confiscated, so restricting everyone to their homes should provide enough security. They won't resist if they think Oihata's son will come to save them."

"And he *will* come, won't he?" said Kazuchiyo. "How many days would it take for him to gather forces and come for us?"

"Several days at least, no matter how good those shinobi of his are." Waseba cast him a measuring glance. "We'll be well ready for them."

"I am not concerned," Kazuchiyo said. "I'm only asking so

as to be prepared."

Waseba grunted. "In the next battle, more will be expected of you than to sit in your saddle and tremble. You *ought* to be prepared."

Hot with shame, Kazuchiyo stared straight ahead. "Yes, General Waseba."

CHAPTER TWELVE

Kazuchiyo and General Waseba toured the compound, confirming that each of Oihata's samurai had been relieved of their weapons and detained. Next came the village, civilians aiding in clearing bodies from the streets before being shuttered back into their homes under General Ebara's watchful eye. As Waseba had said, they encountered no resistance from the battered and mournful townsfolk. All the while Waseba dictated their duties and strategies, and Kazuchiyo absorbed what he could. His heart and mind were heavy with the weight of what his lies had begun.

As the sun set, Kazuchiyo was finally afforded a proper reunion with Yagi. Samurai and foot soldier alike crowded around pots of rice for the evening meal, sharing subdued celebrations of their victory. Anything more raucous would have earned the ire of General Waseba, though Ebara passed around a few jugs of saké, stolen from Oihata's private storage. Yagi took a long drink, and Kazuchiyo a few sips, as they sat together in the main compound entranceway overlooking the village.

"How was the battle?" Kazuchiyo asked, though he was uncertain what manner of answer he hoped for. "Did you learn anything?"

"It wasn't much of a battle once we got inside." Yagi's eyes were lowered as he ate from his bowl. "There were too few of them compared to us." He grumbled quietly. "But Ebara said I did well."

Kazuchiyo watched him closely. "Do you remember it all this time?"

"Yeah." Yagi brushed his hair back, showing off a spatter of red welts stretching down the side of his face. "Hard not to when they're throwing boiling water over everything."

Kazuchiyo grimaced, reaching reflexively toward him before pulling back. "There must be medicine we can get for you."

"It's fine." Yagi let his hair fall. "I heal quickly." He ate a few more mouthfuls of rice, but Kazuchiyo presumed he had more to say. At last he came to it. "I guess I have to say I'm not sure how I feel about it yet. Being good at it, I mean."

"I'm sorry," said Kazuchiyo, with sincerity, "but you're going to have many opportunities to reflect upon it, once General Oihata's son arrives."

Yagi nodded. "At least we'll be fighting an army then, instead of peasants." He finished off the wine and turned to Kazuchiyo. "What about you?"

Kazuchiyo averted his eyes. "I did nothing," he confessed. "I watched with General Waseba from the hill, far from danger." The meal turned over in his stomach, but he forced himself to continue eating anyway. "I couldn't stop thinking about Shimegahara."

"It's not as if you were needed on the field anyway," Yagi clumsily attempted to console him. "Watching from hills is what generals do."

His effort was far more convincing than the words. Kazuchiyo nodded.

They were drawn from their conversation by the approach of a man on horseback, dressed in indigo Sakka robes. He slowed and dismounted with grace, seizing Kazuchiyo's attention even before his identity became clear.

"My lord," Amai greeted Kazuchiyo. He handed his reins to a nearby attendant and then strode forward to drop to one knee in a bow that could only be viewed as condescending. "I'm glad to see you so well after the recent battle."

"You have some nerve," Yagi grumbled while Kazuchiyo sat very still beside him. "I thought you said you weren't on our side."

"Is that what I said?" Amai stood once more, a smirk flitting across his lips as he headed into the compound. "Best of luck to you both."

Kazuchiyo hesitated only a beat longer before setting his bowl down and giving chase. "What are you doing here?"

"I'm making my report to General Waseba," he said breezily. "You're welcome to listen in, if you wish."

Kazuchiyo waited for a pair of low-ranking samurai to pass. "Where did you go after that night in Ninari?"

"Does it matter? I don't report to you."

Kazuchiyo bristled, furious with himself for having ever wasted concern on the man. He increased his pace and grabbed Amai by the back of the neck, using weight and momentum to shove his chest up against the closest wall. All he wanted was for the nasty little imp to show some respect for the suffering he had caused. But even when he had Amai pinned, he felt the sharp poke of a kunai in his groin, right where his armor offered no protection.

"You ought to have me teach you a few things," said Amai, as sarcastic as ever. "You're not very good at this."

Kazuchiyo seethed with frustration, and though he hated to do it, he backed up enough for Amai to turn around. "There," said Amai, and he began smoothing down the front of his robe. "Now if you want to—"

Kazuchiyo struck again, this time catching both of Amai's wrists before closing the distance between their bodies. He forced him back to the wall and trapped his hands beneath his chest. When Amai tried to shift his footing, Kazuchiyo bore into him with his knees, and at last the fox's silvery eyes reflected surprise. It was only a flash, but it was a triumph to young Kazuchiyo.

"All right," Amai said, relaxing beneath Kazuchiyo's pin. "That's a little better."

"Whatever you're about to tell Waseba, you'll tell me as well," Kazuchiyo ordered. "Along with whatever you *weren't* about to tell him."

"I already invited you to listen in," Amai retorted. "You're the lord's son, after all." He smiled, eyes narrowing. "Unless you'd prefer to debrief in private."

Kazuchiyo hardened his heart, though it was a monumental task with Amai watching him so invitingly. Despite his bitterness he had yet to purge weeks of playful artistry from his mind, let alone the anticipation it had planted in him. Amai grew slack and almost docile beneath his hands, and that in turn made his knees weak. But he understood the man's game, and so he released him.

"Let's go, then," he said. "I'm eager to hear your report."

Amai took his time fussing with his robe. He tilted his chin toward Kazuchiyo's shoulder. "Him, too?"

Kazuchiyo turned and was startled to find Yagi a few steps behind them. He flushed with embarrassment. "Of course him as well. He's General Ebara's son."

"Then let's not keep the generals waiting," said Amai, and with yet another smirk he turned to continue.

Yagi fell into step beside Kazuchiyo as they followed. "You said he was trying to kill you, but that looked like something else just now."

"It's nothing," Kazuchiyo replied quickly, unable to help the flush of his cheeks. "A longer tale than we have time for." He glanced to Yagi and didn't know what to make of his steely curiosity. "I'll explain later," he said, though he hoped he wouldn't have to.

They met with Generals Waseba and Ebara in the main chamber of the residence, where they were discussing provisions.

141

Amai bowed to the floor before them, no trace of teasing left in his demeanor. "My lords," he said gravely, "I'm here to report that General Oihata's son, Naoya, is already amassing a force of three thousand men. They're expected to depart from Castle Tettsu by dawn."

"So soon?" said General Waseba, surprised and wary. "How could he have recalled his troops that quickly?"

General Ebara, on the other hand, looked as though he expected it. "Lord Aritaka was right about the Kibaku samurai. They've been expecting this war as long as we have, if not longer."

Kneeling behind Amai, Kazuchiyo did his best not to squirm with the news. "We must owe it to Kibaku's famed shinobi," he said. "If they alerted General Naoya to Lord Aritaka's arrival at Ninari as soon as it occurred, that would have given them plenty of time to prepare."

Waseba stroked his whiskers as he considered the map in front of him. "It is at least a two-day march from Tettsu to here, even with Naoya at the head. We'll abandon the village and form our troops on the eastern hill. They'll want to avoid letting the battle spill into the rice fields, forcing them right into the position we want."

"They'll outnumber us," said Kazuchiyo.

"Not for long." Waseba gestured to Amai. "I trust you've already sent word on to Ninari of this?"

"I have, sir," replied Amai.

"Then our reinforcements will have no trouble arriving at their rear flank in time." Waseba looked to Kazuchiyo. "Well, Kazumune? What would you have me do with Oihata and his retainers?"

Kazuchiyo straightened, determined not to fail his test. "General Oihata we keep captive, but I would set the retainers free. There are too many to reliably guard during the course of the battle, and it would be a nuisance. But once set loose they'll be eager to join with General Naoya and tell him his father still lives. It will force him to be cautious in making his approach and will keep his focus away from his southern flank."

Waseba nodded, and only then did Kazuchiyo resent having to seek his approval. "Yes, I agree. In the morning, they will be freed. Unless you have any objections, Ebara?"

"Every sword you free now is a sword turned on us later," Ebara warned him. "I'll be sure to kill twice as many crows in the next battle to make up for it."

"Then it's settled, and you're all dismissed."

Outside the chamber, Amai took Kazuchiyo by the elbow and leaned in close as they walked. "This younger Oihata will know about the reinforcements," he whispered. "He won't be fooled by them. You should prepare for that."

Kazuchiyo felt the small hairs on the back of his neck rise. "What good will his knowing of them do him, if we outnumber his forces and attack from two sides?"

"I can't say that it will. I'm only telling you what I know." He let his grip slide down Kazuchiyo's arm to give his hand a squeeze. "He's rumored to be a skilled onmyouji. Who knows what kind of trickery he may employ on the battlefield?"

Kazuchiyo gripped him back, telling himself it was only because he did not want Amai to dart away before he was finished with him. "And you know all about trickery, don't you?"

Amai tsked him. "You can only imagine," he teased, and he darted in to lick a stripe across Kazuchiyo's cheek like the feisty beast he was.

Kazuchiyo recoiled, releasing his hand. At the same time Yagi struck from behind, shoving his heavy palm between Amai's shoulder blades. Amai was sent tumbling, only to glide effortlessly into a somersault and then vault to his feet.

"Don't be jealous," he scolded Yagi. "I'll teach you, too." He cast the pair of them a smirk over his shoulder as he darted off down the corridor.

Yagi growled at his back, though his cheeks were red, and from more than the battle. "I should skin that weasel someday."

Kazuchiyo scraped his face clean. "I still want to find you

some medicine," he said, determined not to give any weight to Amai's salacious barbs. "And a room to rest in for the night. It's been a long day."

"I'm fine," Yagi grunted. "But yes, let's find you a room."

They were offered a small room in the compound's interior overlooking the courtyard, with hardwood floors and a low ceiling. It was decorated with hanging scrolls depicting ancient battles with poetry overlaid, which Kazuchiyo was tempted to turn around. The last thing he wanted was to be watched over in his sleep by Kibaku's mighty ancestors.

Once their armor was shed, Kazuchiyo insisted on treating Yagi's burns. He managed to secure a basin of cool water and some bulrush ointment from the storeroom, and they sat close together by candlelight so he could work.

"You mind me too much," Yagi said, holding very still as Kazuchiyo applied the ointment. "I don't understand why."

"Well, it hasn't blistered, but there's still a risk of infection," said Kazuchiyo. He wet his hand so he could smooth an errant strand of hair behind Yagi's ear. "That would be disastrous, so close to your eye."

"I mean other than this." Yagi tried to make a face, only to remember what Kazuchiyo was up to and force himself to relax again. "I'm already fighting in your army; you don't need to pay me special attention."

Kazuchiyo frowned and lowered his hand. "Am I a nuisance to you?"

"Of course not."

Though he spoke as gruffly as ever, that was all the reassurance Kazuchiyo needed. He resumed his work. "You're very important to me," he said from his heart. "You stood as a pillar when I had nothing and no one else." He met Yagi's gaze hesitantly. "Do you think me selfish?"

"No," said Yagi, watching him closely enough that Kazuchiyo blushed. "I'm just not used to it. Someone looking after me, that is."

Kazuchiyo smiled with sympathy as he applied the last bit

of ointment to Yagi's ear. "Then I hope you can become used to it, because I don't intend to leave you alone."

Yagi continued to watch Kazuchiyo with a heart-thumping intensity. Only when Kazuchiyo offered him a length of clean linen to cover his face did he shift and grumble with his usual temperament. "This is fine," he said. He worked his jaw. "I should find a room of my own now."

Kazuchiyo leaned back, allowing disappointment to color his tone. "Would you make a liar of me so soon?"

"Huh? No, I mean..." Yagi fussed with his dampened hair. "I don't make for a pleasant roommate."

"I remember," said Kazuchiyo, goosebumps on his skin as he recalled the nights back in Gyoe, howls echoing through the castle. "But I don't mind. I'd rather you be here with me than anywhere else."

Yagi pulled a face, though Kazuchiyo was coming to understand it as begrudging embarrassment, not irritation. "If you say so."

They prepared for sleep then, curling up among the stolen bedding. Yagi was swiftly unconscious. As he had warned, he tossed and grumbled, but it was the cries in the distance that prevented Kazuchiyo's rest. The voices wailing from the village, in mourning and in pain, reminded him too much of the field for him to find peace. Seeking distraction, he opened the door to the courtyard and sat for a while, watching the moonlight on the stones. He gazed up at the stars and found dragons in the constellations.

He tried to turn his mind to the battle ahead, reminding himself of the maps he'd studied of the terrain, the many war tales and manuals dictating how each hill, valley, and forest line ought to be employed. More and more, the voices of his tutors turned to that of his father, plaguing him with unwanted questions. He wondered, as he tried not to allow himself to do, what his father would say and think of the war he was waging in their enemy's name.

Kazuchiyo shivered. He thought his heart cried out,

only to realize that, just like those first dark nights at Gyoe, it was Yagi crying out after all. His agony was made palpable in the world, a bellow that echoed over the conquered mansion and beyond. Shamefully, Kazuchiyo found nostalgia in Yagi's nightmare-spurred roars. He closed the door back up and crawled to Yagi's side.

Yagi had twisted himself up in the bedding, sweat on his brow as he shouted. Kazuchiyo knew to be wary, but he acted anyway, touching Yagi's shoulder. Yagi lashed out, his hand as heavy and firm as a bear's jaws on Kazuchiyo's wrist. Kazuchiyo did not fight back, instead threading the fingers of his free hand through Yagi's hair. It seemed to do him good, and in time Yagi's hand relaxed, his cries lowered to sleepy murmurs.

"How much you must have suffered," Kazuchiyo whispered, soothing his unconscious comrade with gentle pets. He lay down alongside him, eager to offer whatever respite he could. "I wish I could grant you an easier life than this."

He leaned closer and was surprised when Yagi allowed it, even going so far as to draw them together. Though still fitfully asleep Yagi wrapped his great arms around Kazuchiyo's waist and burrowed against his collar like a child seeking comfort from a nightmare. Kazuchiyo held him in turn, stroking his hair. The heat of another body smothering his was almost unbearable, but he welcomed it.

In time, he even slept.

CHAPTER THIRTEEN

Kazuchiyo roused himself just before dawn. Yagi was still curled up against his chest, looking much smaller than his impressive stature, quietly snoring. He even seemed peaceful, which filled Kazuchiyo with relief. Doing as little as possible to disturb him, he slipped free and changed back into his robe so he could investigate the rest of the manor.

He discovered General Ebara in the main hall, poring over the map again. "Good morning, Lord Kazumune," Ebara greeted him. Kazuchiyo found it ironic how much more agreeable his company was compared to the traitorous vassal he'd known all his life. "Come lend your eye to this."

Kazuchiyo did so, looking over Ebara's placement of the small wooden tiles that represented their forces. Unlike the plan Waseba had discussed the night before, Ebara had positioned them north of the village, which would force a longer march for Naoya's soldiers and put their backs to the tree line. Though Ebara did not have Waseba's strict nature, Kazuchiyo took this to again be a test, and he considered the map very carefully before giving his assessment.

"This would delay the battle some," he said, "and allow my father's archers to assail Naoya's rear with cover from the forest, but it would put the rice fields at risk and would give us less advantage than if we were on the hill. If Naoya chose to reclaim the village, we would not be able to stop him." He frowned thoughtfully. "Though if we tempted him to do so, we could then surround and reclaim it once our numbers were bolstered."

"It is a more defensive strategy, to be sure," said Ebara, his brow furrowing. "Not my specialty."

"You're concerned that our reinforcements won't arrive in time," Kazuchiyo surmised. He wondered if Amai had passed his advice on to more than himself after all.

"There's no reason they wouldn't. But yes, it concerns me." He snorted quietly and then began replacing the tiles where Waseba had left them. "But I am the spear, not the hand holding it. As long as I keep my strength, we'll have victory."

Kazuchiyo frowned, but it was not his place to question either general's judgment. Seeing as it was rare for him to have a moment with Ebara alone, he decided there were better uses he could make of it. "General Ebara, may I ask you something? About your son?"

Ebara chewed on a smirk. "Gave you a fright last night, did he?"

"No," Kazuchiyo replied, earning him a raised eyebrow. "I expected it. But I am curious if he's told you about his circumstances that would...lead to such disturbance of mind."

"That boy," Ebara began, ready to repeat some long-practiced explanation, but then he paused. He looked Kazuchiyo over, and his bemusement faded for sympathy. "He came from Terado Village, but he wasn't born there," he said. "Not that he told me that himself. As far as I know, he's not said a word to anyone of where he really came from, and all his skill is rough and self-taught. They say he's half oni and burst straight out of hell."

Kazuchiyo was no longer satisfied with such dismissive explanations, not with the imprints of Yagi's arms still warm around his back. "As his father, what do *you* say?"

Ebara sighed. "I say that boy is a bone that was broken," he answered with sincerity. "One that was never set and healed crookedly." He straightened his back. "But with some tempering, he'll be the strongest warrior Shuyun has ever known."

"Tempering," Kazuchiyo repeated, concerned as to what that would entail. "I'm sure you're right."

Their conversation was interrupted by a shout from the courtyard; someone was screaming in pain. They hurried to investigate, Ebara pausing only long enough to retrieve his spear. They came out into the manor courtyard and there found General Waseba in his armor, accompanied by a troop of Aritaka soldiers and two dozen of Oihata's retainers. A wooden stool was set at the center of the assembly, and as Kazuchiyo watched, two soldiers shoved one of the retainers to his knees in front of it, while a third pinned his hand to the wood.

"What are you doing?" Kazuchiyo demanded as he approached Waseba. "Did we not agree to free Oihata's men?"

"They will be free," said Waseba, arms crossed over his chest as he watched the proceedings. He nodded to his men. "Carry on."

Oihata's retainer struggled, breathing hard. "Don't," he stuttered as one of the soldiers lifted a heavy wooden hammer. "Wait!"

"General—" Kazuchiyo protested, but the soldier brought the hammer down, breaking the man's thumb. He flinched at the sound of crunching bones and the pained shouts that followed. The rest of the samurai shook with fury and trepidation as their fellow was hauled away.

"General, this is monstrous," Kazuchiyo finished. "They are Kibaku's honorable samurai. You said they would go free!"

"Every sword we free now is one turned on us later," said Waseba with unflinching cruelty. "These men may still be able to pleasure their wives, but they'll never hold a sword. Is that not mercy enough?"

Kazuchiyo seethed, and he looked over his shoulder for

some support from Ebara. Though Ebara's expression was dark with disapproval, he did not speak up or advance as a new Oihata retainer was bent to the stool. Kazuchiyo turned back, ashamed of them both. "This is dishonorable," he insisted. "In this war we are just, but if Kibaku's allies hear of this disgusting—"

"Lord Aritaka has entrusted me with this campaign," Waseba snapped. "If you have complaints, take them to your father."

Kazuchiyo tried to continue his complaints, but Oihata's retainer raised his voice. "I don't need your pity," he spat. "I won't beg."

Kazuchiyo hesitated, burning with frustration and shame. When the hammer came down, the sturdy retainer clenched his teeth and made no sound. But the bones crunched, turning Kazuchiyo's stomach, and as the man was dragged back to his comrades, there was nothing to do but retreat.

"Will you say nothing?" he demanded of Ebara, who remained at the edge of the proceedings. "Will you *do* nothing?"

"Lord Aritaka has given General Waseba command." His face was tight with displeasure but also resignation. "It's his decision."

Kazuchiyo turned away from him. He wanted to return to the manor and not have to watch, but his sense of responsibility prevented him. He forced himself to stay as another man was led to the stool, eyes locked on his face. He held his breath as the hammer was lifted.

"Kazu?"

Yagi took his shoulder, and he startled, spinning to face him. "Yagi?" A moment later the retainer cried out, and he jumped again. With his own temper tested by Waseba's cruelty he couldn't imagine how Yagi would feel, and he quickly urged him back inside. "Come on. We're not wanted here."

Yagi stared past him—Kazuchiyo felt him grow tense once he realized what was happening—but he allowed himself to be guided inside, waiting until they were safely out of sight in the hall to voice his disapproval.

"Weasel-mouthed coward," Yagi growled. "Does he really think crippling this small number of men will make a difference tomorrow?"

"I don't know what he's thinking," Kazuchiyo admitted. "This will only infuriate the Kibaku army. Maybe he thinks that alone will coax Naoya into a useless assault up the hill…" He shook his head, made dizzy trying to anticipate too many competing motivations and strategies. "It doesn't matter," he concluded. "His behavior is abominable whatever his aim, and I will report it to Lord Aritaka." Cold washed over him, and he turned to head deeper into the mansion. "If he's done the same to General Oihata…"

Oihata was being held in a small storeroom toward the back of the compound. As Kazuchiyo drew close he could hear Mahiro's familiar, rough goading and Oihata grumbling retorts. He did not sound angry enough to have heard the truth of Waseba's cruelty, and Kazuchiyo prayed that he could keep it that way.

"Fiercest warrior of the rolling plains indeed!" Mahiro declared as Kazuchiyo and Yagi approached. She had taken up the doorway while Oihata's intentioned guards stood back, watching with wide eyes. "Now he needs *my* permission to take a shit. Is this how you pictured your elderly years, old man?"

"Foul-mouthed cretin!" Oihata spat. He was sitting cross-legged in the center of the storeroom, dressed in simple robes, staring hatefully up at Mahiro. "Were you my daughter I'd have married you to a merchant sailor!"

"I'd've liked to see you try, you lumpy old sack!"

"Mahiro." Kazuchiyo eyed her disapprovingly, though he was relieved by how the tenor of their banter implied that Oihata had not been unjustly harmed. Beyond his pride, at least. "Have you no respect to show our defeated rival?"

"What respect has he shown *me?*" Mahiro shot back, folding her arms. "This old bird has poached our woods for years, insults Father, and—"

"*Our* woods!" Oihata shot back. "*Our own* game! Our—"

He stopped when he fully took note of Kazuchiyo, eyeing him up and down. "So," he said with greater restraint, "Aritaka's young cub comes to lash me, too. Or is it Aritaka's young snake?"

"Why you—" Mahiro began, but Kazuchiyo touched her arm, and begrudgingly she heeded him. "See? He's all venom, this old buzzard!"

Kazuchiyo took a step into the room. Though he was not yet certain what point it might serve, the boy in him was eager for Oihata to know that he did not resemble his compatriots. "Lord Oihata. I do apologize for the treatment you've received here in your own home."

Oihata snorted, though he continued to watch Kazuchiyo very closely. "Hm. You really aren't Aritaka bred after all, with manners like that. I've wondered about you."

Kazuchiyo tried not to let his curiosity show. "I haven't yet accomplished anything worth a man of your legacy's wonder."

"Your father did," Oihata replied, and Kazuchiyo straightened up. "I fought against him and his brother at Fukugawa, when your grandfather still lived. Bright, honorable boys." His eyes pierced Kazuchiyo's defenses. "What would they say to see you now, Kazumune?"

Mahiro shifted anxiously in the doorway, though Kazuchiyo was too eager to navigate this encounter to pay her much mind. "If they could see me, I imagine they would be disappointed in me," he said. "If they could speak to me, less so, I hope."

Oihata snorted again, but the answer seemed to have pleased him. "I imagine so. Then I won't feel guilty about failing to steal you back for your father's honor."

Kazuchiyo leaned back in surprise. "Steal me back?" he repeated.

"If you can't be a dragon, you're better off a crow than a bear," Oihata said with a determined nod. "At least you're still in the sky."

"That's enough," Mahiro snapped. She grabbed Kazuchiyo by the elbow to draw him back out of the room. "Don't rot your ears listening to this senile old fowl."

"Disgraceful girl!" Oihata shouted at her back as they left.

"You shouldn't speak so crudely to him," Kazuchiyo said once they had moved out of the man's hearing. "He's our enemy, but he's an accomplished samurai and we ought to show him respect for that."

"He's a blabbering ball sack, and I don't care what he's done now that he's lost." Mahiro raked her fingers through her hair and shifted her weight back and forth. "What did he mean back there? About stealing you back?"

Kazuchiyo glanced to Yagi, who was leaning against the wall, frowning at the goings-on. "I don't know," said Kazuchiyo. "But he's a fool if he thinks I would choose Kibaku over anyone. My loyalty runs deeper than an animal on a banner."

"Good," Mahiro said quickly. "I mean, I know." She clapped Kazuchiyo heavily on the shoulder. "I'm going to the stable. If you find any breakfast, bring me some, okay?"

"All right," said Kazuchiyo, but when Mahiro turned to leave he quickly added, "Don't go to the courtyard." He winced beneath her curious look. "Or, if you do, don't come back here afterward. Please, Mahiro."

Mahiro's face screwed up as she tried to puzzle out his meaning, but she nodded. "If you say so. Don't forget my breakfast!"

As she moved on, Yagi returned to Kazuchiyo's side. "He was talking about the shinobi, wasn't he? The ones that tried to kidnap you from Gyoe years ago."

"He must have been." Kazuchiyo was tempted to return to Oihata and hear the full truth, though there were still guards to consider and he was not certain if it would help him regardless. "But he doesn't understand the position I'm in. Even if I *wanted* to join Kibaku..."

He looked to Yagi, hoping that his stoic face would give him the confidence he needed. All at once he realized that Yagi was still dressed in his under robe only, as if he had sprung from his futon and marched across the compound without a single care for his state. He sighed. "I'm sorry, I'm rambling on and you're not even dressed."

Yagi rubbed his nose self-consciously. "I woke up and you were gone," he muttered. "And I heard shouting. I was worried."

Kazuchiyo warmed with embarrassment, but he smiled, moved by Yagi's concern. "I'm sorry. You just looked so peaceful, I didn't have the heart to wake you. Let's go back to the room and then find something to eat. We'll need our strength today."

Yagi followed, though his brow was deeply furrowed. "Peaceful?" he said after a long pause. "Really?"

"You seemed so. Did you not sleep well?"

"No, I…" Yagi ground his teeth before surrendering the truth. "I slept very well, actually. Better than in a long time."

Kazuchiyo slowed his pace a half step to put Yagi beside him. "I'm very glad to hear it," he said.

After a visit to the latrine they returned to the room and dressed in their full armor. They still heard men shouting from the courtyard. A group of soldiers had gathered near the rear of the compound to prepare breakfast, likely trying to escape the commotion, and so armed with bowls of rice gruel the pair joined Mahiro in the stables to do the same.

Mahiro's demeanor was much darkened from when Kazuchiyo had seen her not even an hour earlier. He could only guess that coming upon Waseba and his barbarism was the cause, though she would not say as much. Once they had finished their meal and prepared the horses, the trio set out from the village on horseback, riding out to the hill that would serve as their battleground.

"Waseba's strategy is sound," Kazuchiyo said as they toured the long slope. "The Kibaku army will tire trying to scale the hill, and once our reinforcements arrive at their rear, they will be trapped. General Naoya will have to surrender."

"Not too soon, I hope," said Mahiro, though her enthusiasm was noticeably lacking. He wondered if she was trying to spur herself back to earlier spirits. "I don't want the battle to end before I've claimed a few heads."

Kazuchiyo stretched his eye to the south. It was far too soon to catch a glimpse of the approaching army, but his imagination supplied a vivid image of columns of soldiers marching up the road through the plains. He wondered how closely Oihata Naoya matched the rumors.

The rest of the day was one of rest and preparation. By the afternoon Waseba had completed his grisly work and set Oihata's vassals free, kicking them out from the village's southern gate to travel the road on foot. If they were swift, he said, they would reach the next village just after dark. Kazuchiyo kept his continued disapproval to himself.

By evening, the village was buzzing and restless. The remaining captives continued to reassure each other in intentionally ineffective whispers that soon their lord's brave generals would come to rescue them. It fueled the Aritaka soldiers in their preparations and their nerves. Come morning they would abandon the village and set their camp, gambling their fate against a crow's wits and the timing of their reinforcements.

But as night fell and the compound fell quiet, Kazuchiyo was assailed by much more personal concerns. After a short, cold bath, he and Yagi prepared for slumber in the same room as before. Though Kazuchiyo was pleased by their unspoken agreement to again share a room, he was uncertain as to how he might proceed. The night before, his only concern had been to quell Yagi's distress in any way he could; was it not wise to do so again? And if so, ought he wait to see if his interference was necessary, or boldly offer in advance? It seemed a petty concern when faced with an advancing army, but such is youth.

As they laid out their futons, Kazuchiyo chose boldness, drawing his so close to Yagi's as to overlap at the edges. Yagi watched him do so and attempted to comment several times before he was able to get the words past his lips. "I toss. I wouldn't want to hit you in your sleep."

"You won't," Kazuchiyo said as he stretched out beneath the bedding.

Yagi sat down beside him. "But…I do. It's what I do."

"You didn't last night." Kazuchiyo stared up at him, determined to be courageous. "And I was in your futon with you."

Yagi straightened up. "You were?"

"You don't remember?"

"No, I…" Yagi frowned deeply with embarrassment. "I guess I was asleep."

His befuddlement was charming, and Kazuchiyo smiled, even though tension wound beneath his skin. "Would you like me to join you again?"

Yagi considered this for a long moment, the confusion clearing from his face to make way for intense scrutiny. "If you want," he said at last. "But I won't apologize if I hit you."

He lay down, and Kazuchiyo crawled across from his futon. Despite his conviction he wasn't entirely certain how to progress from there. It had been simple and even innocent enough, offering comfort to a suffering Yagi in his sleep; now Yagi was watching his every move, both of them hesitant and alert. Kazuchiyo's adeptness with intricate social interactions didn't prepare him for sliding close to the strong body he'd admired in fantasy throughout his adolescent years. He couldn't be certain of his own intentions, let alone his companion's, and they settled together awkwardly in the dark.

Kazuchiyo held his breath. He waited for a while, considering all manner of actions and outcomes as his heart kept a swift pace, but as his nerves eased and he turned toward

Yagi, thinking he might press for more, he came to realize that Yagi had already fallen asleep. His breath was deep and his eyelids twitching.

"Looks like I'll have to be bolder still," Kazuchiyo murmured, and he relaxed close at Yagi's side, letting the warmth of his body lull him into sleep as well.

The next day, after another relatively peaceful night, preparations continued. Waseba instructed a contingent of fifty men to remain in the village while the rest took to the hillside, setting up camp to brace for the coming army. Kazuchiyo aided where he could, reminding the captains of the formation hat they would be expected to hold until Lord Aritaka himself arrived with the reinforcements. He and Yagi toured the terrain again and were present when a messenger arrived, assuring the generals that Sakka soldiers were positioned on the other side of the southern woods, ready to sally forth the following morning. The trap was set.

It was late in the afternoon when at last they could see green Kibaku banners on the horizon. The pounding of their drums echoed up and down the plains, quiet at first, only barely perceptible. It grew louder as Waseba's men hurried to solidify the camp perimeter. Again and again their eyes were drawn to the march, Kazuchiyo himself not immune. Eventually, three thousand footfalls rumbled on the earth. As they drew closer still, Kazuchiyo joined Waseba at the hill's tallest point to observe.

Naoya's soldiers spanned the width of the southern road. Their marching column was bordered on either side by bannermen carrying tall, broad flags bearing the winged crest of Kibaku. It seemed an unnecessary display for an army racing to save their general's honored father, but as Kazuchiyo looked more closely, he could see a line of mounted captains at the center of the march, half obscured by the flags.

"They're disguising their number of officers," said Waseba. "Mounted bowmen, most likely. They may be aiming to send archers on horseback around the side of the hill to hit our flank."

Kazuchiyo shielded his eyes from the orange sun and turned his focus to the procession's head: a tall man on a white horse was leading the army alongside even more banners, a glint of gold off his helm.

As they continued to watch over several hours, Kibaku's soldiers left the road to make camp. Boldly they erected tents and a rough perimeter of stakes in the center of the open field, no more than an hour's march from their enemy's position on the hill. At last, the two generals could engage in their war of minds face to face. Even before the camp was well established a half-dozen men on horseback set out again along the road. The white horse bearing Naoya was among them.

"I thought we might be entertaining him tonight," said Waseba, all but dripping with disdain. He led Kazuchiyo back toward the center of their own camp. "You should be there for it. As long as you don't let his temper sway you, you ought to get some amusement from him."

Kazuchiyo followed Waseba to the main war tent: walls of Aritaka banners enclosed the broad, square space, torches lit along the perimeter as dusk fell. They were joined by General Ebara, Yagi, eight captains, and a dozen armed guards. Kazuchiyo was relieved to not see Mahiro invited, considering her treatment of the elder Oihata. With Waseba seated on a stool at the head, they made for an impressive reception.

Night had fallen by the time Naoya arrived. He entered the tent along with his entourage, granting Kazuchiyo his first glimpse of their enemy: tall enough to rival Yagi, made taller still by his helm adorned with golden crow's wings spread in display. A long, green coat bearing intricate embroidery draped over his armor and billowed as he marched into the enclosure with poise and confidence. His face was long with deeply pronounced features, younger than Kazuchiyo expected of

158

such a renowned general.

"General Waseba!" Naoya declared with strength and temper to match his father's. "I demand an explanation for this unspeakable barbarism you have heaped upon my lord and house!"

Waseba leaned back on his stool, regarding his guest with only the bare minimum of expected respect. "It is good to see you as well, Young Lord Oihata."

"I will not be condescended to or rebuffed," Naoya snapped as he halted in front of Waseba. "You will release my father and depart from Kibaku territory immediately!"

"You didn't march here with three thousand men to watch us peacefully leave," said Waseba gruffly. "What choice do I have now but the battlefield?"

As furious as Naoya already was, he seemed to expand beneath Waseba's careless retorts. "You are a disgrace to your station," he said, with such overflowing, sonorous passion that Waseba's men found him more amusing than intimidating. Even Kazuchiyo was taken aback. "I will take the utmost pleasure in ejecting you from these hallowed fields. But before then I will know what madness drove you to this course, be it yours or your master's. Why break a peace so hard-fought in this uncouth manner?" He scoffed loudly. "Or shall we blame it on your traitorous nature and not one more word be said?"

Waseba grunted in return. "'Not one more word' from you would be a blessing, indeed."

Naoya's soldiers shifted angrily behind him. To his right, a commander bearing a full moon emblem on their helm clenched their fist as if in want of their sword. Naoya himself was no less offended. "Have you nothing to say for yourself? No defense for your lord, no pretense at all for these abominable actions? That you would assault an aged and honored general in his home and seize his lands is cruelty enough. But to—"

Naoya cut himself off abruptly, and Kazuchiyo was shocked to see a wet sheen to his bright, piercing eyes. "To cripple and shame brave samurai for no other reason than spite," he finished, with visible efforts toward his composure. "And all you offer me is childish barbs?"

Waseba glared back at him, unmoved, and his men reflected much of the same. Kazuchiyo, however, could not claim his heart unstirred by the man's turmoil, all the more so knowing what indignities Waseba would level at Naoya's back once he was no longer present. Even then the man's father, the famous General Oihata of a Thousand Victories, was bound like a common thief at the rear of the camp. Though he should have known no good would come of it, Kazuchiyo could not still his tongue.

"It is the command of our Lord Aritaka," he said, and he managed not to flinch when Naoya's attention snapped to him like a whip crack. "In retaliation for the attempt on my life at Ninari Castle."

Naoya regarded him closely for long enough to become deeply uncomfortable. At last he removed his helmet, granting Kazuchiyo a full view of his face; he could not have been much older than thirty years, his thick, brown hair braided back. His resemblance to his father was stated clearly in the hard line of his brow. Otherwise he was not at all familiar to Kazuchiyo, though there was in Naoya's eyes some familiarity for him.

"*This* is Hidemune?" he asked.

Kazuchiyo was used to being fixed with heavy glares, but Naoya's especially weighed upon him. "My lord, I am Lord Aritaka's youngest son, Kazumune."

Naoya leaned back, and Kazuchiyo saw a pang of emotion flicker across his face he never would have expected. "So you are," he said. "And if that is truly your justification for this travesty, for you I have only grief." He grimaced with mournful restraint. "How it pains me, to see the dragon's son in those colors."

Kazuchiyo's heart stumbled, but before he could fathom a response, Naoya turned back on Waseba. "*Your* colors I have always known," he said with fresh venom. "And I swear to reveal them on the field, for all our allies to see. If you think my Lord Koedzuka will be satisfied with the destruction of this small force of yours, you are mistaken, for he is just and will see you thoroughly punished for this outrage."

"Then I suppose it must be so," said Waseba, without even the slightest civility. "I'm looking forward to it."

Naoya seethed. "Very well. Then I will show you mercy equal to what you have in your heart."

He turned sharply, his coat flaring as he replaced his helmet and marched back the way he had come. His soldiers spared righteous glares of their own and then followed. As soon as they had departed Waseba let out a dismissive sigh. "What did I tell you?" he said to his captains. "He ought to have stayed a poet like his brothers."

"I think he almost shed tears," said one, and they all smirked among themselves, smug and intolerable. Even General Ebara showed no ounce of pity.

Kazuchiyo left the tent, eager to be rid of their apathy. He stepped out among the camp and was suddenly overwhelmed by the scale of their war effort. Men in armor bustled about or crouched around food pots, eager for every bit of preparedness afforded them. Come morning, many would march toward their deaths.

Kazuchiyo followed the path through the tents to where Naoya and his soldiers were reclaiming their horses. His last conversation with Oihata had been fruitful in its own way, granting him some solace in that the man seemed to recognize his actions were not entirely his own. Perhaps he thought he could find such understanding from the younger.

"General Oihata!" Kazuchiyo caught up to Naoya and his entourage just as he was mounting his horse, but he was careful to stop with a respectable distance between them. "Can I have a word with you?"

"As you observed, I have not one word left in me to utter," Naoya replied as he settled into his saddle. "It would shame me to spend another moment longer among these grounded animals." As he turned his horse about he seemed to reconsider, and Kazuchiyo felt some hope that he would not be entirely misjudged. But then Naoya looked tragically away, and any hint of sympathy escaped his features. "You ought to pray, young bear, that I do not encounter you on the field," he said, and he spurred his mount onward, leading his soldiers away from the compound.

Leaving Kazuchiyo little choice but to turn back and rejoin the beasts.

CHAPTER FOURTEEN

Before dawn, Kazuchiyo was roused from a shallow sleep by
the distant pounding of drums. He dressed in his armor,
swords at his waist, dagger tucked behind his back plate, a small
red bead snug against his wrist. He joined General Waseba, and
together they roused the soldiers to their ranks.

"We will hold the hill until our lord's reinforcements
arrive," were Waseba's only instructions, passed from high to
low, each soldier secure in the reassurance that their position
atop the hill would be deterrent enough. Though the slope
was not steep enough to deter a healthy man, Oihata's soldiers,
in full armor after days of marching, would suffer significant
disadvantage against their smaller force. Even so, Kazuchiyo felt
a pang of dread as he mounted Hashikiri. He joined Waseba at
the head of their soldiers and took in the view of the battlefield.

Their army had been spread across the hilltop, with
General Ebara and his vanguard stationed ahead of the main
force. Kazuchiyo could easily spot Yagi's broad shoulders and
the white mane of Mahiro's helmet along the front lines. In
the valley beyond, Oihata's army advanced at a swift pace in
well-maintained columns. Their banners were again on proud
display, this time spread across the army's rear flank in a

163

flowing backdrop of green. A mounted captain rode between each banner, reminding Kazuchiyo of Waseba's speculation the night before. He did not see the familiar shape of a bow rising from behind the captains.

"They put on quite a show, don't they?" said General Waseba. "These crows never pass up an opportunity to flaunt their feathers."

Kazuchiyo stared hard at the approaching line. Already the conflict was much closer than the village battle he had witnessed. He could feel the pounding of the drums in his chest, his eyes burning from the early light reflecting off helms and spears. He felt as if the dirt kicked up from the soldier's footsteps was scratching beneath his skin. If this was to be his test, he hoped to face it with courage, and yet his hands were already aching around the reins.

The sun was still climbing out from behind the trees when Oihata's forces reached their position at the base of the hill and there began to rally for their charge. Naoya himself stood at the front of the vanguard, flanked by his captains from their "visit" the night before. He brandished a sword longer than any Kazuchiyo had seen outside display, using its movements to direct his soldiers. A line of archers moved to the front and readied their bows.

Waseba raised his fan to signal their own archers forward. "Firing up the hill is a waste of time," he said, "but Oihata will do it anyway because he's beholden to tradition, just like his father."

Oihata's troops launched the first volley, and Kazuchiyo shuddered all over at the horrific *thunk* of those that found their mark. Soldiers cried out along the line, and several slumped over or drew back within the ranks. Kazuchiyo closed his eyes briefly against the invading visions of his brother bleeding from the neck. He could still hear that heart-shaking gurgle echoing across years. But then he forced his eyes open, seeking out Yagi and Mahiro at the front; both had held their positions, unharmed.

Waseba signaled for their archers to fire next, and with their advantageous angle more arrows struck true. Naoya himself stood unflinching as one pierced his left shoulder guard, narrowly missing flesh. Though their enemy, Kazuchiyo was relieved not to see him succumb so immediately.

"How bold," he said, "for their commanding officer to lead the vanguard personally."

"How foolish," Waseba corrected him. "He's far too easy to provoke, and no bird will fly with its head severed."

He signaled to one of the mounted captains on his other side, who obediently took up his longbow and slung an arrow. Even while Naoya's men were preparing for their turn, the captain took careful aim and fired.

The arrow struck Naoya directly in the chest, and all upon the hill held their breath. Watching him rock in his saddle sent Kazuchiyo's stomach into his throat; his helplessness in the face of such dishonorable cruelty threatened to burn him alive. But then, to the awe of ally and foe alike, Naoya righted himself. Without having loosened his grip on his sword for even a moment, he ripped the arrow from his breastplate and signaled for his archers to fire as if no interruption had taken place.

Kazuchiyo's shoulders fell with relief, only for him to cringe again at the volley stretching up the hill toward them. Even before all arrows had landed Naoya was signaling again, and the archers stepped back to be replaced by foot soldiers.

"Continue the volleys," Waseba instructed his captain. Though he seemed disappointed that Naoya hadn't been so easily felled, he signaled to Ebara to prepare for the charge. "Tell every man to target their general." He looked to Kazuchiyo with a sneer. "Now watch, Kazumune, as the wave breaks on the shore." He snorted. "See? I'm also a poet."

"Even the mountain, in time, falls into the sea," Kazuchiyo quoted verse. "One stone at a time." Waseba glared at him but did not respond.

Two of Naoya's captains charged up the hill on horseback, leading their soldiers in an all-out assault. Though hampered by the slope as intended, their ferocity was unfaltering, and their footfalls shook the earth. Ebara and his troops held fast, up until the line was a mere dozen meters away. It was then that Mahiro, in a fit of impatience and pride, spurred her horse. As a lone rider she met the enemy charge, a magnificent if foolhardy spectacle, the sun on her armor. With one great sweep of her naginata she engaged the first of Naoya's captains and cleaved his head from his shoulders, an image worthy of a hundred scrolls in her honor, and happily, one that requires no exaggeration.

Her gallantry inspired from General Ebara a mighty bellow, and he advanced the vanguard in a flurry of courageous shouts and clashing steel. The armies collided atop the hillside in near equal numbers, and then all was chaos. Kazuchiyo rose up in his saddle, trying to get a clear view despite the dust and commotion. He heard Yagi's telltale howl above all else and followed it with his eyes to where his champion was fending off four men with spears. After three were hacked down, the fourth fled, only to be picked off and replaced by more Kibaku soldiers, each too blinded by combat to realize they were rushing toward death.

Kazuchiyo watched from atop the hill, as a general ought. Each clash and scream conspired against him, and he did not think he would be able to wield a sword even if the battle called for it. His gaze skipped from Yagi, an unapproachable vision of strength, to the gleefully murderous Mahiro, to Naoya's gold helm flashing in the dawn light. With every painful breath he imagined them cleaved apart, leaving only him and the disgusting Waseba at his side. It was agony, and he regretted ever leaving Gyoe in the first place.

An hour later the sun at last freed itself from the easterly horizon, and with it rose the wail of an oxen horn. Even against the unending cacophony of the battle, its declaration sounded up and down the hill, echoing from the forests at Naoya's flank and turning the heads of his loyalists.

"They've arrived," said Waseba, raising his flag. "Just on

time."

Kazuchiyo leaned forward, squinting into the line of trees. He could see no banners, no foot soldiers, even as the oxen horn was joined by others announcing the arrival of Sakka forces. Instead he saw a cloud of arrows streak from the forest, arching high over Kibaku's eastern flank.

"Did he really not anticipate reinforcements?" Kazuchiyo mused aloud, unable to help mournful disappointment in watching Naoya turn his horse.

"Didn't I tell you he had more pride than sense?" said Waseba. "Look how it crumbles."

Naoya reared his horse, and the captains at his side raised flags as they, too, abandoned the base of the hill. Up and down the line Kibaku conchs sounded the retreat, the advance soldiers fighting ever more fiercely to support the escape of their brethren. "Cowards," Waseba growled at their backs, and he flipped his fan about. "I'm sure it would shame the boy if his father saw this display. Fools fit for each other."

Waseba's secondary force of a thousand men readied their spears while Ebara and his troops redoubled their efforts to make way. The Kibaku front crumbled, much too easily to Kazuchiyo's clever eye. So, too, did it rouse his suspicion to see that none of his father's reinforcements had emerged from the woods, despite the continuing echo of their horns. He watched another volley of arrows spring from the underbrush and realized too late that they were intentionally shot at too poor an angle to strike anything but the hoisted banners.

"General," said Kazuchiyo. "Can you see—"

"Come, Kazumune." Waseba holstered his fan in favor of a spear handed up by his attendant. "If you don't claim at least one head in this battle, you'll shame *both* your fathers."

He charged ahead, and with hundreds of men behind, Kazuchiyo had no choice but to follow. His pulse vibrated between his temples and against his wrist as they plowed down the hillside. A blade glanced across his shin guard, and he could have vomited when Hashikiri trampled a fallen Aritaka soldier beneath his hooves. His hand trembled as he drew his sword. It was as if all his training were for nothing, every body ahead of him smearing and melting beneath a rain that didn't exist. Yet somehow, he saw very clearly when Naoya reached the line of banners and halted his retreat. His captains turned their horses again toward the battle and brandished their spears.

"General!" Kazuchiyo called, but Waseba had pulled away from him and was already at the bottom of the slope, Aritaka's finest following blindly. Though Hashikiri was more than willing to slow his charge at Kazuchiyo's prodding, the rest of their forces were drunk on Kibaku blood and could not see the emerald banners falling away to reveal Naoya's true gamble.

Fifty armored captains on horseback sprang to the field. The foot soldiers parted in well-practiced maneuvers to make way for their charge, Naoya at the head like the point of an arrow. The thunder of their hooves was deafening. Waseba and his men crowding at the base of the hill were unprepared for the piercing assault, and as Naoya struck, sword flashing, Waseba's horse reared in panic. He was thrown from the saddle and quickly disappeared beneath the stampeding beasts.

Kazuchiyo watched as if in a trance as the cavalry split their forces in two. As soon as Naoya reached the hill, his foot soldiers flooded after, soundly dividing Waseba's army. Those with their backs now to the forest were assailed by arrows—this time expertly aimed—while Naoya and his horsemen reformed their ranks on the hill. Within minutes they were charging back down the slope toward their enemy's western flank to divide it further. They passed Kazuchiyo's position, and he was certain that Naoya looked directly at him.

With one simple deception, the battle was lost. Kazuchiyo could no longer see familiar faces among the melee, except for a decorated gelding that was Waseba's horse fleeing on hobbled legs. How tempting it was to stand rooted and senseless until a crow came to take his head, but then he heard a demon shouting, and after a great deal of prodding he convinced Hashikiri to continue down the slope.

Waseba's troops were in chaos: divided, battered, leaderless, helplessly striking out at any green armor. Kazuchiyo came across a small group gathered in the wake of the cavalry attack, and upon approaching realized they were sheltering the fallen General Waseba. His left arm was grotesquely broken, his knees unsteady, and he was glaring into the mayhem with blind wrath.

"Charge!" he screamed at no one, blood on his face. "Charge! Kill them!"

"General!" Kazuchiyo jumped from his horse. He could not blame the beast for quickly abandoning him, spooked by the surrounding battle. Instead, he rushed into the circle of defenders and tried to steady Waseba. "General, we must retreat!"

"Nonsense, charge!" Waseba insisted. He shook his fist as if expecting a spear to be clutched in it. "Our reinforcements are here!"

"There are no reinforcements," Kazuchiyo tried to tell him. "Oihata tricked you—our army is fallen! We *must* retreat!"

"No!" Waseba pushed him aside and nearly toppled himself with the effort. "Charge! Kill them all!"

He continued to wail in mindless hate until Kazuchiyo put his sword through his throat.

As vengeance, yes. You can easily imagine how many nights Kazuchiyo spent imagining a gruesome end for each of his father's killers. As punishment, even, for proprieties breached and arrogance tendered. And also, I must confess on his behalf, an act of sheer panic and desperation, by a young man flung to pandemonium on the dawn of the war he had instigated. A thoughtless, instinctual murder of a dying creature who deserved no better.

Waseba stared back at him. He had a few seconds, as blood poured down his chest, to comprehend the fate he had earned. Then Kazuchiyo cast him down, and he crumpled, gagging, his life quickly spent.

Kazuchiyo swayed on his feet. He could feel again an

unearthly burning against his wrist, which was swiftly drowned out by shock. There was little time to contemplate it, as when he lifted his head it was to find Waseba's bannermen gaping at him.

"What have you done?" one said, his eyes wide. "The general—"

Something struck him in the side of the neck, and he stumbled, wheezing. Kazuchiyo had enough of a glimpse to recognize the metal handle protruding from his throat before another man attacked him. Following the instinct of many years of training, he parried and countered, slicing through the cords of the man's armor and into his armpit. A third man struck him in the back. He felt the blade rake across his armor, drawing blood at the nape of his neck. By the time he turned the man was collapsing, a dagger wrenched from his torso.

On the other end of that dagger was Amai. He was wearing only light armor, blood splashed across its front, his face harried and hair tousled. "What the hell did you do?" he demanded, though there was panic in his eyes he could not will away with anger. "Have you lost your mind?"

Kazuchiyo blinked, half expecting that Amai was a hallucination and would vanish. When he was proved wrong, he turned in place, taking in the nightmarish state of the valley: bodies everywhere, banners snapped, horses stomping screaming men underfoot. He felt rain on the back of his neck, seeping down his spine. Then he looked back to Amai and déjà vu turned his stomach.

"We have to retreat," he said, and he sheathed his sword. With trembling hands he yanked Waseba's helmet free and replaced his own with it. Blood smeared across his chin close enough to his mouth to taste. He went back for Waseba's war fan, which was snapped, but he took it anyway. "I need a horse!"

"A horse?" Amai repeated, dazed. He stripped a bow from a nearby corpse and found an arrow intact. "Fuck me."

One of Naoya's horsemen turned their way, and having spotted the general's helmet atop Kazuchiyo's head, he abandoned his formation to charge at them. "My name is Unatsu Jinzaburou!" he declared with his spear brandished. "And I will have your—"

Amai fired and struck the man through the face. Kazuchiyo flinched at the sound. Though it wasn't enough to kill him outright, the man slumped from his mount, and the well-trained horse slowed to a halt. Amai cast the bow aside as he moved to finish off the soldier. Meanwhile, Kazuchiyo wrangled the animal.

"We need to retreat up the hill," he said as he pulled himself into the saddle. "Up along the western slope, close to the fields."

"The crows will ride us down," Amai warned as he pulled himself up behind Kazuchiyo.

"He won't risk the fields." Kazuchiyo spied Naoya among the fray, green coat thickly stained but sword arm as strong as ever. He swallowed. "We can only depend on his mercy, now."

Kazuchiyo spurred the horse onward, heading for the larger grouping of surviving Aritaka soldiers. "Retreat!" he shouted at the top of his lungs, waving the shattered fan. "Retreat!"

Many of the Sakka forces were already making such an attempt. They fled in groups up the hillside, some crawling when their legs couldn't carry them. As Kazuchiyo drew closer to those still fighting he was relieved to see Mahiro heading toward him atop Suzumekage. Though a fearsome, red-bathed sight, she was more intimidating than she was injured.

"Kazumune!" she called. "Why haven't the reinforcements arrived?"

"I don't know, but it's too late for that!" Kazuchiyo gestured with his fan; he ached to order Mahiro up the hill, for her own safety's sake, but he knew she would never heed such a command. "I need you to take up the rearguard so our forces can retreat!"

"These fucking crows," Mahiro muttered, but she straightened her helmet and gave Suzumekage a pat on the neck. "Go! Oeyo's Unyielding Gate will watch your back!" She galloped back into the fray, shouting, "Behind me! All behind Mahiro!"

Her figure was striking enough that the soldiers obeyed, hastily reforming their ranks. As the churning bodies retook a semblance of order, Kazuchiyo at last found General Ebara in their midst, having lost his horse but still battling fiercely.

"General!" Kazuchiyo shouted. "Move your men west, away from the woods!"

"We should retreat to the village!" Ebara replied, kicking a Kibaku soldier off the end of his spear.

"Oihata's already retaken the village," Amai said in Kazuchiyo's ear. "I came from there."

"What? How?" Kazuchiyo looked for himself, but there was nothing unusual to see from the village they had claimed so easily. An arrow clipped the side of his helmet, startling him back into action. "No!" he shouted to Ebara. "Get out of the range of the archers and head back up the hill! Where is your son?"

Ebara scoffed as he raised his horn to his lips. "Can you not hear him?"

He sounded the retreat, and as Kazuchiyo struggled to turn his horse, he once again caught the sound of Yagi's voice over the battle roar. It was coming from the western flank where the cavalry had broken the ranks nearly beyond repair. "Can you see him?" Kazuchiyo asked of Amai as he spurred his horse across the battlefield, back the way they had come.

Amai leaned close against his back to be heard. "We don't have time to—"

"Tell me if you see him," Kazuchiyo insisted. He had no patience for a lecture on priorities. "There's a tanto in the back of my belt if you need it."

Amai slipped a hand beneath Kazuchiyo's armor and drew the dagger free. "That group ahead and to your left," he said. "That must be him."

Kazuchiyo looked. Whatever line the Aritaka soldiers had been able to form was thanks to the enemy being drawn like a swarm to a single point, where they had encircled their most dangerous foe. Though Kazuchiyo could not see Yagi among the jostling bodies, there was no mistaking his furious bellow or the flash of his spear striking through Kibaku helmets. As much faith as he had in his champion, he couldn't bring himself to hope that such numbers could be overcome alone.

"Get off," Kazuchiyo said, drawing his horse to a stop.

"No," Amai said incredulously. "Don't you dare go in there."

Kazuchiyo's fingers ached around the reins. He had no plan and only shreds of courage to cling to, but with Yagi facing a legion of spears, to not act would have destroyed him more completely than the enemy ever could. "I have to aid him," he said, though he was shaking. "If you won't help me, get off!"

"The rest of Ebara's troops are headed this way," Amai reasoned. "He can hold out until—"

"*Aritaka Kazumune!*"

Naoya's voice split the battlefield like a thunderclap. Even among the chaos dozens of heads turned, and Kazuchiyo shuddered at the sight of Naoya atop his white steed, pointing with his bloodied sword. The Kibaku soldiers parted to make way, and Kazuchiyo could barely breathe.

"Amai," he said. "Get off."

Amai did so, and I suppose we cannot blame him for that. "You have to run," he said as he backed away. "Get out of here!"

"Protect your lord!" shouted an Aritaka captain, and the surrounding fighters struggled to pull together, forming a rough line just as Naoya charged. Valiant though they were, they had little hope of defending their lord's son with such shallow numbers. Kazuchiyo put his hand to his sword but was shaking too badly to draw it. What good would it have done him against his enemy's stampeding fury, in any case? No training could have prepared him to deflect such a foe. Too inexperienced and weighed by trauma to properly defend himself, too bound by the dragon's honor to flee, he stood his ground, an accidental beacon of courage to hopeless and wounded men, as Naoya galloped ever closer.

Then, from the churning ranks, a projectile—a spear larger than most men could carry—streaked across the field, striking Naoya's white horse in its flank. The poor creature reared and stumbled, crashing to the ground with a terrible cry. With it went Naoya, sword wrenched from his grasp as he was thrown down among the fallen.

Kazuchiyo stared in bewilderment, and after a struggle to reclaim his wits he beheld Yagi shouldering through the enemy lines. With bare hands Yagi toppled the foot soldiers in his path, bloodied and roaring, as much a demon as he had been that fateful day when first they met. As he bludgeoned the gathered crows, the Aritaka soldiers regained their courage, attempting to surge forward even as Naoya's allies braced themselves for his defense. With Ebara and his troops approaching there might have even been momentum enough to sever the Kibaku chain of command, but the unceasing shouts, the stomping and gnashing and the heavy thud of his own heart, were threatening to drown the shattered Kazuchiyo. He raised Waseba's broken flag.

"Retreat!" he cried, signaling to the captain that had come to his aid. "Retreat to the hill!"

"You almost have him!" said Amai, staying close to Kazuchiyo's flank as the men began to stream past them in retreat. He drew Kazuchiyo's dagger. "I could finish him—"

"No," Kazuchiyo said, with strength he hadn't believed was still in him. He watched as Naoya was dragged to his feet by a very concerned captain; Naoya was unsteady, holding his right arm to his chest, but his intensity was unwavering, and Kazuchiyo could not stand the thought of extinguishing it. "No, he must live. Help the men retreat up the hill—take the horse!"

Kazuchiyo tossed the reins at Amai and then dropped from the other side. Ignoring Amai's startled cursing, he managed to draw his sword as he ran closer to the fighting. "Retreat!" he called as he went. "Return to the camp!" He bypassed shouting captains and bewildered soldiers, intend on the warrior least likely to heed the retreat.

Yagi had wrenched a spear from one of his opponents and was using it against the rest, fighting through the throngs of angry crows to get to their general. "Yagi!" Kazuchiyo hollered, though his was not a voice yet accustomed to splitting a field. "Yagi, stop! Yagi-douji!"

A sword came at him, and thanks to his sharp reflexes Kazuchiyo parried in time. He sliced at the attacking Kibaku soldier, but his armor was stronger than expected, and it took several blows from different angles before he managed to fell the man. By then several more had spotted his helmet and were rushing toward him in search of glory, only to be gutted by Yagi's spear. The soldiers retreated out of range to rethink the merits of attack.

"Kazu!" Yagi glared at him, a ghastly sight: he was covered in blood, eyes wide and wild, teeth bared as he gasped for breath. "What the hell are you doing here?"

"We're retreating! Please, Yagi, we must go!" When Yagi's attention clawed away, intent on the wary enemy, Kazuchiyo tried again. "I need you to protect me!"

Yagi growled low in his throat and reached out to drag Kazuchiyo behind him. Without another word he backed away from the line, keeping Kazuchiyo protected with his broader frame and masterful spearwork. As more and more Aritaka soldiers joined the retreat, Yagi maintained the rear, Kazuchiyo with him, signaling to and encouraging their soldiers.

At long last, Ebara joined them with the rest of their men, holding Kibaku back long enough for the remaining Sakka forces to flee up the hill. Kazuchiyo watched, anxious until ill, as Naoya was brought a fresh horse and retook command of his troops. But with his sword in his left hand Naoya signaled for his armies not to give chase up the slope, and by the time Mahiro joined her brother, they were able to make their final escape back into their hilltop camp.

CHAPTER FIFTEEN

K azuchiyo stared out over the valley. It was barely midday, and his father's army lay strewn across the hill, some of Kibaku among them but not nearly in equal numbers. General Waseba was dead, as were all who knew who was responsible, save one. Amai was nowhere to be seen.

Yagi was close at hand, still breathing hard from the battle, a wild look stretched across his face and blazing in his eyes. Kazuchiyo touched Yagi's arm and gulped when the man's ferocity was fixed on him. It was a different kind of intensity then: harried and concerned, his gaze scanning heavily for injuries.

"Are you all right?" Yagi asked, his voice hoarse from yelling.

Kazuchiyo stared at him. He felt wild himself, heart still swiftly pounding, a bloodied haze over all his senses. He met Yagi's gaze and was overcome with panic and relief as if they were the same emotion. Obeying his deepest of instincts, he took hold of the front of Yagi's armor, tugging him down and rising up on his toes so he could join their lips in a kiss.

He did not care who might see or what they might think of it. In the center of the grinding pandemonium there was only Yagi, his pillar, standing quite still beneath his hands in what he hoped was welcome. For just a moment he was able to block out the shouting and crying, even the smear of blood across their mouths. He leaned back and held Yagi's startled gaze with his.

"Someday," he promised, "it will be *me* that saves *your* life."

Yagi blinked at him, breathless and baffled, but Kazuchiyo had already drawn from him much-needed momentum, and he could not let it go to waste. "We need to move the wounded to the inner tents," he said, "so they can be tended to out of sight from the other soldiers. Can you help carry them?"

"I—yes." Yagi's wits were still askew, but he nodded. "Yes, I will."

"Thank you," said Kazuchiyo, and he hurried off to other duties.

He found General Ebara at the edge of the hilltop, struggling to reform their soldiers into ranks. They were shaken and disoriented, a pitiable lot compared to the rows of indomitable warriors that had begun the battle. Or perhaps only Kazuchiyo's perception had changed. "General Ebara!"

Ebara did not cease in hollering commands to his captains, but he did motion Kazuchiyo closer. Only once he was better satisfied with their formation did he tear his eyes away. "I would ask what became of General Waseba," he said, "but judging by that helmet you're wearing, I already know."

Sweat crept down Kazuchiyo's neck, its sting reminding him of the shallow wound just above the lip of his armor. "He fought bravely but was cut down by General Naoya's horsemen." He turned his gaze down the hill, where Naoya was still in command, directing his men to reform their lines as well. "I've never heard of mounted warriors being used like that."

"He didn't learn that from his father, that's for certain," said Ebara, unable to hide his appreciation. "They've trained those horses into beasts. And here I thought only your sister had that talent." He looked to Kazuchiyo. "What is your command?"

"*My* command?" Kazuchiyo echoed, his heart thudding.

Ebara nodded, watching him with steely patience that reminded him of his dragon father. "You are my lord's son. With Waseba dead, it is my duty to serve you."

From another man, Kazuchiyo would have taken his fealty to be merely another test, but he suspected that Ebara was as straightforward as his adopted son, and he could sense no bitter or malicious motive beneath his words. He considered the state of their army, obedient but exhausted in every sense; he considered Naoya's troops rallying in outrage for the wealth of dishonorable treatment Waseba had heaped upon them. He remembered his father's hand trembling around his spear.

"The Kibaku army outnumbered us from the start," he said. "And we can't be assured now that reinforcements are coming at all, whatever might have happened to them. If General Naoya chooses to charge the hill, our advantage here will evaporate." He swallowed. "We mustn't give him any reason to pursue us now."

"You sound like you have a plan for that."

"I do," said Kazuchiyo, reaffirming his conviction. "I'll need a horse."

Kazuchiyo rode to the center of the encampment, where a group of white-faced guards hushed their chatter as he approached. He straightened his back and did his best to properly wear the general's helm, growing ever heavier atop his crown. "Fetch me General Oihata," he ordered. "And be respectful."

The soldiers complied, and soon Oihata was escorted from the tent. He was as pale but fiery as ever, his chin held high with as much stern self-assurance as was possible for a man's face to portray. "It must be over," he said, and with his wrists still bound behind his back he dropped to his knees. "Give me a sword and I'll finish it. I won't be paraded out and murdered in front of my own son for your spite."

"General, I have no spite for Kibaku," said Kazuchiyo, aware of the many eyes and ears upon them. It put him at ease to have a role to play. "And I have no sword for you. Please, come with me."

Oihata glared at him, and at length he pushed to his feet. With as much pride as he could muster, he followed Kazuchiyo through the camp. All along their path soldiers turned to look, and once they were among Ebara's ranks, even Mahiro stopped encouraging the troops to watch. Kazuchiyo feared her interference, but she remained atop Suzumekage and did not utter a sound.

Once Kazuchiyo had returned to the front of the column, he dismounted. Oihata bristled. "Well, here we are," he grumbled. "For my son and all his samurai to see. To think I had such hopes for you."

"My actions do not hinge on your approval," said Kazuchiyo as he drew his sword. "But I won't lie to a general of your caliber ever again. Humbly I ask, save some hope for me."

He severed Oihata's bonds and handed him the reins. Though Ebara's brow was heavy with disapproval and the surrounding men murmured and shifted, Kazuchiyo sheathed his sword as proof of his good intent. Oihata resumed his untrusting glare.

"You prefer to shoot me in the back?" he accused the lordling, but when Kazuchiyo returned his temper with calm, he began to come about. "This will earn you no mercy from me or my son," he said as he climbed into the saddle. "I would have rather you given me a sword in the first place!"

"The armies of Sakka Province do not require your mercy," Kazuchiyo replied. "Our poor behavior brought us misfortune, which we have paid for in full." He forced himself to stand taller and face Oihata without pause or weakness. "My only wish is to clear the stain from this battle's history, so that when we fight next it can be with respect, as warriors of equal valor."

Oihata harrumphed, but he seemed pleased by Kazuchiyo's answer, and he spurred the horse. As he raced down the hill toward his son's army, Ebara stepped forward.

"Now there is nothing to stop Naoya from attacking the camp in full force," he said.

"We're retreating from the camp," Kazuchiyo replied. "We can mask ourselves just like he did." He motioned for the captains to come closer. "Take half our banners and set them across the top of the hillside. We'll set them on fire to create a smokescreen so we can move our encampment to the field just north of the village." Ebara raised an eyebrow; Kazuchiyo nodded. "Yes, as you previously suggested. We can hold out there until we hear from my father."

Ebara nodded in return; he could hardly debate a strategy of his own design. "If Naoya does already hold the village, he'll be even more anxious about leaving the fields intact. How did you know he had taken it?"

"It was…" Kazuchiyo glanced about, though he had no hope of spotting the little weasel. "One of father's foxes told me. Where did he run off to this time?"

"I suppose it doesn't matter. I'll have my captains see to the banners if you lead the retreat."

"Of course," said Kazuchiyo, drawing his focus back. "Wait until my signal to set the fires, and if you see anything from General Naoya, raise an alarm."

"Yes, sir."

Kazuchiyo gathered a few of Waseba's remaining captains to assist him, but as he ordered them to their tasks, Mahiro rode up to him. He hastened through his instructions so that he was no longer distracted by the time she dismounted. She was just as intimidating away from battle as in it, her mane matted with blood, her eyes cold. "Brother."

"You fought magnificently," said Kazuchiyo. "No one could blame one grain's worth of our defeat to you."

Mahiro planted her naginata in the ground and advanced,

and for a moment, Kazuchiyo was even afraid. But then she pulled him close, embraced him as a sister ought, and he felt shame for having doubted her.

"I saw you on the field," she said. "Are you all right? I was so sure that pig-headed bird would ride you down."

"I'm fine," Kazuchiyo assured her, though she was pinning him too tightly to return her embrace. "I wasn't in nearly as much danger as you." He hesitated before adding, "I hope you're not too cross with me for freeing Oihata."

"Oihata! What do I care about that old goat?" Mahiro gave him a shake that would have felt more playful if he were not already so weary. "I'll miss tormenting him, but you're probably right. What Waseba did was…"

She grew quiet, but more concerning still, she did not let go. Kazuchiyo hated that he found her silence so unnerving. When she did resume, it was softly, close to his ear. "Kazumune," she said. "I've been a good sister to you, haven't I?"

Kazuchiyo tried hard not to let his imagination stray any further than the words from her mouth. "Yes, Mahiro. You're very dear to me."

"Good." Mahiro lingered a moment longer and at last held him at arm's length. Her eyes were glossy with emotion. "You're the dearest to me—except for Suzumekage, of course." She fixed him with a grim and determined smile. "And this Iron Gate will always have your back."

Kazuchiyo stared, mystified. He was too exhausted with too many concerns ahead of him to worry long on puzzling out the secret meaning beneath her words, if one existed at all. "Thank you, Mahiro. I will try to be as good a brother to you as you have been a sister to me."

Mahiro's smile deepened, but when a tear rolled from her eyelash, she swiped it away and retreated from him. "I'm going to help tear down the tents," she said. "And ready stretchers for the wounded."

"Thank you," said Kazuchiyo. He watched her climb into her saddle again and hurry to those tasks.

The Aritaka soldiers worked swiftly, spurred on by the voice of Oihata Naoya that occasionally drifted up the hill, ordering his men to their ranks. His mounted units had been refreshed and taken formation behind a row of wooden barriers to block any arrows until they were ready to strike. The threat of another pointed charge, this time through their home camp, kept Kazuchiyo's men on task and obedient until they were ready to abandon the hill. As they had planned, Ebara set fire to the banners and their army marched down the north side of the hill, away from Naoya and his scouts, retreating past the rice fields and into the relative security of the plain beyond. Naoya and his soldiers did not pursue, and in time, their forces withdrew from the battlefield as well.

It was as Kazuchiyo was overseeing the reassembly of their encampment that they were interrupted by Sakka horns coming from the woods.

All eyes turned to the east. Kazuchiyo hurried to the edge of the camp and was met there by General Ebara and their captains, everyone anxious of new traps. All activity and conversation ceased across the camp.

A line of soldiers emerged from the forest: Aritaka soldiers in indigo armor, raising their lord's banners. Kazuchiyo recognized two of his father's generals leading the troops as if they planned to charge straight into battle, nevermind that they had deployed at the north side of the hill, a most inconvenient position even if the conflict hadn't ended in failure hours earlier.

"What the hell are they doing?" Mahiro demanded in exasperation. "Did they get *lost?*"

As the columns continued to emerge, Kazuchiyo could make out the collection of banners that indicated Lord Aritaka himself was deep within the lines. "Please don't speculate until we've heard from Father," he said, a tremor in his hands. As much as he could claim not to pay mind to Aritaka's approval, he was fearful of how he might be received after the disastrous outcome on the hill. "He will have an explanation."

One of Aritaka's generals broke from the army with a small group of mounted samurai and rode hard across the field to the new encampment. The deer antlers mounted on his helm gave away his identity as General Fuchihara, better known for his caution than feats of bravery. Kazuchiyo made little effort to receive him with ceremony, trusting the state of their army would forgive any impropriety. Indeed Fuchihara's expression was one of mighty concern as he approached.

"General Ebara," he greeted without even bothering to dismount. "My young lords. Did your messengers not say you would be holding position on the hilltop?"

"Didn't *your* messengers say you'd be attacking from the *south?*" Mahiro shot back before Kazuchiyo could stop her. "Or do you not know the difference?"

Fuchihara wrinkled his long, hooked nose at her. "We encountered... difficulties... in the forest. Though it looks like yours were far greater."

"General Fuchihara," Kazuchiyo interrupted, and thankfully Mahiro heeded him. "Please request that my father stations his troops on the hill. I will join him there to explain."

"Very well, but be swift," said Fuchihara, and he and his men rode away from the camp.

Once he had gone, the three of them looked to each other. "I would accompany you," Ebara offered, "but someone ought to remain in command here."

"I will," Mahiro grunted. She shifted in place and cast a glare at Fuchihara's back. "I don't need to hear Father's excuses." When she noticed the looks they were giving her, she reacted not with temper but with sincerity. "I'll talk to our captains to make sure the wounded are being looked after, then shore up our defenses. They'll all be relieved to see the reinforcements; it won't take much to keep order."

Kazuchiyo wanted to express equal sincerity after her show of emotion earlier. He was just as eager to face his father with Ebara beside him. "I know. I trust you. Thank you, Mahiro.

Our men are in your hands."

Mahiro nodded, taking her duty seriously. As she left to pass commands to the men, Kazuchiyo and Ebara found two of the few horses they had left. It was as they were saddling up that Yagi approached with his own mount in tow.

"I'll come with you," he said, and his eyes looked much clearer than Kazuchiyo had seen him last, though still dressed in his full, bloodstained armor. It was only in looking at him that Kazuchiyo realized he, too, was caked with dirt and death from the field.

"We are only going to give our report," said Ebara. "You're of more use here."

"I want to come with you," Yagi insisted, his eyes hard and only for Kazuchiyo. "As protection."

Kazuchiyo's heart gave a thump. "Of course. I always want you at my side." When he remembered Ebara watching them, he quickly added, "I want to be sure Father commends you for your bravery on the field as well."

Ebara didn't protest, and the three of them rode up the hill to meet their lord.

The Aritaka reinforcements made camp where Waseba's army had before them, for with their numbers now bolstered and Naoya out of clever tricks to draw them down the hill, there was every reason to assume the same strategy. While half the men were put to the task of erecting tents and barriers, the others ventured down the hill to collect the Sakka dead. Naoya's men had cleared their own long before. Waseba's body was returned to the camp, but not his head. Kazuchiyo wondered which of Naoya's captains had claimed credit for it, and if they were at that very moment presenting it to their general at supper.

Lord Aritaka received them in his tent, joined by Generals Fuchihara, Utsukawa, and three others that had set out from

Gyoe. Kazuchiyo bowed his head to the floor before his father, as did Ebara and Yagi, and once prompted he explained the circumstances of the battle: Waseba's sound plan to remain atop the hill until reinforcements arrived, Naoya's uncharacteristic trickery which had lured him down, and the devastating efficacy of the mounted samurai. He did, quite rightly, omit the exact circumstances of Waseba's death, saying only that he fell beneath the cavalry's onslaught and was killed in the ensuing melee. He was, as to be expected, especially generous in his praise toward Yagi's feats of heroism, as well as Ebara's and Mahiro's efforts to command their scattered forces.

Aritaka listened to it all in silence, ignoring the stiff discomfort of his surrounding generals. At the end, he remained quiet a while longer, and at last he sighed. "How many casualties?"

"Some five hundred dead," reported Ebara. "And just as many too injured to fight. With my lord's two thousand men here, we are roughly equal in number to the Kibaku army."

"That will not be for long," said General Fuchihara. "By now word will have reached Lord Koedzuka. He will send reinforcements of his own."

"We're all aware of that," replied Aritaka gruffly. He looked back to Kazuchiyo. "Who holds the village now?"

"I was told Kibaku retook the village during the battle," Kazuchiyo answered dutifully, "though I do not know how, and I have not been able to confirm."

"And General Oihata," Aritaka continued. "He was released to his son."

Kazuchiyo took in a deep breath. He could see and feel the judgment of the other generals, ever mindful that each of them would have no more respect for honor or mercy than Waseba did. "Yes, I released him," he said, determined to project confidence. "I felt it was necessary to ensure our safe retreat from the hill. If Naoya had decided to reclaim him, or if he believed his father was already dead, he could have easily run us down. Then we would not have even the thousand that remain."

Lord Aritaka did not look pleased, but he did look convinced. The surrounding generals appeared much the same. "Well," said Aritaka, "we knew that courting the Oihatas was a risk. Waseba was outdone by his own overconfidence. You did well to preserve the forces you did."

"Thank you, Father," said Kazuchiyo, bowing his head. There he hesitated, uncertain if he should press for greater explanation, given that he had so far performed well.

"My lord," said Ebara, "might we ask how your reinforcements came to be delayed?"

Aritaka frowned deeply, and again his generals shifted and exchanged looks. "We were attacked in the woods by archers," he explained. "It couldn't have been more than two dozen men, but once they retreated and we resumed our march... our direction had changed."

Kazuchiyo stared at him, dumbfounded. "You were misdirected by archers and got lost?"

The generals bristled, especially Fuchihara. "We were misdirected by Oihata's sorcery," he retorted. "There can be no other explanation."

"Sorcery," Kazuchiyo repeated, earning more of their ire. He sought to smooth over his obvious doubt. "Then we are lucky he did not deploy even greater trickery on the field."

It didn't seem to console them at all, and Aritaka cleared his throat. "In any case, our numbers may not overwhelm them as we had hoped, but we still have the advantage of positioning. This time we will maintain the hill at all costs."

"How will we convince Naoya to assail the hill?" Kazuchiyo asked.

Aritaka hesitated just long enough for it to be apparent that, true to his impulsive nature, he had not yet thought that far ahead. "General Ebara, you will return to the camp north of the village. Kazumune, you will remain here. Once we've determined the state of the village, we can plan our next attack."

"Yes, Father."

"Sir," said Yagi, and Kazuchiyo startled, having not expected him to speak up at all. "I'll remain as well."

"You are your father's to command," said Aritaka.

Yagi stared back at him brazenly. "I'd rather remain here."

Kazuchiyo was tempted to intervene, but again he was rescued by Ebara. "My son is best suited to the front lines, my lord. Better to keep him where he's most useful."

"Fine." Aritaka was losing patience, and he gestured for them to be dismissed. "All but Kazumune, leave. Rest well for tomorrow."

The generals left, though it took Ebara's insistence to urge Yagi out. Once they were alone, Aritaka rose from his stool and encouraged Kazuchiyo to stand. "This was your first real battle," he said, watching Kazuchiyo's face. "How did you find it?"

Kazuchiyo returned his probing stare with what he hoped would be seen as deference, though his stamina for mask-wearing was swiftly thinning. "I am disappointed in myself," he said. "I realized Kibaku's trap too late and lost many men. I should have been quicker."

"That wouldn't have been your mistake to make, if only we'd arrived in time," Aritaka admitted, which startled Kazuchiyo. "It sounds as though you performed admirably, given the circumstances. In any case, I am glad to see you safe."

Kazuchiyo's stomach roiled. "Thank you, Father."

"Besides, it is far from over. There will be plenty of opportunities for you to prove yourself on the field, here and elsewhere."

Kazuchiyo nodded. "Of course. I will not shame you again."

Aritaka nodded, and he clapped Kazuchiyo soundly on the shoulder. "See that you don't," he said, his tone a curious mix of sternness and warmth. Kazuchiyo did not know what to make of it. "A tent is being prepared for you. You're dismissed."

"Thank you." He bowed and then showed himself out.

Once outside the tent, Kazuchiyo's momentum began to

fail him. Neither Aritaka nor his generals had expressed any doubt in his recounting of Waseba's death, and overall he had received little rebuke for the defeat. Even so, his knees rattled with his next steps, and he prayed that the tent prepared for him was very close, or else he would embarrass himself in front of entirely new soldiers. But then a hand closed around his elbow, broad and sturdy, and relief flooded over him.

"This way," said Yagi. He drew Kazuchiyo to a nearby tent, with a lantern already lit in its center. There he yanked his gloves off and began undoing the cords on Kazuchiyo's armor.

Kazuchiyo swayed with each hard tug on the knots and had to brace his hand to Yagi's chest plate. "What are you—"

"I asked one of the men to bring water," said Yagi gruffly, eyes locked on his work. He lowered Kazuchiyo's shoulder guards to the ground. "So that I can clean the wound on your neck you've neglected."

It took Kazuchiyo a beat to understand what he meant, such was his exhaustion. "I'd forgotten," he admitted, though even then he barely felt any pain. He smiled at Yagi for his concern. "I didn't think anyone had noticed."

"You should be more careful," Yagi scolded as he took off Kazuchiyo's chest plate. "If it gets worse you could lose your head."

Kazuchiyo's mind skipped briefly to speculations of Waseba's headless body dragged back from the field, dampening the warmth he was eager to draw from Yagi's attention. "I know," he said. "I'm sorry."

"Sir?" A soldier peeked into the tent. Though he startled at Yagi turning his glare on him, he hurried to complete his orders. "I brought water," he said, setting down a gourd, as well as a basin with fresh linen. "And dressings?"

"Fine, good," Yagi grunted. "Go away."

The man scampered out, and as Yagi continued, Kazuchiyo loosened his helm. Upon removing it he took in a deep breath, gasping, as if having finally emerged from deep water. He stared down at the helm in his hands, black and broad, blood dried in each crevice. All at once his fingers seized, and it dropped to the ground as the field rushed back to him—the chaos of the whirling battle, and the terrible, traitorous thing he had done. Instinct had so far propelled him ahead of his guilt, but his strength was spent. He could not keep up so many façades for much longer.

"Kazu?" Yagi took his shoulders, forcing him into the realization that he was shaking all over. "Sit down," he urged.

Kazuchiyo obeyed. Together they removed the rest of his plates, and with the final weight shed, he feared his wits would scatter. But then Yagi drew his hands to *his* armor, saying, "Help me with mine," and it allowed him to focus again.

At last both were completed divested of their armor, and Yagi untied, then re-tied Kazuchiyo's hair to sweep it away from the back of his neck. He thought nothing of dragging Kazuchiyo's robe off his shoulders so that he could clean the trail of blood that had dribbled down his spine. Though his hands were blunt and coarse, he tended Kazuchiyo with precision that suggested long and learned experience in the dressing of wounds.

It was a scene fit for poetry: war-weary Kazuchiyo under the tender care of his otherwise stoic champion, bare hands against his skin. Unfortunate, that Kazuchiyo was in no state to take greater appreciation from it. He shuddered, each breath carefully measured as he tried to maintain his composure, but his strength was spent. As Yagi applied the dressing, he quietly confessed, "I killed Waseba."

Yagi paused only momentarily before continuing his work. "Who knows?"

Kazuchiyo was grateful that he did not ask why; though he was not lacking for reasons, he never would have been able to articulate the impulse. "Amai does, but he helped me kill the rest of Waseba's bannermen who saw." He frowned, shrinking. "Mahiro might as well. I don't know—she was speaking strangely, and..."

Despite his efforts, emotion overwhelmed him. He had

189

to cover his mouth to keep a sound of pain from escaping his throat. Tears welled in his eyes, and he regretted ever asking Lord Aritaka to allow him to leave Gyoe. He didn't have the strength to fight a war of swords as well as lies; he couldn't bear to shoulder so much death and dishonor. What point could there be to a boy like him fighting Aritaka's war?

Yagi finished applying the dressings and leaned forward, drawing Kazuchiyo back against his chest. Without a word he covered Kazuchiyo's eyes with one broad hand, his mouth with the other. The unexpected oddity stilled Kazuchiyo long enough for him to understand his companion's intentions: an offering of peace. In their treacherous world of thin walls and fragile masks all Kazuchiyo wanted was a few moments of peace, to be honest and weak, to be only himself. He twisted about in Yagi's arms and turned his face to his collar, where his cries could be muffled, his tears easily mistaken for sweat. Yagi covered both his ears and granted him blissful silence.

Some might say that Kazuchiyo's deep love for Yagi was born on the fields of Shimegahara, or in their first blood-smeared kiss. But I can assure you with confidence that it was that evening in the tent, when, for Kazuchiyo's sake, Yagi made the world disappear.

CHAPTER SIXTEEN

They slept through the night tangled together on a single futon. At times Yagi groaned and tossed in his sleep but was quieted by Kazuchiyo's soothing whispers. Come morning, they were loath to abandon each other's comfort, even for breakfast. As they redressed in their armor, helping each other tie their cords, Yagi asked, "Why did you kiss me yesterday?"

"I suppose I was overcome with emotion," said Kazuchiyo truthfully. "You saved my life again." It took an extra bout of courage for him to admit, "And I had been hoping to for some time."

Yagi blinked at him. "You had?"

Kazuchiyo smiled; Yagi's blank confusion worked beautifully to calm his boyish nerves. "Yes. A long time."

Yagi considered that as they finished with the armor, his furrowed brow charming. "Well," he grumbled. "How do you feel about it now?"

A gruff invitation, by a remarkably gruff individual, and music to young ears. Kazuchiyo rose up on his toes and kissed Yagi again, lips sweet with gratitude. Though he was expecting it, Yagi again remained very still, only the red in his face giving away any reaction.

Kazuchiyo leaned back. "I feel I wish we had more time," he said, hushed in his boldness. "And more privacy."

Yagi swallowed, the wrinkles deepening along his brow as he took Kazuchiyo by his arms. His fingers worked stiffly, as if afraid of their own strength, and Kazuchiyo shivered, assured more than ever of those sentiments just voiced. But then Yagi came back into himself; he took a deep breath and let go, stepped back. He scraped the back of his glove across his mouth. "Me, too," he muttered, and he stooped down to collect their helmets.

Kazuchiyo regarded the offered helm, a cold pang dampening all thoughts of romance. With a deep breath he drew Waseba's helmet on and secured the cords, trying not to think too long on the dried blood on the straps. Yagi watched carefully as he replaced his own, a strange expression narrowing his eyes.

"Years ago, you asked me to do something for you," he said. "Is now the time?"

Kazuchiyo's breath caught in his throat. His answer was halted by the flap of the tent being drawn back and one of his father's captains peering in at them. "My lord," the man said crisply. "Your father requests you at the main tent."

"I'll be there shortly," Kazuchiyo replied, and as the man left, he faced Yagi once more. "No," he said. "Not yet." There should have been more to say and explain, but Yagi only nodded. Together they left the tent.

The morning proceeded much as it had the day before. Lord Aritaka commanded his men to the front lines, arranging them along the top of the hillside just as Waseba had. Naoya, in turn, led his soldiers from their camp and formed ranks at the hill's base, though far enough out of range to avoid fire from the Sakka archers. Ebara led the rest of Sakka's original forces, battered as they were, to the western hillside. Then, everyone waited.

Hours passed without movement from either side. At first Kazuchiyo found the wait agonizing, memories of the disastrous battle the day before drawing him as tight as a bowstring. As the morning passed to afternoon it became painfully obvious that neither side had any intention of making the first move; Naoya would have had to be an utter fool to scale the hill with Ebara's forces prepared to flank, and Aritaka a larger fool still to abandon his advantage of higher ground. Just after midday a group of Kibaku archers emerged from the village and fired arrows at Ebara's soldiers, but it took only a minor change in position to draw them out of range, with very few casualties.

And so the two armies remained in a stalemate, occasionally pounding their drums or loosing a few more arrows in the hopes of provoking some response. By late afternoon Naoya had proven his point, and he and his army returned to their camp. Aritaka had little choice but to do the same.

"Sniveling coward!" Lord Aritaka raged once he and his generals had returned to the war council tent. "Has he no mind to avenge his father's honor? The great generals of Kibaku, and they sit cowering at the foot of a hill." He turned his glare on Kazuchiyo. "You should not have released old Oihata."

Kazuchiyo bowed his head, grateful that he had asked Yagi not to join the assembly. He had rarely seen Lord Aritaka beyond the limit of his temper and did not know what to expect, or how easily Yagi could be provoked.

"Perhaps we could have Ebara's troops march to their rear," General Utsukawa suggested, stroking his mustache. "Their mounted troops won't be so effective if attacked from both sides."

"The only way to do that would be to circle around the village," said Ebara, "giving their archers plenty of time to fire on us, and Oihata plenty of time to reposition."

Fuchihara, who seemed to have been rustling within his armor ever since the field, scowled at them. "We don't have time for any of that! By now Koedzuka's main army should be underway. We can't perch on this hill like fools waiting for him to ride down our throats."

"We are all aware of that, Fuchihara!" Aritaka snapped, and everyone hushed. They watched in tense silence as Aritaka paced back and forth before his stool. There was little surprise in the faces of the generals, and Kazuchiyo was reminded just how short his five years spent in Aritaka's care had been. Perhaps the beast had always been this impatient and artless in his war-making. The thought made Kazuchiyo itch.

"My lord," Utsukawa finally spoke up. "We will of course follow your every command. Though might I suggest we return to Ninari Castle? The fortifications are plenty strong enough to break Oihata."

Fuchihara scowled at him. "Oihata could not be tempted up a hillside; what makes you think he'll be tempted through the woods to take on your fortress?"

"We'll burn the village," said Aritaka.

Kazuchiyo tasted bile. "Father?"

Aritaka's heavy eyes snapped to him. He did not seem to like what he saw, and he quickly diverted his attention to his generals. "We'll break down the camps and make Oihata believe we intend to retreat. Then we'll set fire to the village and the fields and return to Ninari. I know Oihata and his son. They won't allow that insult to go unpunished."

Kazuchiyo opened his mouth to speak, only to realize that he was the only one. Each of Aritaka's generals returned their lord's ghastly suggestion with grim nods, as if they had already come to the same conclusion. Only Ebara showed any disapproval, though he gave no indication that he would voice it. The tent was suddenly stifling, and Kazuchiyo needed a moment before he could breathe, let alone protest.

"Father," he said, wishing Yagi was at his back after all. "Did we not intend to make use of the village's resources for the campaign ahead?"

"The village is already lost," Aritaka said. "It will only benefit the crows now."

Kazuchiyo gulped, reminded of his first night in the village after the short-lived battle, the cries of the wounded ringing in his ears. "It may not yet be lost," he said, his quick mind put to the test as he groped for some excuse or solution. "With your permission I'll ride farther west—Kibaku's inland neighbors could be convinced to side with us."

The generals looked to their lord, who was in turn glaring at Kazuchiyo red-faced and incredulous. Subtly and without a word, a schism formed between the gathered generals: some waited for Aritaka to deny his son's offers, some waited for him to see the reason in them and accept. In those brief seconds of hesitation and division, Kazuchiyo felt he understood very clearly the impossible task it was to rule men of war.

"You've been outside Gyoe's walls for less than a month," said Aritaka, "and you think you can ride into a whole new province and convince them to war for you?"

None of the generals looked pleased with his stalling, and Fuchihara took it upon himself to rustle some more. "Preposterous," he spat. "After the loss you suffered? We might as well abandon the campaign if we go crawling for aid now."

General Rakuteru stepped forward: a sturdy, square-faced man with whom Kazuchiyo had only the barest acquaintance. "All of Kibaku's neighbors have dreamt of conquering the plains. It would not take much to convince them."

Fuchihara shook his head. "We don't have time to wait for them to decide—Lord Koedzuka is surely coming!"

"What was the point of coming here," Ebara interjected, "if you're so afraid of facing Lord Koedzuka on the field?"

Fuchihara bristled. "M-Me? Afraid? How dare you—"

"*Enough*," Aritaka again halted them. "I've made my decision. Go to your captains and tell them we dismantle the camps at dawn." He gestured to Ebara. "When the time has come to depart, your men will set fire to the fields and village and then serve as the rearguard while we fall back to the woods. General Rakuteru and his son will assist you."

Ebara's jaw worked, but he nodded. "My lord."

"Yes, sir," said Rakuteru, and he and his son, Ginta, bowed their heads.

Kazuchiyo stared, his lungs stinging as if already full of smoke. "What is your command for me, Father?"

Aritaka narrowed his eyes. It wasn't the first time he had judged his son, searching for defiance. Kazuchiyo feared that too much of his frustration and disgust would show in his face—that this time Aritaka would not only sense his resentment, but act upon it. However, he only grumbled under his breath and said, "You'll remain at my side and help lead the main force back."

Kazuchiyo bowed his head. "As you wish, Father."

Kazuchiyo returned to his tent, his heart in turmoil. He paced back and forth, so consumed by frustration that he did not notice at first that Yagi had followed him in.

"What's the matter?" Yagi asked as he removed his helmet. "What's Aritaka's plan?"

"He has no plan," Kazuchiyo said as he continued to pace. "He's no strategist. He never had any plan to lure Oihata up the hill, or any courage to descend." He loosened the cords on his helmet and let it fall to the floor with a clatter. "He's going to destroy the village to cover our retreat."

Yagi straightened, watching him closely. "Are you sure you don't want me to—"

"No," said Kazuchiyo, though he immediately doubted it. He stopped his pacing and gave Yagi's suggestion full consideration. How tempted he was then, to claim vengeance against his hated enemy, leap on a horse with his champion, and ride off into lands unknown. But he had always been too clever for his own good, and he could easily imagine what would happen then: any one of Aritaka's war-mongers could easily take his place on the field, continuing their bloody quest against Kibaku. Hidemune would ride from Gyoe with reinforcements, and the campaign would continue, in even more hateful and inept hands. The thought of abandoning his home province to be embroiled in Aritaka's senseless war was unconscionable to him. His escape meant nothing if Suyama remained beneath the enemy's command.

"No," Kazuchiyo said again, already mourning that freedom he must deny himself. "That wouldn't change anything. If one death alone was enough, I could have found a way years ago." He resumed his pacing. "But there must be a way to change his mind, or else warn Oihata—"

"Either way," interrupted a voice from the tent flap, "you really should lower your voice."

Kazuchiyo whipped about to find Amai watching them from the entrance. He grabbed him by the elbow to draw him deeper inside. "Where have you been?" he demanded. "I haven't seen you since the battle."

"Why would you need to?" Amai countered, slipping free of Kazuchiyo's grip. A smirk flashed across his lips. "Were you worried about me?"

Kazuchiyo's chest tightened. Even Amai's callous betrayals hadn't managed to dislodge the swell of emotion that rose in him every time their connection was made or referenced; they only twisted it into something anxious and fierce he no longer recognized. "I was," he admitted, and he was further confused by Amai's subtle reaction of surprise. "A battlefield is no place for a shinobi."

"You're telling me." Amai leaned back and glanced to Yagi. "And this tent is no place to discuss treason, if that's what you were doing."

Kazuchiyo cast a quick look at Yagi as well; he was watching Amai as fiercely as predator and prey. "It is not treason to want to save my father from himself," he said, drawing his attention back to Amai. "If he attacks the village in such a cowardly manner, he'll destroy any chance we have of uniting Kibaku's neighbors against them."

"And slitting his throat will help?" goaded Amai.

197

"Unconventional and very bold, even for you." He nudged Waseba's helmet with his toes.

"What do you want?" Yagi grunted. "If you're threatening something, I'll take your jaw off."

Amai held his hands up and took a step back. "I'm not threatening to tell anyone. It's not like I couldn't have done it by now, if I wanted to."

"Unless you're planning to hold it over me for some benefit to you," said Kazuchiyo.

"Oh?" Amai smirked again. "Do you have something to trade?"

"Gutless fox," Yagi growled.

He took a step forward, but Kazuchiyo stopped him with a hand on his arm. "Amai, how did Oihata retake the village without anyone realizing? Were you there?"

Amai's answer came a few beats late, as he seemed to be taking great amusement in Yagi's cold glare. "I was," he said, and as he continued, his humor waned. "I was supposed to help watch the battle, to determine if our soldiers holding there would be needed. But just before dawn Oihata's shinobi snuck into the village and caught us unaware. They made quick work of the samurai and had villagers dress in the armor to keep Waseba from realizing."

"If that was before dawn, why didn't you tell us then?" asked Kazuchiyo.

"I didn't have the chance," Amai said with a shrug, but seeing Kazuchiyo and Yagi crowd in on him, he sighed and surrendered the truth. "I was knocked unconscious and thrown in a cell. I was lucky to have escaped at all! I came as soon as I could; you know I did, Kazu."

Yagi snorted. "All your ego and you got caught."

Amai shrugged off his attempts at insult. "We can't all be built of unstoppable iron like you, friend."

"How did they get into the village in the first place?" asked Kazuchiyo before Yagi could go from bristling to battery. "Does Oihata really command skilled onmyouji?"

"If he does or not, I wouldn't know," said Amai, "but there is a tunnel that leads under the moat and into a gully on the far side of the village."

Kazuchiyo turned his head west, drawing the land in his mind's eye. "Then, if they are warned about Aritaka's plans, they have a means of escape."

"Think about what you're doing very carefully," said Amai with greater seriousness.

"Are you worried about me?" Kazuchiyo asked, hating that he was honestly curious for the answer. "If I'm caught and killed for treachery, your work for my brother will be complete."

"But I wouldn't get the credit," replied Amai. "So don't do anything stupid."

In Kazuchiyo's mind, the only unacceptably foolish option was to do nothing. After witnessing the Kibaku army's swift and impeccable strategizing in the face of the unprovoked attack, their honor and courage despite their enemy's lack of honor, he was eager to prove to Oihata that he had not forgotten his dragon heritage. Even if his only course was to spare a few hundred civilian villagers, the attempt for his conscience's sake was worth it.

"I need you to fetch me parchment," he told Amai. "And a brush and ink."

"Any letter you send has a risk of being intercepted," Amai warned him. "And being used against you."

"Let me worry about that," said Kazuchiyo. "But I can't ask for the supplies myself or that will say enough. You know better than I how to fetch them without arousing suspicion."

Amai set his hands on his hips. "Why should I?"

Kazuchiyo stared back at him, determined not to lose his temper or retreat. Every word from Amai was a test of some kind, and he refused to be found wanting. He could think of only one way to truly surprise or impress a vain trickster, and so he took Amai's face in both hands and kissed him.

Amai flinched. With his chin tilted up and eyelashes fluttering he accepted Kazuchiyo's kiss as if caught off guard.

His lips were as soft as Kazuchiyo remembered. Before he could gather his wits, Kazuchiyo eased him back and held his gaze. "Because I'm asking it of you."

Amai gulped, and it took effort for Kazuchiyo to suppress a shiver. Finally, Amai was quiet for a moment, his pale eyes shining with fascination. It was cruel of him to finally look as enticing as Kazuchiyo had imagined him during their false courtship at Gyoe. Then he smiled, which only made it worse.

"All right." Amai stepped back, out of his hands. "Only because you're handsome, though." He cast a smirk at Yagi and brushed past them, out of the tent.

Kazuchiyo's skin crawled with guilt as he turned toward the stone-faced Yagi. "It's not how it looks." He groped after an explanation for his insensitive behavior. "I only—"

Before he could explain, Yagi closed in on him, and wide hands drew him into a fierce kiss. Yagi's mouth was heavy and possessive, and Kazuchiyo's heart thudded wildly as he struggled to meet him in kind. When Yagi released him, he was breathless and had no idea what to think.

Yagi didn't seem to know at first, either; his cheeks were bright red and his eyes ablaze with intensity. He licked his lips as he took Kazuchiyo by the shoulders. "Whatever you need to do to survive, do it," he said. "That's all that matters. You don't need to explain anything to me."

"That's not all that matters," Kazuchiyo insisted. "*You* matter. I don't want you to doubt my sincerity."

"I don't. Don't worry about me." Yagi leaned back and rubbed at his face, as if trying to hide his own confusion. "I'm going to find us some food," he declared, and he stalked out before Kazuchiyo could stop him.

Kazuchiyo shed the rest of his armor, doing his best to untangle his mind from his heart. He had more to worry about than the warmth of lips against his mouth. By the time both his companions returned he had formulated a plan, and as they sat together eating rice gruel, he prepared the ink and the verse.

Would that I could fly
Over gray and swaying fields
Toward home in the hills

"I did say to be cautious," said Amai, "but do you really think Oihata will be able to draw your meaning from that?"

"Yes, I believe he will," Kazuchiyo replied. "Our intent to retreat is clear enough, and why would the fields be gray if not for smoke brought by fire?" Though Amai raised a dubious eyebrow, he remained resolute. "Anything *more* obvious would be too dangerous." He blew the ink dry and then folded the paper small. "I need you to take it to him without being caught."

Amai leaned back and finished gulping down his supper. "You must think a lot of me after all, if you expect me to sneak into the enemy's camp when they're on full alert."

"Don't you still have that Kibaku robe you stole back in Ninari?" goaded Yagi. "Or did you forget it?"

Amai shot him an irritated smirk. "I didn't say I couldn't do it. I'm flattered you're so appreciative of my skill."

"Amai, please," said Kazuchiyo. "You know there's no one else I can ask."

"And you do ask so nicely." Amai plucked the folded paper from his hand. "Will you give me another kiss for another favor?"

"Only if you return."

Amai chuckled as he pushed to his feet. "Keep your lips warm for me, then," he teased, and then he looked to Yagi. "You, too." Yagi scowled at him, and he quickly showed himself out.

"He's obviously useful," Yagi muttered once the tent was closed behind him. He continued to watch the flap as if expecting Amai to resurface at any moment. "But do you really trust him?"

"I don't know," Kazuchiyo admitted. "Right now I don't have any other way to warn Oihata without being found out."

He frowned thoughtfully as he swallowed the last of his meal. "Besides, he did storm the field and save my life. That has to mean something."

"It means wishful thinking," said Yagi. "Be careful."

"I will." Kazuchiyo offered him a smile. "And I have you looking out for me."

Yagi nodded very seriously, which only made him more charming. As night fell the pair of them settled into their bedding together, as before. Though Kazuchiyo was warm and anxious with close memories of lips both tender and fierce, he dared not invite any interest in their tent, not if there was a chance Amai would return. For the time being he contented himself with Yagi's sturdy chest against his back painting vivid images across his imagination, intermittent with worries for the young shinobi he had urged into danger.

Hours passed, and despite his exhaustion Kazuchiyo got very little sleep. His mind ached with speculation, and I must admit, I am no less curious to know just what transpired that night down in the Kibaku camp. For now we have only Amai's account from his own mouth, which he delivered just before dawn.

"Blood," said Yagi, and Kazuchiyo startled upright in time to see Amai dart into the tent.

His manner was far removed from the bravado he had departed with. His Sakka robes were rumpled and askew, his hair helplessly tousled. Blood oozed from a shallow wound in his temple, another in his neck, and his eyes were wild with fright. He made an effort to compose himself as he sat down in the center of the tent, but there was no hiding that his hands trembled as he reached into his sleeve.

"Well," he said, removing the same folded paper Kazuchiyo had passed him hours before. "I'm ready for my kiss."

Kazuchiyo crawled over to him and pushed his hair back

to get a better look at his wounds. "What happened?"

"Nothing I didn't sign up for." Amai made a strong attempt to be glib, but as Yagi lit a candle for them, the lines of worry around his eyes and mouth betrayed how shaken he was. He shoved the paper at Kazuchiyo. "Well? Aren't you going to read it? I worked hard for that."

Kazuchiyo accepted the paper, and as he unfolded it close to the candle, Yagi came forward with the water gourd and fresh linen. "I'm fine," Amai protested, but Yagi would not be deterred. He splashed water over his face to smooth his messy hair back.

"Stay still," he grunted, and though Amai hissed and grumbled about it, he surrendered to his care. Kazuchiyo, relieved, read over the lines that had been added to his poem in bold, curving brush strokes.

Five beats from strong wings, then three
Would be all I require

He read the words aloud as Yagi cleaned Amai's wounds, then whispered them again to himself, pondering. "Did Naoya write this himself? You saw it?"

"Yes," said Amai. He rolled his eyes. "He was very emotional about it, too."

Yagi drew Amai's collar down to better tend to his neck. "I thought you were going to deliver it without being seen."

"So did I! Imagine my surprise."

"Amai." Kazuchiyo scooted closer and took his hand. "Enough teasing. Tell me plainly: what happened?"

Amai stared back at him, and though for a moment he seemed determined to maintain his arrogance, at last he faltered. Yagi's fingertips probing his cuts seemed to draw the truth from him. "One of his shinobi caught me sneaking into the camp. A woman not from Shuyun. She brought me to both Oihatas and I showed them the letter—I didn't say a word! I can promise you that."

"I'm not worried about that," Kazuchiyo said. "What else?"

Amai hesitated, though at long last he pulled from his robe Kazuchiyo's tanto, taken from him on the battlefield. "The shinobi found this on me," he said as he offered it up. "Then Naoya got all teary-eyed and wrote those lines, told me, 'Take it back to your master,' and they let me go."

"What does it mean?" Yagi asked. "Are the numbers..." He growled under his breath. "It's some samurai code or something?"

Kazuchiyo glanced between the poem in one hand, the dagger in the other, and his heart began to pound. "It means... he heard me," he said, his voice frail with emotion. "Five and then three—the strokes that make up the symbol on this dagger—the first character of the name my father gave me." He drew both close to him, feeling he at last understood the message Satsumi had meant to convey to him through her gift. "*Peace*. He knows whose son I really am."

The others fell quiet. Kazuchiyo savored his relief as long as he was able, and then he put the poem to the candle flame, until the words were blackened ash. "Thank you, Amai," he said with full sincerity. "You don't know what you've given me."

Amai gulped. He didn't seem to know how to react for once, and it took him time to recall his usual charm. "You're welcome and all, but I'm still waiting for my kiss."

Kazuchiyo's cheeks darkened, but before he could have that debate within himself, Yagi took Amai sternly by the chin and kissed him hard. It was the last thing any of them had expected; Amai wilted, startled but receptive, and Kazuchiyo flushed even darker. The sight of the slender Amai held captive by Yagi's broad hands and wide mouth twisted in his stomach, though not, he was slow to comprehend, out of jealousy.

Yagi released Amai and went back to wrapping the linen around his neck. "Satisfied?"

Amai's lashes fluttered, and he glanced between Yagi and Kazuchiyo, breathless. Could it be he was considering sincerity for once? Alas, he relaxed with a self-satisfied grin instead. "Yes," he said, watching Kazuchiyo for his reaction. "Very much so." Kazuchiyo's mouth was dry, and he did not trust himself to speak.

"You're not very sweet after all," said Yagi. "You taste like blood."

Amai harrumphed. "I thought you oni got off on that?"

"It's dawn now," Kazuchiyo said loudly. "They'll be preparing the soldiers to take down the camp. You can rest here for a while but not long."

"Don't waste your worry on me. I've had worse." Amai scooped up the gourd and took a long drink. "Your father will be looking for you soon, so you'd better get moving."

Kazuchiyo and Yagi redressed in their armor as the camp began to clamor just beyond the tent walls. He half expected Amai to disappear at any moment, whenever his eyes were off him, but Amai stayed where he was, poking gingerly at Yagi's work.

"Good luck," he said once they were ready to set off, still entirely too smug as he watched the pair depart.

The energy of the camp was very different that morning. The soldiers who had the day before been filled with apprehension and some excitement were now confused and frustrated, and they hurried through their tasks without care for the quality of their work. Kazuchiyo feared for the state of their supplies, as haphazardly as they were being packaged and loaded. "They all marched out here only to turn around and march back without even seeing the battle," Kazuchiyo noted as he and Yagi made their way to the war tent. "Taking the blame for a defeat they weren't part of."

"One general and five hundred men dead over a farming village," Yagi grumbled. "So much for Sakka's campaign."

"Kazumune!" called Mahiro over the ruckus of the preparations. Kazuchiyo was embarrassed for feeling dread at her coming; despite all his time spent in careful secrecy and scheming, he had yet to reach any confident answer on how best to approach her following Waseba's death. When he turned about and saw her, however, those concerns fled, and he allowed himself a moment for joy: she was leading two horses, and one of them was Hashikiri.

"Hashikiri!" He hurried forward and was relieved when the animal seemed to receive him gladly, at least in so much that he allowed Kazuchiyo's fond petting. "I thought him lost," he said, quickly checking the horse over for injuries. "How did you find him?"

"Suzumekage brought him back," Mahiro said proudly, patting her own horse's neck. "They're good friends, you know. She knows how to look after the young ones." She grinned, but she had never been skilled at hiding anything, and Kazuchiyo could see her straining. "Don't you hold it against him that he got skittish. It was his first battle, too."

"No, of course I wouldn't." Kazuchiyo scratched under Hashikiri's chin; he wished there was time to give him more proper care. "Mahiro, shouldn't you still be with General Ebara and his forces?"

Mahiro looked away. "No," she said. For a moment it seemed that she would say no more than that, but as Yagi joined them, she glanced between him and Kazuchiyo and surrendered the truth that was so disturbing her. "He sent me here. Now that I've heard what our father is up to, I know why."

"Not interested in setting fire to peasants?" suggested Yagi.

"Of course not! What the hell does he think—" Mahiro stopped herself, seething. Even her eyes were red with the effort at restraint. "Why did we come here if we're not going to stand and fight against all of Kibaku? I'd go take Oihata's head for him if he asked me to; you know I could!"

"I know you could," said Kazuchiyo, "but it is our father's command."

"I know it is!" Mahiro continued to shift and glower into the distance, and Kazuchiyo was tempted to ease her conscience. Surely she would be grateful to know that Oihata would have seen to the villagers and their safety during the night. Whether she would be grateful hearing how and by whom the warning had come to him was less certain. He thought of her tearful embrace just after the battle and despaired that he could not yet afford to offer her his full honesty.

"Mahiro," he said gently, "stay close to me today, won't you? We'll ride home together just like when we set out. All right?"

Mahiro looked to him, her eyes hard and searching. She wasn't very good at the game then, but she did try so hard to read his intentions from his face. "Okay," she said, leaving both of them to wonder at her success.

The preparations continued. Naoya returned his army to just beyond the base of the hill, as if he expected Aritaka to try his luck another day in their staring contest. It emboldened and shamed Kazuchiyo to see that he was so committed to not giving away his secret knowledge—so committed, in fact, that for a short while Kazuchiyo worried his message had been misinterpreted. He saw no movement from the village except for Kibaku banners in the wind. As Aritaka's armies formed their ranks for the march home, Ebara's archers with their flaming arrows launched volleys into and over the village walls, setting Oihata's modest but respectable homestead afire.

It played out just as Lord Aritaka had expected. Naoya, still too cautious to scale the hilltop, led his army instead to the village's defense. By the time they arrived Ebara's smaller force had fled into the cover of Aritaka's two thousand soldiers, and the Sakka men made their retreat into the woods. It was Aritaka's hope that the rest of Shuyun would consider the village a punishment for Kibaku's unprovoked use of would-be assassins. It was his fear that he would be considered a dullard and a coward. In time, everyone that bordered the plains would fall on one side or the other. But only a clever few would notice that the village did not burn as long or as hard as it should have, considering the sudden and ghastly nature of the attack. Most would attribute the salvation of the Oihata mansion to Naoya's keen foresight, or even his sorcery.

Fewer would ever know the truth. How lucky we are to count ourselves amongst them.

CHAPTER SEVENTEEN

Upon returning to Ninari Castle, Lord Aritaka retreated into his private chambers and refused the counsel of his lords for several hours. The generals whispered that they had not seen him in such a furious state for years, not since before his victories against Suyama Province and the Red Dragon. Had a half decade of peaceful reconstruction dulled the samurai instinct that earned him victory at Shimegahara? General Rakuteru was even bold enough to let himself be overheard suggesting wise Iomori no Jun be summoned before the campaign continued.

Kazuchiyo retreated as well for a time, joining Yagi and Mahiro in the stables to care for their horses. With stable hands bustling about, their gossip was limited to Mahiro's rowdy jokes, which Kazuchiyo attempted to rephrase in poetry format: a favorite game of theirs from over the years. Despite strong effort, neither managed to coax a laugh from Yagi, though he did sometimes grunt or hum, suggesting he found them humorous in his own way.

It was a pleasant enough diversion after days of warfare and uncertainty, though it abruptly ended when Utsukawa's son came to tell them they would be expected to join Lord

Aritaka and the generals for a late supper.

"It's not as if he can blame you for Waseba's failure," Yagi reassured Kazuchiyo as they entered the keep. "He'll rant and complain and plan the next fight."

"'The next fight' is what concerns me," admitted Kazuchiyo. "Father is even less prepared for this campaign than I expected. I need to come to a decision, soon."

Yagi frowned at him. "A decision on what?"

Kazuchiyo took in a deep breath. "What kind of victory I should be hoping for."

They split up to go to their chambers, and there Kazuchiyo finally rid himself of the robes that had accompanied him all throughout his first battle. A proper bath would have to wait, but he stripped down, scrubbed at his skin, and picked the blood and earth out from under his fingernails. The comb felt like heaven through his thick hair. But as he was preparing his hitatare for the formal supper, his attention was drawn to his wrist, and the length of ribbon that had clung to him for so many days.

Kazuchiyo made sure the door and shutters were both secure, and even then kept his back to the door as he unwound the black silk ribbon that Iomori had gifted him. The small red bead remained tucked inside, but when he rolled it back and forth between his fingers, he felt that something was different—that it was heavier, warmer, somehow. He blamed it on finally taking notice of the thing after so long and wrapped it back up for safe keeping.

Supper was more lavish than Kazuchiyo had expected. Utsukawa's sons had prepared overly well for their return, with rice and meats and pickled vegetables. Perhaps they had expected to be celebrating a victory.

Conversation was sparse and awkward, and even Mahiro had nothing to say. They were offered very little saké. Lord Aritaka sat at the head of the assembly, dressed in his fine hitatare and black cap, speaking not one word until the food was nearly eaten. Only when he had no choice but to broach the subject or dismiss them did he straighten his back and declare, "We must be ready for them."

Everyone turned to stare. The tension stretched out among them as the assembly waited for Aritaka to continue. Kazuchiyo saw them as a pack of wolves eyeing a wounded bear in their midst.

"We'll increase Ninari's defenses," said Aritaka. "There are already reinforcements headed this way from all over the countryside. When the Oihatas come to take their vengeance, we must be ready."

"We will be, my lord," said Utsukawa. "Never before was a castle made as heavily fortified as this one. They cannot avoid or defeat us here."

Utsukawa's simpering did nothing to assuage his restless peers. They had stood on the hillside and watched Naoya hold his position with patience and insight, unlike the hot-blooded romantic rumor had painted him as. Each of them was thinking the same thing, hesitant to voice it, and as Kazuchiyo glanced from one to the next, judging them, he was reminded of Aritaka's advice to him his first day at Gyoe.

No daimyo can go on without the confidence of his generals. Fuchihara was a coward but not entirely a fool, sure to always choose the winning side. Rakuteru was logical and strict, ambitious with a powerful family behind him. Ebara had doubted Waseba's methods from the start, and did not seem pleased to see more of the same bull-headed foolishness in his lord. The other two Kazuchiyo did not know well enough to properly assess, but their eyes were cold and wary. Each of them was of one mind, and if no one said it here, they would behind Aritaka's back.

"Father," said Kazuchiyo. "What if Oihata does not come for Ninari?"

Aritaka glared at him, but try as he might, he could not intimidate Kazuchiyo into retracting his question. "Utsukawa," he said. "Have you ever known an Oihata to be a coward?"

Utsukawa straightened. "No, my lord."

"Or to forgive a slight?"

"Certainly not, my lord."

"The road past this castle is the only reliable crossing to reach Gyoe from the west," Aritaka continued gruffly. "It's why we chose Ninari to rebuild in the first place. If he wants revenge for his petty village, he will come."

His words convinced precisely no one. Even Utsukawa hesitated to voice his support again, and Mahiro actively bit her lip to keep from issuing some retort. When Kazuchiyo glanced away, he took notice that Ebara and Rakuteru were both watching *him*. With Yagi by his side, stoic but supportive, he made his gamble.

"If I were Oihata," said Kazuchiyo, "I would not dare march on Ninari Castle."

The air grew thick and sweltering, but he did not relent beneath Aritaka's heavy stare. "You're not a crow from the plains," Aritaka retorted, "with seed for brains and more bile than sense. They'll come."

"Their spies have had their eyes on Ninari for as long as it has stood," Kazuchiyo carried on. "They know the strength of its defenses as well as we do. He would have to be a fool to attack these walls, and he is no fool."

Aritaka's face grew red and contorted with a temper Kazuchiyo had never had the occasion to witness. However, rather than submit to outburst, the great daimyo of Sakka Province was rendered speechless. With his beastly nostrils flared, he looked very much like a childish boar unable to fully commit to his tantrum.

"You should listen to him," said Mahiro. Though her intent to aid her brother was admirable and he was glad for it, Aritaka's fierce eyes shifting to her did their cause no favors. "He's the one that rallied our forces after Waseba's idiocy split us apart."

"I didn't ask for your opinion," Aritaka growled. He took a deep breath, finally ready to unleash some bellow against his children, only to be interrupted by Ebara.

"Lord Aritaka," he said, bowing his head. "We've always known Oihata to be a man ruled more by passion than sense, but as we saw on the field, that is not the case now. It may be he's aided by some other general or strategist."

"And some sorcery, for certain," Fuchihara agreed. "Nothing less than a master onmyouji could have waylaid us in the forest as we were. We ought to meet them in kind."

Aritaka's gaze clawed across the room. One wonders if he even then had caught onto the scent of the wounded animal in the room. "You're suggesting we enlist the aid of Master Iomori," he accused.

"Would it not be wise?" General Rakuteru chimed in. "She has provided many keen insights in the past, and she may be our only way to combat Oihata, if he has become as devious as they say."

Aritaka shifted and chewed, and at last he admitted the truth. "She has already been summoned from Gyoe. It will take some days, so in the meantime we'll focus on strengthening Ninari."

"And if General Oihata does not come to Ninari?" Kazuchiyo pressed.

"Then we will ride out and meet him wherever he *does* go!" Aritaka shoved his dinner tray back and motioned to the servants. "Not another word on it. All of you are dismissed."

Each guest bowed their head. "Yes, sir."

The generals and their children filtered out. As soon as they were away from the room Yagi gave a great snort. "He lives up to his nicknames."

"He's always been blunt, but not like that," said Kazuchiyo. "I've never seen him so out of sorts."

"You've never seen him lose," grumbled Mahiro. "I have. Stubborn old bear..."

She increased her pace to put herself ahead of them; Kazuchiyo did not make an effort to follow. Outside the room he felt as if the air had thinned and cooled, and he found himself faintly reeling, as if on the edge of a revelation. He had little time to compose himself before his name was called, and he turned to see General Rakuteru approaching.

Kazuchiyo knew Rakuteru by reputation, but not so much personally; his clan was an old and distinguished one, with many daughters wed to powerful allies and warriors well praised for their valor. Though he had heard rumors never confirmed, Kazuchiyo was fairly certain it was General Rakuteru himself who had taken the head of his eldest brother at Shimegahara. Despite his service to Aritaka, he was universally acclaimed as a man of strength and good sense, and not one engaged with lightly.

"You spoke very well in there, Kazumune," said Rakuteru as they continued in step down the corridor. "For all the good it did."

"Thank you, General Rakuteru," said Kazuchiyo, and no more than that. He had not secured himself so well in Gyoe by picking opponents carelessly, or speaking too freely.

"Ebara spoke well of you on the field as well," Rakuteru continued. "He said you assumed command swiftly after Waseba fell, and I've heard also that you stood at the front of your men in the face of Oihata himself without flinching."

"I can't say that I did not flinch, sir, but I'm flattered by their kind words."

Rakuteru took his shoulder to halt him, though he quickly let go. Kazuchiyo liked to believe he was very conscious of Yagi paying him intense attention. "Words cannot be kind or unkind," he said. "They are either true, or they are not. Like the words you spoke to your father in there."

Kazuchiyo straightened. "I have only ever spoken true words to my father."

"I believe you," said Rakuteru, though the flatness of his tone suggested that he was more aware of the flexible nature of 'truth' than he was proposing. "Speak truth to me now, then: where do *you* think Oihata will take his vengeance?"

"You're a samurai of Sakka," Yagi interrupted gruffly. "And he's your lord's son. He doesn't have to answer to you."

"It's all right." Kazuchiyo cast Yagi a nod of thanks before returning his attention to the general. "Oihata Naoya is too smart to think he can take Gyoe without full-scale war, and I don't believe his Lord Koedzuka wouldn't allow that. If I were him, I would march south and attack Suyama instead. He'll find less resistance there." Before Rakuteru could take a breath to reply, he added, "Though it puts me in a difficult position to say as much, because of my background. Some would think my judgment is clouded."

Rakuteru leaned back, appraising him. "And is it?"

"No." Kazuchiyo stared straight back at him and could say for certain then that he did not flinch. "My judgment has never been clearer."

Rakuteru considered that and nodded. "Ebara was right about you," he said, with a firmness that indicated he was paying a high compliment. "But I wouldn't push your father any further until Iomori arrives. She'll put sense back in him."

Kazuchiyo bowed his head just enough to acknowledge this advice, thinking it would be dangerous to agree too heartily. Rakuteru, seeming to have concluded his test for the time being, bowed more deeply. "I hope next time I'll be able to see you on the field myself," he said. "Excuse me."

He moved on to rejoin his son, Ginta, who had paused to wait and possibly overhear. Kazuchiyo allowed them to create a sizable lead before he and Yagi continued on. Yagi was quiet until they were in relative privacy, and then he fixed Kazuchiyo with an appreciative look.

"You're really good at this, aren't you?" he said.

Kazuchiyo smiled, though only briefly. "Thank you, but I don't know if I can take credit when I have no other choice."

Yagi grunted. "Of course you can. The Bear doesn't have a choice either, but he still made a fool of himself in there." He scraped his hand across his mouth, realizing he ought to follow Kazuchiyo's example and not speak so openly. "Well. *I'll* give you credit, either way."

"Thank you," said Kazuchiyo again, and his smile lingered

for much longer.

They made their way down to the eastern keep, where the bathhouse was. The fires had been burning ever since their return, as weary lords and soldiers alike took their turns ridding themselves of battle filth. With basins of hot water poured, the pair disrobed, and it occurred to Kazuchiyo with stunning, youthful clarity that they were finally alone.

He shed his hitatare and let down his hair. With goosebumps prickling his skin, he turned—shamefully curious to see Yagi's naked physique after so many years, even more so to know if Yagi had any interest in his. But his first glimpse struck him with a chill and stole his breath.

Yagi's rough skin was puckered with a lattice of scars. Beneath the dark bruises of their most recent battles lay his history in morbid detail: sword slashes, arrow punctures, burns, and knife wounds. The broad, muscular span of his back, which Kazuchiyo had spent so much of his adolescence fantasizing over, was more heavily marred than the rest of him. A few of the marks Kazuchiyo could even fit to his memory of their first meeting at Shimegahara. He stepped closer, aching with sympathy, humbled by it. He reached out to cover a scar just over Yagi's hip that he remembered dressing at Gyoe, and he could have sworn he felt fresh blood pulse beneath his palm.

Yagi turned toward him and leaned down. The sudden proximity of his face was startling, and Kazuchiyo flinched back out of instinct. Yagi flinched as well at his reaction, and they stared, blinking at each other in confusion.

"Sorry," said Yagi. "I thought you were…"

"No, I'm…" Kazuchiyo's cheeks flushed as he became more aware of how closely and how nakedly they were standing together. "Forgive me. I was remembering how you got this."

He touched the scar again, and Yagi held still, allowing it. "How was that?" he asked. "I don't remember."

216

"The tip of a spear at Shimegahara." Kazuchiyo glanced over Yagi's shoulders and chest, easily drawing a map in his mind of arrows protruding from his skin. "There's so many," he lamented. "I suppose it would be impossible to remember them all."

"I remember a few."

Yagi lifted his hand to Kazuchiyo's neck, brushing his thumb against the mostly-healed gash torn by Amai's kunai. The reminder of that night filled Kazuchiyo with conflict, which was muddled by the tantalizingly rough pads of Yagi's fingertips. Reminding himself of his vow for boldness, he took Yagi's hip with his other hand as well. "Can I ask you something?"

Yagi's eyelids drooped, but his gaze was still intense and haunting, locked onto Kazuchiyo's face. "What?"

"Why did you kiss Amai in the tent?"

Yagi's mouth curled in a scowl, but his eyes darted away, more uncertain than irritated, and his cheeks were flushed. He grumbled under his breath for a moment before composing a real answer. "I just wanted to shut him up. He thinks he's so fucking clever."

"He *is* clever," Kazuchiyo said carefully, fascinated by Yagi's disgruntled expression. "I'm still not certain I can ever completely outwit him." He frowned. "Are you still angry with me for kissing him myself?"

Yagi's attention snapped back like a whipcrack. "I wasn't angry with you in the first place," he insisted. "I'd just rather you kiss me instead."

Yagi's idea of courtship was the bluntest Kazuchiyo had ever envisioned or read of, but it suited him fine. His heart fluttered and sang as he tugged at Yagi's waist in invitation and rose up on his toes, seeking the requested kiss. Yagi leaned in to meet him, his breath heavy, but just before their mouths touched, he hesitated. With clear effort at restraint he gentled his wide hands against Kazuchiyo's jaw and kissed him slowly, almost cautiously, as if afraid his lips would bruise. He was clumsy and charming, and Kazuchiyo trembled with him.

"Sorry," Yagi mumbled, even as he threaded his fingers through Kazuchiyo's thick hair. "I'm not any good at this."

"You're perfect," Kazuchiyo reassured him. "Come closer."

Yagi lowered himself to his knees. It stirred Kazuchiyo in ways he couldn't have imagined to see his muscled champion gazing up at him with breathless awe. He sank into Yagi's lap, shivering wherever they touched. After years of dreaming, at last he had Yagi's strong arms wrapping him up, Yagi's sculpted chest against his own. At last he could worship him with deep kisses and blissful sighs. They twisted together, flesh on flesh, simmering with arousal.

Whatever Yagi claimed to be his shortcomings, he was no disappointment. He kissed his lord long and hungrily, kneaded eager fingers into his back, hips, and thighs. His voice rumbled and swelled between their mouths. But he was also in all things restrained, pausing sometimes when his enthusiasm made him ragged.

"It's all right," Kazuchiyo tried again to reassure him. "You won't hurt me."

"You're just as bruised as I am," Yagi retorted. "I might."

He slid one hand down between their bodies, and Kazuchiyo let all other thoughts escape him. The firm stroke of his wide palm exceeded all expectations, and he surrendered himself to Yagi's slow pace and tenderness. What poetry they must have been, breathlessly hushing each other between each grasping kiss, their weary bodies churning and entwined. Yagi's callused hand trapping Kazuchiyo's most sensitive flesh against his own impressive organ. The rhythm of Kazuchiyo rocking against Yagi's thighs like lines in verse. Would that I could count the syllables for you, but that was his talent, not mine. I do hope that I can convey at least some portion of the quiet intimacy of that night, an unexpectedly delicate prelude for many nights of passion that would follow.

At last both were spent, panting into each other's hair. They kept still for a while as the euphoria ran its course, until gradually Yagi's wisdom made itself known. At an even slower and gentler pace, the pair scrubbed each other clean with hot water and rice bran, and dipped into the hot bath to soak their aches away.

"Will your father be angry?" Yagi asked, as forthright as ever, as they relaxed very close together beneath the water. "About you having a lover?"

Kazuchiyo smiled, though the heat was already so great that his face could not have become any redder. "Maybe," he admitted slowly. For once he wasn't in a mind for politics, wishing he could instead dwell on his amazement at having earned Yagi's affection so quickly. "If only because it's you. If you were a servant or a foot soldier, there would be nothing to complain about; it's not as if having a lover prevents me from eventually taking a wife as well. But you're a powerful warrior, with less loyalty to Aritaka than most. He might think we're scheming something."

"Aren't we?" Yagi glanced around the small bathhouse with healthy paranoia. "Scheming for victory for his army isn't something that should worry him," he said, louder.

"Oh, Yagi." Kazuchiyo couldn't help but chuckle as he leaned in close to his lover's ear. "Please, don't worry about all that now. I don't want you to fret over my battles."

"Your battles *are* my battles," Yagi retorted. "But I know I'm no good liar. I'll keep my mouth shut about it, I promise."

"I believe you." Kazuchiyo settled against Yagi's shoulder, wanting a few more minutes of peace. "And I believe *in* you. As long as we're together we'll be all right. Won't we?"

Yagi tucked Kazuchiyo under his arm. "We will," he promised. "I'll look after you."

Once they were finished, they dressed in spare robes and hurried back to the keep. There was no knowing who might have spotted, overheard, or suspected them, but Kazuchiyo was not yet concerned. Yagi had fought bravely in the vanguard and proven himself loyal; no one could fault Kazuchiyo for favoring him, no matter their unusual history.

Still, it was a challenge to leave him for the night. He would have preferred one last kiss, but to do so in the company of such thin walls was inviting more scrutiny than he cared for. "Our days will be full of waiting, for a while," he said as they lingered in the hall outside Kazuchiyo's room. "For Master Iomori, and for more soldiers. I hope you're able to rest well."

"Whatever comes next, I'll be ready," Yagi promised, missing what Kazuchiyo had intended as a subtle invitation to further liaisons. Too subtle, it seemed. As he left, Kazuchiyo resolved to better speak his companion's language in the future.

CHAPTER EIGHTEEN

Kazuchiyo crawled into bed and fell straight to sleep that night. Exhaustion robbed him of his dreams, to his great relief, and with his quiet chamber and stuffed mattress he slept better than he had since leaving Gyoe. By morning his mind raced with possibilities, and he spread out across his floor scrolls and maps, some of which he himself had inked over his years of study. He recited the wisdom of old masters and scrawled notes on possible courses of action. There were so many options to consider, so many men's temperaments to be taken into account and terrains to navigate. One thing he knew for certain: his father had no hope of winning any war if left to his own devices, and though he would not grieve for that loss, he feared what a sound defeat would mean for the lands he was meant to rule afterward, and how he would earn any respect from the generals and lords in such an aftermath.

"Rakuteru and Fuchihara are no more loyal to Lord Aritaka than Waseba was to my father," he explained to Yagi as they sat together alongside the maps, eating breakfast. "If they find strength elsewhere, they'll go to it. That strength must be me if I have any hope to survive, and I can only show it to them by bringing a victory."

"Rakuteru is a brute and Fuchihara a coward," said Yagi. "Why do you need them?"

"Because the two of them, along with your father, make up the strongest of Aritaka's generals. And if they trust in me, they'll support me over Hidemune, when that time comes." Kazuchiyo sighed. "Hidemune. I'd almost forgotten he wants me dead."

"That bitter fox of his won't get past me again," Yagi promised. "When we get back to Gyoe I'll wring Hidemune's neck for you."

Kazuchiyo hushed him, though reluctantly. "I don't know what Amai's really thinking, but at this point it doesn't seem he's still following those orders. Which might mean Hidemune will send someone else."

"Then I'll wring *their* neck." Yagi gulped down the rest of his rice. "Apparently I have a talent for it."

Kazuchiyo watched him thoughtfully for a moment. "We didn't get much time to talk after the battle on the hill," he said, measuring the words as he spoke them. "I know on the way there you said… you're not as fond of war as most think you are."

"I'm not," Yagi replied bluntly, "but I guess I'm pretty good at it, and I saved your life on the field. So I might as well keep at it."

Kazuchiyo couldn't help a chuckle. "You certainly are. And you certainly did. I'm grateful."

Yagi grumbled with embarrassment. "Don't thank me too much, because I plan on doing it a lot more anyway. It's going to get old." That only made Kazuchiyo chuckle more, and when he was certain there was no one passing the room, he kissed Yagi as a more welcome token of his gratitude.

They spent the next several days in relative calm. Utsukawa's men continued to fortify Ninari Castle to the point of absurdity, despite no information from their spies—Amai or any others—that Oihata was headed in their direction. Samurai and their soldiers continued to gather at Lord Aritaka's command, the lowest of them forced to make camp outside the fortress's eastern wall. Lord Aritaka himself overcame his peculiar temper tantrum but still declined to hold another council with his generals. The campaign, though off to an uninspiring start, would stubbornly continue.

Kazuchiyo passed the time in study, as well as tending to Hashikiri, sometimes taking him into the surrounding fields and woods to train with Mahiro. In the evenings he snuck from his room to meet Yagi at the baths. They stole precious, brief moments of intimacy together, hissing in the steam, exploring each other's bodies. They were hungry and foolish, as young lovers ought to be.

At the end of those days, Iomori arrived. But she did not come alone.

Ninari Castle opened its gates to twenty-five hundred new soldiers, many of which were carrying the yellow banners of Yaefu province to the east, where Mahiro and her brother had spent the last several years. Their soldiers were not as well-bred or as well-trained as the bulk of the Sakka force, but the same could also be said of their commander, Aritaka Hidemune himself.

Lord Aritaka and his generals gathered in the courtyard to receive their unexpected guest. He was not pleased to see his eldest son and made only a cursory effort to hide it. Kazuchiyo and Mahiro stood beside him, each baffled by and wary of the visit. The same sentiment was palpable from the accompanying generals, and all were hard-pressed not to share whispers as Hidemune dismounted alongside Iomori. If Hidemune was attuned to their discomfort, he did not show it.

"Father," he greeted, bowing his head. "I have come to aide you."

"If you're here, who's sitting in that big room in Gyoe?" goaded Mahiro. "Aren't you supposed to be running the place?"

"I gave those duties to Lord Oroshibe," said Hidemune, sounding deeply pleased with himself, as if the reassigning of his tasks to another required great skill. "And Mother can manage the castle itself."

"Those were not your orders," Aritaka reminded him coldly.

Hidemune did shed some of his smugness, or at least as much to bring him within reach of acceptability. "You summoned reinforcements," he reasoned. "The samurai of Yaefu were bound by loyalty to respond, and I have led them for years, protecting the east."

Mahiro gave a great snort that turned several heads. Hidemune glared at her. *"For many years,"* he repeated. "Your message said that Waseba is dead, and I am here to take his place."

Again Mahiro interjected with a great huff. "Take his place? At the vanguard, you mean?"

"Enough," said Aritaka, for he must have been as painfully aware as Kazuchiyo was of his generals shifting behind him. He turned his displeased scowl on Iomori. "Is this *your* doing?"

"Each person's actions are always their own doing, Lord Aritaka," said Iomori, her voice as rough and authoritative as ever. "You summoned me, and I am here. And your son is also here."

"So it would seem." Aritaka gave his head a great shake and turned back toward the keep. "Have the Yaefu soldiers join the others. Rest and take supper after your journey. Tomorrow I will hold council for you all."

His children and soldiers each bowed their head, and none spoke another word until after Aritaka had taken his leave. Only then did they disperse, sharing long, meaningful glances amongst themselves. Kazuchiyo looked to Iomori, hoping for a word and especially some privacy, but Hidemune stepped in front of him before he could catch her eye.

"Kazumune," Hidemune grunted, squaring his shoulders to him. All his earlier smugness returned to him. "Are you not glad to see your brother?"

"I am very glad," Kazuchiyo replied. "Though I did not think I would see you so soon." He had expected that when he faced Hidemune next he would feel a swell of righteous fury for the betrayal that nearly slit his throat, but in that moment he felt almost nothing. He had not once considered Hidemune a brother, and he had known since Aritaka first captured him that they could not possibly survive each other. In those circumstances, some betrayal was to be expected, perhaps.

"I heard you fought well at the battle of," Hidemune rolled his eyes, "whatever they're calling that village. Though you didn't take any heads."

"There weren't many heads taken in Father's name at all." Kazuchiyo could feel Yagi moving up alongside him. Goosebumps prickled his arms, and he hurried to anticipate what might come out of his lover.

But Yagi held still, watching Hidemune with a much more intimidating stare than Aritaka had mustered. "Welcome to Ninari Castle, Lord Hidemune," he muttered.

Hidemune eyed him in return. Though he was a proud man, he wasn't entirely without sense; he leaned back slightly beneath Yagi's intensity. "Who's this?"

"Brother, this is Ebara Motonobu," Kazuchiyo introduced him. "Son of General Ebara Toranobu."

"Ah, that's right." Hidemune relaxed again. "The infamous Yagi-douji. I don't suppose *you* took any heads?"

"No, but I killed a hundred men," said Yagi. Kazuchiyo found it difficult to keep from smiling as the truth of that statement made itself clear in Hidemune's rapidly paling face.

"And *I* killed a hundred and forty!" declared Mahiro. She grabbed Hidemune around the neck. He swore and tried unsuccessfully to shake her off. "Which means you're going to have to fight very well against the crows in the next one if you're going to compete with us!"

"Get off!" Hidemune finally wrestled free, and he glared at her as he straightened his armor. "The next one will be the last one," he growled. "I'll take both Oihata's heads myself!"

Mahiro continued to huff, but Kazuchiyo faced Hidemune without humor. "I'm looking forward to it. I've always wanted to see you on the field, brother."

Hidemune waited for him to qualify that statement or to smirk like Mahiro, but Kazuchiyo's unflinching "sincerity" wore him down. With a shake of his head much like their father, he pushed past them. "Then you will," he spat, and he continued on toward the keep.

"So *that's* your brother?" asked Yagi once he was gone. "The one who—"

"Yes," Kazuchiyo cut him off. "I never would have imagined he'd come on his own like this."

"He probably heard you did well taking over for Waseba," said Mahiro, settling her hands on her hips. "He can't out-glory you in front of our father if he's sitting at home in a castle."

"I'm sure you're right," said Kazuchiyo, though his chest tightened with sympathy as he watched uncertainty flicker across Mahiro's face. As despicable as he found the man, he was still Mahiro's brother. "We'll all have to do our best in the war to come."

Mahiro fixed him with a look he couldn't identify. She seemed to consider many responses before pasting her usual grin into place. "Then I'll outperform you both." She cast a smirk at Yagi as well. "And you, too. It'll be two hundred, next time."

"I'd like to see that," replied Yagi.

"You will!" Mahiro punched him in the arm and then followed after Hidemune. "Better hurry to supper, or he'll eat all the pork!"

Kazuchiyo followed, though at a slower pace, Yagi close beside him. "You did say he might send someone else," said Yagi, lowering his voice, "but it looks like he might want to do it himself."

"I doubt he'll risk getting his hands dirty." Kazuchiyo watched Mahiro bound into the keep. "There are plenty of ways to kill someone in war."

"I'll teach him a few if he tries anything."

Kazuchiyo smiled, swelling with reassurance. "You're too good to me, Yagi. I wish I could kiss you right now."

He stepped up onto the *engawa* leading into the keep, but before he could go farther Yagi tugged him back. Broad hands clasped his neck and drew him down for a kiss—hot and possessive, blinding Kazuchiyo to caution. His heart pounded, and when Yagi let him go, his knees trembled as if the wood had pitched under his feet.

"I don't care if they see," Yagi said, red-faced but resolute. He joined Kazuchiyo on the step, reaffirming his greater height. "I don't care if your father gets angry. They might as well all know that to get to you, they have to go through me first. Including Aritaka himself."

Kazuchiyo blinked up at him, speechless. Fear for whatever eyes might be on them held him back only a moment, and then he rose up on his toes, returning Yagi's kiss with his own. "I don't care either."

Despite having instigated the kiss, Yagi squirmed with embarrassment as Kazuchiyo withdrew. "Good," he said, and he marched into the keep, Kazuchiyo smiling to himself close behind.

CHAPTER NINETEEN

They ate supper on the keep's second floor with Mahiro and Hidemune. Hidemune talked loudly about the trip from Gyoe, such as it was, while Mahiro teased him. Kazuchiyo watched his brother closely, but he did not detect anything beyond his usual bitter demeanor.

Once the meal was complete, Yagi walked with Kazuchiyo to his chamber on the upper floor. They shared a kiss before the door, and Kazuchiyo clasped Yagi's hand tight. "I don't want you to risk too much for my sake. You're too important to me."

"You don't have to worry about me," Yagi promised in turn. "Call whenever you need me."

They kissed once more, and Yagi left for his own room. Kazuchiyo was still alight with romance, so he was taken by surprise when he opened the door to his room to find Master Iomori seated inside, waiting for him.

"That's very bold of you, Kazumune," she said with such dull inflection that he couldn't tell if she was chiding or praising him. "You know what your father will think."

Kazuchiyo stepped inside and closed the panel behind him. "Master Iomori. I was hoping to speak to you."

"And I, you. Hence my being here." She motioned to the

space before her; Kazuchiyo took a seat. "I hear you've endured many trials since leaving Gyoe, at least one of them in this room."

"The Kibaku assassin, you mean?"

"Yes." Iomori's brow raised slightly. "The Kibaku assassin."

Kazuchiyo returned her searching gaze with his own, wondering if he dared share the truth with her. "I hope I didn't overly concern you," he said. "I know you hold a special interest in my well-being."

"I do. I didn't spare your life those years ago to see it wasted so easily or so soon." She held her open palm out to him. "Did you make use of my gift?"

"The paper?" Kazuchiyo lifted his left hand, displaying the ribbon still tied around his wrist. "Or do you mean—"

Iomori snatched his wrist in a sudden, strangling grip. The hidden bead pressed hard into Kazuchiyo's tendons, and he thought of the heat he had detected from the thing during the hillside battle, when Waseba gurgled and died beneath his blade. The screams of dying soldiers filled his ears. Just as swiftly, Iomori released him and leaned back once more, composing herself as if she had never moved at all.

"Very bold indeed," she said, and Kazuchiyo felt a new rush of heat with the realization: she knew he'd killed Waseba.

"Master Iomori," he began, "won't you tell me—"

"Your father summoned me to assist in his war-making," Iomori spoke deliberately over him. "I'm certain he will ask me to entice General Oihata to march on Ninari Castle. What do you think of that?"

Kazuchiyo simmered. He considered ignoring her as well until she conceded to answer a question of his. A long look at her stoic face convinced him it wasn't worth the effort. "I think no power in this world would convince Oihata to kill himself on these walls."

"I agree." Iomori reached into the sleeve of her kariginu and pulled out a folded paper, which she spread on the mat in front of them. It was a rough map of Eastern Shuyun. "The rumors about him are true, after all: he *is* a gifted onmyouji. Not a match for me in any particular skill, but if I could wave my hand and convince your father's enemies to slaughter themselves, he would be shogun by now."

Kazuchiyo wound his fingers in his trousers. "But you have used your magic against his enemies before."

"Of course," said Iomori, though then she took his meaning, and she nodded in apology for the careless reference to his former family. "With Oihata even I must be cautious. I don't have a soldier's mind like him. Or like you."

She tapped the paper in front of her. "Where do you believe Oihata will attack?"

Kazuchiyo lowered his eyes. He scanned the narrow brush strokes that outlined their province, and south of that, his birthplace. The names of the castles and villages, forests and streams, bubbled up inside him. He tried to imagine which people still lived there, which temple his mother and remaining brother had been spirited away to. Would he even recognize the flowing hills if he returned?

Kazuchiyo swallowed and forced himself to look westward, where the border of Suyama met Kibaku. "If it were me, I would attack Sabi Castle," he said, pointing it out. "Kibaku held it once before, in my grandfather's time. It's close to their border, and the forests there have been expanding. An approaching army would be difficult to spot." He glanced at Iomori to judge her reaction. "If their spies are still watching Ninari as closely as they were before, they can see Lord Aritaka's forces and attention are focused too far north."

Iomori nodded, and she folded the map to stow back in her sleeve. "Have you ever been there?"

"Yes, as a boy." He leaned back, frowning. "It was promised to one of my elder brothers. I don't know who rules it now."

"I believe Aritaka gave it to the youngest of the three Waseba brothers," said Iomori as she pushed to her feet. "You may have an opportunity to settle with him as well."

Kazuchiyo's skin prickled as he stood. "Master Iomori,

I—"

"Hush, Kazumune," she interrupted him once again. She stepped closer, taking his shoulders. "Don't forget why it was I saved your life: I saw in you a great destiny, true to your name. Trust your judgment, and don't bother explaining yourself to me or to anyone else. Do you understand?"

"Yes," he replied, daring to hope that she was as much an ally as she had been claiming for years. "I understand."

"Very good." Iomori let go and stepped past him. "The Lady Satsumi is very well, by the way. She sends her warmest regards."

"I'm glad to hear it," he said, but when Iomori reached the exit, he gathered himself up. "Master Iomori."

She turned back to him expectantly, and he rallied his courage. "The assassin. He wasn't sent by Kibaku."

Iomori's face withered, as if she had suspected as much but had hoped not to be vindicated. "Keep my gift close to you," she said, and after they had exchanged bows, she departed.

Kazuchiyo moved to his window and gazed out over the clearing and the trees beyond. He tried to picture the rolling green of his homeland, full of apprehension and eagerness for the march that would have to come next. His musings were cut short by a rattle coming from his closet. He put one hand to the tanto tucked in his belt as he threw the panel open.

Amai peered down at him from a hole in the ceiling. "Is she gone?"

Kazuchiyo stepped back, allowing Amai to hop down into the closet proper. "What were you doing up there?"

"Hiding from your brother, of course." Amai smoothed down his robe and took a quick glance around the room. "Are you expecting more visitors?"

"Not tonight." Though wary, Kazuchiyo closed his window and made sure the front panel was firmly shut. "Did you know Hidemune was coming?"

"I wouldn't be here if I did," said Amai. He sat down close to the open closet as if anticipating having to streak into hiding again at any moment. "If he's here, he's probably brought some other fox with him. They'll want to know why you're still alive."

Kazuchiyo hesitated before joining him. He sat down closely enough that they could whisper. "What will you tell them?"

"That you're protected by a ferocious oni the likes of which Sakka Province has never seen. Which is as close to the truth as he needs to hear, if he hears that much at all, because I'm trying to avoid having to tell him *anything*."

Kazuchiyo frowned as he considered Amai. Though the shinobi was leaning in the open closet very casually, his manners as flippant as ever, there were cracks barely visible in his composure. Even the most slippery of eels was wise enough to fear a net.

"How many of my father's shinobi are better than you?" Kazuchiyo asked.

Amai feigned offense, but beneath Kazuchiyo's heavy stare he could not hold up that act for long. "If Hidemune were smart, he would have brought the lot of them," he boasted. "He's not, but I'm sure he'll at least have old man Nanpa with him. The one who trained me."

Kazuchiyo allowed himself a moment of curiosity. He knew very little about Lord Aritaka's spies, where they hailed from or what their training consisted of. His dragon father had not been fond of their manner of subterfuge, but he wondered then what type of man had raised this capricious youth to murder and seduce so effortlessly, to serve and betray as if each were a stroke from the same brush.

"Tomorrow, Iomori will give my father her counsel," said Kazuchiyo. "Preparations will take several days, and then the army will march to wherever Oihata is. You should remain here when we leave. If Hidemune and this 'Nanpa' desire my head, they'll have no reason to linger for you once I'm gone."

Amai raised an eyebrow. "A shinobi master is after your head, and you're asking the only shinobi on your side *not* to go with you?"

"Like you said," Kazuchiyo replied, "I'm protected by a ferocious oni the likes of which—"

"He's very good at spearing horses at ten meters," Amai interrupted. "Among other things, I'm sure." His lip quirked, and Kazuchiyo felt his cheeks redden. "But he's big, and he's loud, and if Hidemune doesn't know about you two, he will soon. If he's your spear I can be your hidden dagger, understand?"

Kazuchiyo leaned back. "If you speak ill of Yagi, I'll turn you in to Hidemune myself."

Amai huffed as if he were joking, but when Kazuchiyo only stared back at him, he was forced to reevaluate. "Don't be like that. You know I wasn't speaking ill of him. I'm only saying... there are things I can offer you that he can't."

He scooted closer so that their knees touched, and Kazuchiyo tensed. Amai was even bold enough to slide one hand to Kazuchiyo's thigh. "He's very strong, but I'm very quick." He followed suit with the other hand. "And I know all the tricks."

Kazuchiyo couldn't lean any farther back without bracing himself or falling. He tried to hide from Amai how uneasy he felt and had no idea as to his success. Amai was a slippery little beast, but Kazuchiyo still remembered the way his heart had thumped whenever he awoke to a folded paper on his pillow. He remembered the warmth of deceitful lips.

"I know you do," he replied carefully. "Tricks are all you have."

"A good match for you, then," retorted Amai. "Between my tricks and your manipulations, we'll have this war won in no time."

Kazuchiyo pushed Amai's hands off him, trying not to shiver at the slender fingers dragging down his thighs and off his knees. "My manipulations? You think I enjoy navigating these old men and their war games?"

Amai smirked. "It comes to you too naturally for me to think otherwise."

Kazuchiyo's stomach clenched with conflict, and he pushed to his feet. "You should leave before anyone finds you here."

"Did I strike a nerve?" Amai teased, but when he realized that Kazuchiyo was heading to the door, he hurried to his feet. "Kazu, wait." He gave chase and tugged at his elbow. "Wait, don't be mad," he said, only to grow playful again. "I'm sorry. You know I'm only being cruel because I'm jealous."

"Jealous?" It was too obvious for Kazuchiyo to even scoff at. "Of Yagi and me?"

"Shouldn't I be?" Amai stepped closer, still holding onto Kazuchiyo's elbow. His voice lowered to a purr. "The two of you get to sneak down to the bathhouse while I'm stuck here hiding in the walls. Won't you invite me down with you next time?"

Kazuchiyo prickled with heat, and he caught himself holding his breath. How shameful it seemed, for him to be so tempted by the sly curve of Amai's tender lips, when his bold champion tended to him so faithfully.

He swallowed, and Amai's eyes narrowed. The room began to swelter. "You should be happy enough that I allow you to hide in my walls," Kazuchiyo said before he could consider anything else. He pulled his arm free and slipped past him to start laying out his futon. "I haven't forgotten how you lied to and used me all those weeks."

"You take it too personally. I've done so much to make up for it since then." He watched Kazuchiyo lay the futon with that same little smirk. "It sure looks big enough to share."

"You can take the closet," said Kazuchiyo without looking up from his work. "It will be safer for you in there anyway, in case someone comes in."

"I'm not worried." Amai slid closer. "I may not be able to smell a drop of blood at fifty paces, but my ears—"

"The closet," Kazuchiyo insisted. "And in the morning you're going to tell me everything I need to know about Nanpa."

"All right, all right." Amai waited until Kazuchiyo was

looking at him to step backward into the closet. "Good night, Kazu," he said, and closed the panel.

Kazuchiyo stared at the closet door for a moment, expecting to hear Amai undressing or even climbing back up into the ceiling. What followed was silence so complete he wondered if Amai was not just standing in place, unmoving, waiting for him to drop his guard. At last Kazuchiyo shook his head and returned to his nighttime preparations. Even as he lay down to sleep, he heard not so much as a creak of the mats from Amai.

Come morning, he felt better prepared to face the man, gain what he needed from him, and not fall to any quips or charms. But when he opened the closet, Amai was long gone.

Kazuchiyo shared his breakfast with Yagi and Mahiro and the children of Aritaka's other generals. They were an interesting lot, some taking after their fathers too much, some not nearly enough. Fuchihara's daughter in particular did not resemble him at all in appearance, broad and muscular as she was, but in temperament was very much as nervous and fastidious. They were, in all, favorable company for Kazuchiyo. Several times throughout the meal one among the group would ask after Hidemune and why he had not chosen to join them, prompting another to supply a very studious and reasonable answer that nonetheless drew smirks from the rest. Even Mahiro joined in. Kazuchiyo offered no questions or suppositions of his own, though he did enjoy them.

Afterward, he was invited to the upper level of the keep to confer with his father. If Mahiro was put out about not being included, she covered it well, promising to spoil Hashikiri for him. As Kazuchiyo ascended he could not help but wonder if Amai was hiding in the walls to listen in, or else, if Hidemune's new shinobi might be.

Lord Aritaka was waiting for him in the broad, low-ceilinged chamber, Iomori at his side. Hidemune stood among the generals, looking none too pleased for it. Kazuchiyo seated himself beside his brother, as was expected of him, though it made his flesh crawl. They shared only enough of a bow to meet their obligations.

Aritaka wasted no time for pleasantries, forced or otherwise. "I have news. Our scouts tell us that Koedzuka has sent fresh troops to reinforce protections of the village, led by one of his lesser generals, but old man Oihata can keep his meager fields. Utsukawa will remain here with his men while the rest of us march south. We will be met at the Suyama border by General Hosoda and his men and continue to Sabi Castle on the western front."

Kazuchiyo took in a slow, deep breath. "Is that where we believe General Oihata will be?"

"The whelp, at least." Aritaka hesitated to admit the embarrassing truth. "He and his men are already underway. He'll likely use the forests there as cover for his advance."

Kazuchiyo looked to Iomori in time to see the corner of her lip turn up a sliver. He did not have time to consider replying, as Hidemune rustled beside him.

"Kazumune should be very familiar with those woods," he said. "He must have a great deal of insight for us."

"I'll aid our father in any way I can," Kazuchiyo replied. "Though I was not more than eight years old the last time I visited Sabi Castle. I don't know that my insight will be much use."

Hidemune snorted as if Kazuchiyo had admitted to some weakness, though none of the assembly were impressed by his half-wit attempts at embarrassment.

"In three days, we march," resumed Lord Aritaka. "The roads will be clear and Iomori promises good weather, so we should make excellent time. Time enough to cut off the crow's head before it causes too much trouble. With Utsukawa and this fortress guarding the north, Gyoe will remain untouchable."

Aritaka looked from one to the next with defiance. "Does

anyone advise otherwise?"

His generals and sons bowed in unison. "No, my lord."

"Very well." Pleased, Aritaka leaned back. "All but Kazumune are dismissed."

The generals departed, Hidemune casting his brother a hateful look in the process. Iomori lingered, assuming herself exempt, until a gesture from Aritaka told her otherwise. Though displeased, she showed herself out among the rest, until only the two of them remained.

"Come closer," said Aritaka, and Kazuchiyo did so, seating himself directly across from his father.

Aritaka considered him for a long time, unspeaking, allowing Kazuchiyo's imagination too much space to flourish. But he was too well-practiced to be tricked into speaking hastily, and he waited. At last, Aritaka cleared his throat and said, "This is going to be a trying time for you."

Kazuchiyo waited for him to say more, knowing that his patience would last longer than his father's. Then he reconsidered; having finally seen the childish reality of Aritaka's hidden temperament, it was time to employ a different strategy.

"Not as trying as it will be for you, Father," he said, bowing his head a hair—just enough that he would not seem too forward or aggressive. "I know you're worried about my loyalty once I'm in my homeland."

Aritaka curled his fists against his knees. "Should I be?"

Kazuchiyo was beginning to see that this beast had no teeth, and he did not falter. "I can't promise that I won't be tempted," he said, allowing emotion into his voice that Aritaka was not used to hearing. "We'll be joining some of my father's old samurai, men and women I knew as a boy, and was betrayed by. I'm certain some of them still harbor thoughts of vengeance against you. I don't know that I can shut my ears to them completely."

Kazuchiyo took in a deep breath and looked to Aritaka's face, which was red and stony. "But I can promise that however I might be tempted, I am not a fool. You've raised me well. I'm stronger now than I would have been if not for you, even if it's sometimes painful to admit. I value that strength a great deal, and I see now how important it is that all of Eastern Shuyun be united under one banner."

Aritaka leaned back, watching him, wanting to believe him. Were he less a villain it may have been pitiable, and maybe someday, someone will tell his story as a tragedy. But I have only a teacup full of sympathy for the man, and Kazuchiyo none.

"Our enemies are in the west," Kazuchiyo said. "My reason will never let me forget that. If any samurai of Suyama makes an offer of rebellion to me, then they've betrayed their lord twice over and will be put to death."

The tension diffused from Aritaka's clenched fists, and his shoulders slowly relaxed. "Our enemies are in the west," he agreed. "It relieves me, that one of you knows that."

Kazuchiyo frowned slightly. "One of us?"

Aritaka pulled a face and looked away. "What do you think of Hidemune joining the march?"

"I think the soldiers he's brought will serve us well in the campaign," said Kazuchiyo, feeling emboldened to take on another of Aritaka's tests. "And… I think he wants to prove his mettle on the field, in the hopes of overshadowing me."

"You're very blunt today," said Aritaka, but it did not sound as if he disapproved. "Yes, I think so, too. And he'll get his chance. You both will." He gathered himself and nodded to Kazuchiyo. "I know you're no fool, Kazumune. Though I worry about…"

He frowned, and Kazuchiyo straightened up, ready to meet whatever new challenge was about to be laid before him. Perhaps Aritaka saw too much of his resolve, or perhaps his courage faltered, because he shook his head. "Nevermind. You're dismissed now. Expect for me to call on you often as we march south."

Kazuchiyo bowed to the floor. "I am yours to command, Father."

He left the chamber, and by the time he had reached his own room he couldn't remember the path he'd taken there. His mind was alight with scheming: the longer he continued his feud with Hidemune, the greater the risks. If Aritaka was more easily swayed than Kazuchiyo originally believed, perhaps now was the time to force him to choose between his two sons, especially when any new assassination attempt could be caught in the act. If he could provide proof of Hidemune's treachery even before that risk made itself manifest, all the better, and if proof existed, only one man would possess it.

"Amai!" he hissed, throwing open the closet door. There was no sign of him there. Kazuchiyo gripped the opening in the ceiling and tried to climb up, managing only a glimpse of the narrow space between the beams. He dropped to the floor again, muttering, "Never when I need him."

Kazuchiyo prepared ink and brush, and on a small scrap of paper he scrawled: *Do you have proof?* Trusting Amai to understand well enough, he tucked the paper into the ceiling and hurried on to his duties about the castle.

The day passed in a flurry of preparation. Now that the army had decided on a direction, supplies were lashed to wagons all over again, armor polished and spears assembled. Hidemune made himself as visible as possible during it all, barking commands and directing his men. It did not seem to impress anyone. Kazuchiyo gave him a wide berth and only had to suffer the occasional glare as he carried out his own responsibilities.

After a quick supper, Kazuchiyo caught Yagi's eye, and the pair retreated up to his chamber high in the keep. There was still no sign of Amai.

"I don't know why you worry about him," said Yagi, leaning against the wall with a small gourd of saké he had pilfered from supper. "He's a shinobi. Disappearing is what they do."

239

"I wanted to ask him something." Kazuchiyo gave up his fruitless vigil of the closet and joined Yagi beneath the window. "At Gyoe, I saw Hidemune leave a message for him in the castle wall. If Amai still has that message, it may be useful as proof against Hidemune, and reveal his treachery to our father."

"I thought you had decided *not* to reveal that."

Yagi offered him the sake, and Kazuchiyo took a long drink. "We have to keep up the pretense for the sake of this war," he explained. "But Amai thinks Hidemune will have brought along some other shinobi to try and take my head. If they make an attempt, *then* we can force Aritaka's hand."

Yagi sat up straighter, his expression hardening. "He's going to try to kill you again?"

"If he wants any hope of keeping his inheritance, he'll have to."

Yagi took the gourd back and stoppered it. "Then I'm not leaving this room."

He said it with such conviction that Kazuchiyo couldn't help but smile. "They won't come *now*," he reassured him. "It would be too suspicious. They'll probably wait until we're in the middle of the fight so it can look like I was killed by the enemy…"

Kazuchiyo lowered his eyes as a chill came over him. "Like I did," he finished quietly. He couldn't stop thinking about Amai's careless accusation. How easy it had been to manipulate Aritaka's trust, and how eagerly he awaited the moment he could convince the man to put his own son to death. How unprepared Waseba had been for his own honorless treachery. His armor on display in the corner of the room bore a new helmet now, one of his own, but he remembered the weight of Waseba's bloody helm. He saw himself from the outside and shuddered.

Yagi gave him no time to be despondent. He dragged Kazuchiyo into his lap and kissed the side of his throat, so firmly he may have left a mark. It seemed a well-meant act of desperation, and Kazuchiyo wilted in his arms, startled by his voracity.

"I won't let anyone hurt you," Yagi promised, "no matter who comes, or how, or when."

"Yagi…" Kazuchiyo shivered, and though there was caution in his mind, his heart claimed a temporary victory as he leaned close to his mouth. "Once we leave the castle, we'll both be in danger," he said, already beginning to loosen the tie around Yagi's waist. "We won't be able to afford distractions."

"I won't be distracted," Yagi replied immediately, though he soon after took Kazuchiyo's meaning. With another kiss he crawled forward, spilling Kazuchiyo onto the mats. The press of his broad, heavy body was almost more than Kazuchiyo could bear; he clung to Yagi's shoulders as if they were rocks along a riverbank, to keep from being swept away. Yagi was, as always, as gentle as his oni makeup allowed, his hands soothing and his kisses long.

"Wait," Kazuchiyo whispered. He could not help his gaze being drawn again to the closet. "What if he really is still hiding in the walls…?"

Yagi followed the direction of his stare. He did not seem as bothered by the suggestion as Kazuchiyo thought he might be. "Then let him watch." He dragged Kazuchiyo's robe off his shoulders as he kissed him again.

Kazuchiyo shivered as he allowed Yagi to undress him. They slipped naked into the futon and twisted together until morning, all the while titillated by the possibility of a watchful audience.

CHAPTER TWENTY

Once all suitable preparations had been made, Aritaka Souyuu set out from Ninari Castle with two sons, one daughter, seven generals, and just over six thousand soldiers.

They traveled south along Sakka's western border, through dry and sloping foothills, the weather as fair as Iomori had promised. Kazuchiyo rode toward the center with his family, Yagi close behind him the whole way. Though it would have been appropriate for Yagi to instead travel alongside his father and their soldiers, no one dared tell him so. Even when it was time to make camp, Yagi remained stubbornly with his lord. Though Kazuchiyo still believed Hidemune would not make any attempt on his life so early in the campaign, he was glad for the company. He slept well with Yagi's head against his chest, occasionally soothing away his dream-state grumbles.

On the third day they arrived at Hibayashi Fort, itself settled on a hilltop, though still deep in mountain shadows by evening. There was no central keep, but the walls were sturdy and topped with tall watchtowers. As the soldiers made camp in the valley below, Kazuchiyo and Yagi climbed to the top of the easternmost tower to get a clear view of the surrounding land.

Many small villages dotted the hills and valleys to the east, their rice paddies cutting into the slopes. The trees were vibrant green, having recently shed their flowers to prepare for plums. Beyond them lay thick forests sprawling down into the plain. Just past them, sunk deep below the visible horizon, lay Shimegahara. Kazuchiyo wondered if the grass was still packed down from the weight of every felled body, the burden of tens of thousands of souls.

"Can you see your home village from here?" he asked, drawing his mind away from somber thoughts. "Terado?"

"It's that one on the highest hill," said Yagi.

"Do you miss it there?"

Yagi snorted. "They were fine enough people. But no." He turned toward the south. "Can you see Suyama from here?"

"Almost." Kazuchiyo pointed into the distance. "That tall hill with the old tree on top? Beyond that hill is Suyama territory, and Sabi Castle. The tree itself is called Hebine. Its roots poke out of the ground in many places, so you have to watch your footing after dark." Kazuchiyo smiled with nostalgia. "Everyone says the roots are actually snakes that slither about at night, tripping trespassers on purpose."

Yagi watched him closely. "How do you feel? Seeing your homeland again?"

Kazuchiyo's smile faded, and he wasn't sure what to make of the weight in his chest, be it anticipation or dread. "I don't know," he admitted, and he led them back down into the fort.

The next day was spent in preparation as even more soldiers joined them from the surrounding villages, the day after that in travel. They camped in the valley at the base of the hill that served as Sakka's southern border, and it was then that Kazuchiyo first heard the news that none of their scouts had reported back from Sabi Castle.

"Two men set out on horseback this morning," related

Hidemune, though clearly he resented having to do so. "One was meant to return straight away with news from the castle, but there's been no sign of him. Father sent another as we were making camp."

Kazuchiyo stared up at the towering hillside, at the branches of the ancient maple tree that had stood there for as long as anyone could remember. It was already mostly dark from evening shadow. "Oihata had a head start on us," he said. "Kibaku's capital is just across the border from Sabi. Plenty of time for them to have marched on the castle."

"I don't care if he is a master onmyouji, no army could take Sabi Castle in a matter of days." Hidemune scoffed. "Shouldn't you have more faith in your father's defenses?"

Kazuchiyo glanced to him, weary of his many childish attempts to out-fox or insult him in such a transparent manner. "Brother, can we not have a truce?" he asked, perhaps thinking too highly of the success his recent boldness had earned him. "It wasn't either of us that put ourselves in this position. There's no need for us to quarrel."

Hidemune regarded him coldly, and the tenor of his malice took on a deeper intensity. "Will you tell Father you don't want to be his heir? That you'll give up any claim to his lands or fortunes, go live as a monk or a priest, like your mother and brother?"

Kazuchiyo stared straight back. "No," he said truthfully. "Even if I said I would, you'd never believe me any more than I'd believe you."

"There. See? Then one of us has to die." Hidemune set a hand on his sword as if he were tempted to do the deed then and there, but Kazuchiyo knew that despite his faults, he couldn't afford to be that impulsive. "Don't forget that you're the intruder here. Father brought you home to *replace* me. So no, we can't have a truce." He turned his back on Kazuchiyo, adding, "I'll see you on the field," as he stalked off.

Kazuchiyo watched him go and then turned back toward the hill, the forests of bamboo creeping up its lower slope, the handsome maple at its peak. He wondered if it would bring him or his family any peace, if he were to at least die in his homeland. Better to settle his bones in the sweeping bamboo, the cloud-touched peaks of the dragonland. But then he thought of his beloved Suyama in the hard, clumsy hands of his ghoulish foster brother. His home and his people deserved far better, and he could give it to them, as long as he outwitted and outlived Aritaka Hidemune.

He heard Yagi call for him and quickly made his way back to the camp.

The army disembarked come morning. General Hosoda and his men, the newest addition to their forces, led the march along the eastern slope of the great hill. For the first time since they had set out from Ninari, the morning was dimmed with fog, with only hazy sunlight to burn it away. Kazuchiyo's mind was still on the missing scouts when they rounded the hill's base, and he was granted his first look of his home in five years.

Even in the cloudy dawn, the countryside was a handsome sight, perhaps even more so because of it. The many hills and deep valleys were vibrant and green with spring, cherry blossoms in bloom. In the far distance the hills grew steeper, craggy preludes to the mountains beyond that sheltered ancient guardian spirits. Somewhere past that breathtaking landscape, high atop Suyama's grand plateau, sat the castle Tengakubou where Kazuchiyo had passed his youth. Kazuchiyo strained his eyes and convinced himself a time or two that he had glimpsed its majestic silhouette, despite how unlikely that was given the distance. Once he had secured himself as Aritaka's heir, perhaps he would distinguish himself to the extent that he would be allowed to visit. It would belong to him twice over by then, after all. His heart ached for it.

He drew his attention closer, searching for smaller huts and villages, but he could make out very little, and to his surprise and shame, he couldn't remember exactly where any of them ought to be, nor their names. His second eldest brother had once been declared Sabi Castle's future lord and had spent weeks at a time traveling between the surrounding villages, learning the countryside as best he could. He had spoken of it so often. Try as he might, Kazuchiyo could remember almost nothing but the enthusiasm in his voice—barely even the shape of his face.

Their path curved westward, and Kazuchiyo turned away, determined not to dwell on it. Hosoda and his men had already thinned their ranks to fifteen men abreast and were entering the forest path that would take them to Sabi Castle. Tall stalks of bamboo, thick as a man's thigh, towered over the old road and crowded together as far as could be seen on either side. Not a breath of wind stirred. As Kazuchiyo crossed the forest boundary he felt a chill, unused to watching such tall trunks stand at such strict, unmoving attention. Normally a forest like this would be alive with the calls of birds and other animals, the unseen tips of ancient bamboo clinking and rustling together. For half an hour they marched amidst near silence into the dreary dark.

"I smell blood," said Yagi. Kazuchiyo looked left and right, though he could still see only mist, and green bamboo climbing out of it.

"An animal?" he suggested, with uncharacteristic optimism.

"I doubt it," said Yagi, and he readied his spear.

The first arrow was meant for Lord Aritaka; how different this tale would be, if not for one of the flag bearers thoughtlessly shifting his burden just enough that the arrow met only wood. The *thunk* of its strike alerted the column, though so few had seen the narrow shaft that every man looked for the enemy in a different direction.

The assault came swiftly after. The caravan was cast into disarray as luckier arrows found throats and temples and gaps in armor. Aritaka's bannermen flocked to him, shielding him and Hidemune from the sudden onslaught, as the captains shouted for order.

Kazuchiyo could make out among the trees a line of hunched figures, draped in cloaks of woven bamboo twigs and leaves, firing into the heart of Sakka's army. An arrow struck his shoulder guard and he flinched, the vibration of it rattling him.

"Ambush!" shouted Hosoda. His keen insight was rewarded with an arrow to his jaw that left him swooning.

To go forward, or to go back? With Hosoda's two thousand men stretched thin ahead of him, Kazuchiyo could not see the path well enough to know if Kibaku soldiers had already closed them off. Three times that number blocked a retreat to the rear, some of them not yet even in the forest and unaware of what was happening. Every second spent in indecision felt like hours as shouts rang up and down the line.

Then Iomori raised her arm, and a gust of wind surged outward from the road like monsoon waves. In seconds the fog was cleared, laying bare the Kibaku ambush party: rows of archers on either side of the path, and behind them, soldiers in full armor waiting with spears at the ready. At the center stood a samurai on horseback wearing green and gold armor, a full moon crest atop their helm. Kazuchiyo recognized the warrior as one who had accompanied Naoya to Waseba's tent, and from the field afterward.

"There the cowards are!" shouted Mahiro. She turned her horse toward the commander, her naginata raised. "We outnumber them! Attack!" Without waiting for a word from anyone else, she charged from the column.

One of Hosoda's captains heeded her call, shouting for the wounded ranks to support her. At last Aritaka spurred to proper response. "Break their line!" he shouted, even as he turned his horse about. "Hold them back, guard the retreat!"

"Make way!" General Ebara signaled for his troops to divide across the road, sending them out against the already retreating archers while clearing a path for Aritaka. "Protect your lord! Call Rakuteru to the front!"

"What are you doing?" Yagi demanded, and Kazuchiyo startled, still partially numbed by the vibrations of the arrow in his shoulder guard. "Get out of here!"

Hashikiri swayed uneasily, and Kazuchiyo struggled to bring him back under control. "But Mahiro—" He looked back to the unfolding battle and spotted Mahiro cutting down archers as they fled. Her aim was the commander beyond them, even as a dozen spearmen moved to intercept her. Just when it seemed she and Suzumekage might be impaled on their crossblades, she leapt atop her saddle and then jumped, sailing over all danger to crash directly into the samurai's chest. The pair of them tumbled to the ground in a clashing tangle.

Yagi cursed loudly; Kazuchiyo sat dumbstruck. "I've got her," said Yagi, and he spurred his horse on, leaving the roadside. "Retreat with the others!"

But Kazuchiyo did not retreat. He could not bear to, here in his homeland, eager to prove himself valiant while his cowardly rival Hidemune fled. He watched Mahiro clamber to her feet and begin attacking the spearmen who were attempting to surround her and rescue their commander. The Kibaku soldiers truly were outnumbered, and with the added threat of Yagi barreling toward them—a fearsome, bellowing sight—many were already retreating. But the samurai Mahiro had unseated would not, batting away her naginata with controlled, elegant sweeps of their longsword.

Kazuchiyo and Hashikiri joined the fray. He did not know what he intended to do, did not even draw his sword at first as he rushed toward the chaotic melee. He watched Mahiro circle her opponent and then strike, swift and violent, her naginata catching in the moon emblem and ripping the helmet free.

Waves of thick, jet-black hair fell across the samurai's armor, and though Kazuchiyo could not see their face, he *could* see Mahiro's light up in a grin. Just before one of the spearmen stabbed her in the side.

Mahiro howled and spun, but Yagi lopped the man's head off before she had the chance to counter. Her confusion gave the samurai commander enough time to reclaim their horse, and as they climbed into the saddle Kazuchiyo finally got a good look.

It was a woman, and unlike one Kazuchiyo had ever seen, with a dark complexion, heavy, thick eyebrows, and a long, sloping nose. She was unmistakably not from Shuyun. "Pull back!" she ordered in a thick accent, and her soldiers obeyed, abandoning their defense against Yagi to retreat at full pace deeper into the forest.

"Cowards!" Yagi hollered, adjusting the grip on his spear. He looked ready to run them down, but it was then that Kazuchiyo realized he could still hear the twang of bowstrings up and down the forest path.

"Yagi, stop!" He hurried closer, boxing Mahiro in between their two horses before she could get it in her mind to give chase as well. "It's another trap," he said, pointing to where the Kibaku archers who had originally fled were reforming their line farther in, their soldiers doing the same behind them. "They're trying to lure our army deeper and deeper into the woods to stretch us thin."

Mahiro growled as she pulled herself back into Suzumekage's saddle. "Let them!" she spat, though she gritted her teeth with the effort of righting herself. "We still outnumber them. Cut them down!"

"No." Kazuchiyo maneuvered in front of Suzumekage, who snorted and pawed. He gulped and could sense the same intimidation from Hashikiri but was resolute. "Mahiro, you're injured, Father is safely away. We have to regroup and retreat!"

As he spoke, another arrow streaked between them, close enough that both their horses whickered in alarm. It was motivation enough, and though Mahiro cast one more long glare at the Kibaku soldiers, she at last uttered a curse and turned to retreat. "Everyone, get the fuck out of the woods!" she shouted, and she raised her naginata like a banner as she weaved her way back to the road.

Kazuchiyo and Yagi followed close behind. "Retreat!"

Kazuchiyo shouted along the way, as loudly as he could. "Full retreat!" He saw General Hosoda's men struggling to keep the unconscious man in his saddle, and he rode closer. "You!" he ordered, pointing to one of the captains. "Get into the saddle with him."

"But this is the general's horse," the man said, aghast.

"I am your lord's son—do as I say!" Kazuchiyo insisted, with such force that the man hurried to obey. With the captain seated he was able to take the reins and spur the horse onward, following the rest of the army in retreat.

At last, the remaining Sakka army emerged from the bamboo forest. In the field beyond Lord Aritaka had set his soldiers into ranks, archers at the ready, prepared to defend against any Kibaku soldiers that might follow. None did. Kazuchiyo did not bother to look back as he rode to rejoin his father.

Aritaka gruffly looked him over. His eyes stalled on the arrow sticking out of his shoulder. "Are you injured?"

"No, Father." Kazuchiyo gripped the arrow and yanked it free, trying to hide his shudder as he did.

"Good." Aritaka faced forward again. "You should have retreated when I ordered it."

Kazuchiyo faced forward as well, refusing to acknowledge Hidemune's stony glare. "Please excuse me, Father. I was disoriented."

"Come and fight!" Mahiro bellowed at the forest. Atop Suzumekage she paced back and forth along the line, still gripping her naginata despite the blood soaking into her pant leg. "Come stand and fight, woman!"

"Mahiro *is* injured," Kazuchiyo told his father, though he knew she'd likely give him an earful for it later. "She shouldn't be on the line."

Aritaka shifted in his saddle, conflict clear on his face; he knew if he called Mahiro back, she would not obey in the state she was in, and now was no time for embarrassments. Thankfully, Iomori took it upon herself to intervene. She urged her horse into Mahiro's path, and when Mahiro began to curse at her, she said only a few words that Kazuchiyo could not make out. Miraculously, they were enough, and with scowls thrown at the forest Mahiro at last followed her back behind the front line.

"I'll tend to her," Iomori assured her lord as they passed.

"Come back quickly," Aritaka replied.

The pair headed toward the rear, and with a sigh of relief, Kazuchiyo turned to Yagi. "What about you?" he asked, noting the splashes of blood against his armor. "You're not hurt?"

"Of course not." Yagi looked like he was about to say more, but then he changed his mind. "We'll talk later," he said, and he sounded cross enough that for the first time Kazuchiyo felt an inkling of apprehension at the prospect.

They waited outside the forest for over an hour. Several times Aritaka ordered his archers to advance and fire into the tree line, hoping to provoke a reaction, to no avail. Mahiro returned with Iomori, full of fury, resuming her pacing though not the taunts. There was not one glimpse of Kibaku samurai through the trees.

CHAPTER TWENTY-ONE

Soon dusk would be upon them, and so Aritaka ordered a
withdrawal from the forest. They marched east for an hour
to get out of easy range, and there set up camp to regroup and
re-strategize.

"Cowards as ever!" Aritaka ranted as he paced back and
forth across the war tent. "Can these flightless birds never stand
and fight?"

"Calm yourself, my lord," said Iomori, and Aritaka's
generals relaxed with relief at her interference. "We have
suffered some losses, but not great ones. And now we know
Kibaku's strategy."

Aritaka scoffed mightily. "Their strategy of attacking from
darkness and fleeing when confronted?"

"Precisely," said Iomori, which gave him pause. "From this
attack we can discern many things, and use them to plan our
counter-strategy."

Aritaka took a seat to listen. "Go on."

Iomori's posture was already impeccable, but she seemed
to grow more composed as all eyes in the tent turned to her.
"We know that Kibaku has spread their army throughout the
forest. Their numbers are great enough to feel confident in

challenging ours, but not so great as to chase us onto an open field. It could be that these are not Oihata's men, but a smaller force sent by Lord Koedzuka to enclose Sabi Castle and stall our forces until a greater army can reinforce them."

"I beg your pardon, Master Iomori," said Kazuchiyo, "but these *are* Oihata's soldiers. I recognized their commander from our meeting on the hill. She was among his honor guard."

"She?" repeated Aritaka, and the generals exchanged glances.

"Yes, a foreign woman, wearing a full-moon crest." Kazuchiyo looked to General Ebara. "Did you see her, general?"

Ebara leaned back with arms folded. "Oh, yes. Now I recall. But I didn't notice it was a woman."

"I've heard no report of such a woman in Kibaku's army," said Aritaka, which was enough for Hidemune to feel the need to interject with his opinion as well.

"What difference does it make?" he grumbled. "Man or woman, like Iomori says, we outnumber them. They couldn't have taken Sabi already, so we'll have them march out of the castle, and we'll surround and destroy these troublesome crows."

Iomori cast Kazuchiyo a sideways look, but he did not need her encouragement to speak his own mind. "Kibaku's Ugarasu Castle is not far from here," he said, focusing on Lord Aritaka. "They have plenty of soldiers to send. If they chose instead to send Oihata's troops, who have already been to battle and marched days to get here, it's for a reason. There must be a larger force we haven't seen yet."

Hidemune bristled, but seeing the other generals nod in agreement, he bit his tongue.

The square-jawed General Rakuteru spoke up. "Is there no way to send a messenger to Sabi Castle? They will have greater insight than us."

"None of our messengers have returned," said Aritaka. "What about your tricks, Master Iomori?"

"I sent a message of my own just after we left the forest,"

253

Iomori confirmed. "But I have not received any response either. If Oihata himself is among them, he's likely intercepting."

"Is your magic not more powerful than his?" asked Fuchihara, sniffing.

"It doesn't work that way," replied Iomori, with a crossness that suggested she had no intention of explaining more than that.

"Then there must be some other way to get word to the castle," Rakuteru insisted. "A small force sent to scale the hill from the eastern or northern slope, away from the forest. They would be exposed, but if even one man makes it through, we can have General Waseba charge the Kibaku flank."

Kazuchiyo flinched at the name, only to remember that it was the youngest of Waseba's brothers that he was referring to. "Kibaku will be watching the hill closely," he said. "They'll certainly be intercepted."

Rakuteru nodded but was undeterred. "With a strong enough collection of soldiers, that won't matter."

"Send that oni of yours," suggested Hidemune.

Kazuchiyo's gaze snapped to him with the swiftness of a cobra. "No."

Hidemune smirked, emboldened by Kazuchiyo's reaction. "He brags so often of the number of men he's killed. Why not put him to the test? No one has a better chance of breaking a Kibaku ambush than him."

"No," Kazuchiyo repeated with such authority that eyebrows raised about the tent. "Motonobu is made of strength, not speed or stealth." He wound his fists in his pant legs. "Better that you send one of your shinobi, brother."

Hidemune glared back at him, and Kazuchiyo refused to relent. It wasn't until Lord Aritaka cleared his throat that he dared turn his eyes away, and then he realized how closely each of the generals was studying their brief but meaningful exchange. They were choosing sides. Every one of them must have been fully aware of the feud playing out in their midst, and every one of them was gauging their own chances of victory.

"What say you, Iomori?" said Aritaka. "You implied we had reason for optimism, but you haven't given us any solutions yet."

"Taking young Lord Kazumune's intel into account, there can only be one conclusion," she said. "That Oihata's men, being fierce and loyal, have been sent out only to harry us, and to prevent us from contacting our allies. The bulk of the Kibaku army must being laying siege to the castle, or at least preventing those inside from marching. Maybe they think they can draw us into a trap while trying to rescue them, or maybe they're simply stalling."

"We could burn the forest," Fuchihara suggested. "Flush them out."

"They anticipated our fire attack the first time, back at Oihata's village," countered Ebara. "They'll be even more prepared for it now. Besides, you'd be trapping Waseba and his forces inside the castle."

"Enough arguing and speculation," said Aritaka. "I want to hear from my two sons." He cast each of them a measuring look. "What would either of you do?"

"Send a troop up the hill," Hidemune said immediately. "Making contact with Sabi Castle should be our main concern. How can we fight these dishonorable crows without their information?" He smirked at Kazuchiyo. "I'll send my men from Yaefu if he'll send his oni."

Kazuchiyo forced himself not to return the taunting glare, saving his full focus for Aritaka. "My brother is right. We outnumber the Kibaku force, for certain. Keeping us from the forest is only a means to stall us while they starve out Sabi Castle. We should launch a full assault on the forest."

The surrounding generals showed surprise—some of it approving, some of it far less so. "With so little intel?" said Fuchihara, already a shade paler. "You'd charge into the woods without any idea of where Oihata is or how many men he has?"

"'Your foe may be wise,'" Kazuchiyo quoted. "'Or he may be a fool; still, defy him, always.' We must never do what our

255

enemy expects or wants us to do. If Oihata's intention is to stall, then we attack at once."

"Very well," said Aritaka. Everyone looked to him, surprised to have an answer from him so quickly. "In that case, we will do both."

Hidemune swelled with accomplishment; Kazuchiyo tightened his fists against his knees. Before either could voice a response, Aritaka continued. "Hidemune will select a captain among his Yaefu soldiers to lead a band up the hill and attempt to contact Sabi Castle. We will use our push through the forest to force Oihata back. But Ebara Motonobu will join the vanguard with his father, where he belongs." He stroked his whiskers. "I have not seen the infamous Yagi-douji display his strength in many years. I'll take the chance to do so now."

Hidemune scowled as he lowered his head to the floor. "As you command, Father."

Kazuchiyo bowed deeply, too. "Yes, Lord Father."

Aritaka went on to describe the formation for the battle, with Ebara and Rakuteru's forces at the front spanning a wide line across the forest entrance to prevent any attempts to flank them. Kazuchiyo listened closely to every word, trying to paint a picture of the coming battle in his mind. He wanted to plan for every possible contingency so that he would never be seized with motionless panic again.

It was dark by the time they were dismissed, and Kazuchiyo was eager to return to his tent, knowing that Yagi would be waiting. He made it no more than a few steps before Iomori approached him, and he was forced to stop and offer her a courtesy bow. "Master Iomori, what can I do for you?"

"You've become very bold, Kazumune," she said, and though her voice was flat, the tilt of her chin suggested approval. "But you should be more careful."

"I can't afford to be meek. I must make my father proud."

"And I am certain you will. I've seen it, after all." She leaned in closer, her voice lowering in secrecy. "But you mustn't let your judgment be clouded. Tell me you didn't advocate a blind charge just to save your precious oni from death on the hillside."

Kazuchiyo gulped, but he remained resolute. "My judgment," he said firmly, "has never been clouded. Father asked for my advice, and I gave it. I stand by it."

"Very well, then." She nodded. "May the gods watch over you on the battlefield." Then she left, and Kazuchiyo hurried on to his tent.

A lantern was already lit inside, and as he approached he could hear a pair of familiar voices conversing. He pushed open the flap to find Yagi blocking Amai into a corner of the tent, his hands on his hips, making every attempt to intimidate the shinobi.

"Kazu!" Amai declared as soon as he spotted him. "Tell this oaf of yours that I'm welcome here, won't you?"

Kazuchiyo made sure the flap closed behind him as he entered. "What's going on?"

"He was trying to steal from your rations." Yagi gestured to the meal that had been laid out.

"I was only looking for a taste," Amai retorted. "Not everyone in the camp is getting a strip of dried herring tonight, you know."

Kazuchiyo loosened the cords on his armor and was flattered but a bit embarrassed when Yagi approached to help him with it. "You can have mine," he said, enduring Yagi's sour look. "But only if you have some news for me."

"There you go again. Always negotiating." Amai straightened his robes as he took a seat near the food, but when he reached for one of the bowls, Kazuchiyo chided him with a tap from his foot.

"News first," he said.

Amai rolled his eyes in dramatic fashion. "You could have some sympathy, you know. I've been through a lot because of you."

"If you regret not ending my life as ordered, that's your own business." Kazuchiyo finished shedding his armor with

257

Yagi's help, and the pair of them took their seats. At closer range he could see that Amai wasn't speaking entirely in jest: healing bruises crept out from under the hem of his collar, fresher than any he had sustained from Yagi or the battle in Kibaku, and dark circles weighed his eyes.

"I didn't say I regret anything," Amai retorted, still eyeing Kazuchiyo's bowl. "I'm just looking for a little gratitude."

Kazuchiyo reached out, tugging Amai's robe off his shoulder to reveal more sickly yellow stretching down his clavicle. Startled, Amai jerked back and drew his collar tight again. "What?" he demanded, though a moment later he regained his humor. "Getting started so soon?"

Kazuchiyo plucked the herring out of his bowl and offered it to Amai. "Who did that?"

He accepted, and for a moment it seemed he would laugh off Kazuchiyo's question as always, but the first bite seemed to change his mind. "It was that shinobi I warned you about. Master Nanpa, punishing me for failing to kill you. I'm lucky to be alive."

"So that's where you've been all this time?" asked Yagi. "Hiding from your old man with your tail between your legs?"

Amai cast him a hard look. "You ought to take my caution seriously. He's here now, in this camp, and when he sees his opportunity, he will strike."

"We have only your word on that."

Kazuchiyo gulped down a mouthful of rice, eager for any sustenance after the long march and unexpected battle, even if his stomach was tight and anxious. "No, I believe him," he told Yagi. "Even just now, Hidemune was trying to separate you and me for the battle ahead. It will be his best chance to attack."

"Then I'm not leaving your side," Yagi blurted out. "And you need to be more careful."

Kazuchiyo frowned. "You think I haven't been careful?"

"Not careful enough." Yagi's face contorted against the words. "Aritaka was right for once: you should have retreated today when he gave the order."

Kazuchiyo swallowed. He had never had Yagi's ire focused on him, and had never imagined it would feel so heavy. "And left Mahiro behind?"

"Mahiro fights at the vanguard for a good reason," Yagi continued passionately. "If you can't hold your own on the line you have no business being there. You're too important."

His insistence sparked defiance and anxiety in Kazuchiyo in equal measure, causing him to fidget uncomfortably. "I'm not more important than—"

"You *are*," Yagi insisted. "You are to *me*." He scraped his hand across his mouth in sudden self-consciousness and tried again in a more even tone. "You're important to me. So be careful."

Kazuchiyo shivered, his emotions teetering. "I will," he said. "I'm sorry."

Yagi shook his head, then nodded, seemingly just as affected by his own outpouring. As he shoveled rice into his mouth Kazuchiyo glanced to Amai and found him watching with eyebrows raised. He appeared similarly unsettled and even sympathetic, rocking Kazuchiyo's composure further. Kazuchiyo reached for his bowl again.

"Here." Yagi offered the slice of dried herring from his dish. "Have mine."

"No, eat it." Kazuchiyo managed a wry smile. "You'll make better use of it than me."

"I don't want it."

"I'll take it, then," piped up Amai as he nibbled on his portion.

Yagi glared, but Kazuchiyo took the opportunity to nudge Yagi's hand back toward his own bowl. "Please, eat it. Tomorrow will be a difficult battle."

Yagi pulled a face, and after a thoughtful moment he bit down on the fish, tearing the hunk in two with his teeth. He placed half in Kazuchiyo's bowl with a mumbled, "There," and then devoted himself again to eating.

259

Kazuchiyo smiled as he took a bite. "Thank you."

Amai glanced between the two of them for a moment and then smirked. "That's really something," he said, leaning toward Kazuchiyo. "You have him eating out of your hand almost literally."

Yagi stopped eating, and Kazuchiyo cast the daring shinobi a warning look. "Amai."

"You're very lucky," Amai went on around small bites of his prized herring. "Few generals can boast having soldiers as loyal and devoted as your friend here. And all it took was a few small acts of kindness and some trips to the baths." He chuckled. "If I'd known it was so easy, I would have started on him a long time ago."

"Easy?" Yagi repeated, setting his bowl down.

Amai swallowed the last of his fish. "No offense. For someone like Kazu here, even I—"

"You think kindness is so *easy*?" said Yagi, his full temper rising. "That it's some trinket for you to bargain with?"

"Yagi," said Kazuchiyo, his skin prickling. "Don't—"

But by then Yagi had already lashed out, snatching Amai by the collar of his robe. He dragged him closer, and Amai went stiff, finally registering the depth of his miscalculation.

"You really think it's so plentiful?" Yagi snarled. "So simple? That it can be offered so easily and without a cost?" His fist shook against Amai's throat. "I've gone without one word of kindness from anyone my entire life until him, do you understand? Not one—only fists and blades. So go on thinking it's just that easy, but don't you dare mock his kindness in front of me again, or I'll have your head on my spear, understand?"

Amai blinked back at him, stunned and breathless, so Yagi gave him a hard shake. "*Understand?*"

"Y-Yes." Amai gulped. "I'm sorry."

Yagi held tight to be sure, before finally shoving Amai back. His hands were still shaking, his eyes wild and disoriented. With a series of muttered curses he stumbled to his feet, snatched up his spear, and stormed from the tent.

Kazuchiyo startled at the snap of the fabric. A flash of panic and indecision not unlike the one on the battlefield took momentary grip of his heart, and it wasn't until Amai slumped onto his side that he jarred back into proper function. "Yagi!" He pushed to his feet, however unsteady they were, and started after him.

"Kazumune," Amai called, and when Kazuchiyo turned back, he wasn't surprised to see the weasel's shock giving way to guilt. "Sorry."

"Don't you dare leave," he said, and he hurried outside.

Following Yagi was not difficult; several soldiers were still milling about the camp, all stopped to stare in a singular direction. Kazuchiyo darted down the line of tents, picking up his pace when he heard a loud clatter of wood from a few rows down. "Yagi!" he called, and the soldiers that were starting to gather parted for him.

He found his companion at the intersection of two grassy paths through the camp. Yagi had overturned a supply cart and was tearing it apart with heavy swings from his spear. Kazuchiyo flinched with the percussion of the wood as Yagi rendered one wheel to splinters. As more soldiers came to investigate the commotion they began whispering to each other, confused and far too mindful of the spear to interrupt. Even Kazuchiyo hesitated, fearful of how much worse things would be if he ordered Yagi to stop, only to have him not obey, cementing him as an uncontrollable demon in the eyes of their men. But as Yagi's strikes grew weary, Kazuchiyo took a deep breath and forced himself closer.

"Yagi?" He crossed to the side so that Yagi would have plenty of opportunity to see him. "Yagi, that's enough."

Yagi brought his spear down one more time, and his audience jumped in alarm at the tremendous crack of the cart splitting in two. But then Yagi let the spear go and stepped back, to their relief. He smoothed his hair from his sweaty brow and gradually slowed his heaving breath. "Kazu?" He looked to Kazuchiyo, and his face twisted with shame. "I'm—"

"It's all right," Kazuchiyo said quickly, and he crossed the distance between them. He would have liked to touch or console him right away, but with so many eyes on them, he worried about how that would be perceived. "Did that help?"

"I…" Yagi gave his face a rub and took a breath. "Yes."

"Good; I'm glad." Kazuchiyo glanced behind him and spotted General Ebara among those gathered; they shared a nod of understanding. "Let's go back to the tent and finish supper," he suggested. "I think I spotted a little wine…?"

"Yes." With one more breath to calm his remaining temper, Yagi wrenched his spear from the wooden carcass of the cart and turned with Kazuchiyo back the way they'd come. "Yes, your sister left it for you." Kazuchiyo released a quiet sigh, and the two of them returned to the tent.

At first glance, Amai was gone, and Kazuchiyo seethed with dissatisfaction, but as he and Yagi settled around their meal once more, he realized that part of the tent opposite him was bowed inward, as if a man's back were leaning against it from the outside. He let it be for the moment, focusing instead on sharing the saké with Yagi. The poor man seemed more embarrassed than anything, and Kazuchiyo made an effort to converse normally.

"Tomorrow, Hidemune will send a troop of soldiers up the hillside," he explained as they ate and drank. "To approach Sabi Castle from its northern side, and deliver a message to its soldiers. But Oihata will certainly have planned for that. I don't have much hope for those men."

"Better they run through the forest," muttered Yagi. "It'll cover them as much as it does the crows."

Kazuchiyo was not convinced that Oihata wouldn't have planned for that as well, but he didn't want to contradict his friend when he was in such a delicate state. "Regardless, he first tried to offer up *you* to the task. Thankfully, Aritaka agreed you'd be more useful down here."

"I'll be useful, all right." Yagi gulped down the rest of the wine, little though there was. "This time I'm going to get a samurai head for you. Then Aritaka won't be able to say one word about the two of us."

Kazuchiyo finished his meal, which was already growing hard in his stomach the more he watched Yagi's creased expression. He chose his next words carefully. "About what you told Amai just now..."

"It was the truth," said Yagi, hints of his temper still making his ears red. "But I don't want to talk about it."

"All right." Kazuchiyo squirmed, unable to keep his swirling emotions in check. "I just want... I need you to know that any kindness I've offered you wasn't currency to buy your loyalty. The affection I have for you doesn't depend on you being useful to me."

"Of course it does," said Yagi, though seeing the hurt splash across Kazuchiyo's face seemed to make him regret it. He scrubbed his fist across his mouth and pushed to his feet. "If I wasn't the strongest man on the field at Shimegahara, you wouldn't have come looking for me afterward," he reasoned as he began moving about the tent, laying out only one of the two straw mats left for them. "You wouldn't have sought me out years later if I was just another soldier in Aritaka's army. I'm only alive at all because I'm useful to you."

"That's not..." Kazuchiyo stood, though he was suddenly weak, his skin crawling. "I didn't—"

"And it's not any different the other way around," Yagi continued as he stretched the mattress flat. "I saved your life, too, and only because you were kind to me when no one else was. Because I know what that's worth! That's just the truth." He straightened up, but looking at Kazuchiyo again unsettled his nerves, and he shifted on his feet, the rest of his words tangling in his mouth. "I'm not saying... It's not that I don't..."

He growled and pushed his hair back. "It's the way the world is," he said firmly. "The way *everything* is. Say you're using me for my spear. I don't care. I don't! So just..." With a heavy snort he sat himself on the bedding. "Just come help me sleep, and I'll keep killing for you. Okay?"

Kazuchiyo did not heed him. Though he might have sensed Yagi's words came from his agitation more than from his heart, burdened by youthful inexperience he could feel only the hurt and uncertainty they caused. He could not help but remember Amai's callous words deeming him a manipulator. "You said you didn't want to talk about it," he said, "but I think tonight has held the most words I've ever heard you speak at one time."

"Don't tease me," Yagi muttered, but then he realized that Kazuchiyo had yet to move, and his brow loosened. "I'm sorry."

Watching his frustration give way to shame finally urged Kazuchiyo to action; he put out the lantern and joined Yagi on the mattress, but without any words he trusted himself to speak. Instead he wrapped his arms around Yagi's neck, drawing him in, and Yagi sank into his embrace. Gradually they settled beneath the bedding together. Understanding and honesty would have to come later. For the moment, each could be only a salve for the other, woefully unaccustomed to the intricacies of a wartime romance.

Once Yagi was asleep, pillowed against Kazuchiyo's aching heart, Amai slipped beneath the wall of the tent once more. Oh, what frustrating misunderstandings he could have caused then, had he a mind for cruelty. But patience and restraint are the surest tools in a shinobi's trade, and for once he put them to proper use.

"I didn't mean to cause such a stir," he whispered as he crept to Kazuchiyo's bedside. "He's more sensitive than I thought."

Kazuchiyo used his sleeves to staunch Yagi's ears. "Yes, he is," he said wearily. "You shouldn't provoke him."

"I've learned my lesson." Amai settled next to him, and though the inside of the tent was almost fully dark by then, his pale eyes seemed to flash with moonlight. "Are you all right?"

"Of course," Kazuchiyo replied, though without much conviction. In truth he was as fragile as he had ever been, with far too many concerns weighing upon him. As Amai continued to watch him, unconvinced, the deepest of his worries wriggled free. "Do you think it's cruel of me to use him like this?"

Amai scoffed quietly. "If giving a man the only pleasure he's ever had in his life is cruel, then yes, you're quite a villain."

"You know what I mean," Kazuchiyo retorted, but when Yagi grumbled into his collar, he stroked Yagi's hair until he was calm again. He sighed deeply. "He's suffered so much more than either of us. He deserves a more peaceful life than I can give him."

"Probably he does. But if you can't give him that, why worry about it?"

Amai reached down to card his nails through Yagi's coarse hair. Kazuchiyo held his breath, but Yagi did not stir again, and even seemed to relax more deeply. "You fret over enough already," Amai continued to whisper. "Focus on the things you can do, like keeping him happy, and keeping yourself safe from Hidemune."

Kazuchiyo watched him for a moment in contemplation, but Amai was ever an enigma to him, and it did nothing to settle his crowded mind. "You really have that much interest vested in me surviving my brother?" he asked.

"As I've been telling you from the start," replied Amai.

"Why?" Kazuchiyo continued to study his soft face for any twitch or change in shade. "Because you regret helping to kill my father?"

Amai continued to stroke and gently tug at Yagi's unruly hair, his expression never changing. "Shimegahara was my first battle, too."

Kazuchiyo frowned. Amai's down-turned eyes and distant smile were nothing like the aching regret he had seen in the face of the monk Houshin, his father's betrayer, but he sensed a common thread beneath. Perhaps it was not so different even from the unshed tears in Oihata's proud eyes back in Waseba's tent. The Red Dragon of Suyama was such a figure in the minds of Shuyun's warriors that all of any virtue rightfully mourned him.

"Guilt," Kazuchiyo whispered. "That seems like a

dangerous weakness for a shinobi to have."

"It is," said Amai. "Believe me. But there's one other that's worse."

"Which is?"

With a smile, Amai leaned down and kissed him. Kazuchiyo had been expecting it, and he held very still, breath caught and pulse throbbing. He told himself he had no other choice if he was to keep Yagi from startling awake and putting his spear through the man. Amai's lips were soft and well-practiced, sweet for their own sake, and Kazuchiyo was too raw with emotion to be unmoved by them.

"Get some sleep, if you can," whispered Amai as he straightened up. "I'll be keeping watch." He gave Yagi's hair one more playful caress and then snuck back the way he had come, under the wall of the tent.

Kazuchiyo let out a sigh. As he resettled and did his best to calm down, he thought he felt Yagi's eyelashes flutter across his bare collar, but nothing came of it; there was only the all-enveloping heat of a broad body draped across his own, a taste of tender lips on his. He did not expect to get much sleep at all.

CHAPTER TWENTY-TWO

In the morning, Yagi rose early and left without a word. He returned with their rations, another piece of dried herring topping each bowl of rice. They sat close together as they ate, but it wasn't until they finished and were helping each other into their armor that either spoke.

"I'm sorry I raised my voice at you," said Yagi, refusing to look Kazuchiyo in the face as he tied the cords on his shoulder guards. "Last night."

"It's all right." Kazuchiyo hesitated to say more; Amai had been right. There were too many worries for them to fret over to allow for childish romantic sentiment. "Let's focus on the battles ahead. Anything else we can discuss later."

"What else is there to discuss?" said Yagi, and though his manner was not cold, Kazuchiyo's throat tightened. "Let's get ready."

Kazuchiyo agreed, and they left the tent together.

The camp already bustled with activity. All around the soldiers hurried to prepare their armor and weapons, counting arrows and reinforcing shields made of bolted wooden planks. Generals Ebara and Rakuteru each made for an intimidating presence as they ordered men into their ranks. Though they were clearly readying their men for the vanguard, General Hosoda and his soldiers—who had taken the duty the day before—were not among them. Mahiro, however, was.

"Yagi-douji!" she shouted as soon as she saw them. She rushed over, already clad in her full armor and mane. "I heard you made a ruckus last night." She smacked him in the hip with the blunt end of her naginata. "Destroyed three carts and butchered their horses."

"I did not," Yagi grunted, his reddened cheeks scrunching. "It was one cart and no horses."

"Lucky for you, then. I would have beaten you senseless if you had." She laughed heartily. "Next time you want to spar, come find me, and I'll give you a better a challenge."

Kazuchiyo eyed the bloodstain on Mahiro's armor that she had done nothing to clean or hide. "Are you all right to fight today, Mahiro? You were injured."

"A scratch! It's nothing." Mahiro gave her side a pat, though it was a decidedly reserved one. "Iomori slapped one of her paper things on it, so you don't have to worry about me." Her smile turned devilish. "I'm not going to miss a chance to pay that woman back for distracting me."

"If you were distracted, that's your own fault, not hers," said Yagi.

"Then I'll pay her back twice as hard," Mahiro retorted. "And have her pretty head for my saddle."

"Mahiro." Kazuchiyo fixed her with a gentle but serious look. "Please do be careful."

Mahiro sobered a bit as she nodded her understanding. "I will. I'll be with Rakuteru and his son at the front. I have to be at my best if I'm going to look after them."

Kazuchiyo frowned at the thought of her positioned so far ahead of their forces, but nothing out of his mouth would have changed her mind. "And General Hosoda's men?"

"With their general behind the front line, I'm sure." Mahiro gestured toward a far corner of the camp. "You should go see him."

There was something gruesome in her expression that made Kazuchiyo wary, but he and Yagi made their way over to General Hosoda's tent. There were men on guard outside, though they were happy to let them through. Inside, General Hosoda was being tied into his armor by his attendant: a sturdy, bright-eyed young man with broad ears who fought to contain a grin as Kazuchiyo entered.

General Hosoda turned toward them. Though nearly prepared for battle his face was in as terrible a state as Mahiro's wince foretold: his lower jaw and neck were dressed with white linen stained red, his cheeks swollen and eyes bloodshot from pain and a sleepless night. Though he could move his head very little and doubtlessly could not speak, he finished tying the cords of his plated armor skirt by feel. He offered Kazuchiyo a very short, very stiff bow.

"Lord Kazumune," the attendant greeted, bowing low at the waist in his stead. "Please excuse my lord that he cannot receive you more formally."

"That's quite all right," Kazuchiyo assured him, bowing in return. "I wanted to inquire after the general's health, after yesterday's ordeal. I'm very glad to see you up and in your armor, sir."

General Hosoda beamed with the attention. He was by all accounts already a quiet man, not wise but devoted, the few accolades to his name earned in much younger years. He was not handsome or refined. To receive a compliment from his lord's son despite having blundered into an ambush must have thrilled him; he even tried to reply, only to be silenced by the painful arrow wound.

"My master is honored by your thoughtfulness," the young attendant said. "As you can see, despite this minor scratch, he is more than ready to fight for Sakka Province against our enemies."

"How will he give his orders if he can't speak?" asked Yagi bluntly.

The young man puffed himself up. "I'll be assisting him

by calling out instructions issued by his war fan," he said. Yagi nodded, satisfied.

"You serve your master very well," said Kazuchiyo. He nodded to them both. "I'm sure your fortitude will bless us with victory."

General Hosoda's brow furrowed, as he was deeply moved. Kazuchiyo and Yagi showed themselves out, only to be halted a moment later by the attendant following them out of the tent. "Lord Kazumune," he said, once again bowing deeply. "Forgive me, but I also wanted to thank you, with all my heart, for what you did on the battlefield."

"What I did?" Kazuchiyo echoed, puzzled.

"You forced the general's first captain into my lord's saddle," he explained. "If not for that, I don't know what would have become of him."

Kazuchiyo frowned. He knew nothing of this boy and was concerned that if he said too much or too little about the appropriateness of that situation, it might be all over the camp. "In that moment, the general's life was more important than propriety. I hope the captain was not punished for it, as any fault was mine."

"No, sir, and you're too good to say so." He kept his head bowed low. "You've done a greater service to me than I can say."

Kazuchiyo glanced to the tent and back again. "What is your name?"

"It's Tomoto, my lord."

"Tomoto." Kazuchiyo touched his shoulder to urge him upright. "General Hosoda is very important to my father's ambitions. Please take good care of him for me."

Tomoto beamed, eyes glossy with emotion. "I will. Thank you, my lord." With yet another deep bow he returned to the tent. Just before the flap closed, Kazuchiyo caught a glimpse of Tomoto gingerly touching his lord's face.

"Why is Hosoda so important?" Yagi asked as the two of them made their way toward Lord Aritaka's war tent. "Is he another powerful general?"

"Not really," Kazuchiyo admitted. "From what I know, he gained most of his land from his family and hasn't distinguished himself in any other way since he was young. But he has a lot of men, and they seem to like him." He smiled to himself, warmed by the thought of Tomoto rising to his lord's defense. "Or, at least, one of them does a great deal."

He wondered if Yagi had taken notice, but he was facing only forward, distracted. Kazuchiyo chose not to elaborate.

Preparations continued throughout the morning. Kazuchiyo participated as much as he was able, memorizing every squad in the formation, their generals and commanders. The soldiers formed into ranks with tall wooden shields brandished across the line, close enough that the men were shoulder to shoulder. The generals on horseback dragged their shoulder guards far forward and secured extra armor to their jaws and necks, mindful of the fate of General Hosoda. As soon as the army disembarked from their hastily assembled camp, the sound of drums echoed out from the forest.

"There could be any number of them in there," Hidemune taunted Kazuchiyo as they rode behind Lord Aritaka and his bannermen. "Are you so sure about charging in without more knowledge?"

"I am not afraid of drums." Kazuchiyo stared straight ahead. "But if you're nervous, Brother, you can always join your soldiers as they charge up the hill."

Hidemune shot him a hateful look but was interrupted by Aritaka loudly clearing his throat. "Kazumune, to me."

Hidemune's scowl deepened as Kazuchiyo spurred Hashikiri to bring him alongside his father. "Yes, Father?"

"Send that oni of yours to the front." Aritaka did not make eye contact as they continued down the gentle slope to the forest. "He belongs in the vanguard."

Kazuchiyo cast a quick glance behind him. Yagi was close

enough to hear; his brow was already furrowing in preparation for a rise in temper. "Father, would you not feel more at ease if—"

"That was the agreement," Aritaka talked over him. "Your brother's men on the hill, your man at the front." Instead of looking to Kazuchiyo, he looked to Iomori on his other side, who nodded. "Motonobu is his father's to command. That is my wish."

"Very well, Father," said Kazuchiyo, and he slowed his horse.

"I won't," Yagi said as soon as they were side by side again. Even in his attempt to lower his voice, his tone was fierce. "The both of them are—"

"You must go," Kazuchiyo said. "It's our lord's order." He dared not risk a look at Hidemune but could feel the smug victory radiating from him. Even as he simmered with anger, he felt a pinch to the back of his calf, and he glanced down to see a foot soldier who had ventured close to his saddle. Though clad in a wide helmet and sparse armor, Kazuchiyo recognized the slope of his shoulders very well.

"I'll be fine," Kazuchiyo reassured Yagi once more. "Please, go look after Mahiro for me. She's likely to get herself into trouble if she charges ahead of the line again."

Yagi shifted in his saddle. "If anything happens to you, that's the last order I'll take from *anyone*," he said, loudly enough that no one could mistake him. Then he quickened his horse's pace, stiffly avoiding Lord Aritaka on his way toward the van.

"Impertinent, savage man," huffed Hidemune. "But if he kills as many as he boasts, fair enough, I suppose."

"Yes," said Kazuchiyo. "I pray he succeeds in all he's promised."

CHAPTER TWENTY-THREE

After an hour's march they once again reached the line of towering bamboo. Rather than narrow their ranks for the road, the brave soldiers at the vanguard put only their southern corner to the path. They strode into the forest a hundred men abreast. General Ebara and his son entered first with their men, with Rakuteru and his covering the southern flank and Hosoda and his, the north. In one great, rectangular column they plunged through the bamboo, shields parting only around the stalks like a rake through water. The forest echoed with the crunching of foliage under their bearskin boots.

Kazuchiyo held his breath when it was his turn to cross the threshold. He was soundly in the ranks, too far from either flank and too deep among the trees for a wayward arrow to find him. Even a skilled assassin keen on blaming his death on the enemy would find the distance too implausible. The drums continued to pound from the woods, quickening his pulse, and Amai stayed close by his ankle, sharpening his focus to a fine needle of anxiety. Over and over he promised himself that, this time, he would not freeze in the face of battle. There would be no hesitation or confusion, only action, only the warrior expected of him. There was no Yagi to protect him, after all.

Soon after Lord Aritaka and his entourage entered the woods, they could hear from the north a muffled echo of clashing steel. Hidemune's face betrayed concern as he squinted between the trees, but there was no path through the bamboo to see anything of the hillside. He gripped the handle of his sword until his knuckles whitened.

The drums intensified. Kazuchiyo began to sweat, wondering if Iomori and perhaps even Hidemune had been right after all. Naoya and his forces had totaled three thousand last they clashed, and with reinforcements from Ugarasu they could number thousands more. There was no way of knowing until the force appeared; even without the advantage of a cavalry charge, it would be simple enough for Naoya to overwhelm the column.

Kazuchiyo thought back to his years of study, the great battles of his ancestors and their enemies, the heroes of ages past. The forests of Sakka Province were not well suited to guerrilla warfare and its generals unaccustomed to its intricacies, but Kazuchiyo had spent his youth poring over whatever texts he could find, even those of outside provinces. Now was the time to make use of that knowledge.

If Naoya outnumbered them, he would wait until the entire army was deep into the woods and surrounded them on all sides, he reasoned. But if he lacked even a hundred men, the wiser choice would be to divide, and with Aritaka's army already proven quick to retreat...

"Father!" Kazuchiyo nudged Amai back with his foot and urged Hashikiri forward again. "Father, we should send a soldier down the column to warn General Fuchihara. He's the most vulnerable to attack."

Aritaka stared at him in bland irritation. "Fuchihara is not the center nor the rear, both of which are well prepared for their ambush. What is your logic?"

"They will shave our numbers wherever they can. The rearguard is brave, but Fuchihara is not—he is still close to the forest edge and will retreat back to safety if overrun."

"You slander our father's general?" Hidemune sneered, having moved closer as well. "Men of Sakka are not so eager to flee!"

Kazuchiyo shot him a quick glare, then turned his full attention back to Aritaka. "The drums were meant to stall us. Oihata's numbers must—"

From far down the line came a flurry of shouts and heavy *thunks*—the sound of arrowheads striking that Kazuchiyo would never forget. The army slowed, and many turned, drawn to the southern flank. As word spread the rest of the column reaffirmed their ranks, squaring their shields to the woods in expectation of the attack expanding to consume the line. Archers nestled into the spaces between foot soldiers and set their sights ahead, though they had no targets to take aim at.

Kazuchiyo turned his horse. Swearing again to himself that he would suffer not one moment of inaction, he abandoned his father's side and hurried down the line as fast as he could while still allowing the soldiers to part for him. He was distantly aware of Amai calling after him but gave no heed as he rushed past the startled captains. As he grew closer the shouting intensified, and when he looked to the woods he finally spotted the Kibaku soldiers behind shields of their own, firing arrow after arrow.

General Fuchihara had retreated deep behind the line of fire, his bannermen surrounding him with flags raised as a shield. "We're still within reach of the field," he was saying to his captains as Kazuchiyo approached. "We could easily—"

"General Fuchihara!" Kazuchiyo struggled to find an opening through the banners to be heard. "This is another of Kibaku's ploys! We must press the attack!"

"Attack?" Fuchihara repeated. "Should we not wait for the column to solidify its ranks?"

"No, we must act at once," Kazuchiyo said determinedly. "The rearguard will lead. Follow without breaking your line; we'll swing the formation outward like the blade of a sickle, forcing their men west to pin them against Rakuteru."

"Swallow-wing formation," said one of the captains with

275

understanding, and Kazuchiyo nodded to him gratefully.

Fuchihara remained unconvinced. "Swallow-wing at a time like this? We have no idea of their numbers!"

There was no time to explain a string of logic to the man, so Kazuchiyo made no effort. "Trust me, General, we do. Spread the orders to your men!" As Fuchihara continued to sputter, Kazuchiyo hurried on to the last thousand men at the rear, where he passed on his plan to the generals there.

"You can't just usurp the chain of command," Amai warned him, somehow having found his place back at Kazuchiyo's side. "Your father won't approve."

"I don't care as long as we hold the line," said Kazuchiyo, and with the ranks prepared, he signaled to the generals.

The rearguard general blew his ox horn for attack, and with shields still held man-to-man, the column's rearmost troops marched on a diagonal into the woods. Arrows split the wood and men screamed, those that were too wounded to continue falling back, but the captains understood the plan well enough to quickly compensate, ordering fresh soldiers to take up any fallen shields and replenish the line. Step by step they swung outward, until even General Fuchihara and his men were forced to join in. Kazuchiyo stayed well within the ranks, Amai close beside, inching closer to the Kibaku force.

"I see him," said Amai. Kazuchiyo followed his gesture toward the far end of the enemy line, where a man in a green top-coat and gold-crowned helmet was mounted among the command force, the full-moon warrior at his side.

"Oihata," said Kazuchiyo, and he could have sworn the man looked his way. His heart gave a thud. "Press forward!" he shouted to Fuchihara. "Force them west!"

At last they were within clashing distance; the archers stepped back to be replaced by spear- and naginata-wielders, who jabbed wildly at the holes in the Kibaku defense just as they dodged the same. As the Sakka rearguard curved along Kibaku's unguarded flank, their line began to shift, retreating westward, deeper into the forest and farther along the waiting line.

Ox horns blew, and Rakuteru, having assessed the situation just as Kazuchiyo hoped he would, spurred his soldiers into a swift attack. Rather than the stoic march of shields he led his men in a charge, Mahiro bellowing at the front. Kibaku's full-moon commander rose to meet them with a roar of her own, though Kazuchiyo quickly lost sight of both women among the melee. All around could be heard the splitting of bamboo as swinging blades caught in the trunks. Men locked swords with the enemy only to leap out of the way of plummeting trees, some with force enough to split helm and head together. Still the men fought, shouting and shoving, until the rearguard pushed forward with such fervor as to surrounded Oihata's smaller force entirely.

Conch shells bleated the retreat. As the green-armored Kibaku soldiers made their escape, Kazuchiyo was able to again spot their ferocious female commander holding the rear without Mahiro to challenge her. So, too, did his eye catch the flash of Naoya's handsome coat as he led his men in a full withdrawal. Emboldened by their flight, Fuchihara and Rakuteru both ordered the pursuit. Ever the tactician, Kazuchiyo sensed the victory too easily won.

"We've seen this retreat of Oihata's before," he told Amai. He winced as Fuchihara's archers picked away at Kibaku's rearguard until they, too, were in flight. "They must be headed to the river."

"Chibatake Bridge," agreed Amai. "If they cross it, they'll be able to reestablish their defensive line."

"That's not the only bridge, though. I think there's another farther north..." Instinct squirmed like eels in Kazuchiyo's belly, and he slowed Hashikiri. "Climb on," he told Amai. "I don't like this."

Amai pulled himself onto the saddle behind Kazuchiyo and leaned close. "You really are good at this, you know," he said against Kazuchiyo's ear.

Kazuchiyo shivered at the touch of his breath. "You

should be praying I'm wrong," he retorted, and he hurried them onward.

He found Lord Aritaka well protected among his bannermen, following Rakuteru's charge from a safe but eager distance. Perhaps the lord was especially hopeful to see Oihata dragged from his horse in person. As Kazuchiyo rejoined the procession his apprehension grew; though Rakuteru was a fierce and wise general, the chase was spreading them thin, men forgoing their shield line in favor of speed as they weaved through the bamboo. They passed many trampled Kibaku soldiers along the way.

Amai prepared to jump clear of the horse. "I don't want him to see me with you."

"Don't go far," said Kazuchiyo, to which Amai scoffed, and he leapt to the ground so Kazuchiyo could continue alone.

"Kazumune!" Aritaka growled as soon as his son was beside him. "There you are! What's got into you, boy, running off like that!"

"I'm sorry, Father," Kazuchiyo said, bowing over Hashikiri's mane as best he could. "I was only eager to carry your will to the rear, for the counterattack. Your plan was a success."

Aritaka puffed himself up, glaring back at him incredulously. But there were a great many soldiers around them now, their attention drawn, and predictably, Aritaka declined to press the issue in front of them. "Very good, then," he said. "We have the fools on the run now."

"Lying snake," Hidemune grumbled, but a sharp look from his father silenced him.

"They're making their retreat to Chibatake Bridge," Aritaka continued. "We must catch them before they cross, or they'll reform their defenses and put us at a disadvantage."

Kazuchiyo drew maps of the terrain in his mind. "Must be we so hasty?" he asked. "At this rate we'll soon pass Sabi Castle completely. Even if Hidemune's soldiers are faring well, they won't be able to rouse the garrison there in time to assist us."

"Why should we need their assistance? See how they flee!"

Aritaka gestured to the bamboo swaying out of the paths of retreating Kibaku soldiers ahead of them. "If there is some trap ahead, Rakuteru and his men can bear it."

Kazuchiyo looked left and right, but the forest was only growing denser, making it difficult to see very far in any direction. The Sakka line would only loosen further at their pace. This race to the bridge must have been intentional, with a wise general's design behind it.

"Father," Kazuchiyo urged, "if you'll permit me—"

"No," Aritaka said. "No, you'll not leave my side again. I command it."

Kazuchiyo ground his teeth but answered, "Yes, Father."

He slowed Hashikiri enough to put him behind Aritaka, though he dared not risk more than that with Hidemune casting him wary looks. As he struggled to think of some way to convince the man, Iomori joined him, drawing their horses close together. "What are you thinking, Kazumune?" she asked. "What do you know?"

Kazuchiyo was caught off guard and needed a moment to answer. "I'm thinking this is another of Oihata's traps. There must be another force waiting to ambush either from the north or south."

Iomori considered his words and then rode just ahead of him, slowing her horse to force him to do the same. "Watch my back a moment, if you wouldn't mind," she said, and she dismounted.

Kazuchiyo halted, turning Hashikiri to provide better protection to the horde of warriors charging from behind. The flash of his helmet gave warning enough for them to steer clear. "What's going on?" He watched anxiously as his father and brother continued on. Hidemune had noticed their absence and relayed it to Aritaka with bitter glee.

"Just a moment," Iomori insisted, and Kazuchiyo put Aritaka out of his mind. He watched as Iomori bent over one of the trampled Kibaku samurai, whose legs had been broken and twisted by the Sakka army and their racing footfalls, and yet his eyes were wide open, scanning back and forth blindly. If she intended to question the man, Kazuchiyo was certain she'd have no success—who could hear a dying man's utterings above the commotion of the hunt? Instead Iomori drew a tanto from her sleeve and plunged it into his throat, ending his life.

Then she did something peculiar that Kazuchiyo was at a loss to explain: she reached forward with her other hand, prayer beads dangling from her wrist, and pressed her palm to the man's temple. Kazuchiyo felt a tingling heat, like a fever-sweat, radiate up the length of his arm, and the dead man's eyes twitched. Seemingly satisfied, Iomori tucked her weapon away, remounted her horse, and motioned for him to follow.

"My lord!" she called, drawing up to Aritaka's side. "My lord, you must reconsider this pursuit. There is an ambush force waiting ahead, north along the riverbank."

Kazuchiyo was relieved to see Aritaka taking her advice more seriously than his, even though it was still unwelcome. "You've seen this? In your visions?"

"I have, my lord. Let me ride ahead to General Ebara and warn him."

"Very well," Aritaka grunted. "Go. But we do not retreat. Tell Ebara that he and Hosoda must defend our northern flank while Rakuteru and Fuchihara continue to press Oihata before he can reach the river." He motioned to Hidemune. "Ride ahead to Rakuteru and deliver my orders."

"Yes, Father!" crowed Hidemune. He gave his horse a heavy kick to spur it on.

"As you say, Lordship," said Iomori, and she, too, rode on to her task.

Kazuchiyo rejoined Aritaka in their absence. "And I, Father?"

"You stay with me," Aritaka said without hesitation. "And witness our victory."

Kazuchiyo conceded, though he was struck by the notion that Aritaka was not merely exerting his authority, but also eager to prove himself to his own son.

They rode on, sounds of chaos to all sides. Kazuchiyo sweated through his armor as he listened to shouts in the distance. He looked for Amai among the foot soldiers, but their helmets all looked too similar, and he knew better than to call for the man with Aritaka paying him such close attention. All he could do was charge forward, his faith resting on the generals that had necessitated this war in the first place. With Yagi guarding the northern flank, there was nothing to fear, especially now that Iomori had delivered the warning. A warning from the dead. He shuddered at the thought.

Light gleamed up ahead, and Lord Aritaka and his men slowed even as they burst from the dense forest into a clearing. Once a natural parting of the bamboo, it was now hacked larger, with fallen trunks littering the ground. The wood could be heard snapping and shifting beneath beast and man. Kazuchiyo's ears stung with the sound of arrowheads, fearing he would feel one in his flesh at any moment. He saw open combat resuming at the clearing's edge: General Ebara had reformed his line behind their shields and was taking the brunt of the volley. Yagi was among them, crouched behind the wood. Kazuchiyo's breath caught at the sight of blood on his armor, which he prayed was only the enemy's. He glimpsed Mahiro's white mane farther down, Hosoda's war fan signaling for the line to advance, and in the thickets beyond, more Kibaku samurai. *Many* more Kibaku samurai.

It was almost impossible to make out their numbers among the bamboo. Kazuchiyo could see spears and naginata raised in every space between the stalks, their helmets crowding together like a second forest floor. Up and down their line were generals on horseback bellowing orders to continue the archery barrage, even as Ebara ordered his men to march forward. Far beyond the conflict, barely visible among the trees, fluttered thick green banners that indicated the presence of the Kibaku daimyo himself.

Any thought Kazuchiyo might have given to the man was cut short, as already Aritaka was turning his horse. His bannermen struggled to keep him shielded with the canvas flags as they retreated from the clearing. Kazuchiyo shook himself from shock and followed, only to have Hashikiri buck suddenly beneath him with a sound of distress. He clung to his mount with his thighs, but the saddle had shifted. In a terrible, heart-skipping instant, he knew he would fall.

Kazuchiyo hit the ground hard. The edges of his armor dug into his sides and slashed bamboo trunks jabbed welts into the unprotected patches of his arms and legs. He thought of the trampled Kibaku samurai and struggled to right himself, startled to find that his feet were still tangled in the stirrups of his saddle. The straps had been severed, and when he looked up, he saw blood on Hashikiri's flank.

"My lord," said a rough voice, devastatingly familiar even among the chaos of shouts and arrows planting—perhaps even more so because of it. "Let me help you."

Something rushed toward him, and Kazuchiyo had barely enough of his wits to throw his hands up in defense. He caught a man's wrist, though not quickly enough; the tip of the arrow clutched in the man's fist skittered across Kazuchiyo's throat, drawing blood along the scar already there. Kazuchiyo fought back, but the man knelt on his chest, stealing his breath and ruining any attempt at leverage. Choking on a call for aid, he stared blearily up into a gnarled face he remembered too well.

"Why bother fighting?" goaded the patchwork mercenary, the one who had severed his brother's head from its body, back at Shimegahara. "You know it's going to end like this anyway."

The man had only one full arm—the other protruded from the sleeve of his soldier's robe as a ragged stump—but he was limber and strong and shoved the curve of his foot into Kazuchiyo's bicep to drive his arm down. Kazuchiyo squirmed, trying to angle the arrowhead away from his throat, but he was shaking, panicked and furious, barely able to move.

The gnarled man reared back suddenly, the blade of a sword swinging through the space his head had just occupied. He rolled to his feet, and with little more than a hateful look at his attacker, he beat a hasty retreat toward the tree line.

"Kazu!" Amai snatched Kazuchiyo by the cords of his armor and pulled, dragging him to his feet. By then more soldiers were hurrying forward, grabbing Kazuchiyo from all sides; he panicked again, fearful that he would see the gnarled face among them. Someone took up his saddle and another Hashikiri's reins as they hurried him out of the pandemonium of the clearing.

"Are you all right?" Amai asked. He tore a strip from his sleeve to press against Kazuchiyo's throat. "Is it deep?"

"No," Kazuchiyo said blankly, not that he knew either way. The Sakka samurai had closed in tight around him, men he didn't recognize shielding him with their bodies, swords drawn and ready. It took him a shameful length of time to regain his wits. "I'm...I'm fine."

"Kazumune!" called Lord Aritaka. Kazuchiyo was startled by the seemingly honest concern in his tone as he rode closer. His bannermen expanded their circle to draw Kazuchiyo and his protectors into them. "Are you injured?"

Kazuchiyo peered up at him, unsure how to respond. He finally registered the blood flowing down his neck, realized that it must have been Amai's Master Nanpa on the other end of the arrow—after so many years, a name put to the face of his brother's killer. It had never occurred to him that the man still existed in the world. With that revelation came anger and indecision, his clever brain spinning between strategy and emotion, what he ought to tell Aritaka in that moment. What good it would do to say anything at all. He found himself clinging to Amai's hand.

"My lord," said Amai, "Lord Kazumune is—"

"I'm fine," Kazuchiyo interrupted quickly. "These crows can't hurt me."

Aritaka straightened. He did not have Kazuchiyo's sharp wit, but he seemed to understand the intended message all the same, and his expression grew dark and troubled. "Bring a fresh horse," he told one of his captains, who snapped into a bow and ran to do so. He turned to the nearest general. "Send all available men to reinforce Ebara and his men. Make sure the eastern flank is especially secure so that our retreat to Sabi Castle is clear, if need be."

The general relayed the orders to his captain, and men began rushing in all directions, forming their lords into a more secure encampment of bodies while the rest hurried to the fight. Kazuchiyo stayed close to Amai's side, scanning every face for deep lines and snarling jaws.

"He won't try again this battle," Amai tried to reassure him. "He can't risk being seen." But Kazuchiyo did not believe him, and he remained painfully vigilant for the remainder of the fight.

CHAPTER TWENTY-FOUR

The first day of open war to visit Sabi's bamboo forest was a fierce one. Bodies littered the ground from its eastern to western edge, and great swathes of land were trampled down by man and horse. The jagged remnants of bamboo trees shook and men shouted and swayed, as if they were all caught up in some devilish whirlwind. The front line pushed back and forth on two fronts long into the afternoon hours.

And then it ended, in a very abrupt and anticlimactic fashion. As exhaustion took its toll, both sides relented to the other in a lull of hostilities. The sun was beginning to drift too low in the sky, turning the green forests orange, and neither army was keen on prolonging a battle until nightfall. In the tangled thickets it would only get harder to tell friend from foe, and easier for reinforcements to approach at unseen angles. And so, both mighty warlords signaled their retreats. Neither pursued the other.

Bidden by his father, Kazuchiyo did not leave Aritaka's side during those long hours of waiting. He watched the melee as best he could, many times recognizing Yagi's familiar bellow as it echoed down the line. It gave him a chill each time. Amai stayed close beside him, occasionally pinching the back of his ankle to reassure him of his presence. Kazuchiyo was grateful but otherwise paid him little mind. Even once the retreat had been called, he was not allowed to venture down into the ranks. He was swallowed up by his father's banners, which conveyed him back through the forest, to the path they had abandoned that morning. The trail took them, at last, to Sabi Castle.

Kazuchiyo had only visited the castle once, as a boy. It was smaller than he remembered, broad and squat in the shadow of the great hillside behind it, with black eaves dulled by sun and weathered palisades surrounding the compound in a ragged oblong. The castle's gates had been thrown open, samurai in armor and some on horseback just emerging as Aritaka and his men approached. Their general rode forward, and though Kazuchiyo was weary, the sight of a familiar face jolted him into focus.

It was Waseba Usaburou, youngest of the three Waseba brothers who had once served the Red Dragon. He was taller than his first brother but shorter than his second, and his eyes were small and beady. The face mask of his armor was decorated with horse hair to form an impressive beard his real chin could never muster. Kazuchiyo recognized his armor. It was the same black-lacquered plates he had worn for his former master; he had merely changed out the cording from red to indigo.

"My Lord Aritaka," Usaburou greeted, bowing over his horse as best he could. "We just received word that you were engaged in the forest. We were preparing to come to your aid."

"It's a little late for that, General Waseba," Aritaka scolded him. "Have your men instead prepare to accept our wounded."

The Sabi Castle garrison made way for them. Without enough time or light to prepare a proper camp outside the walls, the several thousand of Aritaka's men piled into the fortress and its long courtyard, picking benches and patches of grass wherever they could to collapse in exhaustion. Soldiers became nursemaids as supplies were rushed from the keep. Men groaned and shuddered everywhere that could be seen. Kazuchiyo took it all in, unable to fit the horrific scene to the

Sabi of his young memory, when the cherry blossoms were in bloom and his elder brother had been promised this castle to rule.

"Kazu," said Amai, pinching his ankle again. "Look. Seems like Hidemune's men made it after all."

Kazuchiyo followed his gesturing to several men in yellow armor huddled together along one of the outer walls, the Yaefu men that had been sent racing up the hillside. Only three were more or less upright, a fourth collapsed at their feet with blood matting his hair and face. Kazuchiyo cast his gaze about for the rest and found none. "How many did Hidemune send?" he asked.

"Fifty," Amai replied grimly.

Lord Aritaka dismounted from his horse outside the main keep, and Kazuchiyo did the same. He checked quickly with the soldier leading Hashikiri by the reins to be sure his companion would be looked after, and even once assured, he hesitated. There was no greater urgency in him than to throw himself into Ebara's ranks and seek out his champion.

"You should go with your father," Amai urged, nodding to Aritaka and Usaburou, who were headed to the interior. "I'll go find Yagi-douji for you, if you want."

Kazuchiyo swayed on his feet, but then he saw Hidemune climb roughly down from his horse and make for their father. The cold in his chest blazed white-hot. "No, come with me." He took Amai's elbow to be sure he wouldn't try to slip away. "Don't leave my side."

The elder men did not go far. Once inside the keep attendants rushed to them, setting out stools so the lord and his sons could rest. "I want a report on casualties as soon as it is available," Aritaka said. "General, send three of your captains and their men and one of Fuchihara's into the woods to retrieve the wounded, if there are survivors. We have no need for prisoners."

"Yes, Lord," said Usaburou. He passed the orders on to his nearest captain, who hurried to carry them out.

"What a disaster," grumbled Hidemune as he sat down. "Charging into the woods like that without any plan or foresight. If only—"

He spotted Kazuchiyo then, but it was noticing Amai kneeling at his side that drew his mouth into a sneer. "If only we had waited for a signal from the castle, we could have routed them."

"We knew all along that Kibaku would have men waiting for us," said Kazuchiyo, choosing instead to stand in front of his father. "Our Sakka generals fought bravely and kept the line, and now both Kibaku forces have withdrawn to the river."

"At the cost of how many men?" Hidemune snarled. "If only—"

"I don't know yet how many," Kazuchiyo retorted. "Three crows to every two of ours, at least. And even they fared better than your men on the hill."

Hidemune flushed with anger, but Aritaka interrupted with a wave of his hand before they could fall to further argument. "I won't permit squabbling," he said, and he fixed Kazuchiyo with a look of dull amazement.

Kazuchiyo realized then that he had never permitted Aritaka to see him out of sorts of any kind, and he quickly bowed his head. "Excuse me, Father. The excitement of the battle is yet in me, and I spoke poorly."

"Won't you punish him?" Hidemune asked abruptly, making no such effort to hide his disgust. "He abandoned our formation just as the battle was starting." His voice lowered to an accusatory slither. "*Just* as the battle was starting, as if he had some foresight—"

"I said no squabbling," Aritaka interrupted again. "Mind your surroundings, boy."

Hidemune's mouth snapped shut, his eyes darting to the half-dozen lower-ranking soldiers around them. "Excuse me, Father."

"Now." Aritaka turned his attention again to Kazuchiyo. "Who is this soldier you've brought? Does he have something to report?"

"I do, my lord," Amai replied, keeping his head down. "Though I beg a private audience to relay it."

Aritaka straightened his back, recognizing Amai by his voice. His gaze leapt from Kazuchiyo to Hidemune, then back, and in his expression Kazuchiyo saw a familiar streak of disquiet. "If it's not an emergency, it can wait," he said. "There is much to settle first."

"My lord!" called a man from the entrance. He hurried forward and into a bow before Aritaka. It looked to be one of Ebara's soldiers, his armor heavy and stinking of blood. "My lord, it's your daughter."

Kazuchiyo stiffened, trying to remember the last he had seen of Mahiro among the line.

"What of her?" Aritaka asked stiffly.

"She's wounded," the man said. "They've taken her to the healers. Master Iomori is with her."

Kazuchiyo shifted back and forth, anxious to leave immediately; then he remembered himself and looked to his father. He expected a curt dismissal and was surprised when Aritaka instead stood and approached him. He held very still as Aritaka put one hand on his shoulder and the other on his jaw, prodding his head to the side. Kazuchiyo found himself holding his breath beneath the unusual attention being paid him.

"You're also wounded," Aritaka said, quietly enough that not many around them would hear. "Go to the healers. Have them tend to you and see how your sister fares. Then come report to me." His eyes narrowed. "You and your fox."

Kazuchiyo blinked back at him, his mind whirling to interpret the words. Could it be the man was ready to hear a fuller truth? Swallowing, he nodded. "I will, Father."

"Be quick," said Aritaka, and he stepped away.

Kazuchiyo dashed from the central keep, following the soldier who had come to give them the report past many lines of wounded men, to the smaller, western keep where men and women in plain kimono were receiving the most salvageable warriors. "You know," Amai said along the way, "I told you before that I *didn't* want them to see us together."

"Can I assume that was Nanpa who cut my saddle?" said Kazuchiyo.

"It was." Amai had the decency to calm his sarcasm. "I know it's not the first time you've seen him."

"I didn't know his name until today." Kazuchiyo clenched his fists for a moment before forcing them to unravel. "He knows now that you're betraying your orders by protecting me, doesn't he?"

"Oh yes, he knows."

Kazuchiyo spotted true concern hiding beneath Amai's ever-careless expression. "Can I assume that means he'll be out to kill you, too?"

Amai's lip turned up bitterly. "Naturally."

"Then stay close to me, and we'll look after each other." Kazuchiyo caught a moment of sincerity splash across Amai before cynicism could squash it. He hurried them on.

The rooms were overflowing with wounded soldiers trying, mostly in vain, to stifle or smother their sounds of pain. But one among them was swearing so openly and so loudly that it caused commotion over all the others: Mahiro, bloodstained and scowling, shoving at the soldiers who tried to free her of her armor.

"Leave it!" she snarled, going so far as to slap Iomori's hands away. "I'm going back out! I'm going to take her head!"

"Mahiro!" Kazuchiyo reached her side. Before she could protest or resist, he snatched the bloodstained mane from her head. "Sister, please, calm down."

"Kazumune!" Mahiro tried to grab the decoration back, but he had already passed it to one of the soldiers and out of her reach. "Give that back! I want her to know it's me!"

"So she can pluck it off your corpse?" said Iomori, and she pressed both hands to Mahiro's chest. "Now *lay down*."

Mahiro's knees buckled, and she collapsed onto the

hardwood with a thud that left their audience wincing. "Witch!"
she squawked as she fought to get her arms beneath her. But
once on the ground with her momentum sapped, exhaustion
collected its due, and she relented.

Kazuchiyo knelt among the cautiously approaching
healers to help divest Mahiro of her armor. It was only then that
he noticed the shaft of an arrow sticking out of her shoulder
guard, which she had snapped off very close to the lacquer.
"You fought magnificently," he told her. "Despite your wounds
from the last battle. You have nothing to prove to anyone."

"That woman," Mahiro hissed, though she had to clench
her jaws as the blood-stiff armor was peeled away from her
body. Kazuchiyo helped her to sit upright so her backplate
could be removed. "It was that woman again! She aimed right
for my side!" Mahiro pointed emphatically at the stain her left
hip had become, the fabric of her under-robe soaked through.
"She's a beast, and when I see her next, I'll devour her!"

Her eyes gleamed with fervor that bordered on the
rapturous. "Tell me about her," Kazuchiyo said, still eyeing
the arrow piercing her shoulder. He slipped his hands beneath
the armor and could feel that point was deeply buried, even if
Mahiro was determined to behave otherwise. He gestured to
Iomori to call her attention to it. "I didn't get a good look at
her yesterday."

"She's *horrific*," Mahiro said passionately. She stared
straight back at him and babbled on in a too visible effort to
pretend she didn't know what was coming. "The strongest
woman I've ever seen outside a mirror! Faster than a falcon,
and how dare her hair be so full and straight!"

Iomori wrapped her hand around the arrow, as little as
there was to grip. Kazuchiyo braced himself and was surprised
to find Amai beside him, helping to keep Mahiro's arm still.
"She was wearing some fucking stupid saucer on her head,"
Mahiro continued to rant, though her body was winding tight.
"Gold! She must think she's really beautiful!"

Iomori ripped the arrowhead out; Mahiro jolted, teeth

gnashing and tears in her eyes, but she didn't make a sound. As soon as they went about removing the shoulder guard, she resumed. "I'd never wear something that flashy. I'm going to take it right off her head and pull on that hair of hers. She'll feel *that*."

"You'll have to rest up first," said Kazuchiyo, putting pressure on the arrow wound until Iomori was ready with strips of linen to bind it with. "A rival like that deserves you at your best."

"Damn right she does!" said Mahiro, but at last her strength was failing, her skin cold and beginning to shiver. "Make sure no one kills her but me." Gulping, she closed her eyes. "I just need to rest…"

At last Mahiro relaxed, but seeing her head loll drew Kazuchiyo to deeper concern. Iomori was quick to reassure him, saying, "She's lost a lot of blood, but no organs were injured. She'll recover with rest and time."

"Thank you," said Kazuchiyo, scraping his bloodied hands against his armor before he pushed to his feet. "Please, take good care of her."

He was loath to draw any of the other healers away from their work, but he had no choice in the matter; as soon as the commotion surrounding Mahiro had passed, several men and women took note of his father's crest on his armor and sleeves and insisted on devoting themselves to his care. They drew him into a private chamber and removed his armor, and would have undressed him completely if not for his protests. They satisfied themselves in cleaning and binding his throat, and then applied a bit of salve to the bruises in his side.

Kazuchiyo was instructing them that he be replaced in his armor before leaving—he wanted to be no less than fully presentable for his meeting with Aritaka—when they heard shouting in the courtyard outside. Amai, who had kept to his duty of remaining close by through the treatment, peeked out through a small crack in the doors. He snorted with amusement. "I think you can guess who that is," he said.

Kazuchiyo hurried through the rest of his dressing, and with helmet on but not fastened he threw the door open. Sure enough, Yagi was stomping through the lines of wounded men, his head swinging back and forth in search. He was as ever a ferocious sight: his armor slicked red, helmet dented, and shoulder guards twisted askew. He was even missing a boot. But when he spotted Kazuchiyo in the doorway, the battlefield fell from his shoulders, and he plowed forward.

Kazuchiyo retreated several steps into the chamber, so that by the time Yagi reached him they were safe from the majority of the courtyard's prying eyes. Amai even had the presence of mind to slide the panel shut behind him. For when they met their greeting was not one that ought to be shared with so many subordinates in view: Yagi tossed Kazuchiyo's helmet from his head, grabbed him and kissed him deeply.

His passion sent a shudder through Kazuchiyo's already unsteady knees; Kazuchiyo wavered, gripping Yagi's armor to keep hold of his balance. His fingers curled against the snapped shafts of arrows embedded in the lacquer. But Yagi would not allow him to dwell on concern, the heat of his heavy lips stealing away all conscious thought. He tasted like blood and bamboo.

At last Yagi leaned back, and the pair of them panted dizzily. "Are you all right?" Yagi demanded. When he spotted the linen wound around Kazuchiyo's neck, his cheeks flushed. "You're injured!"

"I'm fine," Kazuchiyo quickly reassured him. "Really, it's only a scratch." His cheeks were their own shade of rosy as he looked to the healers who were still in the chamber, watching them with eyes wide. "You're dismissed."

The men and women bowed deeply and then bustled outside. There was sure to be gossip, but Kazuchiyo could not bring himself to worry about that now, instead gingerly exploring the scars in Yagi's armor. "*You're* injured," he said. "Let's get your armor off."

"Only scratches," Yagi retorted, resisting Kazuchiyo's attempts to reach for his cords. He carefully prodded

Kazuchiyo's chin to the side so he could better see the tended wound. "I'm sorry," he murmured. "I should have been there to protect you."

"It happened so fast—there wasn't anything you could have done." Kazuchiyo glanced past him and swallowed. "Amai was looking after me, and he saved my life, at great risk to himself. The shinobi Nanpa will be after us both, now, and maybe even you as well. The three of us need to look out for each other."

Yagi ground his teeth, but eventually he nodded. Without sparing Amai a look he grumbled, "Thank you for protecting him."

Amai's eyebrows shot up. He could not keep victory from his face, but when he opened his mouth to ruin everything with some smart reply, a fierce look from Kazuchiyo made him wisely reconsider. He cleared his throat. "You're welcome."

Yagi nodded, and his hands moved to Kazuchiyo's jaw; his palms were sweaty and hot, huge against Kazuchiyo's cheeks, and he drew them together for another, slower kiss. Kazuchiyo granted it, returned it, his entire body growing buoyant as if he could rise higher to those lips. Whatever awkwardness they had shared in the tent the night before, he felt reassured then that their bond was rooted in deeper soil than mercenary convenience.

Then he remembered Amai's eyes on them, and his skin prickled.

Kazuchiyo eased Yagi back once more to catch his breath. He dared a glance at Amai, but the man's half-lidded stare only drew his stomach tighter. "I have to return to my father," he said. "He asked me to give a report, and... I'm going to tell him about Nanpa. I can't fool about with Hidemune any longer, not with so many lives caught in our... squabbling." He frowned around the word, disgusted by how carelessly Aritaka had cast the two of them against each other, how little gravity he felt from his own actions. "You should stay with your father, let the other men see you. Let them be inspired by you."

"Inspired?" Yagi pulled a squeamish face. "By me?"

"Of course. You're the strongest man in Aritaka's army. You must be a good example for them." Kazuchiyo touched his face. "All you need to do is let them see that you're sturdy and unharmed. Maybe take a tour of the grounds with your father? It will do the men good to see you about."

"Really?" Yagi frowned even as he leaned into Kazuchiyo's palm. "That's all I have to do?"

"Yes, that's it. I'll find you later." Kazuchiyo rose on his toes for one last kiss to Yagi's cheek. "Go on. And find a new boot! We'll have supper together once our duties are finished."

"Very well," said Yagi, warmed by the promise of privacy and food. With a deep breath he turned and left, casting Amai a heavy but thoughtful look on his way out.

"Straight out of your hand," Amai teased once Yagi was a very safe distance away. "I sound flippant, but I *am* impressed."

Kazuchiyo watched him a moment, his pulse still fluttering between his ears. "You mean, you're jealous, don't you?"

Mischief gleamed in the little weasel's silvery eyes. "I am," he said proudly, as if it were a badge to wear. "*I'm* the one that saved your life, after all. Where's my kiss?"

Kazuchiyo took in a deep breath, very slowly. "It's right here," he said, staying very still. "Come and claim it."

Amai glowed. His gaze darted to Kazuchiyo's lips, then back to his eyes, tempted and hesitant at once. He let out a breathless chuckle. "Well now I'm worried this is some kind of trap."

"You would know, wouldn't you?" Kazuchiyo struggled against his instinct to fidget. He was not so good at this as Amai claimed, not by his own estimation; his heart thundered and sweat slicked his palms as the air between them grew thick and warm. "Your lips are well-practiced at deception."

"They are," Amai agreed. He stepped closer, tense and testing. Kazuchiyo did not stir. "But so are yours."

Kazuchiyo did not reply. He did not have the confidence to deny it. He was not even fully certain he could grant Amai what he sought then, if it was crueler not to, or if it was treachery with the taste of Yagi's blood still on his tongue. So he remained where he was, watching Amai cautiously close the distance between them, until it was Amai rising up on his toes, Amai's lips angling for his.

And then Amai stopped. They were close enough to feel each other's breath but neither breathed, each of them waiting for the other to extinguish that final gap between their mouths. But then Amai smiled and leaned back again.

"I think I'll save my kiss," he said. "Until after I've killed Nanpa for you."

Kazuchiyo swallowed, unsure what to make of the threads of tension still encircling his ribs. He could not tell which of them had won their brief contest of wills. "As you like," he replied, the spell binding him a few heartbeats longer. Then he stooped down to retrieve his fallen helmet. "Let's hurry back to Aritaka, before Hidemune can poison his mind further."

They left the keep, and Kazuchiyo took his own advice, striding tall and proud down the path that would allow him to be as visible to the soldiers as possible. He managed to tug the lip of his armor up enough to hide the bandage around his throat. Though he stared straight ahead he could feel many eyes drawn to him, and he could not help but assume at least a portion of the murmuring in his wake was about him. He allowed himself a moment to return a look from General Hosoda, who was still atop his horse among his men. The man bowed his head deeply, as did Tomoto beside him. Kazuchiyo nodded back with relief at seeing them well. So, too, did he catch the eye of General Rakuteru at the gate to the main keep, who moved to intercept him.

"Lord Kazumune," Rakuteru greeted him, bowing at the waist. "Allow me to commend you on your performance today."

Kazuchiyo nodded back, though he was distracted. "I

thank you. Though humbly I confess I'm not worthy of praise. We claimed no victory today."

"Victory is not always in the rout, young sir," replied Rakuteru. "Fuchihara told me it was you who employed the swallow-wing formation at the rear. I wanted you to know I'm aware of that."

It seemed like a compliment, though Rakuteru's manners were so gruff it was difficult to know for certain. Kazuchiyo gathered himself to his full height. "Then I must commend you as well, for reading my intent so swiftly. It was the strength of Rakuteru samurai that drove Oihata to the river, under your decisive leadership."

Rakuteru snorted, though it was clearer then that it was out of appreciation. "I'm honored by your words, but it was the strength of *your* single samurai in particular that brought us greatest renown today."

Kazuchiyo swelled with pride he made no effort to conceal. "Motonobu fights under his father's banner," he said regardless. "Not mine."

"But under your command, and for your honor. No one here mistakes that." Rakuteru may have even smiled, however fleeting the expression was. "My men and I will strive to follow his bold example."

Kazuchiyo sorely wished Yagi could have been at his side to hear him say so; the thought of the embarrassment those compliments might encourage very nearly made him smile as well. "I look forward to that very much, General," he said. The pair bowed to each other and continued to their duties.

CHAPTER TWENTY-FIVE

Kazuchiyo ascended to the lord's chamber of the central keep, where Aritaka was being attended to by his closest bannermen. All were dismissed upon his approach, and father and son faced each other while Amai bowed his head to floor at Kazuchiyo's side.

"I know you have something to tell me," Aritaka groused from his stool. He was still in his armor, and it creaked around him as he shifted uncomfortably. "And I am of a mind to hear it. But understand first that you must be reprimanded for your conduct today."

"I understand, Father," Kazuchiyo said dutifully, bowing low. "I acted without your permission and exaggerated my motives. I'll accept whatever punishment you see fit."

Aritaka shifted again. "Your intentions in doing so were clear. These words from me are punishment enough. Next time, seek my permission before you act."

"Yes, Father, I will without fail."

"Very good." Aritaka was quiet for a long moment, and when Kazuchiyo risked a glance, he found him to be glaring at the far wall indecisively. "All right then," he said at long last. "Let's hear what happened."

Kazuchiyo took a deep breath. Though he had expected and even desired that this day would come, he still felt unprepared. For as much insight as he had recently gathered on his father's mind and manners, there were still so many pitfalls waiting to swallow him up. "When we came upon the bulk of the Kibaku army, I was attacked from within our ranks," he began slowly, carefully. "A man cut the straps on my saddle, and I fell from my horse. This man then attacked me personally by attempting to stab me in the throat with an arrow. I believe he wanted others to think I had been felled by an enemy archer."

Aritaka listened, the folds around his eyes and jowls growing ever more pronounced. He did not comment, so Kazuchiyo continued, saying, "Luckily, through swift action this man, Amai, was able to intervene on my behalf and repel the attack. He saved my life."

"He is to be commended," Aritaka said, though his voice held little praise.

"Twice over, in fact, for it was he who warned me to be mindful of such an attack." Kazuchiyo swallowed. "An assassination attempted by the shinobi Nanpa."

Aritaka did not stir. His heavy expression convinced Kazuchiyo that he had expected such an accusation, though much like in Kazuchiyo's case, that had not led to preparation. "Well?" he said. "Does Sakka's Black Fox corroborate?"

"I do," said Amai, having not lifted his head from his bow the entire exchange. "As the task was given to me first."

"By whom?"

"My lord, if you'll permit me, I'll show you."

Aritaka grunted an affirmative, and Amai righted himself enough to reach into his sleeve for a rolled-up bit of paper. This he passed to Aritaka, then quickly returned to his former position as the message was read. Kazuchiyo ached with curiosity, but he was unable to catch even a single character.

The paper was small enough that Aritaka must have read it over several times, his expression unchanging. At last he sighed and tucked it into his sleeve. "I see," he said, and he held the pair of them in suspense a while longer before more words followed.

"Kazumune, I made you a promise," he said. "I see that the time to keep that promise is near. However…"

"However?" Kazuchiyo prompted breathlessly.

"However, it is not *now*." Aritaka rubbed his mouth and then forced himself to look Kazuchiyo in the eye. "I need you to be patient for me."

Kazuchiyo straightened his back as frustration welled up inside him. "My brother, your son, has—"

"I know," Aritaka cut in swiftly, though he just as quickly calmed his temper. "I know. But this is no simple accusation, Kazumune. If I act now, and word reaches Gyoe before we return, the Lady O-ran will act in turn. You know what difficulty that will cause us."

Kazuchiyo bit his tongue. The truth was that he had spared little thought for Lady O-ran outside her feud with Lady Satsumi, but he understood Aritaka immediately; she was a rich woman in her own right, from a powerful family of Yaefu. Many of Aritaka's advisors were her close or distant kin, and many of his generals were her allies. With Hidemune accused and executed for treason, there were many ears for O-ran to spill her poison into while the campaign against Kibaku dragged on.

"You have proven yourself to many of my men," Lord Aritaka continued gravely. "None here doubts your character. Including me." He drew himself up in an effort to live up to his lofty title. "Once we have returned to Gyoe, I will name you my heir and root out your enemies. But until then you must be patient and continue to prove your honor earned."

Kazuchiyo clenched his fists against his knees, and he bowed his head to keep Aritaka from seeing the unsteady conflict in his expression. He was well-versed in these games, and as Aritaka said, he could see only one route forward. "Then I have no choice but to keep myself alive by my own strength," he said. "And win this war for you as soon as possible so that we can return to Gyoe."

Aritaka did not reply. He was, in his heart, a coward after all, though Kazuchiyo did not pity him for it. Instead Kazuchiyo lowered his forehead to the floor one more time. "If you permit me, I'll leave at once to carry out the preparations."

"You are dismissed," said Aritaka, wearily. "Speak nothing more on this for now, and tomorrow morning we will convene to discuss our next attack."

"Yes, Father."

Kazuchiyo rose, Amai beside him, and they left.

As soon as they were far enough away from the chamber, Kazuchiyo tugged Amai into an empty room and demanded, "What did the letter say?"

"It's the original note Hidemune left for me at Gyoe," Amai replied, leaning back against the wall. "'Black Fox, to my chambers tonight, urgently.' It's not much, but Hidemune's sloppy penmanship is impossible not to recognize." He smirked. "I liked your notes much better."

Kazuchiyo blushed at the reminder of those foolish but exhilarating days. "You've kept it all this time? You could have shown it to him all along."

"But the timing is so important, as you know." Amai's face darkened with gravity. "I know it's your life and future on the line, but keep in mind what you're asking the man to do here. He's going to have to kill his wife and son for you."

Kazuchiyo seethed with an ill heat. "By his own doing! He knew it would come to this when he kidn—"

Amai put his hand over Kazuchiyo's mouth. Despite another flash of anger, Kazuchiyo allowed it to stifle his temper. The unspoken words quaked in his stomach—a bitterness he had never allowed himself to fully voice. It burned his eyes and throat, startling him with its potency. Maybe it had been foolish, thinking he would receive true judgment or action from Aritaka under the circumstances, yet still he felt cheated and helpless and furious at it all.

"Shh," soothed Amai, and with the two of them still in

their armor, he touched Kazuchiyo's cheeks and pressed their foreheads together. "I know. But it's only a while longer. All right? Your oni and I will look after you."

"A while longer," Kazuchiyo repeated wearily. "The rest of our lives, you mean. Even if I can best Hidemune now, there'll be some other enemy that comes next. All Aritaka's generals expect nothing but war."

Amai sighed shortly. "You're a samurai. That can hardly be avoided. But you're already better at it than most of these old fools. A few more years, and you'll command them all. You just need to be patient."

Amai licked his lips, and Kazuchiyo tensed, expecting... But then Amai leaned back, his hands falling from Kazuchiyo's face. "Let's go back to the generals. You've got three of Aritaka's finest up your sleeve now. I know you have every reason to hate the man, but you should speak to Waseba, too. You'll want to be on good terms with him, as lord of this castle."

Kazuchiyo watched him for a long moment, his head spinning too fiercely for all of those spoken words to fully penetrate. "Patient," he echoed, taking the advice in a more deeply personal context. He stared long enough that Amai seemed to regret not taking that kiss when offered. How much longer would fox and dragon wind about each other so? But then Kazuchiyo rallied himself, and he nodded. "Then let's go. You're right; I'll speak to Waseba." He brushed past Amai on his way back into the hall. "I have to offer my condolences for his brother."

Waseba Usaburou had never been a particularly social man, and he was at a loss as to deal with Kazuchiyo's seemingly heartfelt sympathies for the death of his eldest brother. He accepted Kazuchiyo not with General Waseba's callousness, nor Houshin's guilt, but with clear and awkward discomfort. Their interaction did not last long.

The sun had slipped beneath the horizon. As the soldiers made the most of their hastily assembled camp and crowded together in the lower chambers of the keeps, Aritaka hosted supper for his generals and their children. A meager portion of wine was given to each with their meal, and at the end of it, a group of the lord's attendants brought to display before them a box of black lacquer, elegantly carved. The lid was lifted, granting everyone in the assembly a view of a man's severed head: washed and seated on a bed of silk, his long hair drawn in an elegant topknot.

"The head of General Sasahara Enkichi," declared the attendant. "Killed honorably in single combat against the indomitable Ebara Motonobu."

Kazuchiyo raised his head and glanced to Yagi seated across from him. Yagi pursed his lips as the assembly around him murmured in appreciation. Their attention on him lingered, though it took Ebara nudging him with his elbow for him to realize he was meant to respond. After much hemming, Yagi stepped over his dinner tray and dropped to his knees next to the box with a thud. He bowed his head to the floor in front of Lord Aritaka. Kazuchiyo held his breath.

"He fought... strongly," said Yagi. "They told me he commanded seven hundred men. But I won." The muscles along his jaw worked anxiously. "I fought, and will continue to fight, for the honor of my lord."

"You've brought honor to your father and to me," said Aritaka. "And your feats shall be rewarded."

"Thank you." Yagi slouched back to his spot in the assembly, but as everyone returned to the meal, he looked to Kazuchiyo. Many of them looked to Kazuchiyo.

"Your spear is going to win him just as many allies as that godly tongue of his," Amai told Yagi that evening as the three of them at last shed their armor. "Sasahara is a well-known name.

303

Kibaku can't claim to have killed any of ours as important as him."

"I didn't know his name when I killed him." Yagi shrugged out of his shoulder guards. "He challenged me, and I cut his head off."

Kazuchiyo smiled to himself as he stretched his weary back. "If only all our challenges were so straightforward," he said, and he drew on a clean robe. He had been granted a private chamber on the second floor of the keep, with a small window facing north. No one had protested when he brought Yagi and Amai with him, and in fact he could hear many more men in each of the surrounding rooms: guards assigned to him by Aritaka. He might have found the gesture more convincing if not for the room itself.

"I remember this room," he said, and Yagi and Amai stilled their banter. "I stayed in this room with my brother, Wakunaga, when I was a boy and he was destined to be Sabi's master." He stared out through the narrow window slats at moonlight hitting the tall tree, lonely atop the great hill to the castle's north. "Ten years ago, now."

He moved to the window and ran his fingers along the underside of the sill. There were small grooves there that he remembered, though it took him a while to recall the sequence of tugs and slides needed. As he worked, Yagi stepped gingerly up behind him.

"You should sleep, Kazu," he said. "You need it."

"In a moment," Kazuchiyo replied, and at last he succeeded. A piece of the wood came loose in his hands, and he set it aside so he could reach into the narrow, hollowed space beneath. He pulled free a bamboo flute, inelegant but lovingly carved, with a crude replica of the Tatsutomi's dragon crest notched into one end.

"I was my father's fourth born," he continued, turning the instrument over and over in his hands. "I wanted to go to war with my brothers, but I was never going to rule a castle like this. My mother used to say I would be trained as an administrator. To play music and write poetry, and handle the affairs of stronger, more war-minded men. That was my duty."

"None of us are who we were intended to be," said Amai, "but that's the way of the world."

"You should sleep," Yagi said again.

"I will. Please, will you lay the futons for us?" Kazuchiyo took a deep breath and raised the flute to his lips. "I just need a little while."

And Kazuchiyo began to play. The music that sprang from the old flute was raspy at first, thin and mournful and weary. But as his fingertips adjusted to each note, the melody gained strength. He wanted the wood to sing of older days, better days, days when Suyama was proud and protected, its red banners strung high and its cloud-top castle a symbol for all. But politics got the better of him, and to avoid ire he chose instead an old song that all of Shuyun's samurai would recognize: a ballad set to the rhythm of ancient poetry, which in turn chronicled the life of their country's most famous hero, the First Emperor. Though many would take from its somber tunes a sense of conviction from duty served, to Kazuchiyo it was a dirge. Shuyun was, in its heart, a lover of tragedy, and he felt that weight very clearly in his heart as well.

Yagi and Amai didn't bother laying out the futons. Amai leaned against the wall to listen, and Yagi stayed close. He wound his fingers in Kazuchiyo's robes by his waist, pressed his nose to Kazuchiyo's hair. Kazuchiyo had no way of knowing if he recognized the song or understood its significance, but he took comfort from the sturdy, unwavering support of his broad body.

Once the song was done, Kazuchiyo tucked the flute back into its hiding place. They laid out only two futons, Yagi insisting without speaking that Kazuchiyo would share his. So, too, did he use a look rather than words to indicate Amai truly was welcome to stay. Again Amai was wise enough not to taunt him in return. And then, at last, the three of them found solace in sleep.

CHAPTER TWENTY-SIX

By the next morning, Amai was gone. Kazuchiyo did not worry after him much. He felt as if he could smell him in the walls.

Dressed, fed, and steeled for the day ahead, Kazuchiyo and Yagi joined their lord and the rest of his counselors in the high chamber of the keep. Hidemune regarded them warily but said nothing. As the group came to order, they sat around a map stretched on the center of the tatami, with Usaburou at the head.

"The Kibaku army arrived four days before you did," he explained, using small wooden tiles on the map to show the layout of their forces. "They loosed not one arrow on us, choosing to only ever attack our scouts and messengers. We tried many times and lost many men attempting to alert our Lord Aritaka of the danger without success."

"How many men do they have?" asked General Rakuteru.

"Seven thousand, at least. Though likely more." Usaburou nudged more tiles onto his map. "They've been obscured by the forest all this time, and have had little trouble killing our scouts. We haven't been able to accurately assess their numbers."

Rakuteru reached over the map, requiring that Usaburou

withdraw his hand. "Oihata and his twenty-five hundred retreated across Chibatake Bridge yesterday," he said as he arranged the pieces to show as much. "We passed their camp during the rout. I imagine they'll be retaking it as we speak, to keep up their enclosure of the castle."

He leaned back, and Ebara took his turn to position the troops he was aware of. "The rest of their army numbers at least five thousand," he said. "They retreated as far as the Nodo Bridge farther north, but we do not know if they crossed the bridge or not."

"They did not," said Iomori.

All eyes turned to her. "You've seen this?" asked Aritaka.

"I have. General Ebara is right. Lord Koedzuka himself stands at the head of five thousand men." She produced a folded fan from her kariginu and used it to nudge another pair of tiles onto the map, on the other side of the river. "With a thousand more reserves on the opposite bank."

Fuchihara tutted, unimpressed. "So, your magic is now besting Oihata's after all?"

Iomori stared at him for long enough that he began to sweat, and only then replied, stoically, "It doesn't work that way." No one pressed her for an explanation, least of all Fuchihara. "I imagine he's also preparing to retake his position. They'll have to surround Sabi thoroughly for a blockade to be effective."

"That cannot be allowed," said Aritaka.

"In that, I'm certain we can all agree." Iomori began pushing Sakka tiles outside the border of the castle. "But Koedzuka will not be eager to engage in another full-scale battle so soon. We are in the superior position, with the castle to fall back to. If we send a thousand soldiers to pound their drums, I believe he will think twice about retaking all his camps. He may content himself with a western front only."

Aritaka grumbled thoughtfully, and seeing this, Ebara cleared his throat. "My lord, *we* are not yet prepared for another full-scale battle either. Our troops are weary from travel and have dead to bury. Let us stall them a while, to regather our strength."

"They could call reinforcements in that time," protested Fuchihara.

"So could we," replied Ebara, and to this Usaburou nodded fervently.

"With the eastern road open, we could send word to Tengakubou," Usaburou said, and Kazuchiyo's heart skipped at the name of his birthplace. "Another five thousand men can arrive in a matter of days."

"No," said Aritaka, his arms folded across his chest.

Usaburou leaned back. His eyes went unexpectedly to Kazuchiyo, who did not know what to make of the attention. "My lord, all of Suyama is yours to command now. If you'll allow me—"

"No," Aritaka repeated with finality. "By all the numbers stated so far, ours are superior. If we need to call for more from the north, we will do so. They would be in a better position to outflank the crows from there anyway."

"Yes, I agree," spoke up Hidemune, to the surprise and interest of no one. "We don't need reinforcements from that snake nest."

Usaburou scrubbed at his face, and Kazuchiyo thought he saw a flash of bitterness there. "Very well. Then allow me to lead my men out of Sabi to harry the enemy. We've been able to do nothing but sit all this time, and they're anxious to put their spears in Kibaku bellies."

Aritaka considered that as well, and then took in a deep breath. "I want to know what my sons suggest."

Hidemune rushed to speak first. "Let us stall only long enough to refresh the men, and then strike in full force. Now that we are sure we outnumber and out-position them, there can be no reason to hesitate." He cast a sneer in Kazuchiyo's direction. "Was that not Kazumune's strategy? To charge forward to victory?"

"Charge forward in which direction?" asked Kazuchiyo,

and when Hidemune started to scoff, he continued. "The Kibaku forces are divided across two bridges. They are not equal distances from us, and if we attack one, the other will certainly move to flank. How do you intend to deploy our 'full force' between the two?"

Hidemune gaped at him angrily; Kazuchiyo gave him only enough time to look foolish, then carried on before he could supply a proper answer. "I agree with Master Iomori. We should send a force comprised mostly of General Waseba's men into the forest, to form a line along the western flank, where the Kibaku soldiers themselves were camped." He reached over the map to nudge the tiles into place. "A smaller force will raid the abandoned camps to the south for supplies. We won't need to position men there as long as the western flank holds. This should buy enough time for our soldiers to regain their strength, so that we can launch a two-pronged attack against Lord Koedzuka's and General Oihata's forces when the time is right."

"B-But what if Kibaku has moved already?" countered Hidemune. "They could be retaking those camps as we speak, and then what good would Waseba's thousand men do? If we're going to leave the castle at all, we should march in force!"

"I can assist with that," said Iomori. "I'll ride with General Waseba and use a spell that will trick their forces into thinking there are more of us than there are. If Kibaku has sent some men, they will not be any more interested in fighting than we are. We can force them to withdraw."

"Very well," said Aritaka before anyone else could interject. "As you say, General Waseba will lead his thousand men to form a line along the western edge of the forest, with Master Iomori's help. My captain Joushiki will lead five hundred men to raid the Kibaku camps and then reinforce General Waseba. Then in three days' time, we attack."

"My lord," said General Rakuteru, "how shall we divide our forces when the time comes?"

Aritaka started to answer, but then he stopped himself and

gave the matter greater thought. "That will be decided later. First we must gather what information we can from General Waseba at the front. The situation might change in that time."

General Rakuteru was pleased with his answer, and the assembly dissolved. Kazuchiyo stayed close at Yagi's side as they departed, thus managing to avoid any confrontation from the steaming Hidemune.

Afterward, the pair joined Mahiro in her room for breakfast. She was in fine spirits despite her injuries, even with her left arm bound tightly to her chest to aid the recovery of her shoulder. She gulped down several portions of rice and requested wine more than once.

"I'm going to find out who that woman is," she promised between mouthfuls. "I know I could have taken her if not for the fucking arrow." She poked at her shoulder and then grimaced. "Next time, I'll have her."

"I'm certain you will," said Kazuchiyo diplomatically. "Though I hope you don't intend to try until you're fully rested."

"Yes, yes, I know." Mahiro chomped through a pickled radish. "It'll be up to you and Hidemune to handle things until then."

Yagi raised an eyebrow, but Kazuchiyo remained unmoved, replying, "Yes, of course."

"She's going to have to confront the truth sooner or later," said Yagi once they had left her to her rest. "And pick between the two of you."

"I know," said Kazuchiyo, vexed by that eventuality. "But if I can delay that until Lord Aritaka has declared his intentions openly, at least she can say he made the choice for her, if she wishes."

They left the keep to take part in the final preparations for the day's deployment. Usaburou and his men were just coming into formation at the gates, all of them hard-eyed and eager for a fight they weren't meant to encounter. They straightened their backs at the sight of Yagi prowling down their ranks. Kazuchiyo passed his well-wishes on to the captains, assuring them that he would offer a prayer to Sabi's local gods to bless their march. Some met his overtures with gratitude, others with discomfort, which was not unexpected from a mixed army of Sakka and Suyama soldiers.

At last he bowed a greeting to Iomori, who was wearing a hunter's light armor over her kariginu. Her hair had been fixed tight beneath a straw hat, and her horse was even saddled with a quiver.

"Do you mean to disguise yourself, Master Iomori?" Kazuchiyo asked, fascinated. He had never known her to pass up the opportunity to boast of her profession. "Or will you be joining the line?"

Iomori returned his amusement with a dry snort. "The former, if you must know. Oihata may know I'm here, but that doesn't mean I have to make it easy on him." She stepped closer, inappropriately so, and her eyes grew harder. "Your father summoned me last night," she said quietly. "I'm sure you can guess what he wanted to consult me about."

Kazuchiyo took in a slow breath. "And how did you advise him?"

"I told him he ought to settle this nonsense as soon as possible and leave the repercussions to me. Unfortunately, he disagreed. But the next time you're on the field, I'll be at your side." She gave another snort. "I've hunted fox in my time."

"I'm relieved to hear it," said Kazuchiyo, and he bid her good fortune out in the woods.

The Sakka forces, lead by Usaburou, departed from Sabi Castle amidst a mighty roar of horns and drums. Once the last soldier had cleared the gates, the might of their heraldry swelled even further, so that even those within the castle could have been forgiven for thinking their numbers miraculously doubled. Kazuchiyo climbed to the top of the gatehouse to watch for as long as they were visible, marching stoically across the open field that surrounded the compound, and then as they weaved into the swaying bamboo. In time, their boastful calls were the only trace of them.

Kazuchiyo kept himself busy throughout the day with a variety of chores both essential and less so, each with the purpose of separating him from his father and brother. He visited Hashikiri in the stables and was pleased to find him well-tended; he toured the courtyard with Yagi to encourage the men and receive reports from their captains as to each squadron's casualties and remaining strength; he saw to it that his armor was in steady hands to be cleaned and mended. The continued pounding of Sakka drums in the distance reassured all that Kibaku had not risen to battle, and by midday, a scout returned with news that confirmed as much. Kibaku had contented itself in claiming a defensive line along the western border of the forest. Usaburou and his men were ideally placed to stall and intimidate them. The drums quieted, and the stalemate had begun.

Kazuchiyo took his supper with Yagi in his chamber, and only then was joined by Amai. "You shouldn't disappear for so long at a time," Kazuchiyo scolded him. "What if something happened to you?"

"I'll try not to enjoy your concern too much," said Amai, thumping down next to him. He helped himself to one of the pickles on his tray. "Don't worry—Nanpa is smarter than Hidemune. He won't try anything within the castle."

"You're too cocky," said Yagi. "Kazu is proving himself more and more. If Hidemune becomes desperate there's no telling what they'll do."

Amai rolled his eyes. "I have a lot more experience with 'desperate' men than you, friend. I know what I'm doing."

He reached for Yagi's tray, but Yagi slapped his hand away. He laughed, and before he could move on to some other taunt, Kazuchiyo intervened. "What *have* you been doing all day, Amai?"

"If you must know, I've been following Hidemune." He pulled a small bundle out of his robe, and when he peeled the fabric away, it revealed a collection of dried plums. He passed two to each of his companions; Yagi scoffed but accepted his eagerly. "He spent most of the day with your father, as I think you know," Amai continued, "sucking up as if it were his profession. Not to mention warning about how dangerous it is for you to have so formidable an ally as Yagi."

"There's not much I can do about that," said Kazuchiyo as he ate. "Hidemune will always be in his ear."

"Only action will sway the generals," Amai assured him. "And Aritaka will defer to them if pressed. Hidemune can simper all he wants, but I'll let you know if he takes it any further."

"Good. Thank you."

By the time they finished the meal, the sun was sinking below the hills. Kazuchiyo lit a lantern and hoped to spend an hour longer in study, only to be distracted before he'd begun.

Something tapped against his window. Amai heard it as well, and with an uncharacteristic seriousness eye he motioned for Kazuchiyo to stand back. Slowly he crept to the window, his hand dipping into his belt for a weapon, but after a peek through the wooden slats, he snorted and reached his hand through.

"What is it?" asked Yagi, his hand on his spear.

"Paper," said Amai. After another look through the window, he drew the intruder in: a piece of white parchment folded into the shape of a small doll, with a round head, spread arms, and joined legs.

Kazuchiyo accepted it and began carefully unfolding the message. "It must be from Master Iomori," he mused aloud, flattening it to reveal his own name. But the brush strokes were broader and more fanciful than he was accustomed to from Iomori, and his heart began to pound as he turned the paper over. It read:

His wings bring him home,
But he sings of tragedy,

313

His voice so heavy.

Kazuchiyo read the words over several times without taking a breath. The long, swooping strokes of ink impressed on him a sonorous voice full of passion, and before he could think better of it he leapt to his feet. Ignoring the alarm of his peers, he moved to the window, but only the distant, hilltop tree greeted him.

"What does it say?" Yagi asked. "Is there trouble on the line?"

"It's not—" Kazuchiyo quieted himself and returned to the pair. He drew them in close before revealing the lines of poetry, which he recited for Yagi's sake. "It's not from Iomori," he whispered. "This is Oihata's brushwork."

"Only another onmyouji could send a messenger shiki," Amai agreed with a sigh. "Too bad ours has already flown off. You couldn't send a reply even if you dared to ask her."

"Master Iomori did leave one of her shiki with me," said Kazuchiyo, "but its intended recipient is her. I wouldn't know how to direct it otherwise. We'll need some other messenger."

He and Yagi both looked very pointedly at Amai, who, once he caught on, flushed darkly. "No," he said. "I'm not taking any messages from you again."

"He needs an answer," said Kazuchiyo, urgency tightening ribs. "He'll be expecting one."

"Then go ahead and answer him, but not through me!" Amai checked his tone then, folding his arms as he eyed Kazuchiyo. "Last time I was caught, remember? And that was between camps, not a castle."

"But then Oihata let you go," said Yagi. There was a note of gruff teasing in his voice that gave Kazuchiyo goosebumps. "He knows you, which makes it your job now."

"No, it does not. It doesn't make it my *anything*."

"We can't risk having Amai sneaking in and out with Nanpa about," Kazuchiyo reluctantly agreed. "I'm more worried about what he would do than Oihata." He turned the paper back and forth, seeking some extra message or instruction, but there was nothing. With great reluctance, he lifted the lamp's shade and put the message to the flame. "But Oihata understands the position I'm in. He must have had something else in mind..."

"An arrow shot over the wall?" Yagi suggested.

Amai snorted. "It's a long wall. You would have to signal Oihata for him to ever find it, but do that and the guard towers will see, too."

Kazuchiyo set the message down on his dinner tray to burn out. He watched the fire consume each character and tried to picture Oihata's brush moving over them, his face down in passionate concentration. Was it one particular note in his musical homage that had drawn Oihata's ear so well, that he would risk treason for them both to deliver these handsomely rendered syllables?

Kazuchiyo returned to the window, and from its hidden sill he retrieved the bamboo flute. Though he was quick bringing it to his lips, he hesitated to breathe song through it. To repeat the same melody would assure Oihata that his message had been received, but no more than that. With a clever choice, he could answer.

And so Kazuchiyo began to play. It was a livelier song than the night before, composed of long, drawn-out tones that rose in pitch like asked questions, which were then answered with a fluttering of staccato notes. In his heart he held a vision of a crimson dragon spiraling across the sky, winged companions swooping between its coils, a song of joy and camaraderie.

When he had finished, he returned to his two companions. "What did you say?" Yagi asked, with such charming earnestness that Kazuchiyo could not help but kiss him. He tasted like sweet plums.

"Hopefully, I said that I got his message and am glad for it," said Kazuchiyo, alight with a confidence he had not felt in days.

"I can see him already," teased Amai. "Those big brown eyes of his full of tears." He didn't spare one moment or thought to modesty as he stripped out of his gi and replaced it with a sleeping robe. "Not that I can imagine anything coming of it. We're still at war, you know."

Kazuchiyo would not allow any cynicism to dampen his spirits. In fact, he was cheerful enough to lean deeply into Yagi's side in youthful retaliation for Amai's exhibitionism. "As long as he knows my heart, we can broker peace after this skirmish has passed. That's all I want."

His revenge only seemed to pique Amai's interest further; his eyes gleamed, reluctant to leave Kazuchiyo's as he helped himself to one of the futons. "That's a lot to ask for," he teased as he spread the mattress. "Is your heart so easy to know?"

Kazuchiyo did not know how to respond, but he did not have to. Yagi wrapped his arm around Kazuchiyo's shoulders possessively and said, "What about my fist? Would you like to get to know *that?*"

"Don't tempt me," Amai retorted, and Yagi's expression tightened and went red.

"Always teasing," Yagi muttered. "No wonder you have so many enemies."

"What do my enemies matter if I have the two of you?" Amai's smile softened as he slipped beneath his covers. "Aren't you going to sleep? It's getting late."

Yagi scowled, but he left Kazuchiyo's side to unfurl their futon as well. Kazuchiyo could feel Amai's gaze on him as he changed into his sleeping robe, heavily enough that he wondered if the little devil was counting his goosebumps. But as he slid into bed with Yagi alongside, that chill was swiftly banished, and he lay between the two of them, his pulse thrumming.

"You have us, but we have you, too," Kazuchiyo said as he returned Amai's stare across their pillows. "We're in this together."

"I know," Amai whispered, smiling secretively. "I wouldn't have it any other way."

Kazuchiyo leaned back into Yagi's chest, Amai's turned-up lips the last thing he saw before falling asleep.

CHAPTER TWENTY-SEVEN

Come morning, Kazuchiyo looked to the window. A small paper doll leaned against the sill.

Kazuchiyo crept out from between Yagi and Amai to retrieve the new message. His heart fluttered with eagerness, just like those days in Gyoe, as he unfolded Naoya's finely pressed paper, revealing that not only had the man written further lines to his previous poem, he had also felt compelled to repeat the first ones so that it could all be read at once.

> *His wings bring him home,*
> *But he sings of tragedy,*
> *His voice so heavy.*
>
> *Would that I could offer him*
> *A more peaceful home than this.*

Kazuchiyo huddled beneath the window and allowed himself a few moments of fantasy. He imagined the rolling rice plains of Kibaku, its green pastures, its bustling towns. He pictured himself climbing the gold-trimmed eaves of the Ugarasu keep to greet Lord Koedzuka, not as a captor but as a safe harbor and ally. He longed for men of honor to welcome him as a peer and maybe, he dared to hope, rally for vengeance in his name. All those things he could feel in the notes of Naoya's simple letter, and all those things called to him with a gravity that brought tears to his eyes.

But then Kazuchiyo glanced to Amai's sleeping face and was given pause. How well he had been tricked by sentimental poetry before. There was little reason to believe Naoya intended to take him as a hostage, as the youngest and thus least valuable of Aritaka's children, but he could not console himself with that logic. Even men of outwardly good appearance could fall to treachery for petty reasons.

But neither could Kazuchiyo bring himself to put the notion from his mind. He folded the note up tight and tucked it into the hidden alcove in the window, then moved to wake his companions.

The day passed in tense anticipation. Regular reports arrived from Usaburou's via his scouts, assuring all that the Kibaku army was just as eager to stall for time as they were. Both sides beat drums without taking a single step. At Sabi Castle, preparations continued. Kazuchiyo spent a great deal of time with Generals Ebara, Rakuteru, and Hosoda, poring over maps of the terrain and debating strategy. Though Hosoda was still recovering and could not voice his opinion well, he contributed as best he could by nudging tiles across the map and seemed very pleased to have been included at all.

Though Kazuchiyo was concerned that Lord Aritaka would resent not being included, they insisted he not fret. In the end, the lord of Sakka appreciated having his mind handed to him more than he would ever admit.

As the day drew to evening, Kazuchiyo's worries took another course: Naoya would be expecting a reply. All through supper his mind and heart waged war, leaving his poor stomach a helpless casualty. After forcing down a half portion of rice he could not stop himself from pulling his flute from the window.

"How will you answer him?" Amai asked. "Are you really

considering abandoning Aritaka after all these years carefully biding your time?"

Yagi hushed for his quiet and then looked intently to Kazuchiyo. "It doesn't matter to me which side I fight on," he said firmly, "as long as it's by yours."

Kazuchiyo smiled gratefully. "I'm honored. And I wish it were so simple." He sighed and drew the flute to his lips. "If only I could speak my mind directly to him."

His melody was the same as the night before, notes sweeping low only to be spirited up again, but at a slower tempo. His joy had not been squashed, but it was wiser now, hopeful and cautious at once. He could only pray the message came across as intended. By the time he finished the sun was long down, and a pair of round, dark eyes were peering back at him through the window slats.

Kazuchiyo startled but did not recoil. So swift and soundless had the intruder's approach been that it wasn't until he flinched that Amai took notice; Kazuchiyo quickly motioned for him to stay back. The eyes blinked at him, long lashes batting and thick, black eyebrows drawing in. The rest of the stranger's face and hair were covered, but there was no mistaking it: it was a woman, and one not from Shuyun.

"Hush," the woman said, and even that short order lit the spark that ignited Kazuchiyo's recognition. "I am not an enemy."

Yagi put his hand on his spear, and Amai crept forward, his hand inching toward his belt. Kazuchiyo again signaled them for calm. "Who are you?" he asked. "How did you get here?"

"No time for that." The woman reached through the bars holding a slip of paper. "Look, quickly."

Kazuchiyo accepted the paper and held it to the light of the room's lantern. Though it wasn't poetry this time, the brushwork was unmistakably Naoya's: *Let us speak*.

"Is he here?" Kazuchiyo asked incredulously, his heart in his throat.

"He waits on the far side of the hill," said the woman, and

she motioned for him to hand the paper back, which he did. "I will take you to him."

Amai joined them at the window, eyeing the woman with distrust. "And how do you expect us to leave the castle without being detected?"

"Clumsy fox could never manage," she retorted, "but is easy for Purnima." She looked impatiently back to Kazuchiyo. "Are you ready?"

"I can't just leave in the night to meet the enemy," he protested, even as he bent down to tighten his leather sandals.

The woman snorted at him. "My lord risks everything for you. If you will not do the same, you do not deserve him."

She turned away from the window, and Kazuchiyo snapped upright again, pressing himself up against the bars. "Wait," he whispered as loudly as he dared. "Wait, don't leave. I want to meet with him."

The woman returned, still eyeing him with as much caution as Kazuchiyo's two companions were eyeing her. "Your name is Panima?" he asked. "You're General Oihata's commander, the full-moon samurai that fought my sister."

"*Pur*nima," she corrected him stiffly. "Make an excuse to leave the keep."

Kazuchiyo's head spun; he ignored Amai shaking his head beside him. "Can I meet you at the bathhouse?"

"That will do," she said. She stood and then braced her foot on the window sill to climb onto the roof.

Kazuchiyo hurried away from the window to prepare. Considering he had nearly lost his life to Kibaku assassins in the past, as far as anyone knew, he figured he could wear his swords even to the bathhouse without raising suspicion. As he tucked the pair into his belt and his dagger into the back of his robe, Yagi followed close behind.

"I'll come with you," he said, not seeking permission.

"To the baths, yes." Despite the circumstances Kazuchiyo blushed. "You and I have spent enough time in them that no one will think to disturb us once we're there. But after that it would be too dangerous for you to try to leave the castle."

"But you—" Yagi shifted back and forth as he watched Kazuchiyo retie his hair to keep more of it against his scalp. "I can be quiet," he insisted. "I won't get caught."

"Shh," scolded Amai. Kazuchiyo flinched as he took over the job of securing his hair. "There are guards in the next room even now, and you can't keep quiet."

Yagi glowered at him, but he didn't open his mouth for fear of proving Amai right. "It'll be all right," Kazuchiyo reassured him. "I'll be as swift as I can. Naoya is a good man; he won't hurt me."

"He's a samurai," Yagi insisted. "Just because you were good to his father doesn't mean he'll remember."

"He will. And if he doesn't, Amai will remind him." Kazuchiyo glanced back. "Won't you?"

Amai finished securing Kazuchiyo's bun with a firm tug. "I'm not about to let you take a secret route out of here without me seeing it," he replied. "And especially not with that woman." He thumped Kazuchiyo between the shoulders. "Go on, I'll meet you at the bathhouse."

Yagi hefted his spear, and though it might complicate things, Kazuchiyo wasn't about to ask him to leave it. "I don't like this," he said as they moved to the door. "It's a trap."

"It might be," Kazuchiyo admitted, "but I have to see him, if only to know for myself."

They left the chamber and had only turned one corner before running into one of the guards on patrol. He frowned at their weapons, but then Yagi slung his arm protectively over Kazuchiyo's shoulders. It did the trick, and the guard gave him an understanding nod as he moved on.

They remained uninterrupted all the way to the bathhouse, but upon arriving Kazuchiyo was dismayed to find it already occupied: General Hosoda and his attendant, Tomoto, were soaking together in one of the tubs. They were not seated especially close to each other, and yet they put further distance between them as soon as they realized they were not alone.

"I'm sorry," said Kazuchiyo, bowing his head. "We thought it might be empty this late."

"No, please, excuse us," Tomoto replied quickly. "We're just finishing."

Both men bowed their heads and rose from the bath. As they stepped out to dry off, Kazuchiyo and Yagi moved toward the washing bins. Yagi was coiled tight, unsure what to do, and so Kazuchiyo urged him to set his spear down and then boldly started untying his belt. When he cast a glance at Tomoto, he startled to find the young man casting him a similarly anxious look as he helped his general into a clean robe.

"General Hosoda," Kazuchiyo said, hoping to ease all their minds. "It's good to see your wound healing so well."

Hosoda put a hand to his jaw, where the scab was beginning to turn to scar. "Thank you, my lord," he said, voice quiet and rough, but sincere.

"Tomoto is taking good care of you, then?"

Both men blushed, the pace of their redressing hurried. Though it must have hurt, Hosoda managed a brief smile. "Yes, my lord, very much so."

Kazuchiyo smiled at them in return, and the pair retreated, embarrassed but relieved. As soon as they were gone, he drew Yagi down for a quick kiss.

"Stay here," he said. "Splash some water around. If someone comes I'm sure you can ward them off."

"Be careful," Yagi replied. "You know what I'll do if anything happens to you."

Kazuchiyo shivered, already able to hear the demon wail ringing through his ears. Before he could reply, Yagi kissed his forehead and urged him toward the servant's exit. "Don't be long," he said. Kazuchiyo nodded, took a deep breath, and slipped outside.

Amai was already hunkered down next the wood pile, waiting for him. "You're sure about this?" he asked as he straightened up. "The three of us could just stay in the bath, you know. Make a night of it."

Kazuchiyo was swift to prevent his imagination from dwelling on that invitation. "I'm sure," he said. "You don't have to come."

"No, I'm coming. Apparently it's my job now."

"Quiet." Purnima hopped down from the roof, granting Kazuchiyo his first up-close look at her: she was tall for a woman, strongly built, dressed in dark-green robes cinched tightly to her frame. Her face and hair were still covered by a cloth wrap, but the flutter of her long eyelashes reminded Kazuchiyo pointedly of Mahiro's infatuation with the woman.

"Stay close," she said as she pulled a few slips of paper out of her robe. "And do not speak until we are beyond the walls—later, if you can."

Amai harrumphed. "So, that's your secret?" he said. "Shiki? You shouldn't boast when you're the one relying on someone else's magic."

Purnima glared back. "No speaking." She slapped one of the papers onto Amai's chest.

She took greater care in affixing another to the front of Kazuchiyo's robe, and as soon as it was in place, his vision dimmed briefly as if a fog had fallen over him. His skin tingled, and when he looked down at his hands, the shape of them appeared muddy and blurred.

"Are we invisible?" he asked, stunned and impressed.

"Only almost. So be careful." Purnima added the last to herself, and already in her dark robe she seemed to become little more than a shadow. "Stay close," she said again. "No speaking."

Purnima led them on a twisting path through the outbuildings, toward the compound's northern wall. The courtyard to the west was still full of camped soldiers, lights gleaming from fires as they worked late into the night on their armor and weaponry. The trio was far enough away, and indistinct enough due to the sorcery, that they defied detection. They reached the wall without incident and crouched down in tall grass that had been allowed free growth for too long. There, hidden behind a small pile of discarded saddles, was a narrow tunnel dug under the outer wall.

"The castle warden is mighty careless," quipped Amai.

Purnima pushed at his shoulder. "Go first."

Amai pulled a face before he could recall his bravado. "If you insist." He slid a kunai into his hand and then crawled beneath the chipped wood. Though he needed to twist onto his back to pull himself through, he passed through to the other side and then called back, "I'm through."

Kazuchiyo took his swords out of his belt to follow. The path was narrow and the dirt stung his nostrils, but Amai took hold of him from the other side to help him free. They kept close to the wall as Purnima joined them, and then they were off again, hugging the border until they had reached the westernmost edge.

"Wait," said Purnima, and they did so until the man at the guard tower turned away from the north. They sprinted across the clearing and were soon safe in the cover of towering bamboo.

"Your castle guards are as dull as beasts," said Purnima as she led them through the forest, following the curve of Sabi's mighty hillside. "We have been digging that tunnel for days. If not for my lord's mercy I would be taking Aritaka's head tonight."

"Oh?" Amai hurried his step to put him beside her. "Did he not give you a shiki for that as well? I can show you the traditional method, if you—"

"No speaking," Purnima snapped. Amai chuckled, far too pleased with himself.

They did not have to travel far before Kazuchiyo glimpsed the light of a torch through the trees and heard the scuff of horse hooves. He put the shinobi squabbling to the back of his mind as he came to realize he had not had any time to prepare for what he might say. It was true that Naoya was risking much, for certainly his Kibaku peers could not be any more thrilled at entertaining an enemy than Aritaka would have been. Still

324

Kazuchiyo marched on, hopeful that his wits would find a way to knit themselves together.

Naoya and his party were grouped in a small clearing among the trees. He was dressed in his fine coat but not his armor, and the two men with him were dressed in the same simple, dark robes as Purnima. As they approached he swiftly turned his head, catching notice of their footsteps quite easily. "My lady?" he called.

"Here, my lord," Purnima answered, and she removed each of their shiki as they entered the clearing. Surprisingly given the formality of her address, she offered only a slight nod as greeting as she moved to his side. She tugged her mask down to reveal the rest of her face. "There was no trouble."

"Good. Thank you for your efforts."

Naoya turned to Kazuchiyo, overcome with joyous relief. "Kazumune, you've come!" He strode boldly forward. "I knew that you would."

Kazuchiyo froze. By the time he had even thought of a suitable greeting Naoya was upon him, and he grabbed Kazuchiyo up in a brotherly embrace. It was so unexpected Kazuchiyo couldn't bring himself to react in thought let alone anything else, and he stood paralyzed.

"My poor lad, what you must have suffered," Naoya said with an overabundance of sincerity that would have seemed comical on a lesser man. "My father suspected you still had your dragon's honor, but I didn't dare hope until I received your letter! Such a clever poet you are, and just as clever a musician. Only a man of great valor could play the Twilight Ballad so faithfully, I know it."

Naoya leaned back, tears in his eyes. Kazuchiyo could only stare. "Thank the heavens that old bear couldn't smother you to death," he carried on. He grimaced with sympathy and then rallied himself again, clasping Kazuchiyo's shoulders. "But that's all over with now. It may be many years too late, but at least now I can fulfill my father's wishes and escort you home among friends."

Even then, Kazuchiyo could not bring himself to respond. He stared up into Naoya's hopeful grin and felt small and ashamed. It was not a dragon's honor that had bowed his head before his father's enemies for so long, that had taught him to lie and scheme. It was only a boy's cowardice and spite that had driven his sword through General Waseba's neck, only selfishness that tore his heart between two men. And still, here stood a stranger ready to shed blood and tears for him. Kazuchiyo dreamed again of grassy fields like rolling clouds, a hearty welcome from trustworthy allies.

But how could he accept? After so long a struggle, his heart was convinced that if he turned his back on Suyama, even for an instant, his home would be lost to him. The strides he had taken to earn honor among Aritaka's generals would have been for nothing, leaving him to depend instead on the courage of strangers to war in his stead. Would it be honorable to win back Suyama under green banners and pray Lord Koedzuka would let him keep it, if he even had a mind to take the dragonlands at all? Could he have borne to accept that none of his own efforts had been enough, that the strength of the Tatsutomi bloodline in him might never be enough?

Yet, still, he was tempted. Was afraid of how strongly he was tempted—was brought to tears by how strongly he was tempted.

Seeing him distraught, Naoya tempered his smile. "Oh," he said quietly, and as Kazuchiyo's shoulders began to shake he drew him close again. "Oh, dear boy, I'm sorry." He wrapped Kazuchiyo up and sighed. "You can't, can you? I understand, I truly do. I understand."

And my poor Kazuchiyo, he had no idea how badly he had longed for those words until they broke against his ears, and he gripped Naoya tightly as he cried.

Naoya gave him some time, standing sturdy as Kazuchiyo soaked his collar. Only after he had exhausted his grief did Naoya ease him back. They both had tears on their cheeks, and Kazuchiyo scrubbed his sleeve against his face. "I'm sorry," he said, and then he cleared his throat to try again. "Sir Oihata, forgive me, that's... not how I meant to greet you."

Naoya chuckled warmly, making no effort to conceal his emotion. "Please, think nothing of it." He motioned to Purnima behind him. "I only wish we had more time. If you intend to go back to the castle, we'll have to be quick."

"Yes, of course." Kazuchiyo accepted a bamboo flask from Purnima and took a long gulp of much-needed cool water. As he handed it back, he was surprised to see her discreetly wipe her eyes as well. He could feel Amai close by but didn't dare look. "I wanted to thank you for your generous offer, but I can't leave Aritaka yet. That would only unify his forces against us, and I fear that would drag this conflict on for much longer than necessary."

"Yes, you're right, of course." Naoya sighed, resigned and seemingly a little embarrassed. "I sometimes let these passions of mine get the better of me, you see." He gathered himself up. "But I couldn't bear to face you on the field again without you knowing my heart. If we must be enemies, let us be honorable ones."

Kazuchiyo couldn't help a quiet huff of laughter at the sudden change. "It's my hope we don't have to be enemies at all, because I certainly don't want to find myself across the field from you again."

He had hoped for levity, but instead was met with Naoya's deeply furrowed brow. "Then I fear you'll have to find some way of convincing that fool Aritaka to stay his hand," Naoya said. "My Lord Koedzuka has the will of the heavens on his side, and he will not bow to a scavenging beast."

"I would not ask him to," Kazuchiyo replied hastily. "I only hoped..."

He paused. Again he felt the eyes of Amai on him, and that time he chose to look. It did him little good; Amai was watching him with a peculiar intensity he could not place to its proper emotion. Amai himself had always been a sobering reminder for Kazuchiyo: even now, his mind was turning toward the impulse to scheme. Naoya was honest and emotional; surely that would make him easy to manipulate. The thought, along with his eagerness to bow to it, made Kazuchiyo ill.

"Sir Oihata, my brother is trying to have me killed," Kazuchiyo said plainly, to the shock of everyone in attendance. "Aritaka has promised to punish him for it and name me his heir, but only if we can finish this battle and return to Gyoe first. I need to end this conflict as soon as possible."

Naoya leaned back, hate on his face. "Such despicable...!" He took a breath to calm his temper. "Are you certain you won't come away with me tonight?"

"I am." Kazuchiyo clenched his fists and thought of Yagi waiting for him at the bathhouse. "I'm sorry, but I can't. Once I am lord of Sakka there will be no reason for us to war. If you can help me find a way to finish this battle, I give you my word that the samurai of Sakka will never march on your lands again."

"I believe you," said Naoya, with such ease and immediacy that Kazuchiyo was staggered by it. "I understand perfectly. How Lord Koedzuka will act on my counsel, I do not know, but he will have it." He clasped Kazuchiyo's shoulder. "I will do what I can to end this, as you said. One way or the other."

Kazuchiyo gulped and then nodded, determined not to let Naoya's sincerity overpower him. "Thank you, sir. I'm in your debt."

Naoya's seriousness melted into another radiant smile. "No, Kazumune, it is I who am grateful." He clapped Kazuchiyo soundly on both shoulders and then stepped back. "You should return now, before you're missed. And I should, too, for that matter. But I'll be listening for your songs."

Kazuchiyo gathered himself up, spending one moment more to try and clean his face. "Do you have a request?"

Naoya lit up as one of the shinobi brought the horses forward. "Well, there can be none other! 'Enmei's Willow Garden,' if you know it?"

Kazuchiyo blinked, taken aback momentarily by such

a romantic choice. Then he smiled, thinking that he should have expected the man to be of impeccable and refined tastes. "There can be none other," he replied.

"You're a good man, Kazumune." Naoya mounted his horse. "I will pray for both our fortunes, as for now they are the same." He turned about, and as he and his two men rode off, Kazuchiyo could hear him already humming the first few lines of his chosen melody.

Purnima remained, and as she watched her master depart, Amai cleared his throat. "Aren't you going with them?" he asked.

Purnima scowled at him and then quickly drew her mask back up to hide her expression. "Someone has to carry you back." She pulled three fresh shiki from her robe, slapped each on, and then motioned for haste. "Come on."

CHAPTER TWENTY-EIGHT

They headed back through the trees the way they had
come. Kazuchiyo was exhausted from the short encounter
and grateful that Amai stayed close by his side. "Did I say too
much?" he asked quietly. "About Hidemune?"

"I don't know if it will help," Amai said, "but I don't think
it will hurt, either." He hummed with amusement. "I don't
blame you for it. That Oihata is pretty intense, isn't he?"

"Mock him at your peril," said Purnima ahead of them.

Amai flinched but was undeterred. "Keen ears, she has," he
teased, and then he raised his voice. "I'm not, and I wouldn't.
But you have to admit, he's a little overwhelming."

Purnima scoffed. "Only if you find truth and honesty
overwhelming, fox."

"I kind of do," Amai replied, his voice oddly wistful. "I
think a lot of people do."

Kazuchiyo frowned, not daring to offer his opinion as
they continued back toward Sabi Castle.

The trio arrived at the outer wall, still managing to avoid
all detection. "Thank you for your help, Pa—*Pur*nima,"
Kazuchiyo said, wincing guiltily at his fumbling with the
unfamiliar pronunciation. "Lord Oihata is very lucky to have

you."

"Thank you," Purnima replied, taking the compliment seriously. She hesitated for a moment and then added, "There are only two good, luminous men left in the world, and one of them is Oihata Naoya. Do not ever forget that."

Kazuchiyo nodded, taking her just as seriously. Amai offered a smirk as he crouched down next to the tunnel under the wall. "And the other is...?" he prompted, playfully hopeful.

Purnima made a sound of disgust. "Our Lord Koedzuka, of course!" She pushed him with her foot. "Go." Chuckling, Amai crawled under.

Kazuchiyo started to follow, but then Purnima touched his arm. It took her another thoughtful moment to call up the words she intended. "Your sister," she said. "The maned warrior." The mask over her mouth twitched. "Tell her I look forward to beating her on the field again."

Kazuchiyo smiled thinly. "I can't, but I can tell you for sure she feels the same way." Purnima's eyes pinched happily, and the pair bowed to each other before splitting up.

Kazuchiyo crawled through the narrow tunnel, and as soon as he came out the other side he was met with an unexpected struggle. He had only a glimpse of bodies grappling in the dirt, and then a blade struck toward him, light from the courtyard fires reflecting off its chipped edges. With his swords in hand Kazuchiyo managed to guard himself just in time. His wrist trembled with the impact of a throwing dagger embedding itself in the scabbard of his long sword.

Kazuchiyo scrambled to his feet and barely had time to register the scene. Amai was chest down in the dirt, blood on his face, Nanpa leaping from his back. In a blur of motion the man attacked, the swing of his arm giving Kazuchiyo only enough time to again raise his scabbard as defense. The strike threw him back into the outside wall, forcing him to one foot as the other hit the empty air of the tunnel, and then Nanpa was upon him, pinning his sword to his chest.

Nanpa snorted. Close up, his face was as gnarled with

age and scars as Kazuchiyo remembered, his rough voice gut-twisting. "We always knew you'd turn traitor eventually," he snarled. "Aritaka was wrong to keep you as a pet."

Kazuchiyo shifted, trying to gain some kind of leverage, but Nanpa was broader and stronger than him, and it took everything he had to keep the dagger away from his throat. "I haven't betrayed anyone, because I was never his!" he retorted, thinking he could stall for Amai to help, though he couldn't see him and didn't know if he was in any state to do so. "And I'm going to kill you for what you did to my brother!"

Nanpa laughed in his face. "You are?" He shifted his feet, preparing for some new attack, and Kazuchiyo tensed as he concentrated on trying to predict it. "Boy, if I still had both arms you'd be dead already." Nanpa's eyes narrowed. "And I remember whose fault it is that I don't."

Kazuchiyo remembered, too. The threat against Yagi scattered his thoughts of self-preservation, and he let go of the scabbard with one hand. Nanpa pushed his weight forward to take advantage, but then Kazuchiyo wrenched out the kunai already embedded in the scabbard and struck, raking a gash down Nanpa's chest.

Nanpa retreated, cursing. The cut wasn't deep enough to truly threaten him, and he looked ready to launch himself at Kazuchiyo again, but then he realized that Amai was climbing to his feet. Though bloodied, Amai's pale eyes were piercing, his grip around his dagger unwavering. As Kazuchiyo pushed away from the wall, Nanpa reconsidered his odds. He took a step back.

"I don't have to kill you anyway," he said. "I just have to tell your father." And he turned to run.

Amai flung his kunai at him, but he was off balance, dirt and blood on his face, and the blade only managed to tear Nanpa's robe. As he cursed, Kazuchiyo hurried to support him.

"Go after him!" Amai said, trying to push Kazuchiyo away. "If he tells your brother—"

"It's too late," Kazuchiyo interrupted. He was already

winded from the short skirmish and knew he had no hope of overtaking the man, let alone overpowering and killing him without drawing attention. Already he could hear the curious shouts of guards heading in their direction. Hastily he shoved the discarded saddles over their tunnel and snatched up both his swords. "Come on—we have to hurry."

Kazuchiyo grabbed Amai by the elbow and led the way back through the maze of buildings. Those that had heard the commotion were heading in the other direction, so they were cautious, pausing at corners to be sure they wouldn't run into anyone as they retreated to the bathhouse. They all but crashed through the servant's entrance and were greeted by Yagi supporting them each with one arm.

"Are you all right?" he demanded, and though Kazuchiyo pulled away he continued to offer the shaky Amai the support of his elbow. "He's bleeding."

"Grab water," Kazuchiyo said as he dropped his weapons and scrambled out of his clothing. "Hidemune is coming."

"I'm sorry," Amai murmured as he fumbled with his belt. Now that they had halted Kazuchiyo could see the shallow gash in his scalp; he was teetering on his feet dizzily from whatever blow Nanpa had landed. "I should have expected that."

"Quiet." Kazuchiyo wrenched Amai's clothes off and knelt down to untie his sandals. "Yagi, dump that water on him."

Yagi overturned one of the wash basins on Amai's head; Amai clapped both hands to his mouth to keep from yelping. As Kazuchiyo hushed him again, he could hear voices from the lower keep. In desperation he snatched up a strip of rough hemp fabric to wrap around Amai's head as if to protect his hair from the bath. "Please, Amai," he said, dragging him onto a nearby bench. "Don't say anything stupid."

Amai blinked at him, realizing for the first time that they were both stark naked, huddling very close together next to the wash bins. "Stupid?" he echoed, and a slow grin stretched his lips as Kazuchiyo scrubbed the remaining blood from his face and neck. "But that would be so out of character for me,

Hidemune would—"

"*Amai*," Kazuchiyo snapped.

The door to the bathhouse flew open, and he held his breath.

Hidemune stormed inside. He had General Fuchihara and a handful of other samurai with him, all of them wearing swords. But the scene gave them pause: three men crowded close in the bathhouse, each of them naked and soaked, Kazuchiyo with his hands perched tenderly on his young companion, the immaculately-bodied Yagi standing over them. A sight better suited to pillow-books than to a scroll-painter hoping to capture Hidemune's triumph over his bitter enemy.

Hidemune flushed and sputtered. "K-Kazumune!" he bellowed as if hoping to rekindle his proper outrage. "You are the snake I've always known you to be. Sneaking out in the middle of the night to meet with our enemies? Father will have your head for this."

"What? I don't know what you're talking about." Kazuchiyo wanted to cringe at how rough and out of breath he sounded, but then he saw that Fuchihara and the others were only blushing more darkly. Though his heart was pounding and his head faint, he played into the ruse, ladling more water onto Amai's shoulder. "We've been here all night."

He glanced to Amai as if to confirm it, and was almost knocked out of his wits and character; Amai was leaning heavily to one side, eyes half-lidded as they regarded the samurai with lazy indifference. It may have been the effects of a still-bleeding head wound, but his limbs were so lax and face so content no one would second-guess that he really had been vigorously engaged all evening. Kazuchiyo swallowed.

"You've got real nerve barging in like this," said Yagi. He was still a very poor liar and sought to make up for it with the force of his tone. Judging by the way the men shifted, he was successful. "Don't you have any manners?"

"You deny the accusation, then?" Fuchihara looked down his nose at the trio. "You weren't outside the walls tonight?"

"I was not," Kazuchiyo replied, praying he sounded calm. "How could I have been?"

"A tunnel was discovered under the northern wall," he said, and Kazuchiyo busied himself with the ladle again to keep from showing any of his nerves. "And a shinobi's kunai there as well. The guards heard a scuffle."

"I don't know anything about that."

"Then why is he bleeding?" asked one of the samurai next to Hidemune.

Kazuchiyo stiffened and could not help looking to Amai, likely giving them away further. A spot of blood had soaked through the hemp covering Amai's crown. He took a breath without having any idea what he would say or do, whether come up with a lie or fake ignorance.

Amai took his hand and squeezed it tight. "My lords play rough," he said, smirking at Hidemune. "Especially the big one."

Fuchihara and the rest of the men shifted uncomfortably, but Hidemune only grew in anger. He gestured sharply at Amai. "Come over here so I can see," he said, his other hand gripping his sword.

Kazuchiyo rallied a protest, but he didn't need to; Yagi stepped in front of them both, shoulders squared to the entourage. "Come and get him yourself," he snarled.

Hidemune shrank back. Yagi was ever impressive, and with his skin red from the warm bathwater, he resembled his oni namesake more than ever. After much hesitation Hidemune looked to his samurai, but their faces reflected just as much apprehension. He was working up the gall to order them to it when another group approached from the outside.

"Hidemune?" called Lord Aritaka. The samurai parted from Hidemune's side to bow for their lord. "What in the world is going on?"

Kazuchiyo slipped off the bench and grabbed up his robe, drawing it on just as Aritaka entered the bathhouse. A few of his own men trailed just outside, and Kazuchiyo recognized some as those who had been ordered to guard his bedchamber. Among them was General Hosoda, and his eyes sought out Kazuchiyo's. Kazuchiyo held them for a moment and then lowered his head to properly greet his father.

"Father, I'm sorry to disturb you," he said. "There's been some misunderstanding between my brother and I."

"He and that rat-fox were outside the walls tonight," Hidemune said quickly. "They were conspiring with the enemy, just like I said! First he knew about Oihata's attack just before it happened, and now this? He's a traitor!"

Aritaka frowned, looking a little too willing to believe it. But Kazuchiyo was humbly bowed, and Amai with his bloody head was well hidden behind the imposing Yagi, and unsurprisingly the lord of Sakka, too, was not keen to order Yagi-douji to do anything. "Kazumune," he said. "What say you?"

"I don't know what's inspired my brother to spread such a malicious lie," he replied. "All I care about is victory for Sakka; I've been here bathing since just after sundown."

Hosoda cleared his throat, and Aritaka glanced to him. "It's true, my lord," he said, covering his wounded jaw with one hand. "I was here when he entered."

Hidemune puffed up indignantly. "That's just their excuse," he ranted. "I *know* they left the castle! Left and came back to hide their betrayal!"

Aritaka did not spare him a look, continuing to watch Hosoda. "They were here the whole time?" he asked.

"Yes, lord." Hosoda rubbed his jaw again. "My mouth is injured, but not my ears."

Aritaka snorted, and he may have blushed as well as he turned on Hidemune. "Are you satisfied?" he asked roughly. "Apologize to your brother for your slander."

Hidemune shuddered hatefully, his eyes leaping between Aritaka and Kazuchiyo. "Never," he snapped. He spun about and shoved his way out of the bathhouse.

Hidemune's samurai wavered awkwardly behind him.

336

They offered conciliatory bows to Kazuchiyo and their lord and then scuttled out. Fuchihara bowed low with a muttered, "Please forgive me, Lord Kazumune," before doing the same. General Hosoda offered and received a grateful nod from Kazuchiyo before following Aritaka's dismissal. It warmed Kazuchiyo's heart.

"Now's no time for trysts in the bathhouse," Aritaka scolded his younger son. "Get dressed and return to your room. The captain here will escort you."

"I understand, Father," Kazuchiyo replied obediently. "Please excuse my... impropriety." Aritaka harrumphed awkwardly and showed himself out.

Kazuchiyo waited until he was far gone before turning to his companions. There were still guards just outside the door, preventing him from expressing all his relief and gratitude, but he couldn't help a heavy sigh and a tired grin. "Amai, are you all right?"

"Never better," purred Amai. He grabbed Yagi's bicep, using it to help himself upright. "With my two heroes looking after me."

He pushed up on his toes, took Yagi's face in both hands, and kissed him. Though Yagi was surprised, he did not try to pull away as Amai's naked body swayed into his. A shudder ran the length of his muscular frame, and his hand hesitated before gripping the back of Amai's neck. Kazuchiyo could only stare. He wondered, heat in his cheeks, if he looked like that when caught in Yagi's kiss. Their heights and proportions were so mismatched, and yet Amai curled to Yagi's chest like he belonged there. His heart twisted and fluttered at the sight of them, and it wasn't until Amai leaned back and cast him a sly glance that he understood the sensation for the arousal it was.

Then Amai turned, his intentions painted clear across his face. Kazuchiyo had only a moment to decide if he would allow it, and he spent it looking to Yagi. The heady expression he found there tightened his stomach, and when Amai leaned into him for his kiss, Kazuchiyo granted it, welcomed it, took

Amai by the shoulders and pulled him in. Whatever Yagi's complaints, he had always found Amai's lips sweet, and the frustration of their tumultuous courtship made him want to gnaw at them. He kissed Amai forcefully, and for once was granted a clear victory, Amai wilting happily in his arms. Even that might have been part of the game, but Kazuchiyo didn't care, and when Amai eased back, he was panting.

"We make a good team," said Amai, breathless himself. He tried to be suave as he stepped away, but his footing betrayed him, and he needed Yagi's hand against his spine to catch his balance. He chuckled. "A better one, once I've had some sleep." After his balance was assured again, he moved to grab up his discarded clothing. "And some wine."

"Sleep," agreed Kazuchiyo. "And a proper dressing for your head." Amai made some retort, but by then he wasn't listening, his attention returning to Yagi.

They watched each other for a long moment, breath held and eyes seeking an answer for the question neither had the courage to ask. Both looked to Amai and back. When Yagi moved forward, took Kazuchiyo's chin and tipped it for a kiss of his own, it wasn't with the anger of jealousy or the desperation of possessiveness. There was only excitement, however incredulous, only reassurance. The realization that he wouldn't be forced to choose between them after all shook Kazuchiyo with relief, and the burden of guilt drawn from him left him weightless.

"Well, we've all had our fill now, haven't we?" goaded Amai. He tossed Yagi's robes at him. "Let's get out of here before your brother comes back for his share."

Kazuchiyo smiled weakly. It was a night of rawness and newness for him, and he wasn't sure how to react to either of them, what to do or think. Thankfully, his companions resuming their usual banter rescued him from that embarrassment. Yagi and Amai bickered as they dressed as if nothing had transpired, and they stayed close by Kazuchiyo's side as they made their way back to his chambers for badly needed sleep.

CHAPTER TWENTY-NINE

When Kazuchiyo awoke the next morning, the first thing he did was to retrieve his flute from the window to play "Enmei's Willow Garden." A courtly ballad was a strange choice for a warrior's son on the eve of battle, but no one could hope for a more heartfelt and faithful rendition. He prayed that Naoya would hear it.

As he returned to his fellows, he was a touch surprised to see that though Yagi was awake and waiting for him, Amai was still curled beneath his blanket, deeply asleep. Carefully he parted Amai's hair and was relieved to see the healing progress of his wound.

"He's been sleeping with one eye open for some time, I'm sure," Kazuchiyo whispered. "He should take this chance to recover."

"What about you?" asked Yagi. "Are you well?"

"I feel rested now, but I'm sure that won't be for long," Kazuchiyo said with a grim smile. "I was able to speak with Oihata last night. I'm so glad for it, but to be honest, I'm not certain how much good it did. He has no more power to stop this war than I do."

"But he knows you want to stop it, right?" Yagi pressed.

"If he understands, that's good enough. You were so happy to know he at least understood, the last time."

Kazuchiyo straightened up, and seeing the calm, thoughtful focus Yagi was regarding him with warmed his chest. "Yes, you're right," he said. "I am happy."

"Then it was worth it," said Yagi, and he stood to start collect their clothing. "We should eat breakfast outside with the soldiers, so they can see us before your brother starts spreading rumors."

Kazuchiyo watched him for a moment, struck by how well he was adapting. Following a sudden urge, he pushed to his feet and snagged Yagi by the front of his robe. Up on his toes he kissed him, and, though caught off guard, Yagi reciprocated.

"Thank you," said Kazuchiyo. "For everything, last night."

Yagi glanced to the still sleeping Amai and back. His cheeks went red and he struggled over a response. "He's not so bad," he mumbled.

"I didn't just mean that, but… yes, that, too." Kazuchiyo blushed as well and leaned back. "I know you don't really get along, but—"

"He's not terrible," Yagi interrupted, still deeply embarrassed. "But if he tries any more fox tricks I'll still wring his neck."

"He might enjoy it," Kazuchiyo teased with a smile, and the two of them dressed for the day.

Breakfast among the soldiers was a well-meant but short-lived affair. Kazuchiyo and Yagi barely had time to swallow a few mouthfuls of rice while listening to tales of the evening's ruckus before one of Lord Aritaka's attendants came to summon Kazuchiyo. Without complaint, and gifting his remaining rations to his companion, Kazuchiyo followed the attendant to the upper level of the main keep.

Lord Aritaka had assembled his generals in the war hall,

340

each of them looking just as harried by the sudden summons. He wasted no time in stating his business.

"I received a message this morning from Master Iomori no Jun, who has lately observed the Kibaku army changing formations within their camp. By her account some messenger came to them in the night. It may be news of reinforcements arriving, or whatever else, but we have no time to waste speculating. We attack tomorrow."

The generals nodded and mumbled in agreement, while Kazuchiyo held his breath. He could not help but wonder if it was merely Naoya returning to camp after their meeting who had been mistaken for an incoming messenger. It pained him to think of them facing each other on the field again so soon.

"Based on her recommendations and those of the rest of this council, I have formed a plan of attack," Lord Aritaka continued, and all eyes and ears on him sharpened. "A two-pronged attack against each of the bridges that the crows now occupy." He used his fan to nudge the various tiles representing their forces into place across his map. Everyone leaned forward to see.

Five hundred men remained at Sabi Castle. To the northern bridge, where the larger Kibaku force of five thousand and reserves were positioned, he had set out seventy-five hundred, leaving only a thousand Sakka samurai to fend against Oihata Naoya's southern force of more than twice their number. His intent was clear and not unsound: to overwhelm Lord Koedzuka's force with numbers and to prevent their reserves from crossing the bridge. With Naoya's soldiers already pinned on the western bank, a smaller force had a chance of holding them without fear of being outflanked or overrun. It was a dangerous gamble that would be won or lost by men willing to sacrifice everything for their lord.

Kazuchiyo prickled with ill ease as he recounted each tile to be sure of his sums. Though Aritaka's face was stoic, beside him, Hidemune smirked boastfully. There was still some piece to be laid.

"A bold strategy, lord," said Fuchihara, eyeing the board critically. Certainly he and each of his peers were curious as to who would be assigned the crucial, undesirable defense of Chibatake Bridge. "We must attack both at once, that's certain. But can such a small force reliably hold back Oihata?"

"It can," Aritaka replied with confidence. "That bridge is the narrower of the two, and so far General Waseba has prevented them from crossing. Their superior numbers will matter little in such a bottleneck. With a larger advantage over Koedzuka we can destroy him ever faster and leave the Kibaku army leaderless and in disarray."

The men shifted. It was Rakuteru who at last asked outright, "Who does the task fall to, my lord?"

Aritaka hesitated only a beat, but long enough for Kazuchiyo to dread the answer. "The honor will go to General Ebara and his men."

Kazuchiyo's stomach twisted as fiercely as if a spear had been thrust into it. "You mean, General Ebara and his *son?*" he said.

Aritaka took a deep breath before turning his gaze to Kazuchiyo. "Of course."

"No," said Kazuchiyo before he could stop himself. He sat very still, drawn too tight with panic to even tremble.

"Ebara Motonobu wields the strongest spear in our army," Aritaka said firmly, as if he had rehearsed. "He belongs nowhere else."

"No," Kazuchiyo insisted, only vaguely aware of the many other eyes on him, two of them particularly gleeful at his misery. "No, he belongs at the vanguard. If it's swift victory against Lord Koedzuka we need, let the sharpest spear lead."

Aritaka only sat up straighter, resolute. "It's numbers we need in the north, skill in the south. My mind is made up."

"Your mind?" Kazuchiyo repeated, and at last a shudder worked through him as he scoffed. "Your *mind?*"

"Lord Aritaka," interrupted Ebara, hoping to save Kazuchiyo from speaking too far out of turn. "I am honored to accept this task from you. Oihata will not cross Chibatake while we stand."

Kazuchiyo shook his head. "Father, please—"

"Don't be so worried," Hidemune jeered. "He's going to be in good company."

"He will," agreed Aritaka. "You'll be joining him."

The color drained from Hidemune's face. "What?"

"Hidemune will be taking command over Captain Joushiki and his five hundred men," Aritaka explained to the stunned room. "They are already positioned at the bridge opposite Oihata, and it will only disturb our defenses to withdraw them. General Ebara," he glanced to Kazuchiyo, "and his son, Motonobu, will join and overtake their ranks to form the defense." He continued to point out tiles on the map. "Rakuteru and Waseba with their forces will lead the vanguard at Nodo Bridge. Hosoda and his two thousand men will be positioned toward the southern flank, Fuchihara to the north. Mahiro will remain at Sabi Castle with five hundred of my men, which will be more than enough to hold should Oihata break through. Kazuchiyo will remain with me at the command."

Kazuchiyo's knuckles whitened against his knees, and as the room wound tight in confusion, he found himself meeting Hidemune's wild look. For the first time he felt that they were equaled, if only in their outrage and desperation.

"Let me take Hidemune's place," he said. "You said I performed admirably during the charge. Allow me to take command of Captain Joushiki and his men."

"No," said Aritaka.

"Why not?" demanded Hidemune. "Let him command that oni of his—it's what he wants!"

"*No.*" Aritaka leaned back. "The rest of you are dismissed to pass the orders to your men. We depart at sunrise."

The generals were slow to rise, each of them exchanging glances. Though Kazuchiyo remained where he was, awash with frustration and silent, Hidemune could not restrain himself. "Father, I don't question your strategy, but you can't be serious about Kazumune and me. What good will he do you at the command post? All he does is betray your orders and race ahead. Let him throw himself against Oihata!"

"Hold your tongue, boy," Aritaka snapped, one eye on his generals still filtering out of the room. "Your cowardice only convinces me more that you ought to prove your mettle on the field."

Kazuchiyo clenched his teeth, waiting only until the panel shut behind him. One can easily imagine the men lingering in the hall to overhear, but he could not restrain himself any longer. "Everyone can see whose cowardice is on display here," he said, and Aritaka's face went red. "You can't bring yourself to choose between us, so you'll let Kibaku arrows and spears do it for you."

"I will not forgive disrespect from either of you!" Aritaka stood, his fists tight at his sides. Both sons followed suit. "You are men of Sakka, and you will accept your duty with honor!"

"How can you talk about honor?" Hidemune cried. "You'd drown your own blood in the river to protect the son of our enemy—"

"He is *my* son now!" Aritaka bellowed, and Kazuchiyo quaked through to his bones. "You have brought this fate on your own head!" He took Hidemune by the front of his robe, twisting the Aritaka crest embroidered there beneath his shaking fist. "To have conspired against your own house behind my back with that mercenary? You will order Nanpa to abandon his mission, and then reclaim your honor by waylaying Oihata. Do you understand me?"

Hidemune stared back at his father, tears of frustration in his eyes. "You promised me," he said, but seeing that his words did nothing to move Aritaka, he shrank back in bitterness. "He will destroy our clan someday, I know it."

"Have you no spine?" Aritaka pushed Hidemune back and scowled. "I am giving you the chance to prove yourself. If you won't rise to meet my challenge, you are no son of mine."

Hidemune grimaced all over, and as he scraped his sleeve

across his face, Kazuchiyo stepped forward. "And how will you challenge me, Father?" he asked, his composure nearly as tenuous as his brother's. "How does it test my mettle to waste Sakka's finest spear while I cower beside you in safety?"

Aritaka turned on him, anger and a sliver of fear drawing his features tight. But as he returned Kazuchiyo's anguished glare, his shoulders began to sag. "You have proven yourself to me well enough," he said, once again drawing from some prepared script.

"So you say," Kazuchiyo replied, "but it seems to me that you don't trust me at all, if you're so eager to sacrifice the only samurai loyal to me."

Aritaka stepped toward him, Hidemune utterly forgotten, map tiles snapping beneath his feet. "Ebara Motonobu belongs where the fighting is thickest," he said, "as you yourself have argued."

Kazuchiyo held his ground. "You're sentencing him to death because he's mine!"

"I am!" Aritaka said forcefully, and before Kazuchiyo could react with outrage he stepped closer still, close enough to take his son's shoulders. "I am," he repeated, quieter then. "For your own good."

Kazuchiyo rooted his feet to the tatami, his fists to his sides. His lungs were full of fire, and he knew that to move any muscle at all would set him down an irreparable path. Lord Aritaka, even more coward than fool, must have seen as much, as he clasped Kazuchiyo tight. "You chose war, Kazumune. In war, men die—powerful men, invincible men you thought would be beside you forever. You can't place so much hope on one man, not ever."

He took in a deep breath, and even if he had given Kazuchiyo space to interject, he did not trust himself to fill it. "When my brother died, it fractured our clan," Aritaka continued gravely. "When the Red Dragon's brother died, it broke his spirit, and he never recovered. Suffer your losses now, while you're young. You'll be better for it."

345

Kazuchiyo stared straight back. Seeing that he was not prepared to answer, Aritaka leaned away. "Well, you overcame your hatred for me once already," he muttered. "You'll do it again." He let Kazuchiyo go and stepped away. "Save some blame for Master Iomori while you're at it. Much of this design was part of her council."

Kazuchiyo blinked, shaken from his fury by the unexpected admission. "Iomori?"

"You let that mystic decide our fates?" Hidemune said, appalled. "But why—"

"Enough!" Aritaka barked. He turned his back on them both, broad shoulders sloped with sudden exhaustion. "Both of you are dismissed. You should use the rest of today to prepare yourselves for tomorrow."

"Father!" Hidemune tried again, but met only with Aritaka's turned back and silence, he at last accepted defeat. With one more heavy, hateful glare in Kazuchiyo's direction, he stormed out. In time, Kazuchiyo had no choice but to follow.

"This is *your* fault!" Hidemune ranted as soon as Kazuchiyo joined him in the hall. "If not for you—"

"Did you not listen to a word from his mouth?" Kazuchiyo interrupted, all his bitterness welling forth outside of Aritaka's presence. "If you hadn't left Gyoe bent on killing me in the first place, you wouldn't be anywhere near Chibatake Bridge now!"

"H-How dare you!" Hidemune's gaze darted about, certainly concerned by the number of ears that had to be nearby. "If I wanted you dead, all I'd have to do is draw my sword."

"Then draw and be done with it," Kazuchiyo retorted, his hand going to his scabbard. "You've never bested me before, and you won't now."

Hidemune scowled. He reached for his katana, only for his hand to shake around its grip. Before he could commit to a humiliating retreat or a doomed attack, a blade appeared at the side of his throat, and Amai's familiar voice buzzed in a thoughtful hum.

"Relax, Hidemune, I'm here to help you," Amai said, leaning against Hidemune's tensed shoulder. "Now that I'm threatening to cut your throat, you can walk away without embarrassing yourself any further."

Hidemune let go of his sword, his face contorted in hate. "You backstabbing rat!" he snarled. "If you weren't such a gutless whore—"

"You'd still be on the other end of my knife." Amai angled the tip toward Hidemune's jugular as he moved alongside him. "And your own father is calling for your head now, so I won't think twice about flicking my wrist."

Hidemune took a quick step back and flinched when Amai faked that he might follow. "I'll have you killed for this," he stuttered, and then turned, hurrying away in full retreat.

"You'll have to hire better shinobi!" Amai shouted after him, but by the time he turned toward Kazuchiyo, his flippancy had vanished. "Are you all right?"

Kazuchiyo didn't know how to answer. "Did you hear everything?"

"Yeah." Amai stowed his kunai and came closer. "I think a lot of people did."

He nodded toward the far end of the hall, and Kazuchiyo turned, spotting Ebara and Hosoda standing close together in conversation. Kazuchiyo's breath caught, and before he could think better of it, he rushed down the hall toward them. "General Ebara!"

Amai chased after him. "Kazu, wait—"

"General!" Kazuchiyo halted in front of Ebara. His hope withered in the face of the man's calmly resigned expression. "My father asks too much of you," he said anyway. "Won't you say anything to him?"

Ebara sighed. "His strategy is sound, and it requires sacrifice. It is an honorable duty."

"It's a punishment not meant for you," Kazuchiyo insisted. "He thinks it won't matter if you're overrun, because by then he'll have Koedzuka's head and Oihata won't have momentum enough to overcome Hosoda's numbers." He glanced to General Hosoda; though the man reflected sympathy, it comforted Kazuchiyo very little. "You and your son will die."

"If you believe that, you also believe Koedzuka will be dead," Ebara reasoned, "and that is victory for Sakka."

Kazuchiyo struggled to reply, and in his lapse, Ebara offered him a fatherly smile. "Kazumune, I understand. But our lord has spoken." He patted his shoulder. "Have a bit more faith in Motonobu and me."

Kazuchiyo shook his head, but it was too late. Ebara turned to leave. "But… but General!" Kazuchiyo called after him, only to whirl next on Hosoda. "General Hosoda, *please*."

"I'm sorry," said Hosoda. Though he seemed to mean it, the plea did nothing to sway him. He bowed his head and departed after Ebara, leaving Kazuchiyo flustered in their wake.

"Kazu, calm down," said Amai. "We'll think of something."

Amai touched his back, but that gentle contact startled Kazuchiyo out of his brief stupor. "We should have left," he said, and he spun to head off down a different corridor. His every effort to compose himself failed. He was desperate to find Yagi, to let a stronger body support him and reassure him then. "We should have all gone past the wall with Oihata—"

"You can't talk like that here," Amai hissed. "Just take a breath. It's not as bad as it seems."

"Not as—" Kazuchiyo didn't break stride as he cast Amai a hard glare. "Aritaka is throwing Yagi to his death because of me, and I'm supposed to remain calm?"

"We have all day to come up with something. Maybe you can think of some better strategy that will win him over." Amai's lip quirked. "You're the smartest man here, after all."

But Kazuchiyo would not be swayed. "I was a fool to think so," he rambled on as they turned a corner, heading for the stairs. "I thought I was a step ahead of him, that I could finally sway him." He scoffed. "But he's a coward and a fool, and so was I. What's the point of getting any kind of revenge if it costs Yagi his life?"

"Kazu, I'm serious, you can't—" Amai tried again, but it was too late. They turned the final corner and nearly collided with General Rakuteru.

At last Kazuchiyo stopped. He met Rakuteru's stoic gaze, knowing immediately and with certainty that Rakuteru had been waiting for him, and that he had heard everything. The heat that had propelled him from Aritaka's chamber sharpened to biting cold, so that he could barely take a breath through his aching lungs.

Rakuteru took Kazuchiyo's shoulder, and though he at first thought the worst, it soon became clear that he meant only to steady the poor, reckless boy. "Catch your breath," he said, and with effort, Kazuchiyo did so.

Amai bowed deeply, as required, and Kazuchiyo regained his senses as he did the same. "Excuse me," he said. "I wasn't... watching my path."

"I could probably say something witty about that," replied Rakuteru, "but I don't think you're in any temper to hear it. You ought to return to your room and compose yourself before seeking Motonobu, for both your sakes."

Kazuchiyo lowered his eyes, ashamed of his behavior and fearful of what Rakuteru had overheard. "Yes, you're right. Thank you, General."

Rakuteru stepped aside to let them pass, but as they set foot on the stairs, he called after them. "Kazumune." Kazuchiyo flinched, but then the general lowered his voice. "You *should* have more faith in Yagi-douji, and in the rest of us, too. There is more than one samurai here who serves you."

Kazuchiyo blinked at him, again speechless. He did not have time to recover himself before Rakuteru, too, moved on, deeper into the keep.

"Let's take his advice," said Amai, tugging Kazuchiyo's elbow, and the two of them retreated to their bedchamber.

Once behind closed doors, Kazuchiyo sank to the floor. The small portion of breakfast he'd eaten churned in his stomach as he realized what he had said and how he had acted.

"What if he tells Aritaka?" he said, struggling anew to regain use of his wits. "What if anyone else heard?"

"Then you won't have to worry about hiding with the old bear at the command tent," said Amai. He sat down very close in front of Kazuchiyo, nearly in his lap. "Take a breath, okay? Look at me." He took Kazuchiyo's face in his hands. "It's going to be all right. We have time."

At last Kazuchiyo was able to fully embrace his advice; though his emotions were as twisted and fragile as spiderwebs, he breathed slowly until his raging pulse had calmed.

"I'm sorry," he said quietly. "I don't know what came over me in there."

"I do. I'd call it 'sheer panic.'" Amai chuckled. "You know, after seeing you cry all over Oihata last night, I figured there weren't many sides to you left that I didn't know. Guess I was wrong."

Kazuchiyo's cheeks flushed; he could still feel that rawness behind his eyes. "I don't need you teasing me right now."

That only made Amai's smile deepen. "That's more like you." He leaned in for a quick kiss and then let Kazuchiyo go. "So, talk. I really meant it—there's no one here smarter than you. What can we do, and what *can't* we do?"

Kazuchiyo licked his lips as he considered. "We can't trust Aritaka," he said, feeling more like himself with his mind put to work. "Even that plan he laid out for us today—anything could change his mind. Especially..."

He crawled away from Amai and began rummaging through his personal effects. "He said to pin half the blame on Iomori," he recalled. "Aritaka is no strategist. If she offered him this plan, she can convince him to change his mind."

"Would she?" Amai joined him, and when Kazuchiyo handed him an inkstone, he obediently retrieved a flask of water to prepare it. "Does she really care who risks their life on that bridge?"

"She said once that she saved my life *and Yagi's* for a reason." Kazuchiyo unearthed the strip of parchment Iomori had given him when he first struck out from Gyoe and smoothed it out on a writing tray before him. "She wouldn't waste his life lightly. Maybe she meant for Rakuteru to take the bridge and Aritaka changed that part of the plan just to spite me." He shuddered at the thought and then stopped for a moment, taking a deep breath so that his hand wouldn't shake around the brush.

"You're not going to ask me to take that to the front, are you?" asked Amai. "I doubt Nanpa's given up, and I don't want to leave you."

"No." Kazuchiyo wet his brush in the ink. "If Iomori was right about this paper, you won't have to."

Lord Aritaka has tasked the Ebara clan with defense of Chibatake Bridge, he wrote, *but I strongly believe they are better suited to the vanguard at Nodo Bridge. Please assist me in convincing our lord of the same, and let General Rakuteru's larger, more seasoned force defend from Oihata.*

Amai leaned back on his hands, watching as Kazuchiyo blew the ink dry. "Rakuteru did just pronounce his fealty to you, in a way. Though he might not have if he knew you would have him take Ebara's place."

"He is the stronger general," said Kazuchiyo without looking up. "In command of more numbers, but not so great as to upset Iomori's strategy. He's the better choice."

"His son isn't any older than Yagi."

"So?" Kazuchiyo caught himself, his stomach once again turning over. "If you want me to admit I care more about Yagi than all the rest of them put together, I do. If there was a wiser strategy, I would follow it; if I could have stopped this war before it started, I would have!" He gave his message a shake and then began folding it into the shape of a doll. "But if Aritaka won't be satisfied without blood and death, let it be someone else's."

"I'm not blaming you," Amai said. "I just want you to be prepared."

"I am." Kazuchiyo paused, forcing himself to take Amai's words to heart. He truly did, after all, remember that *he* had started the war in the first place. He took in a deep breath and let it out slowly. "I know."

He set the folded paper onto the open window sill, and after a few moments, it stirred. Its paper wings stretched and fluttered, and just like a strange sparrow, it took off and headed west.

"Here's hoping," said Amai. "If that doesn't work, what else?"

"I don't know." Kazuchiyo busied himself with cleaning up the ink as he tried to draw a map of the territory in his mind, but all his thoughts turned to one direction. "I just want to find Yagi."

"All right." Amai helped him tidy up and then pulled him to his feet. "Let's go."

The pair headed down from the keep, and all along their path whispers ceased with every corner they turned. Kazuchiyo kept his gaze straight ahead, determined not to pause or pay any mind. It was too late to worry about who had heard what or what they now thought of him because of it. As they came out into the courtyard, however, he found himself face to face with Mahiro, without any means or excuse to avoid her.

"Kazumune!" Mahiro latched immediately onto his sleeve. She was simply dressed, her left arm tucked into her robe and lashed to her torso. Her eyes were red and strained. It pained him to see her so uncharacteristically out of sorts.

"Are you all right?" she asked. "I heard you were upset after the meeting with Father."

Try as he might, Kazuchiyo could not keep his distress completely out of his face. "I'm all right now," he tried to reassure her. "I'm just... concerned, about the upcoming battle." He offered her a sympathetic smile. "I heard you won't be joining us."

Mahiro gave a great huff, but he could see her lip tremble with genuine emotion. "Damn Sabi healer refused her consent. Said I could split open an organ or something. But I know..." Her expression twisted. "I'm sure Father made her say that because he doesn't want me out there. He doesn't want me to choose sides."

Kazuchiyo's breath caught. As much as he should have anticipated having to face this crisis with her, he was wholly unprepared. "Mahiro..."

"You two shouldn't have this conversation out in the open," said Amai quietly.

"Then come on," said Mahiro. She yanked on Kazuchiyo's sleeve, dragging him further away from the keep. "Walk with me."

Kazuchiyo let her lead him, and soon saw her aim: they were headed toward the stables, Amai trailing close behind. "Mahiro," he said again, stalling. "I'm sorry. You shouldn't be involved in this."

"I'm sister to both of you, aren't I?" She sniffed and shook her head. "Just come on, I need to tell you."

Kazuchiyo went with her into the stables. They came across a pair of workers, but one fierce look from Mahiro sent them scuttling away. "Hashikiri's okay," she said as she dragged Kazuchiyo down the line of stalls. Kazuchiyo had only a moment to look over his gray gelding, who was eating happily, before he was pulled onward. "His side is gonna heal up fine, but you can't put a saddle on him now. It'll itch his wound, and he'll buck you."

"I didn't think of that," Kazuchiyo admitted. "But there's—"

"Here." Mahiro drew him to a halt in front of the last stall.

Suzumekage leaned her long head out of the stall, and her ears flicked curiously as she and Kazuchiyo regarded each other. She was as ever an impressive animal, sturdy and attentive. When Mahiro slipped a chunk of radish into Kazuchiyo's palm, he was happy to pass it on.

"I want you to ride Suzumekage tomorrow," said Mahiro, and Kazuchiyo instantly sobered, understanding her meaning. She faced him with tremulous determination. "She's strong and smart, and she likes you. She won't do me any good here, so I want you to have her."

Kazuchiyo's chest tightened in painful sympathy. "You don't—"

"It's all I can do!" Mahiro blurted out before he could finish, her cheeks and eyes red with emotion. "I can't just do nothing, I have to... to choose, and I want *you* to have her, okay?"

Tears rolled down her cheeks, and she swiped at them with her sleeve. "I'm sorry," she said. "I'm so sorry. Maybe if I was smarter and better, Father could have picked *me,* and you and Hidemune wouldn't have to fight at all!"

"No," Kazuchiyo said quickly, and he took her shoulders. "No, Mahiro, please don't. It's not your fault." Anger and guilt gnawed at his throat as he fought to keep his own emotion at bay. "It's not at all your fault—don't talk like that. You're Sakka's finest and exactly how you should be." He ground his teeth. "It's not even about Hidemune and me, really; it's about us and Father. This was always going to happen, and he *knew* that."

Mahiro couldn't speak for a while as she tried to staunch her tears. Gradually, she calmed. "Please say you'll take her."

"I will. I'll be honored to ride her. Thank you."

Mahiro nodded again, and then with a deep breath she shook him off. "I'm going to stay with her today, to take care of her for you. She'll be fit and perfect."

"Of course." Kazuchiyo struggled after a more meaningful reply, but he could think of nothing to express himself properly. "Thank you, Sister." He bowed his head respectfully and then hurried out.

In the courtyard once more, Kazuchiyo took time to catch his breath. Mahiro's tears had disrupted so much of the composure he had tried to rebuild; he closed his eyes, willing all that bitter emotion back down, deep below his surface. It wasn't until he had succeeded and opened his eyes again that he noticed the subtle pressure of Amai's hand against his back.

"You're being very generous today," Kazuchiyo said.

"Blame the head wound," replied Amai, but then his smile grew more serious. "You've been looking out for yourself a long time now. I don't mind taking a turn."

Had Kazuchiyo been in stronger spirits he might have pressed for more, but in the moment he was too eager for any support to question it. "Thank you," he said simply, and they continued in their search.

CHAPTER THIRTY

Yagi was not to be found on the grounds. Everyone was busy with preparations—or determined to make themselves busy the moment Kazuchiyo appeared—and it took time to find someone willing to offer the truth. Yagi had been spirited away to the lesser keep by his adoptive father soon after Aritaka concluded his war council. Though the temptation to storm Ebara's quarters was a strong one, Kazuchiyo relented. As Amai had reminded him, they had time.

So Kazuchiyo busied himself as he was meant to, with preparations for the coming battle. He polished his armor and tightened the cords. He spoke to the senior captains to be sure that they all understood the formations and troop forces of both sides. He even found a few castle guards born in Suyama who refreshed his memory of the riverbank landscape. In the afternoon, when exhaustion threatened him, he retreated to the training hall and went through simple katana exercises with a few of the younger soldiers.

As the sun dipped into the west, Kazuchiyo drew Amai aside. "Find supper for us and meet me back at my chamber," he said. "There's something I need to do."

"Nothing foolish, I hope," Amai replied, concerned and

teasing at once.

"I hope not either." Kazuchiyo smiled grimly. To give himself courage he leaned in to press a small kiss to Amai's cheek. "I won't be long."

Amai blinked, and then with a smile of his own he nodded and left Kazuchiyo to his unpleasant mission.

He climbed the stairs to the top of the central keep. The samurai on guard outside Lord Aritaka's chamber eyed him uncomfortably, but they were of no rank high enough to deny him anything, and they let him in.

Lord Aritaka was seated by the western wall, taking his evening meal in privacy. Though it churned Kazuchiyo's stomach, he moved to the center of the room and lowered to his knees in a deep bow.

"Father, please excuse my intrusion," he said. "I won't interrupt your meal for long. I just want to apologize for my behavior earlier."

He heard the tap of Aritaka replacing his dish on the dinner tray. "I know you don't really mean that now," he said, "but you *are* here, and that's enough. I accept your apology."

Kazuchiyo bit his lip, staring only at the floor. "Thank you, Father."

Then he left. He felt as if he was being pulled in too many directions, his flesh and bones drawn thin as koto strings. As he returned to his chamber he heard voices conversing on the other side of the door, and he rushed inside.

Amai sat in the center of the room, and across from him sat Yagi. He didn't look any different than when they had parted that morning, however much had changed. Kazuchiyo closed the panel behind him, and by the time he came forward Yagi was on his feet. He was just as sturdy as Kazuchiyo needed him to be; he stood firm as Kazuchiyo threw his arms around his waist in a tight embrace.

"Yagi..." Kazuchiyo buried his face in the collar of Yagi's robe, breathing in the familiar smell of his sweat. All over again he was tempted to drag his companions to the stables, force their way through the castle gates, and flee through the woods to the Kibaku camp. There was still time.

"You've heard, haven't you?" he asked as he clung to Yagi, his hands twisted and trembling in the back of his robe. "What Aritaka has planned?"

"I've heard," said Yagi. He sounded far too calm, and his hands sinking into Kazuchiyo's hair were free of the tremor Kazuchiyo's suffered. "Are you all right?"

"Me?" Kazuchiyo cringed; faced with Yagi's stoicism, he was ashamed of the panic that had driven him forward all day. "It's you I'm concerned for," he said, and he leaned back so that he could see Yagi's face. "You're the one in danger."

Yagi stared back at him. He was far too composed; Kazuchiyo had expected steel anger and bristling indignation. His relief turned sour, and he looked to Amai, who also watched him with grim resolve.

"What did General Ebara tell you?" Kazuchiyo asked. "What were you and Amai talking about before I came in?"

"It doesn't matter," said Yagi, which only made him more anxious to know. But then Yagi's broad palms cupped his jaw, and he went still. He had never seen the man so serious yet so calm at once.

"I'm going with Ebara to the bridge," Yagi told him. "You need to do what Aritaka says and stay with the command troops."

"You'll be outnumbered more than two to one," Kazuchiyo protested. "He doesn't mean for you to survive, let alone win. But if the three of us—"

"I'll win." Yagi's fingers tightened subtly against the back of Kazuchiyo's neck, and his heavy brow grew furrowed, but his voice didn't waver. "I don't want you to worry about me. You don't have to. Everything they've said about me is true."

Kazuchiyo twisted his fingers into Yagi's robe. "What do you mean?"

"I'm an oni," he said, and Kazuchiyo held his breath. "I crawled out of hell just like everyone says. Oihata and his crows can't kill me. I can't die." He moved his thumbs against Kazuchiyo's cheeks. "The best they can do is send me home. I'll keep the fires hot for when you send Aritaka and his gutless weasel son down to Hell."

Kazuchiyo trembled in his hands, and he smiled as the tears he'd been holding back for hours finally spilled free. Yagi was no better of a liar than he had ever been, but his conviction was sincere, and Kazuchiyo could not bring himself to shame the man with his doubt. "Okay," he whispered. "I won't worry."

Yagi sighed with relief. "Good." He drew Kazuchiyo into an eagerly awaited kiss, and though he remained unfaltering, Kazuchiyo could taste the desperation beneath it. They clung to each other, resigned to the fate that lay before them.

The three of them sat down together to eat. Though Kazuchiyo's heart and stomach were too delicate to make the most of it, his fellows had no such reservations. After eating only a small portion, he passed the rest of his meal to them and busied himself with drawing out a crude map of the following day's engagement. "Lord Aritaka believes he can overrun the Kibaku's northern forces with sheer numbers, the southern forces with superior positioning. But he hasn't given a thought to how Kibaku might counter that strategy." He sighed in frustration. "And I've no idea if Master Iomori has either."

Amai sucked on a dried plum. "Suppose you were Oihata, then," he suggested. "Facing these odds, what would you do?"

"I would trust my soldiers to break free of General Ebara's hold on the bridge," Kazuchiyo answered. "As far as we know he has some magic that will assist him. What if he can dry up the riverbed and render the bridges useless?"

"He would have to be an extraordinary onmyouji to accomplish something like that. What if he can turn the clouds into arrows? What if he curses all of us blind?" Amai shrugged. "There's no use trying to predict magic. What else might he do?"

"He'll retreat," said Yagi around a mouthful of rice. "He always does."

"He does," Kazuchiyo agreed slowly, his gaze flicking over his roughly drawn map. "He may move his forces north along the bank to try and draw you across the river, then turn back to overwhelm you."

Yagi gulped his mouthful down. "He can try. I won't take one step off that bridge."

Kazuchiyo nodded, hoping to show his encouragement more than his nerves. "If Oihata's Lord Koedzuka is of a similar mind, we can expect he'll have some trap for the northern bridge as well. He'll deploy his thousand reserves somehow, or have laid an ambush. The riverbank there is cleared; he might even use mounted spearmen like at the village."

"Then the most important thing is not to be baited," supposed Amai. "They know Aritaka's temperament and will use that to try to guide him into whatever they have planned."

"You're right, not that it does much good to know it." Kazuchiyo sighed. "Aritaka's not about to listen to my counsel, but at least I can warn General Rakuteru to be cautious."

"I'll try not to kill Oihata for you, if I can help it," said Yagi, "since it sounds like you like him now."

Kazuchiyo refused to let himself be tempted by the offer. "He's an ally I would hate to lose, but he's also a samurai and an honorable one. He won't hold back, and neither should you." He held Yagi's gaze. "Do whatever you must."

Yagi nodded. "Then let's hope he's too smart to set foot on my bridge."

They finished the meal and prepared for the night's rest. Even with the sun extinguished the castle remained bustling with activity, torches lit along the walls lighting the courtyards as men hurried to finish their tasks and their meals. Kazuchiyo moved to the window as Yagi and Amai spread the futons, contemplating one final song. His musings were interrupted before he could decide by a small paper doll fluttering to rest

360

on the open sill. Kazuchiyo quickly drew the paper inside, and the trio huddled together over a candle to inspect it.

But as Kazuchiyo peeled it apart, he discovered there was no message written on the paper. It instead held only a small red bead.

"A prayer bead," said Amai, poking it gingerly with his little finger.

"From Oihata?" asked Yagi.

"No." Kazuchiyo rolled the bead between two fingers, feeling from it a subtle heat. "It's from Iomori." He tugged at the ribbon still bound to his wrist, showing off the gift she had given him back in Gyoe at the onset of the campaign.

Yagi eyed the thing distastefully. "What does it do?"

"I'm still uncertain," Kazuchiyo admitted. "She said it would protect me, but if it requires an onmyouji's skill, I have no idea how to use it." He lifted his gaze to Yagi's face. "It's for you."

Yagi straightened his back. "Me?"

"It must be." Kazuchiyo's heart beat faster as he crawled to Yagi's armor in the corner of the room. "I asked her to move you away from the bridge, but instead she sends this. If it really is some kind of protection, maybe that means she has a plan after all?" He loosened one of the thinner cords between the plates in the armor's thigh guards so he could tie the bead into it.

"I don't need her sorcery," Yagi muttered, though he made no effort to stop Kazuchiyo. "I'm plenty strong."

Kazuchiyo smiled despite himself. "I know you are." Once finished, he crawled back to Yagi's side. "You're the strongest spear in the country. But wear it for my sake, won't you?"

"I'm not about to take it out now."

Yagi grabbed Kazuchiyo by the waist and drew him into his lap with such fervor and strength that Kazuchiyo had to grip his shoulders to catch his balance. "You worry too much," Yagi scolded him. "I don't want to think about any of that tonight."

He caught Kazuchiyo's mouth in a kiss, and the poor boy felt his heart crack apart with its every beat: half of him wanted only to melt into Yagi's embrace, to give him a night of such pleasure as to make his survival an even more tempting goal; the other was too terrified of the farewell their intimacy could easily become, even more so with the heavy, too-urgent press of Yagi's lips. The thought that this night could be their last threatened to destroy any attempt for him to savor it, and just as he thought he might be swallowed up by that cowardly sentiment, he felt a weight leaning into his back.

"I agree," Amai whispered against his ear just as the kiss ended. He nestled up against Kazuchiyo's spine and wrapped his arms around his chest. "You worry *much* too much."

His hands glided down between Kazuchiyo's and Yagi's pressed bodies, sneaky fingers undoing the sash on Kazuchiyo's sleeping robe. Yagi grumbled low in his chest with jealousy, but he didn't try to intervene; he kissed Kazuchiyo again, possessively, hands clenching against his hips. Caught between the two of them, Kazuchiyo could only shiver, bewildered and breathless.

"It's not the time for this," he said once he had use of his mouth again, but by then Amai had untied his robe. Yagi pushed it away from his torso while Amai drew the collar down his shoulders.

"It's the perfect time for this," Amai whispered, and the long, wet kiss he pressed to Kazuchiyo's throat did wonders to convince him. "He's going to fight very hard tomorrow. It's only right to take very good care of him now."

He drew Kazuchiyo's robe the rest of the way off and cast it aside, then he reached around him again for Yagi's sash. He feigned clumsiness as he worked so that it took longer than it needed to, his hands brushing against Yagi's groin as much as possible.

Yagi shifted and grumbled, his grip flexing against Kazuchiyo's hips. "You've been biding your time for this all along."

"And you haven't?" Amai tugged his robe open, pressing a smile into Kazuchiyo's shoulder as he dipped his hand down between Yagi's legs. "It was you who kissed me first."

Yagi growled, and despite the tangle they were quickly becoming, he reached past Kazuchiyo to take a fistful of Amai's hair. He dragged the smirking imp into a long, breath-halting kiss, while Kazuchiyo squirmed dizzily between them. How surreal it was, to be trapped on either side by Yagi's beastly rumblings and Amai's sultry purr. Worry was suddenly the furthest thing from his mind.

Kazuchiyo eased them apart and then turned to draw Amai out from behind him. He had waited too long to catch the mischievous weasel to be satisfied with no view of him. He demanded of Amai a heady kiss and stripped him of his robe. How sweet Amai's lips were, how lewd every sway and shiver of his naked body. Amai made known his greater experience with every shameless touch and encouraging murmur. As they twisted together, Yagi even lowered his back to the floor to watch. His eyes were dark and intense with fascination. When Kazuchiyo caught a glimpse, he recognized that look: it was the piercing look Yagi had flashed his way after first witnessing him kiss Amai, which he at the time had assumed to be jealousy. There was only arousal, now, proven in the revenant groping of Yagi's strong hands against each of their thighs, the swipe of his tongue along his lips. Kazuchiyo kissed Amai again, deeper, moaning softly with the thrill of it all.

They became a blur of moist, naked skin: Amai boldly exploring Kazuchiyo's mouth with long, suckling kisses; Kazuchiyo squirming and rocking in Yagi's lap, encouraged by Amai kneading into the small of his back; Yagi encouraging them both, stroking each of them in his rough fists, gasping and grumbling when they returned his attentions. Every quiver was bliss, every kiss and caress and whimper a revelation. When all were spent they collapsed atop and alongside each other, a web of sweat-glistening limbs and panting breath.

Kazuchiyo was first to regain some composure. He sat

up and stared down at his two lovers, their skin bronzed by candlelight, Amai draped across Yagi's chest. It stirred in him a fierce determination, and he leaned down to steal a kiss from each of them. He felt as if he had been offered an impossible chance and could not bear to be parted from either one.

With a few minutes spent tidying up and replacing their robes, they curled up together within their futons, warming and soothing each other through their night of rest.

The trio roused before dawn. They moved with brisk but solemn purpose through the dressing of their armor, Kazuchiyo paying special attention to the bead he had threaded into Yagi's thigh plates. With only a look shared among them, they headed out of the keep.

Sabi Castle itself seemed to shudder excitedly with the early morning commotion. The soldiers gathered into their ranks throughout the courtyard, some of them still fastening their armor and tightening their spears. The generals, surrounded by their bannermen and attendants, hoisted themselves onto their horses. Wherever Kazuchiyo looked, he was blinded by yellow light reflecting off blades and helmets. The low drone of unintelligible voices gave him goosebumps.

Of his family, he spotted Hidemune first, as he was already on his horse, standing ready among Ebara's troops toward the castle gates. Though pale of face, his scowl was unflinching. Further away, Lord Aritaka awaited with his own attendants, Mahiro beside him in her full armor, Suzumekage's reins in her fist.

Kazuchiyo took in a deep breath as he gazed about at the hurried preparations, the grim but determined faces of their soldiers. Then he looked to Yagi. "There's something I need you to know," he said with determination. "Whatever happens today, I'll still come to you tonight." He quaked with emotion. "Even if Kibaku breaks both your arms so you never fight again,

I'll always be at your side, to help you sleep."

A tremor ran through Yagi; rather than reply, he took Kazuchiyo's chin and tipped it up. Without one care to the throngs of soldiers surrounding them, he leaned down and kissed him boldly, passionately. Kazuchiyo was too overwhelmed to move, and he stared, blinking and flushed, as Yagi leaned back.

"Not one Kibaku crow is going to step foot across that bridge," he declared. "And when they're spent, I'll come back to you."

Kazuchiyo nodded beneath dozens of watchful eyes. "I know."

Yagi put his helmet on, and the surrounding men parted for him as he marched across the courtyard toward his father. One of the bannermen handed him his spear reverently, another held his horse steady as he mounted. Every samurai present held him in awe, and even Kazuchiyo needed a tap against his arm to spur him back to his senses.

"Don't I get a kiss, too?" Amai teased.

Kazuchiyo blushed even darker as he pulled his helmet on. "Stay close, if you can," he said as he led them onward to join Aritaka. "We might still see Nanpa."

"I'm ready," Amai replied with much greater seriousness. "None of your enemies are getting past me either."

Kazuchiyo approached Lord Aritaka and bowed to him deeply. Aritaka greeted him with a stiff nod, either irritated by the romantic display of moments ago, or, I would like to suppose, made to feel guilty by it. Mahiro's heart was much easier to glean; her smile was grim as she bowed her head to Kazuchiyo, her mane spilling down her shoulders. "I'll take care of Sabi while you're gone," she said, "and Suzumekage will take care of you."

"I'm honored," said Kazuchiyo, and he pulled himself up into the saddle.

Looking out over his father's army was a far different view atop Suzumekage than his own Hashikiri, much more so than Kazuchiyo had anticipated. Her flanks were broad and her back taller than any horse he had ever attempted to ride, and it occurred to him that an hour of practice would have been wise. But soon after he was situated, Aritaka signaled for the march to begin. The castle gates swung open, and General Ebara, Yagi beside him, led the first of their troops onward, out to battle.

CHAPTER THIRTY-ONE

On the ninth day of the fourth month of 1487, Lord Aritaka Souyuu led his army from Sabi Castle intent on destroying his Kibaku enemies. He had never laid eyes on the Fukugawa River that would be their battleground, whereas Lord Koedzuka and his many generals had all cut their teeth on its banks in their youth, when Kibaku's black crows clashed often against red dragon banners. With Mahiro and five hundred men left behind to guard Sabi Castle, the two armies were nearly equal in the measure of their soldiers. It would be strategy and mettle that determined the victor.

Kazuchiyo rode close to his father during the march west. All about them the bamboo swayed and rattled, and above, thick, gray clouds roiled. The smell of distant rain sent chills coursing along Kazuchiyo's skin, but he kept his chin high, watching the column of samurai and their foot soldiers stretching far down the road. He could barely see the tip of Yagi's spear at the front.

Half an hour into the procession, the road split, and General Ebara and his troops took the southern fork that would lead them to Chibatake Bridge. Kazuchiyo watched Yagi's spear bob and sway until it was swallowed up by the shifting bamboo.

Amai pinched the back of his calf, and Kazuchiyo glanced down. "I'm all right," he said. Amai nodded, and they continued on.

Drums echoed through the forest. Kazuchiyo tightened his grip on the reins as Suzumekage tried to pick up her pace, eager for the fight, so different from his timid Hashikiri. In time the pounding grew louder and was joined by the trumpeting of oxen horns, the roar of men's raised voices, pounding footfalls. The soldiers ahead hurried as they reached the edge of the woods and caught their first glimpse of the field beyond. Rakuteru's voice boomed above it all as he ordered his men into broader ranks; the battle at Nodo Bridge had already begun.

The column marched on, faster, though still at an agonizing pace for Kazuchiyo, who was trapped far behind the forward ranks. Sweat trickled along the scar at the back of his neck as he made his way to the last bamboo sentinels along the road. Finally, he was granted his first view of Fukugawa River in many years.

From the forest, the road flowed in a long, gentle slope to the river and to the broad Nodo Bridge that crossed it. The field along the bank was already a fearsome and eerie sight: General Waseba's thousand soldiers had taken up a defensive position along the hillside, though the slope was not great enough to provide much of an advantage; beyond them, five thousand Kibaku soldiers pressed the attack amidst a blanket of heavy fog. Despite strong gusts of cool air from the west, waves of mist flowed off the river's back, making each crow a shadow. The far bank, said to hold Kibaku's thousand reserves, was obscured save for the tips of green banners flying high above the mist.

Rakuteru signaled for attack, and he and his men barreled down the hillside to Waseba's aid. As more of Aritaka's soldiers emerged from the woods they fell into their commanded ranks and hurried into position. Lord Aritaka halted Kazuchiyo and the rest of his forces just outside the tree line to watch as his strategy was put to effect.

Kazuchiyo watched, unblinking. It was an awesome and terrible sight: thousands of soldiers streaming down the hillside in measured rows, spears at the ready to meet thousands more. The sheer number of wind-swept banners was itself overwhelming. Suzumekage swayed with the rising shouts and the thunder of footfalls shaking the earth beneath her hooves. Kazuchiyo could do nothing to calm her, his entire focus locked on the clashing spectacle.

"See now how terrain makes all the difference," said Aritaka, and Kazuchiyo startled. He had to edge closer to hear his father above the commotion. "Koedzuka camped his forces just north of the bridge, where the slope is at its most shallow, and the earth stronger. But if he seeks retreat, he will find it a difficult thing to press south against Hosoda."

Kazuchiyo looked back to the formations. As Rakuteru reinforced Waseba on the hill, Fuchihara and Hosoda had moved north and south respectively to flank the Kibaku army. Though the Kibaku generals were already stretching their line to try to keep from being surrounded, they could not hope to match the sudden superior numbers.

"But there are reserves on the other side of that bridge," Kazuchiyo reminded Aritaka, staring hard into the thick mist obscuring what should have been an entire second camp. "If Hosoda pushes too hard from the south, he could put his men in position for an ambush."

"Worry not, Kazumune. He knows that."

Kazuchiyo forced himself to take a breath. The air stank of dust and blood already. He spotted General Waseba himself among the throngs, ordering his exhausted men to make way for Rakuteru's fresh troops; he looked to General Hosoda, the smaller figure of Tomoto close beside him, as their ranks were absorbed into the roiling fog.

"Doesn't this fog remind you of the other day?" asked Amai, one hand on Kazuchiyo's calf. "When Kibaku ambushed us the first day in Sabi?"

"It doesn't seem natural," Kazuchiyo agreed, "but that would mean Kibaku has another onmyouji in their army." He scoured the field and at last caught a glimpse of a familiar straw hat toward the south of the melee. "And why hasn't Master Iomori dispelled it?"

"Or it's Oihata, and he's stronger than her after all."

Kazuchiyo shook his head, but looked again to the Kibaku ranks. Their generals were not difficult to spot, as many were wearing helmets leafed in gold or bearing tall crests. Banners hoisted toward the center of their army indicated the presence of Lord Koedzuka, though the man himself was not visible within the fog. Nor did Kazuchiyo see the familiar gold wings of Oihata's helm.

"I don't like this." Kazuchiyo turned toward Aritaka. "Father, there's something unnatural about this fog. With your permission I'll order Master Iomori to dispel it, as we've seen her do before."

Aritaka eyed him suspiciously, but when Kazuchiyo only stared back, unwavering, he at last nodded. "Go," he said. "But know that I'm watching you."

"I welcome it," said Kazuchiyo. He nudged Amai with his foot, who then climbed up into the saddle with him; they rode out from among Aritaka's command forces without looking back.

Suzumekage raced down the slope, her sights set on the front lines; it took a great deal of coaxing from Kazuchiyo to steer her away, and she snorted in complaint the entire time. Such respect he had for his sister then. As the battle raged on, he managed to wrangle Suzumekage down the rear line, past Rakuteru's onslaught to the wide-spread ranks of Hosoda's loyal soldiers. Once at the bottom of the slope the fog seemed to envelope them all at once, cold against his neck and stinging his eyes. It seemed to tug at his armor like a living beast, and the bead nestled against his wrist throbbed.

"Master Iomori!" Kazuchiyo spurred Suzumekage through the rearmost soldiers, working his way toward the figure of

Iomori, sitting tall in her saddle. "Iomori!"

She turned, and the soldiers around her parted to allow Suzumekage a wide berth. "Kazumune," she greeted him calmly. "Should you be so close to the front?"

Kazuchiyo pulled Suzumekage alongside her. "This fog is the work of magic," he said. "My father orders that you dispel it at once."

Iomori stared back at him, utterly unconcerned, to such a degree that it chilled him. "Lord Koedzuka cannot see through it any better than he can," she replied. "He likely hasn't realized just how badly we outnumber him. You'd give up that advantage?"

Kazuchiyo frowned at her in confusion. "Then is it *your* doing?"

Iomori turned to face the battle again, and it took Kazuchiyo several beats to realize that she planned to ignore him entirely. "Master Iomori, I'm ordering you dispel this fog," he said, louder. "On behalf of our lord."

Still Iomori did not respond. As Kazuchiyo gaped at her, confounded, Amai leaned into his back. "Do you think she can't?" he suggested, loudly enough that she would hear. "Or should we tell your father she's on the wrong side of the field?"

Iomori cast him a glare. Kazuchiyo could all but see map tiles sliding behind her eyes as she weighed Amai's threat against whatever motivation kept her silent. Before she could reach a conclusion, though, their attention was drawn by a shout from Tomoto, and the heavy, resounding *twang* of a hundred bowstrings.

Arrows hailed down out of the mist. Men and beasts reared back as they glanced off armor and spearheads, far too many finding their marks in muscle and bone. One pierced Kazuchiyo's shoulder guard with a familiar, shuddering impact that left him breathless.

When he had recovered, Kazuchiyo craned to look at Amai behind him.. "Are you all right?"

"I'm not hit," said Amai, still leaning close against his

back. "That asshole really did turn clouds into arrows, huh?"

"Brace!" someone at the front hollered. "Brace!" And Kazuchiyo yanked on the reins, drawing Suzumekage, stomping and snorting, further away. A line of green banners charged forth amidst the fog. The impact of their surge against the Hosoda line washed over Kazuchiyo like a strike to a bell, and his ears ached with the clawing of metal and the screams of the injured. A hundred men separated him from the fighting, but still he tasted each blow in his throat.

"Kazumune!" Iomori grabbed him by the elbow. "Go back to your father," she commanded, and when another volley of arrows flew their way, a flick of her hand sent those aimed at them spinning away on a gust of wind. Kazuchiyo watched the mist part from her with the action, only to reform itself a moment later.

"Not until you dispel this fog!" he insisted. "We're only at a disadvantage now because of it!"

"Stubborn boy," Iomori grumbled, but she raised her hand.

An arrow struck through her palm; Iomori cursed and drew her hand in. The crowd around them surged with another push from the Kibaku soldiers, and their corner of the battlefield became a churning mass—bodies backing into those behind them, spears jostling, hunks of grass and earth turned up under raking feet. Hosoda's men were being driven back, and distantly Kazuchiyo understood; just as Aritaka had supposed, the whole of the Kibaku army had turned their might southward, eager to reopen their path to the Nodo Bridge.

"Forward!" Hosoda bellowed over his troops, his volume a shock after so many days of imposed silence. "Do not let them retreat!"

Kazuchiyo's mind spun in want of strategy. Kibaku had only ever retreated as part of some gambit, and he was rightfully wary of the choice now. But the soldiers had become a mob, and Suzumekage was tossing her great head back and forth as she tried to push forward with the surge. Men boxed them in from all sides so closely that he doubted he could draw his long sword without hitting an ally. It was during this pressurized chaos that Amai turned abruptly in the saddle. "Kazu—"

Amai jerked, and Kazuchiyo felt a blade scrape across the front of his chest plate. Looking down, he had only a moment to grasp that a kick from Amai had diverted a dagger strike meant for the gap in his armor. Among the mob of soldiers, beneath a plain Sakka helmet, stood Nanpa, his face upturned in a snarl.

Amai lashed out again with his heel; he caught Nanpa in the temple and sent him tumbling into the nearest soldier. "Try to get back to Aritaka!" Amai drew his dagger as he leapt off Suzumekage's back.

"Amai!" Kazuchiyo drew his katana, but the hiss of the metal in Suzumekage's ear only heightened her eagerness for the battle continuing beyond her reach. She pushed forward, forcing the soldiers to make way, all while bodies squirmed and shoved in every direction. "Amai!" Kazuchiyo shouted again, but with the fog and the masses he may as well have been caught in swirling rapids, and the two shinobi were quickly lost to his vision.

"Iomori!" Kazuchiyo gestured to her; they had been separated by the flow, but she was still nearby, trying to snap the arrow shaft still embedded in her palm. She looked up at his call. "The old fox is here!"

Iomori straightened, finally showing some urgency as she scanned the field. "Where?"

Kazuchiyo twisted about, trying to spot the pair to no avail. "He was—"

A wide hand grabbed Kazuchiyo at the thigh and pushed; he tried to brace his foot against the stirrup, but Suzumekage was so much broader than he was accustomed to, and already half turned in search, he couldn't keep his balance. A familiar, sick vertigo twisted his stomach as he was sent tumbling off the horse's back.

Kazuchiyo landed hard, the edges of his own armor

forcing the air from his lungs. There was no time to catch his breath; boots and sandals pounded all around him, shin guards and thigh plates knocked his shoulders, and most frightening, Suzumekage's broad hooves clomped heavily in the dirt beside him. He struggled upright as quickly as he could. Dizzily he turned, gaping at each indecipherable figure. "Amai?" he called, and a man in light armor pushed toward him. Soon enough, he recognized the man's gnarled face in the mist.

"This time, I'll sever your line for good," Nanpa growled. He flipped the dagger around in his hand. In the oppressive gray he looked so much like he had when Kazuchiyo first saw him, stalking out of the rains at Shimegahara, and his hand trembled around his sword.

A gust of powerful wind swept through the ranks. It howled like a typhoon, and a few men lost their helmets as the fog was at last stripped away. Kazuchiyo flinched back, his eyes stinging in the wind. Nanpa paid it no mind. Even with the surrounding soldiers able to see them clearly now, the shinobi closed in on Kazuchiyo, trapped among the packed crowd, his dagger upraised.

Nanpa grimaced suddenly, and a sound of pain hissed through his clenched teeth. He swayed against an impact to his back. Even then he didn't stop, but the hesitation was enough; Kazuchiyo braced himself, forcing his gaze to the man's rough, gnarled face, forced himself to remember his brother's head slumping from his neck. Frustration and fury overwhelmed him as he forced both hands to the grip of his katana. Heat flooded along his arm like a whip of fire. It spurred him on with an unnatural outpouring of strength he'd never felt, as if his body had become a conduit to the same hellish might that drove Yagi's spear.

In one smooth, clean swing of his katana he split Nanpa apart—straight through armor and bone with inhuman voracity, cleaving off his arm at the shoulder and his head from his neck. The body teetered a moment, the cut so swift and razor perfect that it barely seemed to register its own death.

Then it crumbled, leaving Amai standing behind it, bloody dagger clutched in hand, eyes wide in surprise.

He gaped at the severed body at his feet. "How did you do that?"

Kazuchiyo staggered, barely aware of the many other soldiers staring at him as well. His arms shuddered and burned, but within moments the sensation dissipated, leaving only the throb of his pulse against his wrist. He looked to the impossible smoothness of his sword's cut through Nanpa's armor, and when he raised his gaze again, it caught on Iomori atop her horse, smiling at him.

"Lord Kazumune!" called Tomoto. Kazuchiyo sheathed his sword as he struggled to reclaim his wits. Hosoda's young attendant was shoving through the soldiers to reach him. "Are you all right, my lord? What happened?"

"An enemy," Kazuchiyo said thoughtlessly, but then he took a breath and found clarity. The sky was still undulating gray, but with the mist gone his head began to clear, and he forced himself to take in Nanpa's corpse stretched before him. Blood poured from the neck and was quickly stamped beneath the sandals of nearby soldiers. Even with the pandemonium swirling around them, he found a moment of relief.

"It was a spy in our midst," he told Tomoto. "Sent to kill me."

"What?" Tomoto exclaimed; he looked to the corpse and back. "Thank the gods you're safe. Please allow me to help you back to your horse."

"Yes, thank you." He gestured to Amai. "Take the head."

Amai tipped Nanpa's helmet aside and grabbed up the head by its hair. "Are you going to throw it at your father's feet?" he asked.

Kazuchiyo gave Amai's shoulder a tight squeeze as they came together. "Thank you," he said. "I'll give you your kiss later."

Amai gave a snort. "You're thinking about that now? When you just cut a man in half with one stroke?"

375

Kazuchiyo pressed his thumb into the bead tied at his wrist, but its heat was already fading. He gave his arm a shake, and the last of it dispelled. "I can't explain it now, but I suspect Iomori can, once this is over." Amai nodded, and he and Tomoto helped convey Kazuchiyo through the crowding soldiers.

Without her rider, Suzumekage had taken it upon herself to continue toward the front lines. She had reached General Hosoda by the time Kazuchiyo caught up with her, who took the reins personally to prevent her progress. "Lord Kazumune," the man said, fresh blood on his face. "Are you injured?"

"No, General." Kazuchiyo drew himself into the saddle and then took Nanpa's head from Amai. As gruesome as it was, he tied Nanpa's hair through the pommel so he could be sure not to lose it.

Amai pulled himself up behind him. "How fares the battle?"

Kazuchiyo looked out over the field. With the mist parted the positions of both armies became clear: Kibaku, overwhelmed by Sakka's superior numbers, was continuing the push south in an effort to reach the bridge, despite heavy resistance from Hosoda's stalwart samurai. Aritaka's entire force had shifted to prevent their escape: Rakuteru's men had become intermingled with Hosoda's, Fuchihara abandoning the northern flank to make up for the loss at the center. Their half-moon enclosure was shrinking with every passing moment.

"They're trying to retreat across the bridge," said Tomoto as he remounted his horse. "If we allow that, this battle will draw out for days."

Kazuchiyo frowned. "But the reserves..."

He looked to the opposite bank, expecting a rank of mounted samurai to be waiting, only to realize that only a handful of men stood guard. The banners he had spotted at the start of the battle were mounted alone in a line down the shore, as if deliberately staged.

"Where are they?" He stood in his saddle, despite Amai

tugging on his armor. More banners at the center of Kibaku's formation indicated the command force, and at last Kazuchiyo could see among them the tighter collection of flags and men that indicated Lord Koedzuka. A group of fifty horses pawed the earth nearby, their riders fresh and watching the battle. At their head, a samurai with a gold-winged helmet awaited his lord's order.

"Oihata," Kazuchiyo breathed, and he finally allowed Amai to drag him back down into his saddle. "He *is* here—but not all his men. Where are Kibaku's reserves?"

A great ball of golden light burst from the field. Like a false sun it flashed and burned, sending all Aritaka's men cringing back and covering their eyes. Even Kazuchiyo had to shield himself from the unnatural gleam. Through parted fingers he traced the source of the glare to Naoya himself, the gold of his armor lit up like a beacon. He charged, fifty horses and their riders chasing him northeast, straight toward Fuchihara's straggling forces.

Kazuchiyo could only watch, his heart in his mouth. Naoya's riders blazed across the field like holy lightning and struck at the weakest link in the Sakka army. Fuchihara himself soon vanished amidst the overpowering light, and then, from farther north still, came a trumpeting of conch shells. Just as Kazuchiyo had feared, another fifty horses streamed out of the woods where they had lain in wait all along, spears at the ready and aiming at Aritaka's command unit.

Another fake retreat, to cover another clever ambush; everyone had suspected as much from Kibaku's generals, but in their eagerness to finish the battle swiftly, they had laid themselves open to the revolutionary use of speared cavalry. As Naoya and his horsemen trampled their way through Fuchihara's forces, the second group of riders pierced the Sakka army at its throat by dashing behind Waseba and Rakuteru's line. Aritaka's command force retreated farther up the slope to avoid being speared, only to cut themselves off from the rest of the army. Even fifty excellent horsemen wouldn't have been enough to make up for the several-thousand-man advantage held by Aritaka's army, but with their lord separated from his generals, already Kazuchiyo could see the beginnings of disarray.

The Kibaku banners parted then, just enough that Kazuchiyo could see Lord Koedzuka safe within his protective ranks. He wore a fine green coat over his armor not unlike Naoya's, his helmet proudly bearing the curved sigil of his clan. He raised his war fan, and his generals trumpeted and shouted his commands to their men, distributing their focus away from the south for a more even advance.

Across Kazuchiyo's eyes played a vision of the man's strategy coming to fruition: With Fuchihara's flank obliterated, Kibaku would press their advantage north and east, stretching the line so as to prevent themselves from being surrounded again. It would crowd Sakka against the slope and leave them ripe for assault from behind—from Naoya's remaining twenty-five hundred men at Chibatake and the rest of the thousand missing reserves. They were forming the hillside into a gauntlet.

"Hold tight," Kazuchiyo said to Amai. He pulled at the reins, demanding that Suzumekage heed him. Reluctantly she did, and due to her great size and efforts they pulled free of Hosoda's crammed bodies. They rode hard down the line until they reached General Rakuteru, who had spared some of his men to guard their rear in case the Kibaku spearmen changed their course. His men were bold, but from blinding fog to blinding light they were confused and distraught, and they were being pushed back.

"General!" Kazuchiyo called as Suzumekage shouldered her way to the man's side. "General, they're folding the fan. We cannot allow them to control our line!"

"Do you think I can't see that?" growled Rakuteru, continuing to signal for attack. "Back away, Kazumune, we still have our numbers. If Oihata is here, who knows who's leading his men, but we can still turn this around before they break through the bridge."

"Purnima," said Amai against Kazuchiyo's ear. "It must be her."

Kazuchiyo agreed, though he could not spare any concern for her safety. "General, there were a thousand men camped on the Kibaku bank," he insisted. "Those men are gone now."

Rakuteru looked to him, baffled, and then turned his gaze toward the river. His steely confidence turned to strain. "Cursed Waseba! Is he blind? Why did he not report as much?"

"If those men are not here, they're either farther north still," Kazuchiyo shuddered, "or they've gone to Chibatake."

They looked to the south, just as a trumpet from approaching soldiers echoed up the river.

CHAPTER THIRTY-TWO

A dozen riders hurried their way along the riverbank, a stream of foot soldiers behind them struggling to keep up. Kazuchiyo was at a loss to understand their unruly formation until he recognized the rider at the head: Hidemune, harried but unbloodied, led the haphazard charge. Even General Rakuteru was struck witless as they watched Hidemune making his way toward General Hosoda's troops.

"Has he lost his mind?" Rakuteru spat and motioned to one of his captains. "Go collect the young lord and bring him here to explain himself."

Kazuchiyo looked past the scrambling Hidemune. The battlefield and all its scraping, stabbing, mashing chaos fell away from his senses. All he could see was bamboo sloping toward the shore, their swaying trunks preventing his gaze from reaching any farther. Cold claimed his limbs and lungs. He knew very well why Hidemune had come.

"Kazu…" Amai slipped his hand beneath Kazuchiyo's shoulder guard to grip his bicep, hard, in trembling sympathy. "Kazu, I'm sorry."

"The bridge has fallen," Kazuchiyo whispered. Hearing the words come out of him, however frail, shook him to his bones.

He took a deep, gasping breath as he drew himself back from the ledge of his despair. He turned back to Rakuteru. "General, if the bridge has fallen, there are likely three thousand Kibaku soldiers headed this way."

He felt a thrill of dread at the cold resignation behind Rakuteru's eyes. His instincts cried out in defiance of it; before his courage could wane, he continued. "Give me your horses. I'll ride south to delay them as long as I can."

Surprise interrupted what might have been Rakuteru anticipating his battlefield death; he stared at Kazuchiyo as if not understanding the words. Then he nodded. "Ginta!" he shouted, and his soldiers parted to make way for his son to approach atop his horse. "Ginta, take your best captain and what remains of our riders. The enemy is approaching from the south."

Ginta leaned back, his expression reflecting all of his father's grim pride. "At your command," he said, and he began calling for his troops.

Kazuchiyo drew Suzumekage back; she pawed the earth impatiently as Ginta rallied the available men. Kazuchiyo himself was no less anxious. He felt as if his breath were whistling through great holes gouged in his lungs. If he allowed his momentum to slow, he would suffocate.

"Three thousand crows," Amai said. "If Yagi couldn't stop them at the bridge, thirty horses won't stop them once they're loose on this side of the river."

"There's nothing else we can do," replied Kazuchiyo. "If they attack now, we'll be surrounded and overrun."

"We don't have to stay at all!" Amai insisted. "You don't have loyalty to either of these lords. If Yagi is dead, there's nothing keeping us here."

"*No.*" Kazuchiyo quaked but stayed resolute. "No, I haven't fought all this time for it to mean nothing. Go if you want. I'm going to stall Purnima."

Ginta drew his men away from the line, and he nodded to Kazuchiyo. The hard set of his square jaw reminded Kazuchiyo of what Amai had said in the keep the day before: here was a young man only a few years his senior, prepared to charge into death at the bridge, just as Kazuchiyo would have ordered him to. Without allowing himself to dwell upon it, Kazuchiyo turned Suzumekage about and spurred her to the south.

Having been denied the front lines, Suzumekage was eager to contribute; she tore down the line toward the riverbank and then curved to run alongside it at such a speed that Kazuchiyo had to cling to her with all his might. Ginta and the rest of his meager troop hurried after, each man and beast conscious of the impossible task before them.

Amai twisted his fingers in Kazuchiyo's belt to keep from being thrown. He had to yell to be heard. "I'm not leaving you! But think, Kazu. Kibaku has all the momentum. Stalling Purnima won't be enough!"

"I know that!" Kazuchiyo leaned forward, trying to escape Amai's unwanted reminders. "But he didn't give up, and neither will I!"

They had to slow as they came to where the forest crept down toward the bank. Kazuchiyo glanced behind him; he could see Hidemune's tall helmet as he tried to push his way through Hosoda's troops to the front, perhaps thinking he could stumble on some Kibaku general's head to bargain for redemption with. He turned forward again, bile in his throat.

The sounds of the battle dulled, and again Amai leaned into Kazuchiyo, stubbornly trying to be heard. "Kazuchiyo," he said, sharply enough that his lord flinched in the saddle. "Yagi went to the bridge because he thought he could win. Don't go there now if all you're thinking about is losing. You know what he'd say."

Kazuchiyo clenched his teeth to aching, and with a sob of frustration he reined Suzumekage to a halt. Ginta and the rest followed suit despite their confusion. Behind them, spears clashed, and men shouted and screamed. Somewhere far ahead were more spears and more men, but for a few moments Kazuchiyo cast them all aside so he could breathe. His gaze went to the river, its waters silvery even in the gray of the cloudy morning.

How many times had the Red Dragon gone to war on the banks of the Fukugawa? Kazuchiyo had grown up on such stories of valor and cunning. He watched the currents roll by and tried to remember the sound of his father's voice.

"Kazu?" Amai nudged him, and when he received no response, he at last resorted to climbing off Suzumekage's back to stand in front of him. He reached up to touch Kazuchiyo's hand, clenched and shaking, around the reins. "Kazu!"

Kazuchiyo shivered at the familiar image of Amai's heart-shaped face peering up at him from beneath his helmet, hair matted and eyes wild with fright. "Amai," he said. "How fast is Hidemune?"

"What?" Amai frowned up at him with concern. "Not very. What do you mean?"

Kazuchiyo lifted his head. "I don't see Purnima yet." He scanned the line of the river as far as the curve that took its bank out of his sight. "If she made it over the bridge, she'd be here by now."

"There could be any reason for that," said Amai. "What are you thinking?"

"My lord?" Ginta drew up alongside Kazuchiyo as well. He clenched his hand around his spear to try to hide that it was trembling. "Are we not going to the bridge?"

"No." Kazuchiyo sat up straight in his saddle. "If Yagi's still alive, then the bridge is held. And if he's dead..." He took a deep breath. "If the bridge has fallen, stalling Kibaku will not save us. There's only one way to victory now."

Kazuchiyo guided Suzumekage to turn. "You were right all along," he told her as he aimed at the riverbank. "You belong at the front." He spurred her on, and she understood at once, leaping from the grassy bank and into the river.

Ginta and his riders stared, flabbergasted, as Kazuchiyo and Suzumekage struck out for the opposite bank. Though the Fukugawa was especially known for its depth, here where the forest reached the shore was its narrowest point, and the recent lack of rain made for a gentle current. "Follow me, if your horse can bear it!" Kazuchiyo shouted to the others, the water up to his saddle as Suzumekage plowed ahead. "There is still victory for Sakka!"

Ginta rallied himself, hoisting his spear. "Victory for Sakka!" he cried, and he dug his heels into his horse. The beast obeyed, quickly following Suzumekage's lead. One after another the rest joined them, until only Amai and one other were left on the shore.

The man offered Amai his hand, ready to bear him across the river, but Amai shook his head. He faced Kazuchiyo with a strange, crooked smile, and then turned and ran. He soon disappeared into the woods.

Kazuchiyo set his jaw and faced forward, saving any emotion he might have felt for a later time.

Thirty-two Sakka warriors crossed the river that day. Each of them had resigned themselves to certain death on Kibaku spears, only to have their hopes reignited as they followed Kazuchiyo's leadership. As they reached the opposite bank, now in the enemy's territory, Kazuchiyo drew them together so the horses could catch their breath.

"Our aim is Lord Koedzuka," he told them, clasping his courage tight. "The command unit's defense is loose at the rear. We'll cross the Nodo Bridge and take him from behind. Nothing else matters."

"We're with you," Ginta assured him, and the soldiers young and old nodded their conviction.

Then they were off again, racing back toward the battle. The clashing and pounding resumed in Kazuchiyo's ears, but he forced himself to be numb. As they drew closer, he could still see the distant golden light of Naoya's beacon storming through the Sakka line, though Rakuteru and the other generals valiantly resisted. Aritaka remained cut off at the rear. The battle would drag on for hours more, with insurmountable casualties, if something did not change soon.

A shout went up along the bank as they passed the Kibaku soldiers that had been stationed to hold the misleading banners. There was no time for squeamishness nor mercy; Kazuchiyo and his riders ran the men down who tried to halt them. Ginta put his spear through the throat of a man just as he raised a conch shell to his lips. They continued on, throwing themselves upon the old wooden planks of the bridge. The pounding of their hooves was lost to the cacophony of battle beyond, but Kazuchiyo felt each echo through his frame. He drew his sword. He did not know if he could depend on Iomori's sorcery to aid him again, so he set his sights on the cluster of samurai at Kibaku's heart and prayed that his resolve would not falter.

He and his men were halfway across the bridge before Kibaku realized, and by then it was too late. Soldiers flowed in from north and south to defend their lord; Suzumekage showed no fear as she leapt from the bridge and plowed through their line, as if they were blades of grass. Lord Koedzuka turned, his bannermen throwing themselves loyally into Kazuchiyo's path. The tip of a spear glanced off Kazuchiyo's thigh guard, but he refused to relent. With sword upraised, he led the charge across the short span of field leading up to the command unit, then into their midst. He saw shock in Koedzuka's face, and with breath held, he struck.

Koedzuka threw his war fan up in a parry. The katana cut through the wood and paper easily, but the force was great enough to divert Kazuchiyo's strike from his neck. The blade sliced through the gold adornments on his helmet and sent them spinning away. Kazuchiyo shook with fiery emotion as Suzumekage thundered past the man and then turned, eager to whirl about for a second attempt. But by then Ginta and the rest had descended, and two men put their spears in the flanks of Koedzuka's horse. With a cry of pain the animal reared and threw its master to the ground.

Kazuchiyo raced back. He adjusted his grip on his katana over and over, a dozen outcomes fighting for prominence in his mind as he faced down the Kibaku lord. Koedzuka locked eyes with him as he drew his katana; he was younger than Aritaka, handsome, with a thick, finely groomed mustache and beard. His eyes narrowed with regret more than fear or pride. When two of Ginta's men attacked, he retaliated with speed and precision, cutting them open at their thighs. Even with the fearsome Suzumekage bearing down on him, he did not flinch, and Kazuchiyo knew at once he could not bring himself to destroy such a man.

The riders closed in on their cornered prey; several dismounted and taunted Koedzuka with their spears while the others rode in circles around them, driving back or trampling any man who dared intervene. He would soon be overpowered. Kazuchiyo rode closer, the well-trained Suzumekage passing behind their enemy. Perhaps she hoped he would put his sword through the man's spine, but Kazuchiyo passed his sword to his other hand, and just as Koedzuka was fending off another spear, he reached down and grabbed the man by the back of his helmet.

Koedzuka tried to turn, but already Suzumekage had continued on; gasping and choking, he yanked at the cords digging into his chin and neck as Kazuchiyo dragged him back toward the bridge. His sword flailed, and Kazuchiyo flinched as the blade clashed against his armor and helm.

Just as they reached the foot of the bridge, Koedzuka managed to wrench himself free of his helm. He staggered and turned only to find Kazuchiyo's blade at his throat, a dozen Sakka spears at his back. Regret eased again into his weary features as he gazed up at Kazuchiyo.

Kazuchiyo shuddered with adrenaline, his composure held by a thread. "I don't want to kill you," he said.

"If you don't, your father will," replied Koedzuka.

"No." Kazuchiyo took in a deep breath, determined that the words would come out just as he meant them. "I am no son of beasts."

Koedzuka's eyes widened, and in that moment he looked very much like Naoya, understanding and relief in his face.

"Surrender to me," Kazuchiyo continued, placing the blade of his katana close to Koedzuka's throat if only for the pageantry of it. "Show your men the battle is over."

Koedzuka betrayed a flash of pain, and his gaze darted to the field. An army of thousands was not so easy a thing to halt, but his generals had come to realize what was happening. Their horns blared as men turned to see what had become of their lord. Confusion spread among the ranks as Kibaku soldiers hesitated after orders, and Sakka's pulled back in exhaustion. To the north, Naoya's golden light at last extinguished.

That, it seemed, was the final blow to Koedzuka's resolve, and he lowered himself to his knees before Kazuchiyo in a humble bow. "I surrender."

The call went out; conch shells and oxen horns blared the battle's end, and Kibaku's flags were laid down. Pockets of continued fighting along the line were gradually brought to a halt, and samurai and foot soldier alike retreated from their enemies, exhausted and shaken. Upon the hill, Aritaka's forces trumpeted victory as the lord himself made his way down the slope, all men parting before him. Kazuchiyo dismounted from Suzumekage as they waited, fearful of any over-eager gambit from a loyal Kibaku crow or even from one of Sakka's, blinded by glory, seeking a lord's head.

Kazuchiyo motioned to Ginta's lead rider, who had joined them across the river. "Captain, ride to Chibatake. If there are any left alive, let them know the battle is ended."

"Sir," the man said crisply, and he took to his horse.

The soldiers beyond the bridge parted, and Naoya burst from the line. His armor that had shown so brilliantly during the battle was dulled with blood, his features contorted in panic. "Lord Koedzuka!" he cried as he leapt from his horse. He advanced on Kazuchiyo and drew his sword.

Kazuchiyo's heart rushed into his throat as Ginta and his men surged forward protectively. "Don't kill him!" he shouted without thinking. "This battle is over!"

But Naoya continued toward them, seething. "Get away from my lord!" he hollered, and he lashed out with his sword, severing one of the spears pointed at him. "Release him now, or—"

"Naoya!" Though still on his knees, Koedzuka faced his vassal with authority. "Throw down your sword. I command it."

Naoya shuddered; closer now, Kazuchiyo could see his teeth gnashing, tears on his cheeks. He threw his sword to the ground and marched ahead anyway. Even when men braced their spears as a barrier to him, he fought and shoved, trying to make his way to Koedzuka. "Don't you touch him!" he continued to yell. "You sniveling beasts, how dare you! I'll smite each of you to Hell!"

Ginta thrust the butt of his spear into Naoya's knee and crumpled him. It took four men to wrestle him to the ground and keep him there. Even then he struggled, and Kazuchiyo ached to see it.

"Sir Oihata," he said, and Naoya wrenched his gaze from his lord. Kazuchiyo faced him with his best sincerity. "Please, trust me."

Naoya's expression contorted in anguish, and he let his head fall to the earth to weep.

It took nearly half an hour for Lord Aritaka to arrive. By then his generals had approached as well, leaving their troops in the command of their captains. Kazuchiyo was relieved to see that Rakuteru had brought Hidemune to his side after all, and was gripping him by the scruff of his neck. He did not see Fuchihara at all. Each of them parted to make way for their lord.

Aritaka dismounted with help from his bannermen and

marched over to his son. "Kazumune," he greeted him with as much stern pride in his face as Kazuchiyo had ever seen. "You've done your father proud this day."

"You honor me," replied Kazuchiyo, and he bowed his head.

Aritaka nodded in return before turning his attention to Koedzuka. "Koedzuka Danzou," he said. "I believe this is the first time you and I have met in person."

"It is," Koedzuka replied evenly. "Regrettable as the circumstances may be."

Aritaka snorted. "Regrettable for you, indeed." He looked to Kazuchiyo. "The battle is yours, my son. Let him cut his belly open. His head is yours to take."

The men around them grew tense. Several Kibaku officers dropped to their knees, and Naoya raised his head, breathless in his misery. Kazuchiyo had never felt a weight upon him such as he did then. He sheathed his sword.

"My Lord Aritaka," he said, drawing himself to his full height and summoning his courage. "I have no desire to take his head."

Aritaka's brows drew in severely, but before he could reply, Kazuchiyo continued. "I have been on both sides of the river today, however briefly. I have seen men of Sakka and Kibaku fight with bravery, and cunning, and honor," Kazuchiyo glanced between the two lords significantly, "and I have not seen one single enemy among them. All our enemies lie in the west."

The lords each straightened their back, looking to Kazuchiyo with immediate understanding. So, too, did every general, officer, and soldier within hearing feel emboldened with Kazuchiyo's declaration. Kazuchiyo etched a bold picture of his ambition in the hearts of each of them that day. Sakka's triumph was further sweetened with the promise of greater conquests to come, Kibaku's defeat softened with the relief of their lord's life spared, and both were emboldened by the prospect of a marriage of beastly might and feathered wisdom.

"Our enemies lie in the west," said Aritaka, and then Koedzuka stood to face them.

"Our enemies lie in the west," Koedzuka agreed. When he bowed, Aritaka and Kazuchiyo did as well, in equal degree. Generals from both sides lowered their heads and soldiers took to their knees. And thus Sakka's campaign against Kibaku ended, as it had begun, with Kazuchiyo.

Ginta's men released Oihata, who scrambled to his feet, only to approach Lord Koedzuka and drop to his knees again. He bowed his head to the earth, inconsolable and unable to speak. Kazuchiyo's throat tightened with sympathy, but his heart was already soaring far away. "Sir Oihata," he said as he climbed into Suzumekage's saddle again. "I pray that you can someday forgive me."

Naoya pushed himself up, though he did not raise his head. He scraped his glove across his face. "I can," he said. "I will."

"Thank you, friend," said Kazuchiyo, not caring if anyone heard. For too long he had restrained himself with duty, and in that moment his dignity frayed; he drew his short sword and cut Nanpa's head from his saddle. He tossed the gruesome trophy at Aritaka's feet.

"I'm sorry, Father, that this is the only head I've taken for you this day," he said, "but I trust you know whose it is, and how I came to claim it."

Aritaka hardened. Likely he would have preferred to accept Kazuchiyo's admonishment outside so many eyes, but the shame was his to bear. "I do," he said. Behind him, Hidemune shrank within his armor. "It will be dealt with." He gestured to the south. "Go, then."

"Thank you," said Kazuchiyo, and once again Suzumekage sped him down the riverbank.

They stayed close to the water, Suzumekage's hooves splashing through the shallows at times to avoid slowing between the trees. Kazuchiyo would not remember most of the trip later, nor that several riders accompanied him; he saw only the path ahead of him, his mind desperately blank. He could not bring himself to imagine what scene he would come upon. The battlefield fell away, as did the howling wind, the clanging bamboo. Even Suzumekage, conveying him so faithfully, seemed to disappear beneath him. As far as he was concerned, he soared.

As Kazuchiyo turned the final bend, he heard it: the enraged voice of a demon. The red beams of the Chibatake Bridge leapt into view in all their broad, bloody glory. Kazuchiyo could barely breathe. At the far end of the bridge, Purnima stood with her army, identifiable by the half-moon emblem on her helmet. Her thinned forces still outnumbered what remained of Ebara's by three to one at least, but no Kibaku soldier dared set foot upon the bridge. For at the center, standing tall among dozens of corpses, Yagi-douji bellowed at them in unearthly defiance.

Kazuchiyo reached the foot of the bridge and leapt from Suzumekage's back. He passed General Ebara, wounded but tended to by his loyal soldiers. He passed Amai, to his surprise—Amai slumped against the bridge railing, a bow clasped in one hand, his fingers raw and bleeding from the bowstring. He climbed over a pile of Sakka corpses only to be granted a view of even more dead Kibaku beyond. There were enough bodies to stain the bridge red. It was an image fit for a hellscape, completed with a vision of a blood-drenched demon at the fore. Yagi's armor was battered and stained, his helmet askew. Nearly a dozen broken arrow shafts adorned him, piercing plate and skin, and his spear had been split in two, yet he had not retreated an inch, not for a moment. Even as Kibaku's proud soldiers cowered behind their unsteady captain, he squared his shoulders to his enemy and dared them to advance with wordless shouts.

Kazuchiyo ran to him. "Yagi!" he called, and without any thought to his own safety he rounded Yagi's side to face him. "Yagi, it's over. The battle is over."

Yagi stared straight ahead, his breath heaving, blood on

his face. He resembled a wild animal, and when Kazuchiyo touched his arm, he startled and brandished his spear. "Yagi," Kazuchiyo said again. He remained still and patient as the fury gradually receded from Yagi's face. "It's me."

Yagi blinked at him. "Kazu?"

"It's all right." Kazuchiyo urged Yagi to lower his spear. "It's over."

Yagi let his spear clatter to the bridge, and with a deep sigh he collapsed into Kazuchiyo's arms.

Kazuchiyo bore his weight as best he could as he lowered them both to the ground. Emotion strangled him and burned his eyes. He felt the shafts of arrows pressing into him, blood slick against his gloves, and feared that at any moment Yagi would fall still against his chest, but as heartbeats passed, Yagi's weary breath carried on.

Ebara's troops approached. Amai reached the pair of them first, dropping to his knees at Kazuchiyo's side with an exhausted sigh. "Well, you're here," he said, "so I guess that means we won."

"Yes." Tears rolled down Kazuchiyo's cheeks as he managed a shaky smile. "We won."

CHAPTER THIRTY-THREE

They laid Yagi out on Sakka's largest flag as a sling. It took four strong men to carry him. Kazuchiyo bowed to Purnima across the bridge, who returned his courtesy, though he imagined it was begrudgingly. Then he left with Ebara and his men, hurrying the wounded back to Sabi Castle.

The healers had to sever the cords on Yagi's armor to remove it. They pulled arrows out of him, applied salves to and bandaged his many wounds. Kazuchiyo assisted to the limits of his skill. Yagi grumbled and tossed in fitful unconsciousness through it all, which frightened the healers, but to Kazuchiyo it was a relief to see him retain that much strength. Once he was cleaned, tended, and resting as comfortably as he was capable, the healers departed. Kazuchiyo at last shed his own armor and stayed close at his side, to wipe the sweat from his brow and smooth his hair from his face.

Iomori came next, removing her straw hat. Without a word she began preparing paper and ink, and Kazuchiyo left her to it, though he paid her close attention. She scrawled out a few characters and affixed the paper charm to Yagi's chest; almost immediately Yagi's growls quieted, and his head lolled peacefully against Kazuchiyo's knee.

Kazuchiyo ran his fingers through his lover's hair. "Thank you," he said quietly.

"He might be part oni after all," said Iomori as she cleaned her supplies. "The soldiers are saying he killed two thousand men. I have my doubts, but even half that is a feat for legends."

Iomori dragged a piece of Yagi's armor to her. She swiftly found and untied her red bead from the thigh guard as if she had known it was there all along.

"The bead," said Kazuchiyo, glancing to the ribbon still tied securely around his wrist. "It's magic, isn't it? This bead is the reason I was able to kill Nanpa."

"Magic is a complicated thing," said Iomori. She drew up her left sleeve, granting Kazuchiyo his first full glimpse of the long string of prayer beads wrapped along the length of her arm. With great dexterity she untied the string one-handed to replace the bead among its peers. "Think of the bead as a cup: it can be filled with magic, and when needed, it can be tipped over. Today you learned how to tip the cup."

"Not on purpose," Kazuchiyo admitted. He frowned as he watched Iomori's calm, unreadable expression. "But you were right: it saved my life."

Iomori smiled as she tied her string once more and lowered her sleeve. "I have a vested interest in your safety. Haven't I always said so?"

"Then why didn't you clear the fog when I asked it of you?"

She paused. Kazuchiyo was convinced she was deciding on a lie long before she spoke. "Like I told you, I felt it worked to our advantage as much as Lord Koedzuka's," she said.

"If we had known from the start that the reserves were missing, we could have prepared," he insisted. "It would have spared lives."

Her small smile returned. "This is war, Kazumune. Lord Aritaka has asked me for victory, not lives."

She stood, and though Kazuchiyo burned with frustration and paranoia, he could not imagine any words that would convince her to share her mind. He licked his lips. "Master Iomori, will you teach me how to use these beads?"

"When you're ready," she replied.

She showed herself out, only to reveal that Amai was standing just beyond the open door. Iomori raised her eyebrows at him but said nothing more as she headed away. Amai made a face at her back as he entered and then shut the door behind him.

"Is he still asleep?" he asked as he sat at Kazuchiyo's side.

"Yes, but at least it seems that he's resting." Kazuchiyo stroked Yagi's cheek and was relieved by his quiet snoring.

"He was incredible," said Amai. "I didn't even see most of it, but they were still fighting when I got there. I've never seen anything like it."

He didn't sound like his normal, carefree self, and Kazuchiyo frowned as he gave him his full attention. Amai had changed into a fresh set of robes, his hair loose, his eyes downcast. His hands had been wound with strips of clean linen.

"Are you all right?" Kazuchiyo asked.

"Oh—sure." Amai shook himself, but when he smiled, he could not convince the expression to stay. "I'm not used to firing a bow for so long. My fingers are going to be sore for days. I'm sure you're disappointed."

Kazuchiyo would not be fooled or provoked by Amai's attempts to deflect. "When you didn't cross the river, I wasn't sure what to think. You could have just left, like you wanted to."

"I guess I've given you plenty of reason to assume that," Amai said with a wincing smile. "The battlefield is no place for a shinobi, after all." He hesitated before continuing, struggling to keep his usual flippancy in place. "I thought about it. I wanted to." He started to rub his face, only to remember his hands were bandaged and return them to his lap. "I don't know. When you jumped into the river, I realized you were right: you didn't give up, and he didn't either. What would that make me if I ran away?" He inhaled sharply through his nose. "I wanted

395

to be of use to you, too."

Kazuchiyo reached out and swept a lock of Amai's hair behind his ear. Amai looked to him, startled and even a little shaken. "You saved my life again," Kazuchiyo told him, squeezing the back of his neck. "And you protected Yagi. Thank you."

Amai nodded, tears welling in his eyes as he fought one last time to smirk. "My kiss?"

Kazuchiyo nodded, but rather than draw Amai in, he reached down, taking a gentle hold of Amai's wrist. He lifted Amai's hand and kissed the backs of his raw fingers. Amai shuddered. The final strand of his bravado peeled away, and with a whimper he turned to wrap his arms around Kazuchiyo's shoulders. He felt small; Kazuchiyo held him tightly as he cried into his collar.

"I was scared," Amai whispered.

The admission brought tears to Kazuchiyo's eyes as well. He twisted his fingers in the back of Amai's robe, his other hand running again through Yagi's hair. "So was I."

Yagi slept through the rest of the day and the night, and Kazuchiyo and Amai took turns watching over him while the other rested. Generals Rakuteru and Hosoda came to offer words of congratulation and respect, and Mahiro brought them supper, eager to hear every detail from the battle. Kazuchiyo assured her as animatedly as possible that any credit for the victory lay with Suzumekage alone, to her great delight. They did not speak of Hidemune.

The next morning, one of the captains came to collect Kazuchiyo for his father. Kazuchiyo bathed and dressed in a fine hitatare and joined Aritaka in the courtyard. Horses and a contingent of guards had been prepared for them. Aritaka offered a stiff but seemingly heartfelt greeting, and they set out.

The meeting took place at the top of the hillside north

of the castle. Lord Koedzuka and General Oihata met them there, and together the four of them sat beneath the ancient boughs of the maple tree. They drank saké from the same cup to symbolize the end of their hostilities, and it was only then that Kazuchiyo learned that General Fuchihara had been killed in the battle. Naoya had brought his head for them to view.

"Five years of peace, we had," said Lord Koedzuka once their ceremony had concluded, "and I am loath to give it up. But as you've said, we cannot ignore our enemies to the west much longer. The inner territories have been testing our borders ever since Shimegahara. It's only a matter of time before they invent their own excuse to go to war."

Aritaka did not challenge his choice of words, though he seemed tempted. "Sooner than you know, I'll bet. All of Shuyun has seen that the capital has not one care for how we conduct ourselves. That apathy will be the undoing of our country if one does not rise to take the reins."

"And you believe you are fit for that task?" asked Naoya, making no attempt to hide his contempt. "To bring peace to Shuyun?"

"I am," replied Aritaka without hesitation. "And should I fail, I have a fine heir to carry on in my stead."

Koedzuka and Naoya looked to Kazuchiyo, who humbly bowed his head. He could not bring himself to speak.

After sharing respectful farewells, the lords parted and began separate descents down the hillside. Aritaka motioned for Kazuchiyo to ride close beside him. "I've heard that Motonobu is still resting," he said, "but Master Iomori assured me that she expects he'll recover fully."

"Not a single one of his injuries was severe enough to threaten his life," replied Kazuchiyo dutifully, staring straight ahead. "Though there were a great many of them. He'll recover with time."

"Good. I'm glad to hear it."

Kazuchiyo did not believe him, and for once Aritaka chose to meet that disapproval at once. "I did say it would benefit you to lose him, and I have not changed my mind. But the inspiration he's given to our men is invaluable. Soon all of Shuyun will know what he accomplished at Chibatake, which will only help our cause."

"Father, please excuse me, but you don't have to convince me," said Kazuchiyo. "I understand."

Aritaka cast him a sideways glance. After a time, he began again. "Hidemune is being held in his room," he said, and Kazuchiyo straightened in his saddle. "As soon as Motonobu and the rest of our wounded are fit to travel, we'll be returning to Gyoe. There he will answer for his crimes and his cowardice, and commit seppuku. If I find that the Lady O-ran was aware of or participated in the attempt on your life, she will be made to atone as well."

Kazuchiyo stared back at him. Relief, vindication, disgust, and unease battled each other through his stomach. He could not have expected a better outcome, and no one could assign him any blame. There would likely be many more sacrifices and punishments, earned and otherwise, for him to encounter if war took them westward, but in that moment he felt keenly the weight he would be expected to bear, the cost of his survival and success.

"And you will name me your heir?" he asked, his emotion drawn wire-tight.

Aritaka nodded. "All that I own and command will one day pass to Aritaka Kazumune."

Kazuchiyo bowed his head, and the two of them said no more the rest of the way back to Sabi Castle.

As soon as they returned, Kazuchiyo retreated to the healers' room where Yagi still rested. Any disorientation he felt from his brief discussion with Aritaka and the Kibaku lords was erased when he heard conversation coming from within the room. He rushed inside.

Yagi stared up at him from the floor, weary but awake, relief in his face. "Kazu."

He dropped to Yagi's side and snatched up his hand in both of his. "Yagi," he started to say, but an unexpected surge of emotion got the better of him, choking off the rest. As much as he struggled to get the words out, the warmth of Yagi's broad palm in his hands kept closing his throat. For as much as he had cried already, he could not swallow back a fresh round of tears.

"Kazu?" Yagi touched his face, distraught. "Stop that. I'm all right."

He managed at last to take a breath. "I can't help it," he said. "I'm..." He took a moment to swallow and regain his composure as he held Yagi's hand to his cheek. "I'm so glad you're awake."

"Only for a few minutes," volunteered Amai. "Take it easy on him."

"I'm fine," Yagi muttered, but when he looked up at Kazuchiyo, he softened. "Are you all right?"

Kazuchiyo scoffed. "Even more fine than you," he replied. "Do you need anything? I'll have them bring food—"

He leaned back, but before he could go too far Yagi grabbed the collar of his robe. "Stay," he said urgently. Then he relaxed, smoothing Kazuchiyo's clothing. "Please."

Amai glanced between them and smiled. "I'll go," he said, pushing to his feet. "Some food will do you good."

"Bring saké," Yagi called after him, and with a chuckle Amai let himself out. As soon as he was gone, Yagi gave Kazuchiyo's collar another tug. "Come down here; I can't sit up yet."

Kazuchiyo happily leaned down and kissed him. Yagi's lips were dry and his jaw bruised, so he tried to be gentle, but Yagi would have none of that, sinking his fingers into Kazuchiyo's

399

thick hair. He demanded and was granted a hard, aching kiss of reaffirmation. Determined to remain as close as possible, Kazuchiyo stretched out alongside him, though he was careful not to put any pressure on the man's many healing wounds.

"I heard you stormed the enemy from behind," said Yagi, with appreciation in his voice that made Kazuchiyo blush. "Beat the Kibaku daimyo in a duel."

Kazuchiyo chuckled. "Not quite like that." He twined his fingers with Yagi's as he leaned into his shoulder. "But we won, and we didn't have to lose Oihata *or* Lord Koedzuka. They've agreed to ally with us in the wars to come."

Yagi let out a long sigh. "Has that stupid bear started another one already?"

"No, but..." Kazuchiyo squeezed his hand. "Another will come. There may be no stopping it now." He took a deep breath and then squirmed closer to press a small kiss to Yagi's neck. "But I don't want to worry about that. As soon as you can travel we're going back to Gyoe." He paused. "Hidemune will be put to death."

"Serves him right," Yagi muttered. "He turned and ran as soon as he saw how many soldiers we were up against." Realizing how still Kazuchiyo had grown, he nudged him with his chin. "Hey. He's brought it on himself."

"I know. It's not precisely that which concerns me." Kazuchiyo closed his eyes as he breathed Yagi in. "Once he's gone, Aritaka will name me his official heir. I'll be his son in the eyes of all of Shuyun. Aritaka Kazumune, future lord of Sakka, Yaefu... and Suyama." He shuddered at the thought. "It's what I wanted, but it frightens me. Do you think my father would despise me for it? To reclaim our homeland, but in another's name?"

"I have no idea," Yagi replied. "I didn't know your father." He let go of Kazuchiyo's hand to stroke his cheek. "But *I'm* proud of you. Whatever happens, I'll be with you."

Kazuchiyo wiped his eyes and then propped himself up so he could kiss Yagi's lips. "I love you," he whispered.

Yagi blushed deeply and squirmed as he glanced away. "I lo..." He gulped. "I love you, too." Then with a deep breath he drew Kazuchiyo back down for another, longer kiss.

Yagi dozed off again. He rested peacefully until Amai returned with warm soup and saké. It took both Kazuchiyo and Amai to prop him up. Together the three of them ate and drank and regaled each other with their tales of battle won. Despite the trials that waited ahead, it was the happiest Kazuchiyo had been in many years.

EPILOGUE

Twelve days after the Sakka victory at Nodo Bridge, Lord Aritaka dispersed his armies to their homesteads and returned to Gyoe Castle.

The homecoming was a complex affair. Townspeople gathered in the streets to see their returning lord home, excited to have victory as an excuse to celebrate. The procession weaved through the streets among pounding drums and happy chatter, but as it passed through the gold-eaved gates of the castle proper, the merriment sobered. Aritaka's bureaucrats and remaining generals greeted them in lined ranks, clan banners flying, silent in their respect. They regarded Aritaka and Kazuchiyo with sharp attention, even suspicion. Only Satsumi greeted Kazuchiyo with warmth. The Lady O-ran was not among them.

During supper, some of the tension lifted. Each of Aritaka's generals took their turn telling their part of the battles in the south, some exaggerating more than others. Even Kazuchiyo was persuaded to share the tale of his river crossing, with enthusiastic support from Rakuteru's son. Yagi gave a very gruff, very concise version of his heroics at Chibatake Bridge, while Mahiro scoffed and bragged about the prowess she might have shown in his place. Hidemune did not attend.

"You've done so well for yourself, Kazu," Satsumi congratulated him after the feasting. "I'm so proud. I hope my gift was of some use to you."

"We would not have achieved victory without it," he said. "That dagger won us a powerful ally. I'm very grateful."

Satsumi laughed as they left the hall together. "You tease me."

"No, truly." Kazuchiyo smiled to show his sincerity. "Shall I escort you to your room and tell you about it?"

"Oh, I would like that. It's a rare thing to see you smile." Satsumi's own smile grew mischievous. "But it's not my own room I'm retiring to tonight, which I believe I have you to thank for."

She cast a significant look at Aritaka, still among the merry-makers. Though it sobered Kazuchiyo to take her meaning, he continued to offer her pleasant encouragement. "I hope you're able to make the most of it," he said.

Satsumi hummed gleefully. "I will. Thank you, Kazu. I look forward to having you as a son." She turned back into the chamber, her hair and robes flowing behind her.

In the morning, Aritaka spread word to all his subjects: in three days, Hidemune would commit seppuku to atone for sins against his family.

Out of tact and respect, Kazuchiyo kept mostly to himself and his room during the interim. He did not want for pleasant and encouraging company. When the morning of the fateful day arrived, he was surprised by the arrival of a messenger, saying that Hidemune had asked to speak to him prior to the ceremony.

"You shouldn't go," Yagi grumbled as he and Kazuchiyo changed into fine hitatare for the event. "He might try to stick a dagger in you at the last minute."

"I don't think so," said Kazuchiyo, "but I'll be careful. If I don't go, I'll always wonder."

He reached for his hair, only to have Amai sneak up behind him and begin tying it up himself. "I can go with you," Amai offered. "Just in case."

"No, it's all right." Kazuchiyo held still as Amai fussed with his hair, and, not to be put out, Yagi took it upon himself to straighten the line of his collar. He smiled at them both. "Thank you, though, both of you."

"We'll be waiting for you in the courtyard," said Yagi, and Kazuchiyo shared a short kiss with each of them before making his way to the room in which Hidemune was confined.

There were armed samurai at the door, who nodded to Kazuchiyo as he approached. Despite his confidence in front of his companions, he was glad for their presence. He entered to find that Hidemune was not alone. He stood at the center of the small chamber, Mahiro with him. She was helping to dress him in a pure white kimono.

"Come in," Hidemune invited without looking up. His face was red, and Mahiro's eyes were swollen; Kazuchiyo winced at the thought of whatever argument they'd been having. "Don't worry, I'm not going to try anything. It wouldn't do anything now."

Kazuchiyo came forward, though not close enough to be in easy range of the man. "You asked for me. I'm here."

Hidemune nodded, and he abruptly pushed Mahiro's hands off him. "I can do the rest myself."

Mahiro glared at him. She looked ready to retort but then thought better of it. She dropped the end of the sash she had been holding and stormed from the room, wiping her eyes.

Kazuchiyo, too, stopped himself from commenting. He faced Hidemune and waited, silent and patient, for the man to make his intentions clear. Without Mahiro's help Hidemune struggled some with tying the robe. His hands trembled. At last he tightened it to his satisfaction and raised his head.

"Well," he said, "I guess you won."

"I did," Kazuchiyo replied. "But I don't take any pleasure from it, as I think you know. I didn't want this for either of us."

"I know." Hidemune looked left and right, trying to gather himself. He began fussing with his hair, and the unfamiliar, hard knot that had been tied specifically to make the collection of his head easier. "It's all Father. Did you know he promised to make me his heir? Right up until Sabi? He probably promised you, too."

Kazuchiyo swallowed. "He did."

Hidemune stopped and took a deep breath. At last he looked to Kazuchiyo and seemed to come to what he wanted to say. "Did you know I wasn't his firstborn son?" Kazuchiyo leaned back, startled. "I didn't think so. Genmaru was his name. He didn't live long enough to take an adult one. Died of blood-lung when we were children. Just like our uncle."

Kazuchiyo watched Hidemune carefully, his mind spinning. "No one's ever mentioned that to me."

"Unsurprising." Now that the words had begun, they came easier. "Genmaru was strong and smart. Everyone said he'd take our clan to the capital someday. And then he fucking died." Hidemune began tugging at his kimono again. "It's not my fault I couldn't live up to that, you know. Nothing I did was ever going to be good enough. Him bringing you here proved that." His face contorted in anger, and he glared at Kazuchiyo. "I didn't have a choice, you know I didn't! All of this is *his* fault!"

He lashed out with his foot, kicking over the small tray that had held his final meal. The dishes and utensils clattered across the hardwood. Kazuchiyo held very still. But that seemed to be the extent of Hidemune's temper; he swiped at his eyes and took a deep breath. "Well," he muttered. "You'll see someday. But at least for now, you won."

The pair fell silent for a moment, neither knowing what to say. Kazuchiyo's thoughts were a tangle, and he wasn't sure if it would have made it any easier if Yagi and Amai were at his side. At long last, he took a breath and said, "Thank you for telling

405

me about your brother."

Hidemune's shoulders drooped, and he nodded. "Be good to Mahiro, okay? Or else I'll haunt you."

"I will," Kazuchiyo promised, and he bowed his head before showing himself out.

Mahiro was waiting in the hall. She snatched Kazuchiyo by the sleeve and dragged him out of sight of the two samurai guards so she could grab him up in a tight hug.

"Mahiro..." Kazuchiyo returned the embrace, unsure what other comfort he could offer. "I'm sorry."

She shivered, but just when he thought she might cry, she rallied herself. "I have to go to my mother," she said, and Kazuchiyo's heart sank all over again. "But I want you to know that I didn't know, okay? He never told me anything. I would have knocked him senseless if I—"

"I know," Kazuchiyo hurried to reassure her. "I know, Mahiro. I believe you."

"Please do. Please believe me." Her hands tightened against his shoulders. "I saw you kill General Waseba."

Kazuchiyo's heart gave a heavy thud, but before he could collect himself to respond, she continued. "I know why; I know he hurt you. You can tell me next time, okay? You're my only brother, now. I'm going to take care of you." She squeezed him so tight he could barely breathe. "Please believe me."

"I do." Kazuchiyo shuddered, sick with grief and elation as he held her just as tightly. "I promise, I'll trust you next time." He let out a sharp breath. "I hope there *isn't* a next time."

Mahiro went quiet, and slowly she unwound from him. As she leaned back, he saw in her face a tragic kind of wisdom, as if she already knew better. "Me, too," she said, and she wiped her eyes with her collar. "Will you sit next to me down there?"

"Of course." Kazuchiyo managed to smile for her. "I'll always be with you."

Mahiro darted in for one more hug and then released him. With a weak smile of her own she hurried off down the hall, and Kazuchiyo made his way to the courtyard.

Lord Aritaka gathered all of his top generals and advisors for the ceremony. Like all things samurai, it was a formal affair, every detail well-planned, each member of the audience chosen and meticulously placed. Kazuchiyo took his seat next to Aritaka at the head of the assembly, and when Mahiro arrived, she joined him. Each family head was dressed in their finest, crests on display, except for General Rakuteru: he stood opposite Aritaka dressed in black, his swords in his belt. His was a grim honor.

Hidemune and his mother were led into the square, both dressed in immaculate white. Each knelt a step ahead of Rakuteru to face the crowd. The lacquered boxes containing each of their final words were conveyed to Aritaka by attendants, making all other declarations unnecessary. There was no need to repeat their offenses when the act that they were about to commit would wipe each clean of their sins and debts. Kazuchiyo watched, gripping his knees and holding his breath, as Hidemune drew his sword with shaking hands and plunged it into his belly.

General Rakuteru was as efficient as he was merciful. Long before Hidemune could shame himself with any sound of pain, he brought his sword down, severing his neck and ending his life. The Lady O-ran did not go quite so peacefully; she held Aritaka's gaze for a long time, eyes hard with defiance, before finally putting a dagger to her throat. Throughout it all, the crowd remained silent. Mahiro took Kazuchiyo's hand at the end, and he gripped it tight.

The blood was still fresh as Aritaka led his assembly back into the keep. There in the main hall a new ceremony commenced, which was its own kind of death; with a few strokes of a brush and drinks shared, Kazuchiyo was named the rightful heir to Aritaka's clan and fortune. The generals that had fought alongside him toasted to his success, Rakuteru and Ebara chief among them. Young Tomoto bowed in deep respect, and Ginta goaded him into sharing few lines of verse. Others treated him with curiosity, others still with mistrust and disdain that they were, sensibly, too cowardly to voice.

Aritaka oversaw it all, the Lady Satsumi and Master Iomori beside him, a grim and determined gleam in his face.

In the evening, Kazuchiyo climbed onto the roof outside his chamber window. He drew the flute Lady Satsumi had gifted him to his lips and began to play. He followed no practiced melody, simply giving life to notes as they came to him. His gaze strayed to the west, and the golden hues stretching out from the rolling countryside. To the east and the south, everything he could see would one day belong to him, but the west was home to battlefields, some he'd survived and some yet to come—home to new allies that lived on plains of vibrant green, and enemies that dwelled in mountains and along riverbeds. Beyond that, the capital awaited, a thing of legends Kazuchiyo could only begin to imagine. Despite a day of heartache and trepidation, he found himself comforted by thoughts of a world beyond his own.

"Kazu?"

He turned to look over his shoulder. Yagi and Amai were both waiting in the room, watching him with mixed sympathy and concern. As he lowered the flute, Yagi offered his hand.

"What were you saying?" he asked.

Kazuchiyo smiled as he accepted Yagi's help climbing back inside. "I was calling for you," he said, and he tucked the flute into his robe so he could draw both of them to him. "And you came."

They closed the window, and together the three of them prepared for a night of well-earned rest. Their battles had ended, their enemies rooted out. Kazuchiyo had secured his future and honored both his fathers. For a time, their war was over.

And I wish that I could tell you that a thousand ages of peace can be so easily won, but as we know, there are far more daring tales, to be told another time.

Thank you for reading

I hope you'll join Kazuchiyo, Yagi, and Amai
for the next chapter of their journey in book
two!

ABOUT THE AUTHOR

Melanie Schoen is an indie author born and raised in Michigan. From a young age she enjoyed crafting stories, particularly those featuring historical settings with diverse characters, full of adventure and drama. After studying Japanese language and culture and earning a bachelor's degree in East Asian Language and Studies, she spent several years translating manga for various American publishers. These days she works an office job to lend more time to her passion for her personal fiction, marrying her love of history with a desire for more progressive narratives.

In addition to Kazuchiyo, Melanie is publishing graphic novel *Bang! Bang! BOOM!* along with its prequel novel, *Bang! Bang! BOOM! [NEW YORK]*, a jazz era adventure series featuring LGBT gangsters and magic. For updates, other news, and information about all my current projects, please visit www.melanieschoenbooks.com

CPSIA information can be obtained
at www.ICGtesting.com
Printed in the USA
FFHW020801221019
55671373-61520FF